To Have and to Hold

To Have and to Hold

Marriage, the Baby Boom, and Social Change

JESSICA WEISS

the university of chicago press   *chicago and london*

JESSICA WEISS teaches United States history and United States women's history at California State University, Hayward.

The University of Chicago Press, Chicago 60637
The University of Chicago Press, Ltd., London
© 2000 by The University of Chicago
All rights reserved. Published 2000
Printed in the United States of America
09 08 07 06 05 04 03 02 01 00   1 2 3 4 5

ISBN: 0-226-88670-0 (CLOTH)
ISBN: 0-226-88671-9 (PAPER)

Library of Congress Cataloging-in-Publication Data

Weiss, Jessica.
    To have and to hold : marriage, the baby boom, and social change / Jessica Weiss.
        p.   cm.
    Includes bibliographical references and index.
    ISBN 0-226-88670-0 (cloth).—ISBN 0-226-88671-9 (paper)
        1. Marriage—United States.   2. Family—United States.   3. Baby boom generation—United States.   4. Nineteen fifties.   I. Title.
    HQ535.W435   2000
    306.8'0973—dc21   99-40312
                                                                      CIP

⊗ The paper used in this publication meets the minimum requirements of the American National Standard for Information Sciences—Permanence of Paper for Printed Library Materials, ANSI Z39.48-1992.

Contents

Acknowledgments

This book began in a research seminar with Paula Fass. As I searched for a source that would allow me an inside look at marriage during the Great Depression, she directed me to the Archives at the Institute of Human Development (IHD) at Berkeley. Without her suggestion I might never have discovered this rich historical source.

Mary Ryan has been a true mentor. As I researched, wrote, and revised, she cheered the appearance of each chapter and always encouraged me to go beyond the easy answers. Jon Gjerde, Michael Rogin, and Arlene Skolnick provided insightful feedback, useful questions, and support. Much of the research was supported by the Eugene Irwin McCormac Fellowship and the writing by a Mellon Dissertation Award.

I acknowledge with thanks the IHD for providing access to the data that made my work possible. At the IHD two individuals were crucial to my research. I would like to thank Carol Huffine, director of the longitudinal studies, for securing me desk space during my research, allowing me return visits, and reading the entire manuscript, and Barbara Burek for sharing a corner of her office with me for a few short weeks as I finished up. Barbara, the archivist at the IHD, was helpful at all stages of research. Without her knowledge, skills, and cooperation this book would have seemed impossible. Dorothy Field, of the Berkeley Older Generation Study, whose work on the IHD parent generation also examines the intersection of historical and family cycle forces, shared her interest and encouragement and at a crucial stage in the revision process generously provided office space and much needed assistance with IHD data. Dorothy Eichorn, retired associate director of the institute, read sections of the manuscript and offered guidance on protecting participant confidentiality. Cenita Kupperbusch stepped in to help interpret IHD data.

I have also been blessed with not one but two wonderful writing groups. A special and heartfelt thanks to Jesse Berrett, Karen Bradley, Elizabeth Haiken, Julia Rechter, and Tina Stevens for the friendship and fine dinners. And thanks also to Sue Grayzel, Laura Lovett, Valerie Mendoza, Mary Ryan, Laura Schwemm, Jill Schlessinger, and Linda Song. They all provided succor from the isolation of the writing and research process and invaluable advice. At the University of Utah, our informal gender reading group—Susie Porter, Carol Harrison, and Laura Nym Mayhall—provided community and food for thought. I am deeply grateful to them all.

As I completed my work, I received valuable suggestions from Daniel Horowitz, who took time during his sabbatical to read chapter 2 carefully, from Robert Goldberg, who tutored me in the function of an introduction, from Robert Griswold, who carefully commented on the entire manuscript, and from an anonymous reviewer for the University of Chicago Press who prompted me to think about the meaning of my findings and reminded me about the ongoing struggle over gender roles in families today. Theresa Kaminski read the entire manuscript and offered insights. Matthew Howard and Doug Mitchell at the University of Chicago Press guided me through all stages of the process with good humor and kindness. Jean Eckenfels copyedited the manuscript with care. Larry Schwartz speeded my request through at Archive Photos. All have won my enduring gratitude.

Friends Julia Rechter and Elizabeth Haiken read countless drafts and joined Lois Hedberg, Kirsten Michener, Tina Stevens, and Susan Spath in doling out emotional and spiritual sustenance. Estelle Zinkhen, my grandmother, did not live to see this project in book form, but her experience in the labor force before, during, and after World War II and her constant faith in me guided me as I wrote. Boundless gratitude to my parents Jean and Robert Weiss and to my sister Hilary White for her friendship. Vitaly and Ludmila Luskin shared their encouragement and baked chicken. My husband, Vlad Luskin, lived with this project from its inception. His limitless support and affection made it possible; his editorial contributions made it better. I am deeply grateful to him for brightening my days and believing in me.

Finally, there are more than 200 individuals whose candor and commitment made this book possible. The participants and their spouses of the Oakland and Berkeley longitudinal studies at the Institute of Human Development, University of California, Berkeley, gave of themselves honestly and unstintingly for most of their lives. I have tried to honor their voices even as I analyzed their experiences.

To Have and to Hold

Youthful marriage defined postwar family life but also transformed it. ARCHIVE PHOTOS

Introduction

In the early 1990s, the phrase "family values" crept into American political discourse. Regardless of the speaker and whatever the target—the divorce rate, deadbeat dads, teen pregnancy, or working mothers—American family life in the 1950s is the standard that critics use to judge family life today. Aided by a constant stream of reruns on cable television, Americans in the 1990s persisted in viewing the fifties family as the repository of "traditional" American family values. To contemporary Americans, the 1950s represent the quiet before the storm of social, sexual, and gender role change that rocked the nation over the next four decades. This placid, static view of happy nuclear families composed of breadwinning husbands, homemaking wives, and their requisite three children ensconced in an affluent suburban home may be comforting, but it conceals the swift social currents that were already beginning to transform American family life in the early 1950s. A brief look at one postwar couple reveals this process of change.

Glen and Lois Dyer married in 1957. Glen was a twenty-four year old veteran and Lois was a nineteen-year-old coed.[1] Lois left college to put Glen through school, and the newlyweds moved to a Southern California suburb. Pregnant just a few months after the wedding, Lois gave birth to several children in as many years while Glen worked to finish school on the GI Bill and then to get ahead in his career. The Dyers appear to be a typical baby boom family—a real life June and Ward Cleaver. On the surface, the Dyers fit nicely into our preconceptions of fifties family life—youthful, suburban, prolific, and "traditional."[2]

When our lens widens to scan the following decades, however, a more complex picture emerges. In the early 1960s, when the youngest of the Dyer children was in preschool, Lois resumed her college education. By the time their oldest child applied to college, Lois was running a small school.

In the early 1970s, the picture changed again. College-age children and inflation prompted Lois to look for a new line of work. Her husband's paycheck no longer stretched as far as it once had. When Glen changed jobs, Lois donned a "power" suit and landed a clerical job in a large corporation. She and Glen soon looked to her job to supply medical and retirement benefits that his no longer provided, and Lois had her eye on a managerial position.[3]

Clearly, the term "traditional," as Americans usually understand it, fails to describe adequately this couple's marriage beyond the early years of child rearing and ignores the fact that youthful marriage was a specific postwar phenomenon, not an American tradition. Our tendency to glorify the middle-class family stereotype of the 1950s obscures the fact that the decade encompasses only a single stage in the family cycle of that first generation to form families after the war—the parents of the baby boomers. Their children, the boomers, grew up and went to school, then off to college and independent lives, and parents' lives evolved with these changes and historical circumstances.

To understand the Dyers and their peers, we must look closely at such families and the cultural context in which they made their choices, not only in the 1950s, but across the entire family cycle on through the 1970s. Rarely have historians undertaken such a longitudinal approach. Fortunately, the pseudonymous Dyer family was part of a one-of-a-kind study that makes a long-term examination of postwar family life possible—the longitudinal studies located at the Institute of Human Development (IHD) at the University of California, Berkeley. In the 1930s IHD researchers set out to study the stages of human development and began a project that would ultimately follow the same group of individuals throughout their entire lives. Because the IHD interviewed study members over the life cycle, from childhood to late middle age, we are able to follow the effects of the fifties family pattern over time, permitting a much more nuanced and deeper understanding of postwar family life than the one-decade "snapshot" view historians persist in portraying.[4]

In the following chapters I pair first-person experiences of postwar family life drawn from a sample of 100 couples from the IHD archives with material culled from mainstream and women's magazines, advice books, sociological studies, television shows, and movies from 1950 to 1980, in order to explore the connections and contradictions between behavior and cultural prescriptions. Alongside the actual experiences of ordinary families, I trace shifts in and patterns of American opinion about issues affecting family life. In each decade, articles on parenting, working women, marriage, sexuality, and divorce filled the pages of popular magazines. The advice that journalists and experts doled out and the trends they pointed to may not have directly shaped individual behavior and choices, but these opinions informed the spectrum of options middle-class Americans considered. The interview evidence shows an ongoing dialogue between prescription and behavior. Ordinary Americans were cognizant of the norms and directives purveyed in the press and where they stood in relation to them. This combined social and cultural history approach traces change across three decades and provides a new perspective on the lives of postwar middle-class families, uncovering the early postwar roots of recent family and gender changes.

The unique and fascinating trove of data at the IHD permits this longitudinal examination—from nest building to empty nest—of the family lives of an important and overlooked generation as it moved through American history from the 1950s to the 1980s. I selected one hundred IHD study members and their spouses from two of the IHD studies, the Berkeley Guidance Study and the Oakland Longitudinal Study. Long-term, continuous cooperation with the IHD on the part of both spouses was the major criterion for selection in order to take advantage of the longitudinal potential of these sources. The study members in this sample were both highly committed to contact with the IHD and able to maintain it. According to IHD sociologist John Clausen, the social factors contributing most to lifelong participation were family emotional and economic stability as well as personal success. Participation in the study offered East Bay families incentives such as access to experts, clubhouses, group outings, and the chance to survey their lives periodically with a sympathetic, objective listener. And significantly, study members spoke fondly of the influence of the IHD on their lives, mentioning that they derived a sense of "family" or "esprit de corps" from participating.[5]

Drawing on IHD Adult Interviews I, II, and III, we first encounter the members of this one-hundred-couple case study in the late 1950s when most have been married about a decade, meet them again in the late 1960s and early 1970s when their children were teens, and then finally in the early 1980s, when they faced the empty nest. Unlike cross sectional analysis of census data, which can only provide a static picture of families, frozen in time—snapshots—this study follows the same group of individuals from youthful marriage to retirement, permitting an in-depth and longitudinal study of changes in American family life—a moving picture. This dynamic look at postwar American family life as it developed over time reveals that, far from being traditional, the idealized middle-class family pattern of the 1950s was both transitory and transitional: transitory because the baby boom family pattern was of brief duration and because it represents but one stage of the family cycle and transitional because of innovative attempts to modify the family division of labor.[6]

The baby boom, to which the Dyers contributed, stretched from 1947 to 1964 and is more remarkable for its novel innovations in American family patterns than any stuffy traditions we commonly associate with it. After the war, Americans married at younger ages and had children sooner after marriage than before the war. Most significantly, couples spaced their children closely together, ending childbearing relatively early in adulthood. A few statistics illustrate the singularity of the fifties family. By 1950, the median age at first marriage for women had fallen to 20.3 from 21.3 in 1930 and for men to 22.8 from 26.7 at the turn of the century. More Americans wed than ever before in the fifties; by 1960, only 27.4 percent of American women aged 20–24 were single. And couples stayed married; in the fifties the divorce rate slowed, reaching a low point of 8.9 per thousand women aged 15 and older, or 368,000 divorces in 1958. Baby boom couples also bore more children than earlier cohorts had. At the peak of the baby boom, in 1957, the fertility rate was 122.9 per thousand women compared to only 79.9 per thousand in 1940. Without question, fifties patterns broke from those of earlier decades in the twentieth century.[7]

Scholars, focusing on this distinctive family style, have aimed primarily at explaining its origins. Largely missing from such accounts is a discussion of the lasting legacy of baby boom family innovations. From sociologist Glen Elder's cohort study of children who experienced the Great Depression, based on IHD material from the 1930s and 1950s, we learn that economic deprivation during adolescence lay the groundwork for the postwar pattern of early marriage and large families. Young teenagers prematurely adopted adult gender roles in their families of origin and viewed any disruption of their parents' roles—men's unemployment and women's work—as negative adaptations to crisis. As young adults, these experiences prepared them to embrace traditional gender roles and early marriage and to place a high value on children as a family resource in the 1950s. It is now time to ask how these young adult choices shaped later adulthood.[8]

Economist Richard Easterlin, also drawing on a cohort approach, plots the economic progress of Americans born during the 1930s. This generation's small numbers, which stem from Depression-related family planning, proved to be a blessing in the atmosphere of plenty that greeted young people as they came of age after World War II. The postwar boom opened up vast economic opportunities in the form of the GI Bill and bountiful employment. Young couples in the 1950s, better situated economically than their parents to marry and build large families, did so, producing the baby boom. But Easterlin's focus on the significance of birth year and the economy assumes that early marriage and large families are permanent American goals, untouched by historical change, merely waiting to be put into practice whenever the opportunity arises. Certainly, the culture of the Cold War, for example, influenced Americans' family goals.[9]

Historian Elaine Tyler May illustrates the political and psychological inducements created by the Cold War that encouraged postwar couples to turn their sights homeward. The doctrine of containment, abroad and at home, shaped the American family style, making the family a bastion of defense against a threatening, unstable world. Not just communism, but subversive elements within American society concerned politicians, social critics, and experts. Americans hoped that secure home life could stave off the dangers posed by consumerism, sexuality, and new technology. Healthy, happy families would guide the nation safely through the Cold War. The combination of prewar disruptions, postwar opportunities, and Cold War insecurities all help explain the baby boom, but they do not explore the long-term implications of this radical break from past family patterns.[10]

The uniqueness and brevity of the baby boom family pattern is, by now, well established. Recent revisionist scholars have shown that not only was that pattern unique in U.S. history, it was hardly universal even at its peak. The affluence that underwrote the baby boom did not extend to all Americans. As Americans rediscovered in the early 1960s, poverty still plagued many American families in the midst of plenty. And behind the picket fences of ranch house suburbia, alcoholism and psychiatric problems made the individuals inside miserable. The social mobility that put a barbecue in every backyard and a swimming pool in many and the freeways that permitted the breadwinner to travel from the city to the suburb each day were largely subsidized by government policies that made individual home ownership a weapon of the Cold War. Furthermore, a social contract between corporations and employers that encouraged loyalty and stability financed and sustained family affluence. Therefore, changes in family behavior since 1960 result not so much from declining family values, historian Stephanie Coontz reminds us, but from structural economic changes that made the family values of the fifties less possible to maintain for each successive generation.[11]

The affluent families of the fifties suburbs nurtured conformity, but they also nurtured a generation of young women who would redefine the female experience in the United States. According to sociologist Wini Breines, the contradictions of growing up female in the 1950s in a culture that included rock and roll, beat coffee houses, and a hypocritical sexual double standard also provided the building blocks of a feminist critique of conventional marriage and family life. New options for women would blossom when daughters of the 1950s came of age in the 1960s. Breines concludes that sociologists whose work formed the backbone of college textbooks on family life oversold the convergence of sex roles and underestimated the powerful restraints on women, thereby "reproduc[ing] the paradoxes" of growing up female in the 1950s by teaching girls that they had more equality than social reality in fact permitted. If their textbooks taught them about gender contradiction, from their mothers they learned about self-denial and unhappiness. Breines writes, "Ironically, despite the older women's commitment to children, to us, their daughters, their commitment to domesticity and their denial of their own discontent were ambiguous legacies." One result was that daughters rejected the family patterns they grew up with as they set out to shape lives of their own.[12]

Breines exposed the contradictory undercurrents shaping youthful female identity in the 1950s. At the same time historian Joanne Meyerowitz spearheaded a reexamination of what we have long assumed to be the dominating gender current in that decade, the "feminine mystique." Feminist author Betty Friedan published her best-seller on postwar womanhood in 1963. Since then her telling of the female experience has characterized postwar women's history. Surveying women's magazines and advertisements, she concluded that they spouted one message to American women, and one alone—that marriage and family, homemaking and child care were where women's true personal fulfillment lay. Then, surveying graduates of Smith College, Friedan revealed that behind the facade of fulfillment individual women questioned themselves, their femininity, and their sanity when at the end of the day they dared to worry, "Is this all?"[13]

Meyerowitz studied a wider array of American magazines and found evidence that American culture supported individual achievement outside the home for women; there was a counterweight to domesticity in the 1950s, after all. Recent research has also refuted the June Cleaver image of postwar womanhood by illuminating women's activism in trade unions and Mexican- and African-American communities, as well as the interesting uses of motherhood ideology in the hands of Communist Party women, civil defense protestors, and civil rights activists. These were women whose class and racial position or political convictions denied them access to the happy homemaker image or inspired them to utilize the image for political change. Revised histories of the 1950s reveal the overlooked scope of action for women our focus on the "feminine mystique" hid from view.[14]

For the most part, however, these interpretations locate change only outside the bounds of the middle-class family. And, with the exception of middle-class civil defense protestors in New York City at the end of the decade, decentering the June Cleaver image leaves that image intact for the majority of American women who did not engage in activism or who came of age before the 1960s. What about these real life embodiments of television motherhood—middle-class, married women of suburbia? The mystique surrounding their lives needs to be questioned as well. We forget, for example, that Harriet Nelson, the actress, was a working mother with an accomplished career, even if Harriet Nelson, the character, played second fiddle to Ozzie on the show. Middle-class women, whose lives on the surface conformed with the June Cleaver stereotype, were in fact at the forefront of significant gender change in the postwar years.

Most accounts of the 1950s, then, have left middle-class suburban men and women within the home, constructing cozy if constraining family cocoons out of postwar prosperity tinged with fear; our scholarly gaze follows the younger generation, the baby boomers out of the home to the arenas of social protest—the deep south, the college campus, the city streets. For those changes that did affect family life we look to the daughters of the 1950s who as young women denounced sexism, questioned femininity, and protested for equality. Discontent, if acknowledged, remains at a simmer but primed to blow, like the contents of a faultily sealed, time-saving pressure cooker—every modern homemaker's essential—when the new decade of the 1960s dawns. Explosion is a seductive metaphor particularly for the early nuclear age. But it is not the most appropriate description of what happened to American families in the decades following the 1950s. For change was already afoot. And postwar, middle-class couples—dismissed as cookie cutter versions of June and Ward Cleaver—were early actors in the family and gender transformations that took root in the 1960s and 1970s.

The baby boomers captured the attention of historians interested in postwar social and cultural change after 1960. The baby boomers' history and the changes that their generation sparked in American society have eclipsed those of their parents' generation, masking earlier indications of social and family transition. The cultural mandate not to trust anyone over thirty seems to have carried over to a historical injunction not to study anyone over thirty when it comes to the 1960s and 1970s. The baby boomers' supposed break with the past dovetails with the way historians approach the postwar period, tightly confining discussion of family life in discrete, decade-long time capsules and obscuring continuity and connection. By beginning families early, the parents of the baby boom in fact started the engine of postwar social change in the 1950s. They bore and raised their children in their early twenties, a choice that required a new flexibility in gender roles and set the stage for the relaxation of family demands at an early age. This collapsed period of intensive child rearing and the relative freedom from such demands that followed when they reached their late thirties and early forties provided fertile ground for family change. The gestation period for these changes was lengthy, and they only become visible if the entire family cycle, which lasts considerably longer than a single decade, is examined. The IHD studies make just such an examination possible.

In the 1930s, researchers at what was then the Institute for Child Welfare began these ambitious studies that included over 500 children. Who were these children? IHD subjects are representative of the prewar East Bay population, before World War II migration transformed the ethnic and racial make-up of the region. The vast majority of study members came from families in which both parents were native born, from Northern European backgrounds, and often recent migrants to California, although Southern or Eastern European and a few African-American and Hispanic families do number among those surveyed. Most lived their lives within fifty miles of their childhood homes in the East Bay, although the mobility related to Depression generated economic crisis and postwar economic boom dispersed a few, and many experienced residential mobility within their native region. With regard to social status, a third of the Berkeley families were working class when the study began; 40 percent of the Oakland families were working class. Nearly all study members (90%) were middle class in adulthood—working-class women achieved mobility through marriage, and working-class men entered the middle class courtesy of GI Bill education and home loans. After the war, study members experienced in microcosm the educational and social mobility that transformed the class composition of the nation.[15]

The Bay Area, which IHD study members called home, underwent substantial transformation in their lifetime. In 1930, when the studies began, Oakland's population was 284,000 and Berkeley's 82,000. The university dominated Berkeley's society but both it and Oakland were industrial cities. These cities had changed dramatically in population and economy by the time the men and women in this study came of age.[16]

The Depression hit the Bay Area hard; between 1929 and 1933, study families suffered income losses of between 30 and 40 percent on average. Joblessness was rife and the relief rolls of both Berkeley and Oakland swelled. Nonetheless with the onset of World War II, IHD youths expressed optimism about the upturn in the economy and their future in it.[17]

If the Great Depression disrupted economic conditions, World War II dramatically altered the social composition of the Bay Area. Migration expanded the East Bay population numerically and geographically. In 1950, Oakland had 384,575 inhabitants, and Berkeley 113,805, an increase of 35 percent for Oakland and 39 percent for Berkeley from the prewar figures. White and black migrants to the East Bay resided in developments near the plants and shipyards that employed them but socialized in the downtown districts of Oakland and Berkeley, shocking "old-timers." In the East Bay, the war accelerated the process of white flight, and in the housing shortage that followed the war, it was the white-collar middle class that was able to buy their way out of the shortage and into the suburbs to the south and east of Oakland and Berkeley. After the war, California's middle class increased exponentially. The number of Californians filling professional and technical positions in the state economy grew by 83 percent, reflecting the proliferation of defense-related industries on the west coast. Suburbanization and an expanding middle class provide a backdrop for the lives members of this generation shaped when we first encounter them in the late 1950s, in the early years of marriage.[18]

My sample of the IHD participants was well educated and reasonably well off. In terms of educational attainment, the older Oakland women all finished high school; most stopped their educations there. Gender and the Great Depression limited their access to higher education. Seven attended college but only three earned bachelors degrees. All the Oakland men completed high school and the majority attended college. Fifteen earned bachelors and five went on for further education. For Berkeley women, the educational odds were much improved. Twenty women attended college with half earning degrees and two going on for further schooling. The Berkeley men fared best educationally. Nineteen of them had at least some college, fifteen earned degrees, and 7 went on to professional or graduate school. The majority of male participants and male spouses were white-collar workers in management, the professions, or as proprietors of their own business. The most advantaged group occupationally were male subjects who came of age at the end of World War II to educational and economic opportunity.

So what do the adult lives of 100 of the most consistently cooperative children in a University of California study teach us? How are they like or unlike their generational peers across the nation? The IHD subjects were mainly native Californians, many of whose parents migrated to the state in search of the American Dream to the quintessential state for that pursuit. Their parents, followed from young adulthood to old age themselves, have proven to differ only slightly from the demographic features of their national cohort. Their educational attainment is higher than average, and their incomes slightly lower—factors not surprising to find in a university town. It could be argued that their state of residence sets them apart, but California in the 1950s and 1960s experienced much of the population growth and defense-related economic boom of the other sunbelt states. And of the burgeoning states nourished by Cold War defense contracts, California was America's choice destination. Finally, even as it became a mecca for rebelling youth in the 1960s, the golden state also nurtured the conservative political resurgence of those same years.[19]

Experience as participants points to the idiosyncracies that do set IHD-ers apart from the general population; for example, participation may have prompted higher levels of personal and psychological awareness and promoted a clinical, therapeutic cast to the material. But therapeutic models and solutions to human behavior grew more prevalent and acceptable in the United States during these years, blurring the distinctiveness of the IHD experience. A close reading of the interviews allows a fascinating journey into the inner life of a segment of middle-class Americans during an important time in U.S. history. IHD questions focused on issues of individual development—psychological, social, physical—but reveal a great deal of the social milieu and responses to historical events in the years in question.[20]

These then are the "children of the Great Depression," who have led "American lives." No single study can encapsulate the entirety and the diversity of the postwar American experience, or even the experience of the middle class. But what the IHD studies do extremely well is permit the investigation of middle-class families at a level of continuity unprecedented in social science studies. That is their strength. The IHD material provides the opportunity to peer into the private lives of ordinary families as they lived through the social and cultural transformations of the 1950s, 1960s, and 1970s. And while this book is about white middle-class marriages, in so doing, it explodes the easy stereotypes about happy homemakers and gray-flannel-suited organization men, allowing individual voices to come through, with tales of love, commitment, conflict, and frustration, and replaces the nostalgic hagiography of June and Ward Cleaver or Ozzie and Harriet Nelson with nuance and complexity.

Indeed, the intimacy of IHD material allows the exploration of topics crucial to understanding postwar family life—marriage, child rearing, sexuality, employment, divorce, and retirement. In the following pages, we will explore key questions about historical change, focusing on the overlooked generation that started families in the years immediately before and after World War II: How did the transformation in gender roles, alternatively hailed by feminists and assailed by conservatives, occur? What propelled married women into the workforce even before the launch of second-wave feminism and how did this affect family life? Or, to pose the question a different way, what is the relationship between married middle-class women's increasing participation in the labor force and the women's movement or gender role change? Did baby boomers and feminists invent the nurturing father? How did actual couples negotiate heightened expectations and ideals with the realities of suburban middle-class marriage in the midst of the sexual revolution? And finally, what accounts for the rise in American divorce rates that rocked the 1970s and how did couples (divorced or not) cope?

I have labeled this generation "the parents of the baby boom," drawing attention to what has been seen as their major contribution to postwar history—their children. But they are unquestionably an important historical generation in their own right. The experiences and hidden contributions that make them so are the subject of this book. The 1960s and 1970s marked a new stage in the life course for baby boom parents just as it did for the baby boomers. When their children left home, parents left behind an ideology of family that exalted a home full of young children and adjusted to new roles. They, before their children, began to chip away to traditional gender roles. Upon closer inspection the nostalgic celebration of a single decade's family style appears both misleading and misplaced.

The decade of the fifties does stand as a demographic anomaly, differing from the decades that preceded and followed in terms of marriage rates, age at first marriage, birth rates, age at birth of first child, and divorce rates. But too much focus on these differentiating aspects masks links to family life in the 1990s. Parents of the baby boomers, in fact, have much more in common with their children than we assume. The baby boomers rejected youthful marriage and child rearing but adapted other important patterns their parents set in motion. Postwar parents did more than merely witness the social revolutions of the sixties. The parents of the baby boomers planted the seeds of change which they themselves, as well as younger Americans harvested in the sixties and seventies. By the 1980s, they had traveled a great distance from the 1950s.

The Dyers illustrate this distance. In 1982 Lois Dyer was very conscious of her position as a working woman. She saw the 1980s as a period when women might lose status in the work place. Although she had not yet participated in a protest for women's rights or a feminist consciousness-raising group, she considered herself in the forefront of historical change in the quality of women's lives. That same year her husband reflected back on changes in the three decades of their marriage. In thirty years he had grown to accept shared breadwinning and had dinner on the table for his wife when she got home late from a hard day at the office. Because Lois was so busy with her job, he had also become the parent who maintained contact with the Dyers' grown children, making phone calls and seeing to it that the birthday cards went out on time. The Dyer family chronicle and those of the other families that follow tell the story of the transformation of postwar middle-class marriage and family life.[21]

More than that, their experiences reveal what it felt like to shape and live out that transformation as American society itself changed. Close study of this generation's lives reveals the effort and struggle that went into the incremental, layered changes described above. And we recognize in these struggles—over romantic, companionate, eroticized, but disposable marriages and individual careers, shared parenting and breadwinning—the challenges of family life today, now being lived out by the children and grandchildren of this generation. We have ignored the fact that postwar couples set these developments in motion, but we have also overstated the completeness of the gender revolution in the marriages created by baby boomers and generation Xers ever since. Mothers still struggle with the double day and the mommy track, joined now by fathers who discover that the work place makes room for men's family lives with a daddy track as potentially limiting occupationally as it may be rewarding personally; and home is where these struggles over gender role changes continue to unfold.

In the 1950s, experts celebrated the cooperative partnership of youthful marriage. ARCHIVE PHOTOS

Making the Most of Marriage

Youthful Marriage and Gender Roles in the 1950s

In a popular 1955 movie musical, Debbie Reynolds plays the ingenue eager to make it on Broadway. Before even setting foot on stage, however, Reynolds's character plans early retirement, by the age of 22, to marry, although the groom is as yet undetermined. *The Tender Trap* encapsulated Americans' ambivalent attitudes toward marriage in the 1950s. They celebrated marriage, youthful marriage in particular. Yet, hailed and encouraged for youth in the postwar years, marriage also had its detractors. "You fell in love and love is the tender trap," warbled Reynolds and co-star Frank Sinatra, singing the lyrics of Sammy Cahn. If love led to the "trap" of marriage, women, the script made clear, were both bait and trapper. The carefree bachelor was the prey. Once married, David Wayne's Joe shows, the former bachelor became the linchpin of the middle-class family economy, the supplier of juvenile orthodontia, fencing lessons, and new wall-to-wall carpeting.

He might protest, but Joe willingly returns to the husbandly fold, and by movie's end, Frank Sinatra's character has also succumbed to the marital yoke, won over by the marriage-minded starlet he had once ridiculed. In the 1950s, marriage might be criticized, but it was inescapable. While *The Tender Trap* focused on the entrapment of bachelors and their transformation to breadwinners, by the end of the decade other voices sounded the same refrain in a different key.[1]

According to feminist author Betty Friedan, it was wives, not husbands, that fifties marriage trapped. The women who seemed to have everything—love, children, well-kept and well-appointed homes—lived with deep discontent. In her 1963 bestseller, *The Feminine Mystique*, Friedan rephrased the problem slightly. The prevailing image of women, not marriage per se, was a trap. To critics the American home had become a "comfortable concentration camp" for both male and female inhabitants.[2]

By the late 1950s, then, Americans shared the sense that marriage entrapped its participants. This view contrasted with the celebration of marriage in the early 1950s, particularly in women's magazines and on television. In fact, the ambivalence apparent in *The Tender Trap* was perhaps unintentional. The movie closes with two couples (one not married to each other) arm in arm, singing joyfully of love and marriage. Both the celebratory and the stifling image of fifties marriage have survived to characterize the decade.

Yet, marriage in the 1950s was far less placid and far less static than has been popularly conceived. Confining perhaps, fifties marriages were not all-encompassing traps. Nor were they harmonious or based on a contentedly traditional division of labor. Rather they were a crucible for egalitarian ideals and a site of nascent struggle for a more egalitarian reality in middle-class marriage. Equality and sharing constituted the postwar ideal, but an ideal superimposed over continuing complementary and distinct gender roles. Out of this paradox couples created a transitional marital pattern that I term "contested egalitarianism"—contested because couples struggled over marital power and decision making. Examining the everyday experiences of middle-class couples in conjunction with the advice literature targeting them reveals important dynamic features of marriage in the 1950s heretofore missed. Young men and women discovered that marriage involved a period of "adjustment"—as experts termed it. With marriage, graduation, wartime enlistment, and new jobs occurring in quick succession, a young bride and groom faced a new environment as they crossed the threshold together.

Couples attempted to fill their socially prescribed roles and held their mates to equally exacting ideals. But youthful marriage and parenthood had differing impacts on men and women. Prescribed roles exacted unique pressures on them, and both sexes suffered from anxiety and feelings of inadequacy. Contrary to the nostalgic image of fifties marriage, this was not traditional terrain; rather it was terrain never before traversed, and it involved struggle, conflict, and extreme gender strain. The transformation of gender roles began in this struggle.

Early marriage ushered in a sense of novelty and experimentation. The youthful ages of marriage that characterized the late 1940s and 1950s heralded a shift from prewar assumptions about the place of marriage in the life cycle. Before the war, marriage had signified the end of youth, whereas by 1945 American youth embraced marriage. During the 1950s, the average age of marriage for men fell to 22 and the average age for women to 20. The men and women in this case study (a subset of the IHD study) followed the national trend to youthful marriage. Women born in 1920 and 1921 married, on average, by age 21; those born between 1928 and 1929, by 22. The older cohort of men married at 25 on average, and the younger at 24. As a group, participants' spouses had average ages of marriage slightly higher than those of participants.[3]

Americans born in the twenties and thirties restructured more than just marital timing. They began families soon after marriage and spaced their children close together. In this study average age of Oakland women at birth of first child was 23, while Berkeley women had their firstborns at 24. Most had between two and four children. By having larger families than their parents' generation, couples in the 1950s, particularly upper middle-class couples, reversed a long-term trend in American history: the decline of family size.[4]

Choosing to start families so early in life, postwar brides and grooms hewed a new path to adulthood. Male financial independence was no longer a requirement for marriage. In addition, young women could now expect to work during the period after marriage and before childbearing. These new ingredients of modern marriage caught the attention of scholars interested in understanding postwar family life in the United States.

In the 1950s Americans noted novel trends in marriage beyond youthfulness. Sociologists pointed to evidence of increasing sexual equality and fading sexual differences. Yet scholars since then have for the most part ignored or downplayed this development, concluding that in the 1950s cultural investment in female subordination overwhelmed any glimmer of gender symmetry. But the propensity toward equality in postwar marriage was more widespread than has been assumed.[5]

After World War II, commentators noted greater flexibility in gender roles than previously observed. In fact postwar marital experts concerned themselves with the potential for conflict in marriage that accompanied these new gender roles. They took change for granted and set out to help couples manage it. Sex role prescriptions in the 1950s reveal a sturdy strain of egalitarianism. In his postwar book on marital problems, *Conflict in Marriage*, psychiatrist Edmund Bergler wrote, "The relationship between the sexes is at present in a period of transition—between the full emancipation of women and man's smoldering rebellion against that emancipation." He overstated the emancipation of women in postwar America, but his comments point to developing expert and sociological opinions about the shifting place of women in American marriage and the male response. Marital advisor Frances Strain encouraged couples to adopt a pattern of egalitarian marriage. She noted, "This is an age of progress in international, racial, and sex equality. Let us hope that it will also be an age of progress and equality in the marriage field."[6]

Strain aimed her advice at male readers. She, like Bergler, was sensitive to the fact that men might resist relaxing their hold on marital power but tempted them with the benefits of better marriages. She cautioned, "Authority is easy, cooperation is not; but if it is pursued jointly, it yields the riches and satisfactions that come from the stimulation of two active personalities working toward a common goal." Strain stressed that marriage should be a partnership. Women, she said, had a right to be full participants in a new type of marriage. Her emphasis on partnership reveals the egalitarian views of marriage circulating in the fifties.[7]

Writer Constance Foster, who co-authored the parenting manual, *Fathers Are Parents, Too*, also saw the 1950s as an era of fluctuating sex roles. For couples the consequence was confusion over what was expected of each spouse. She warned that in the midst of a "transition from old ways to new, the traditional sex roles are apt to seem hazy or unsettled at times." She advised couples to "tread a little gently and not build up demands that are out of accord with what the mate is able or willing to do." She urged young couples to adopt flexibility regarding marital roles. In fact, because of what she saw as a gradual erosion of traditional sex roles, she predicted difficulty for brides and grooms who brought differing expectations to marriage. Foster said, "It has become a confusing world of new-fashioned women trying to live with old-fashioned men or vice-versa."[8]

Other experts, while still espousing the moral and natural rightness of complementary male and female roles, condoned the moderate blurring of the division between the sexes that they observed. If women now had work experience and men more interest in the home, Robert Coughlan concluded, this could benefit marriage, so long as the fundamental division of roles was upheld. The husband, he told *Life* magazine readers,

> is also better able to understand his wife's problems of homemaking; while she, perhaps having had a job . . . is better able to understand his. *Without trading primary responsibilities or trying to compete with each other they are able to help each other.* With mutual respect based on understanding he can dry the dishes or tuck the children in, she can paint the fence or write the checks, without any loss whatever of prestige or emotional confidence. [Emphasis in original][9]

Sociologist Mirra Komarovsky, on the other hand, while acknowledging the complementary roles of husbands and wives, criticized the extreme specialization that she observed in prescribed marital and social roles during the 1950s. She attacked the complacency with which sociologists like Talcott Parsons, father of functionalism, welcomed gender complementarity in marriage, remarking that while the complementary roles of "homemaker and provider" protected marriages "from rivalry," "physical separation of the place of business from the home and the great specialization in the occupations . . . create a serious divergence between the spheres of the homemaker and provider." She feared the consequences for American marriage of recommendations for further differentiation between men and women "at a time when marriage in the urban middle classes is already strained by the fact that husband and wife live in two separate worlds." Komarovsky warned against the divisions heightened by complementary marital roles, an issue that other observers tended to celebrate or ignore.[10]

The observations of social scientists spread beyond the narrow confines of academia; they were incorporated into the curriculum of college "education for marriage" courses during a decade when more Americans than ever before attended college.[11] One textbook, *Making the Most of Marriage*, by Paul H. Landis, implied that marriage had entered a transitional period. He visualized, "increasing sex equality and role sharing in the relationship of men and women and greater co-operation and sharing in the experience of parents and children." He urged couples to "cast aside" old-fashioned ideas in favor of a marriage of equals. He also assumed that marital difficulty arose when couples disagreed "as to what is the accepted role for man and wife in our time." The equality he discussed remained incomplete, however. He suggested that college men needed help accepting women's new status. But just as husbands should learn to accept these changes, women would have to realize before they entered marriage that to them fell the heavier burden of adjustment. After all, it was their "way of life that usually reshaped to fit the husband's." Equality in marriage was a relative term.[12]

Proclamations of a new marital equality were not limited to social scientists, educators, and marriage advisers. Empirical sociological studies of middle-class marriage in this decade included egalitarian patterns among their findings. One study of married couples in metropolitan Detroit held that equity rather than custom was the watchword of marriage. While they found ample evidence of the continued persistence of "husband-dominant" couples, Robert O. Blood Jr. and Donald M. Wolfe concluded that the spouse who controlled the marriage no longer depended on gender, but instead, on individual "competence." When they observed greater "husband dominance" in suburban couples where the husbands had high occupational prestige, they speculated that wifely respect and gratitude accounted for this, ignoring the fundamental social inequalities that effectively rendered "competence" male and gratitude female. Nevertheless, Blood and Wolfe's use of their findings highlights two important points. First, they and other scholars announced the demise of the old-fashioned patriarchal family and the dawn of new age of shared partnership. Second, norms that sanctioned gender imbalance were so ingrained in the culture that many sociologists, social scientists, and experts turned a blind eye to the inequities they observed, chalked them up to common-sense adjustments to individual situations, or interpreted contemporary "husband dominance" as milder in form and impact than in the past, in which case it became further evidence of change.[13]

Americans in the 1950s observed and commented on changes in the nature of sexual difference at the same time that they maintained belief in the essential necessity of complementary gender roles. The continued dominance of the traditional sexual division of labor, despite modifications, proved to be a huge stumbling block to egalitarian marriage in both theory and practice. This foray into the popular discussion of marriage and gender roles in the 1950s lends credence to a reinterpretation of gender ideology from that era. A significant few with access to the readers of mass market magazines, the family advice press, and scholarly books spoke to new more egalitarian male and female roles in marriage.

With the exception of Komarovsky, these observers may be guilty of understating the continued constraints and inequalities married middle-class women faced. But they were clearly responding to perceived changes in women's social and economic position. The war had shown women to be autonomous, economically self-sufficient, and even sexual. Historian Elaine Tyler May argues that one proposed function of Cold War family life was the containment of women in the home, easing social concern about the destructive, destabilizing potential of women's sexuality. "Harnessed" in the home with proper male authority delineated, women would channel their energies for family and for good. This may have been the "stick" response to changes in women's status. But what about the "carrot"? A greater stake in family decisions and shared authority, from the experts' perspective, added incentive for women to choose family and marriage over other options, which would not only contain women's independence but, it was hoped, provide a safe arena in which to exercise it. Popular concern about the possibility of divorce given married women's increasing taste for employment indicates the fear that if marriage could not accommodate the postwar American woman's expectations, she might opt out.

The experts called attention to and advocated a growing egalitarian ethos for marriage, still encased by complementary if newly flexible roles. And couples in the 1950s grappled with the tensions between complementary roles, expectations for equality, and still-current views of female subordination in marriage. Add in the factor of youthful marriages and we begin to see the previously ignored potential for change in marriage in the 1950s.

Beginning with World War II and continuing through the 1950s, the timing of major transitions to adulthood collapsed as young people threw over the accepted ordering of the milestones to maturity. For youthful couples, marriage, graduation, and work might all occur in a few months' time, with parenthood quickly following. One observer of early marriage noted, "It seemed as if the depression resulted in a barrier to marriage which, with the intimations of prosperity in the early 1940s, suddenly melted and released a steady stream of youthful marriage." Ten IHD couples volunteered lengthy descriptions of their hectic transitions to adulthood. Their accounts emphasized the speed with which couples rushed through major milestones: high school graduation, military enlistment or discharge, quickly followed by marriage, parenthood, and often, more schooling.[14]

For the older cohort in my study, those who graduated from high school in 1939, World War II played a key role in hastening decisions to marry. Dating couples were anxious to grab what happiness they could in a time of national crisis and they confronted mortality for the first time. Paul and Nan Meeker became engaged at Christmas 1941. They had originally planned a summer wedding, but Pearl Harbor panic was contagious and so their engagement lasted "a grand total of one month." Blanche Warner wondered if the wartime rush had not contributed to her early marriage. She thought, "Maybe we wouldn't have gotten married, if it hadn't been for the necessity of hurrying to make up our minds." Thirty-six percent of Oakland couples said that World War II accelerated their desire to marry and start a family.[15]

Surprise orders, long tours of duty, and brief leaves meant many couples married without knowing much about one another. Couples courted through the mail or married only to separate immediately. Celia and Malcom McKee, who wed at 20 and 23, respectively, went on a total of five dates before Malcom was shipped overseas. They corresponded for a year and then he proposed. Fear that they would not return from the war prompted soldiers to propose, and young women to accept, despite the difficulties of separation that such marriages entailed.[16]

It was not only coping with uncertainty and facing mortality that induced young people to marry during the war. Military allotment policies and job availability made marriage more appealing to the young. McKee decided, "Let's get married and let the government give us dependency pay which we can bank. If the war goes on for four or five years we'll have a nest egg." World War II made marriage financially possible for men and women in their late teens and early twenties.[17]

Youthful marriage was common by 1950; but the Korean War also hurried along juvenile nuptials. It both hastened and impinged on Stuart and Sue White's marriage: "After basic training I came back, married a gal I had met in summer school before I had joined the army, and after a week's honeymoon . . . was shipped out to Korea." The flurry of events surrounding their wedding completely reshaped the young couple's identities, roles, and responsibilities.[18]

Thus war enabled Americans' youthful rush to assume the indicators of maturity. The GI bill permitted young veterans to finance their education and, with their new brides' help, attend school as they embarked on married life. GI loans meant newlyweds could quickly acquire that essential component of the American dream, their own home. In these ways, the war encouraged American youths to marry younger and begin families sooner than couples had before it.[19]

In the heady postwar era, calls for marriage filled the air, and these calls reached young ears, putting pressure on youths, especially girls, to pair off. A walk down the aisle conferred an adult social position on college coeds, recent graduates, and junior executives—a position with responsibilities and roles they would learn to fill. "Young marrieds" viewed marriage as having a maturing effect. While the wedding itself did not instantly confer adulthood, without marriage, Americans thought, true maturity was impossible.

Youthful marriage won the approval of family advisors. For example, Walter Stokes, author of *Modern Pattern for Marriage*, reassured those who worried about the effects of young marriage, saying, "Emotionally mature and responsible young couples who are deeply in love may often feasibly enter marriage at an early age, perhaps *seventeen* or *eighteen*" (emphasis mine). He added that "the marriage usually has a maturing and stabilizing effect upon their emotional lives." Even for experts, marriage became part of growing up, not the endpoint of that process.[20]

Although most couples who married early had not yet attained financial independence, this did little to dampen national enthusiasm for youthful marriage. In 1949, the editorial staff of *Ladies' Home Journal* lent its support for parental financing of collegiate marriages, noting that "with the growing need for lengthy specialization in education, younger marriages during the war as precedent, and a change in thinking on the part of both parents and educators, college marriages are becoming more and more frequent." The cultural consensus blessed the trend of youthful marriage, even if it involved the adults of one generation subsidizing the "adults" of another.[21]

With the popularity of early marriage, girls now faced an old problem at younger and younger ages. In the 1950s it was not uncommon for a young woman of 21 to feel she was an old maid. Psychiatrist Sidonie M. Gruenberg only fanned the flames, writing, "A girl who hasn't a man in sight by the time she is 20 is not altogether wrong in fearing that she may never get married."[22]

Parents joined the experts encouraging youthful marriage, worrying when sons and daughters in their early twenties had not yet walked down the aisle. Dorothy Simon recalled that she met her husband through the careful planning of her father, "who unquestionably thought I was getting along in years and should be married," and the mother of the prospective groom, "who was afraid her shy and diffident boy with the girls was not going to get married either." Daughters, particularly, received the worried ministrations of match-making parents. Rita Frank remembered her fear that she wouldn't meet "the one" and that her father "had just about given up on me. I was about 24 or 25." The specter of spinsterhood haunted many young women after the war, contributing to the downward trend in marriage ages.[23]

Peer, parental, and personal pressure combined to persuade young people to marry as soon as they could. For Max Ames graduating from college and leaving home to begin his first job led him to propose. As his wife Denise put it, "He was going away up north for his first . . . job and he needed a wife up there to [work] also." For young men, too, an expected sequence of events pointed directly toward marriage.[24]

While both young men and young women were eager to marry, the social penalties of not marrying weighed much more heavily on women. Fears of never marrying nearly persuaded Diane Key to stay with an abusive fiance. She said, "I was afraid to give him up for fear I'd never have another man interested in me." Anxiety over spinsterhood was not a new worry for American women, but what is striking is the young age at which these women fretted about remaining single for life and the stigma they believed they would face. With limited educational and occupational opportunities awaiting the single woman after the war, marriage appeared to be the most satisfying option.[25]

Both sexes were drawn down the aisle for other reasons. Bowing to or upholding social conventions that frowned on premarital sex, couples married early in part because they were eager for sexual intimacy. Leonard Stone recalled that he and his fiance were "a couple of kids want[ing] to try it out." He married his high school sweetheart. Ruth Wright had similar emotions: "I was a virgin when I got married and I intended to stay that way, and if we hadn't gotten married I wouldn't have stayed that way much longer." Historian Elaine Tyler May has noted that many family experts in this period approved of early marriage because it was one way of avoiding premarital sex. Similar ideas operated in the minds of betrothed couples, or so they reported in hindsight.[26]

Into the tangle of complex motivations that led a couple to marry early went the desire to set up house on their own. For women especially, marriage was a legitimate path out of their home of origin. Whether merely chafing against parental authority as they attempted to assert independence or wanting to escape an unhappy home, young women saw marriage as the logical route out of their own family. Patricia James remembered, "I had a tremendous drive to get married, to get out of my house. I didn't fall madly in love." Linda Anderson's father gave her more freedom when she was dating her future husband John, freedom "that I had never had before and I grabbed it." She went on to recall that she "would have done anything to get out of the house." By marrying, a woman signaled both her maturity and her independence—for some, before they had reached the legal age of adulthood.[27]

Men unhappy at their parents' homes found their options less limited but marriage followed quickly in any case. David Morris said, "When I couldn't stand it at home, I joined the navy." He followed up this declaration of independence with marriage and, soon after, parenthood.[28]

What explains the youthful eagerness to enter the tender trap? Wartime and postwar prosperity provided one impetus. Young couples were financially able to enact nuptial hopes. For the older of the baby boom's parents, the experience of family deprivation during the Depression taught them to prize family as a resource in difficult times. And the postwar climate, while it seemed to promise prosperity, failed to offer security, at least in a geopolitical sense. Fears of communism and nuclear annihilation prompted a turn to the comforts of home and family. Finally, marriage permitted the proscribed—sex—or legitimized the risky—indulgence in premarital sex. In either case, youthful marriage relieved women of the burden of setting the limits on premarital sexual exploration, worry over pregnancy, and loss of reputation. Married after brief engagements, separated by the crisis of world war, young couples eagerly anticipated peacetime family life. Marriage brought the responsibilities along with the status and privileges of adulthood.[29]

The emphasis on maturity in the 1950s was spurred by the trend in youthful marriage, quieting worries about the instability youth might bring to marriage. Maturity implied the assumption of adult sex roles and responsibility, thereby calming concerns about financially solvent, unattached sexual young people unchecked by parents and at play in the fields of consumer society. The twin specters of communism and atomic war also called for national sobriety and a responsible mature citizenry. If they married and did not mature, divorce might project young people back into society as a destabilizing force. Maturity combined with the potential for egalitarian flexibility would provide the stabilizing counterweight, safeguarding family and society.

While marriage signaled autonomy from parents, financial and emotional separation came more slowly to young brides and grooms. Newly-weds resided close by or sometimes with their parents and in-laws or turned to them for advice, comfort, or financial help. Gail Henderson thought that her marriage was "floundering" so she sought the help of a counselor. She learned "that I had to grow up, that I had to accept the fact that I was leading my own life." She still felt very attached to her parents and this made marriage difficult. Claire and Nick Manning moved to the suburbs in order to gain some distance from theirs. Claire said, "I needed to grow up away from mine," adding that her husband felt the same way about his parents.[30]

Many young couples could not have embarked on these early marriages during the 1950s without help, usually financial, from their parents. Scott Parker's parents subsidized him and his wife, continuing to pay his college expenses after they married. Gordon and Patricia James lived in an apartment her parents rented to them for a nominal fee. Only after Gordon finished school did they move to a home of their own in a nearby suburban community. Another couple secured parental permission and support for their college marriage. After marrying, the Andrews continued to receive help with tuition from both sets of parents. In the 1950s, marriage did not necessarily confer physical, emotional, or financial independence from parents.[31]

Despite ties to parents, after the wedding came immediate responsibility and with it, the young newlyweds hoped, gradual maturity. Men, in particular, took pride in entering marriage. David Morris was proud that he had "married at 20, [was a] father at 21, had responsibilities and earned my keep." Rick Snyder felt that with engagement he "began to mature and think about somebody but myself. I settled down and worked harder on the job." Marriage prompted men to leave behind adolescent behavior and pursuits like going out with the boys. For these men marriage augured maturation.[32]

The first years of marriage, then, were for growing up. The process was not always smooth. Lois Dyer commented, "It was difficult having a family so soon. We had to go directly from childhood into adulthood in a hurry." Spouses looked to one another for help. Cynthia Thornton felt lucky because her "husband had more stability than I. He was patient, firm, and definite and I gradually began to grow up." Gordon James lauded his wife Patricia: "She's the one that really brought me up. I've become an adult through her." Spouses attributed parental qualities to each other. In fact, coming of age together and learning about adult responsibilities as a couple was a bonding experience for many.[33]

Growing up did not always lead to growing closer, however. In a few cases it meant growing apart. Marlene Hill, who had been so eager to marry and live in her own apartment, said of her first husband, "I guess he wasn't very bright. As I started to grow up, I found that I was too far ahead of him." Married as a teenager, she formally dissolved the marriage four years later. Suzanne Miller thought she grew up through marriage and parenthood. She married before she was twenty, because she was pregnant, and had several children by her early twenties. In her opinion she "was just too young and unhappy to have children when I had them, was self-centered and my only techniques in a family were tempers and tears!" She described both her husband and herself as insecure. They had, she said, "a difficult time" growing up after marriage. When marital problems or discontent occurred, immaturity became the culprit. Maturity, as Americans perceived it, held the key to successful marriage.[34]

Marriage meant setting up an independent household; yet, many couples went right back to what they had been doing before the wedding—their educations. College coeds likely heard the wedding march long before they heard the solemn strains of "Pomp and Circumstance." Cynthia Thornton recalled that her husband Grant divided himself between his studies and a part-time job selling garbage disposals, leaving little time for the two as a couple. Young spouses found marriage and student life conflicted. They juggled jobs and studies as well as marriage. Finishing school and establishing a new household concurrently involved difficulties.[35]

While most men who married in college finished school, young women often left school after marriage. Judy Kent's friends made bets over whether she would finish her degree after the wedding, but Judy was determined. In order to graduate she took extra units each semester and went to school year round. But the Kents had married while Clay was a junior and Judy was a sophomore in college, and his education became their priority. When Clay's GI bill ran out, Judy withdrew and took a job in the registrar's office so that he could continue. Although she worked, went to school, and helped Clay earn his degree, Judy felt that she neglected her role as a wife: "Poor Clay, he had the most dreadful meals!" Wives dropped out to work and help their husbands finish or to take better care of their spouses. Seven women, or 14 percent, of the Guidance Study women in my sample mentioned quitting school after marriage. Claire Manning withdrew short only a few units of her degree because her husband Nick was working evenings and going to school days and she wanted to devote herself to making a home and preparing good meals for him. He could earn a living and study concurrently, but Claire saw homemaking as a full-time job. Prohibitions against married students kept other women from completing their programs. Caroline Good was in training in the health care field when she married and gave it up because her program barred married students. The 1950s witnessed a decline in women's higher education. And there was an education gender gap; a higher percentage of college-aged men attended college than did women of the same age group. In the mid-1950s, 25 percent of women college students married while still in school. Youthful marriage's particular impact on women was to narrow their prospects for completed education.[36]

As postwar brides, whether they completed college or not, many women laid claim to the position of breadwinner. Early marriages rarely began on a secure financial footing. Home ownership, the goal of most middle-class couples, became possible only when both spouses contributed to the down payment. Employed young wives did define their employment in terms of family need. Yet, brides of student grooms reversed accepted marital roles by breadwinning while their husbands studied. Working wives of college men were mockingly said to be earning their Ph.T.s, for "putting hubby through," along with their salaries. In fact, the Dames Club at the University of California, Berkeley, annually conferred Ph.T. degrees on wives of graduating students. But the good-humored jests did not change the fact that wives supported husbands, sometimes for several years.[37]

College educations for husbands, homes, and living room sets: the earnings of married women made them possible. But bridal breadwinning had more than just economic import; it contributed to the breakdown in sex role differences that social scientists observed. It was also conducive to egalitarian marital partnership.[38]

This new pattern ran counter to the wisdom of the older generation. Evelyn Mitchell worked full time while her husband Robert studied, "in spite of the fact that my mother thought I was a fool to work and support a husband while he finished his schooling." Evelyn and other breadwinning brides broke with past patterns. Not only did they continue to work after the honeymoon, they became the sole providers.[39]

In student households, working wives' earnings were the cornerstone of the family income. The student marriage years were ones of considerable financial difficulty, especially when unplanned pregnancies upset carefully balanced budgets and threatened to remove the family breadwinner from the workforce. Evelyn Mitchell said her job "was getting Robert through college. It was no pick up job, I assure [you]." Years later, Evelyn still felt pride at the responsibility and salary her employment garnered. Another bride, Patricia James continued to work to put her husband through school even after the birth of their first child. Married women's earnings, by financing husbands' undergraduate, graduate, and professional degrees, helped insure higher incomes and secure futures for middle-class couples.[40]

When brides went to work, a down payment on a suburban home was often their goal. Combined with their husbands' salaries, the money young women earned enabled young couples to become homeowners. Cynthia Thornton continued to work after her marriage to Grant to save money for a bigger house than Grant's salary alone would have provided. Ellen Collins's nest egg, which she saved while she worked before and after marriage, became the down payment on the Collins's house and new furniture. The Gordons, another couple, both worked for several years after marriage, saving up to build their own home and then furnish it. Her salary, although slightly more than half of his was an important part of their financial planning. In the late 1950s the couple counted on Maureen working another year before having children. Max Ames said, "We were married in August and started our first jobs together. Although the salary for neither one of us was high, the fact that we were both earning money made a good income." Together the Ameses claimed a middle-class income, but on starting salaries, neither could have done so alone. Postwar newlyweds pooled earning power; suburban homeowning was, in fact, built on a partial foundation of women's paychecks.[41]

While Denise Ames's contribution made the Ames's aspirations possible, Rose Little's economic contribution made her marriage viable. Middle-class couples in the 1950s shared breadwinning while getting established or saving to obtain the trappings of middle-class life. For those from the working class making the move to suburbia, two incomes permitted financial survival. While Mark Little struggled to learn his trade, making low pay as an apprentice, his wife Rose took on a "split shift" job so that they could both look after their son. Their joint income gave them financial stability for the first time in their marriage.[42]

Their tenure as breadwinning brides may have been brief, but women of the generation that came of age with the war solidified the legitimization of a period of employment for white middle-class women after marriage and before childrearing. At the same time, they improved their family's standard of living. Furthermore, working early in marriage, they set a precedent for further breadwinning later in life.[43]

Brief courtships, new responsibilities, and rapid transitions through the markers of adulthood created challenges for postwar "young marrieds."

After marrying her husband Bill, a "stranger," before either of them had finished college, author Erma Bombeck wrote, "the biggest problem, was that we were poor and totally unprepared for marriage." Like the newlywed Bombecks, couples in the fifties found themselves to be unprepared for the reality of wedded life. They got acquainted after their vows while holding staunchly to romantic expectations. Women faced particular difficulties because marriage turned them into housewives, altering their lives considerably. Once they carried their brides across the threshold, grooms met daunting new responsibilities. Having eagerly embraced matrimony, fifties newlyweds set about transforming themselves and each other into wives and husbands. Together these young couples "adjusted" to marriage, a process that abbreviated courtships made more difficult.[44]

Marrying had little to do with intimate knowledge of one's future spouse. Dating had not prepared couples for the intimacy of married life. Doris Jenkins married her husband Kevin when he returned from a dangerous military assignment. She said, "I knew him a short time and then we decided to get married. I was in love with the idea of being in love, not really in love, nor was he."[45]

Cynthia Thornton described her anxieties after the wedding. She wondered if she would be an adequate wife, but what she found most threatening was "having to live on an intimate basis without some place to go and live and escape to. Every time I got panicky and uneasy, I wanted to run some place and hide. This was quite different from going out, spending the evening, and then separating." The rituals of courtship and brief engagements provided little opportunity for couples to learn about one another.[46]

Getting acquainted was only part of the task at hand for "young marrieds." They also had to learn to get along. Looking back, Leonard Stone remarked, "I had never lived with a woman before, had never read any of the books about marriage or being a father or husband or lover, had to play it by ear. I thought my marriage was the way things were supposed to be." He married when he was 20 and his wife was 19. Claire Manning, who married at 22, told an interviewer how she worried, especially in the early part of marriage: "I was pretty young . . . and I got very little guidance from anyone. Everything came sort of hard."[47]

Spouses criticized their own idealized conceptions of how marriage should be for making their acclimation to married life difficult. Brenda Jones, whose brief marriage ended in divorce, described her "romantic notions about entering this marriage," which were dashed when the only apartment they could afford was a "miserable unaesthetic place." The new-lyweds both felt "a tremendous letdown." Within a few months, Brenda went off to live with a friend and soon divorced. She would not wed again. Nan Meeker said actual marriage disillusioned her. The "sweetness and light" of the honeymoon had worn off and she was now "so busy and tired."[48]

For women like Nan marriage meant a significant change in lifestyle. Janice Rogers quit her job when she got married, but she found that in her and George's small apartment, "There wasn't much to do. I had too much time alone," she said. "I began being afraid I wasn't able to accept the responsibility for a marriage." One young woman simply rejected the changes expected of her after marriage rather than adapt. John Anderson, whose wife Linda was 17 when they married and 18 when they had their first child said, "She would go out without me. I would put the kids to bed and take care of them and out she would go, and come home in the middle of the night." Linda clung to an active social life even though she was a mother with several children. She proved unwilling to adjust to the requirements of marriage, in John Anderson's view, and they divorced.[49]

Adjusting to married life involved resolving unhappiness over unmet expectations and disappointments. Marriage required a greater change in daily activities for young women than for young men. Brides entered a whole new world of domestic tasks and often left behind the familiar social world of work or school. A woman walked up the aisle a bride and back down it a housewife, whether or not she continued to work or study. Her husband may have faced doubts about his ability to support a family, but his career remained his primary responsibility. Unsure of themselves, couples struggled to meet each other's expectations and needs and to adjust to their sometimes shared but often conflicting conceptions of married life. Because marriage became part of growing up and spouses brought each other up, they imparted to matrimony a sense of experimentation and shared teamwork that could become the basis of a more egalitarian partnership. But norms of masculinity and femininity still tethered these postwar couples.

Newlyweds brought ideas about the proper roles for husbands and wives to marriage. For a few, taking on these adult gender roles brought immediate satisfaction, but for others failure to perform up to the ideal bred conflict. Wives expected good housekeeping of themselves and struggled to maintain their standards and their husbands', too. Role expectations for husbands revolved around breadwinning and authority in the home, although husbands also ran up against their wives' demands for sharing household duties.

Ruth Wright took herself to task when it came to housekeeping. She wanted all her rugs to lie straight and everything to be in its place. She described herself as a fanatic about cleanliness. At the same time she admitted the futility of such high standards with a home full of growing children. She said, "There's no point to get yourself in a tizzy about it, but I just can't help it underneath. Every time I see a foot print down on the floor I just cringe." Dorothy Simon also struggled to uphold the expectations she had for herself as a wife and mother. She said, "If I take a nap I feel ashamed . . . and I feel so many women doing so now . . . It's an example of our times. I think we need tremendous standards now; I think today mothers must be all things at all times." These women worked valiantly to keep house and fill the proper feminine role—to be renaissance wives with boundless energy, spotless floors, and sunny dispositions.[50]

For not only did women have conceptions about what wives did, they also had a sense of the way wives should act and worked to conform. Janice Rogers worried that she had "been a discouragement" to her husband George. She said, "It's no fun coming home to a somber-sided wife." She believed that as a wife, she should encourage her husband and maintain at least a cheerful facade. These women shaped their moods and demeanor to their conceptions of proper wifely behavior.[51]

Men's expectations centered mainly around what they did outside the home, that is, on providing for their families. Lloyd Andrews recalled that once married he had been very eager to finish his degree. His wife was pregnant and he was anxious to "get to earning, and feeling that I was acting as a husband and father should, namely, supporting my family and not depending on bounty from relatives." Earning money to support a family defined the husband's role. Men relied on the satisfaction they got from fulfilling this role to temper its strain. Max Ames, who worked three jobs to support his wife and children, said, "Although I'm somewhat tired at the moment, I get pleasure out of thinking the family is dependent on me for their income."[52]

Responsibility weighed heavily in the fifties conception of marriage. Men fully expected to be full-time wage-earners and the primary breadwinners in their homes, and marrying conferred upon them breadwinner status or, in the case of students, future breadwinner. Sometimes the enormity of the obligations involved surprised young men. When Miriam became pregnant, Leonard Stone said, "I suddenly felt overwhelmed with

responsibility." The financial duties and social expectations of husband-
hood remained, even when circumstances worked against their being carried out. Mark Little said of the first few years of his marriage, when he
struggled to find a job, "I'd never had such responsibility in my life and felt
so inadequate to fulfill it." Young men often went directly from financial
dependence on their parents to the responsibility of supporting a growing
family, with perhaps a brief detour in college or the army, and found the
prospect of supporting an entire household frightening.[53]

With breadwinning the norm, housework remained a central issue
around which conflict about role fulfillment revolved. In the 1950s, couples worked out compromises on their own, relying partly on advice literature and partly on experience in their parental homes for their sense of the
right way to balance the running of a home. Immediately after their wedding, Stuart and Sue White quarrelled about how each should treat the
other. Of their "unhappy and confusing" honeymoon, Sue griped, "In the
first place, he expected me to wait on him and get breakfast, and I was
outraged to be subservient to any man. I expected to be catered to and
made over, and Stuart did practically none of it." While Stuart had traditional notions of women's role, Sue perceived such behaviors as demean-
ing. The two still had not worked out their conflicting ideas nearly a decade
into the marriage.

When Stuart studied full-time earning his degree and Sue worked full-
time and commuted to support them, she balked when he maintained that
his studies were of primary importance and refused to reduce her
housekeeping load. Sue expected her husband to share household duties as
she shared those of breadwinning; Stuart, however, held as his ideal a wife
who would cook, clean, and shop, even as she financed his tuition, while
he might occasionally lend a hand by doing yard work. Performance of
labor, or lack thereof, became the currency of the Whites' conflict. Stuart
often withheld his participation from traditionally defined "male" household duties such as yard work as a protest against late dinners, unlaundered
clothes, and a disheveled home. The predictions of experts Constance Foster and Mirra Komarovsky would have rung true in the Whites' home.
Neither could take traditional assumptions for granted.[54]

Other couples also had disputes, although not as chronic or contentious
as the Whites, over the who and the how of household and child-care responsibilities. Mary Smith said the problems she and Norm had when they
were first married came about because she "had some preconceived idea of
'his work' and 'her work.' They had to be ironed out." Society sanctioned

both the traditional division of labor and flexibility in marital roles; it was up to couples individually to work out the blend that worked for them. Women pushed for more egalitarian modes.[55]

Men also complained when their wives did not fulfill their ideal of the wifely role. Mark Little eventually stopped nagging his wife to keep the house cleaner because "she always says, 'Why don't you pitch in and help? I've got [the] children to care for.' And of course it's true so I've learned to shut up." Instead of meeting his wife's expectations for how a husband should behave, Mark chose to let go of his own. Larry Sloan was also disappointed with his wife's housekeeping, but excused her since "she does have to take care of the children." These men relaxed the standards of housekeeping they originally held.[56]

Wives, in turn, complained about the way their husbands tried to reform their habits and shape them into ideal homemakers. May Perkins said of Dennis, "He has an old idea about wives. He felt I was that type. I guess maybe I am really. But everyone is too modern to go for this baloney about the wife being the housewife and that's all, these days. His mother was like that." This couple clashed over parental and prescriptive models of marital roles, but May saw so-called traditional ideals as "baloney." Gail Henderson said that her husband Herbert "had to adjust to my inability to live up to the standards that he sets for me. . . . He's had to realize that I have only a certain amount of energy and things can't be as nice as he might like to have them."

Still, she felt that she, too, had "to adjust to meet his standards at quite a cost to me." Connie Small's husband Walter had "finally reconciled to marrying a nondomestic type." But, he did so only after trying "to make" Connie "over." Connie said, "My husband thinks a wife and mother should be a constant servant. That was his dream—a marvelous cook, housekeeper, child psychologist, and marvelous hostess." She rejected that model partly because her mother had been a consummate but bitter homemaker. These women set their own definitions of wifely responsibility, in contrast to their husbands'. They claimed the right to more independence from the home, a partner who pitched in, and even the freedom to identify as "nondomestic."[57]

Yet, women, too, had their notions of how their spouses should behave and what responsibilities they should fulfill. While Walter Small chided Connie for her haphazard housekeeping, she begrudged the ways in which he failed to be properly husbandlike. She wanted him to take complete charge of the family finances, from bill-paying to budgeting. She said, "I was raised with the idea that the man is to be in charge of the money, head of the household." Gail Henderson also drew on the patterns she grew up with, and her husband did not measure up. She said, "I had an idealized image of my father, and what a husband should be like, and Herbert didn't meet that standard. . . . I expected more of him than he could possibly give in the first place." She relinquished her ideals for him, as did he for her. After marriage, couples' expectations met with their actual ability and tolerance for prescribed roles. Their experiences indicate that many adapted rather than conform to ideals they found to be unrealistic. Traditional role performance was a site of contention, and thus transformation.[58]

Most couples followed youthful marriage quickly with parenthood. Financial problems loomed for young men who had not yet graduated or who earned starting salaries. While, for the most part, once children arrived, men bore the burden of supporting these eagerly formed youthful families, women bore the burden of caring for them. Young breadwinners and young homemakers experienced frustration and depression as they fell into these complementary roles. Youthful marriage offered the opportunity of shared partnership and parenthood; couples looked forward to parenthood, welcomed first pregnancies, and anticipated large families. After children, couples reverted to a more confining division of labor, and yet even this time-honored tradition would begin to give way.

Early parenthood was practically enjoined upon newlyweds. Most wanted three or four children, frowning on families with only one child as well as on those with more than four children. After he married, Murray Borden wanted to have children right away. He told his wife, "I felt it was very important that I have children while I was a still young enough to play with them, play ball, go swimming and so on." He was married at twenty and became a father soon after, long before any signs of aging set in and with a number of years of play ahead of him.[59]

Those who married before college graduation often became parents while mother or more likely father pursued a degree. Lois Dyer said, "Having the children as soon as we did, we didn't have even a year really to get acquainted in." She went on to wonder if "we might have missed a lot of good times because we did start a family so soon." Because couples became parents at such young ages, they often faced difficulties fitting parenthood in with other roles.[60]

Socially prescribed and enthusiastically chosen early parenthood was difficult for many young couples not yet fully accustomed to marriage. Martha Bentley got pregnant "immediately" after the wedding. The Bentleys readied for their first born by reading "embryology books and Mr. Spock." They were "all prepared to do a good job" by their family. Yet,

Martha spent her pregnancy in a new town, lonely and depressed, far from family and friends. Youthful and prolific parenthood followed early marriage and could contribute to marital difficulties.[61]

Having a child each year during the first several years of marriage meant a financial struggle for several families. Ellen and Milton Collins had their first child a year after they married. Ellen said, "This baby was not planned for at this particular time, because we were planning on buying a house, a car, and furniture." She added proudly, "We've done all that and have the baby, too." In this case, parenthood became an achievement and, like the other items on Ellen's list, a symbol of success.[62]

Often associated with abundance, the early years of the baby boom were difficult for couples from working-class or Depression-scarred middle-class backgrounds with material aspirations and large young families. Fifties abundance made a middle-class lifestyle accessible, but maintaining suburban married life required stringent sacrifice. House payments, car payments, medical bills, in addition to the expenses of a growing family, put young couples on tight budgets. Mark Little remembered having started out in marriage "with absolutely nothing in the world." It seemed to him that along with each year's salary increase came another mouth to feed and "we simply could not get our head above water." In 1958, with regular payments made on the house and the car, he could say, "I think we've done pretty well."[63]

The Ameses, whose first child interrupted Denise's first year at work, had difficulty making ends meet later when Denise was staying home with their young children. To supplement his salary, Max took on extra jobs sandwiched around the regular work day. Parenthood and home ownership spurred young fathers to work harder and look for promotions or better jobs, and sometimes supplementary jobs. Fatherhood occurred at a time when young men had yet to reach peak earning capacity; instead they were heavily involved in establishing careers as well as families.[64]

While, overall, the decade of the 1950s was one of economic growth, there were periodic recessions that caused severe setbacks for some families. The 1954 recession, for example, led to Robert Mitchell's lay off. He and Evelyn worried because she was pregnant and she had been planning to quit her job. Kurt Wolf was nearly destroyed financially by a recession in the early 1950s. He described this as the "lowest period" of his life, when, after making a substantial down payment on a house, suddenly, "Bang! the stock market crashed and I was in a big jam financially after having felt so secure." To make matters worse, the Wolfs' first child was on the way and their new house only half-built. Kurt said, "I didn't see how I was going to make ends meet and I felt completely inadequate and terribly worried." These experiences with economic uncertainty reveal the unstable basis of middle-class patterns of consumption. Monthly payments mounted along with larger houses and greater material wants. Men internalized their fiscal responsibilities and interpreted financial straits as the result of personal inadequacies.[65]

Even if their salaries were secure and could accommodate large families, there was still pressure to earn more and consume more in the fifties. Clay Kent half-complained, half-boasted, "Well, married life, now, there's always this terrific money pressure. You know, the more money you make, the more you want and it gets worse. You never have enough. I'm caught up in this horrible economic rat race and social rat race."

Once children entered the picture, this financial pressure fell largely on young men, at least in the first few years, eager to display their success as breadwinners. According to Suzanne Miller, her husband Louis's nervous breakdown came about when he "found that I was carrying another child. That was too much, you know. He couldn't face the thought of trying to raise the children—the responsibility of feeding and clothing them." While their wives might and often did help out, men shouldered the burden of supporting a growing family largely on their own.[66]

Still family life gave meaning to the hard work couples performed, especially for men. When Stuart and Sue White moved into their new home, Stuart felt as though they had arrived: "At last, I thought I was giving her what she wanted—a home with conveniences and we had a child." The job he disliked financed their new life. But the house, all its modern appliances, and their toddler did not bring the Whites happiness. The scurry to get established was followed by pressure to get ahead, or stay afloat.[67]

While these white middle-class men experienced the emotional burdens of financial responsibility, another man, as a minority, faced a different set of obstacles. His employment was steady, and thanks to his wife's salary the couple was prepared to build a home in the East Bay suburbs. Unfortunately, the bank they patronized refused to offer them a loan for the land they wanted to build on in a white neighborhood—their first serious confrontation with racism. The couple did eventually build their dream home in their neighborhood of choice. And, he reported with pleasure and pride, "The neighbors have been pleasant and friendly. We've had no problems at all since we've moved in. We have a nice house and a nice garden."[68]

While pressure to earn money to support the children fell mostly to men, the rearing of those children fell to the mothers who suffered from their own feelings of anxiety or inadequacy. Large families took their toll emotionally on young women who, on a daily basis, watched over and cared for their children. For brides who had worked after marriage, pregnancy marked their withdrawal from the workforce, their first experience with the vocation through which they were, according to fifties ideology, to find fulfillment. While their days were full with the challenges and satisfactions of childrearing, what many found was not fulfillment.

The birth of a first child marked an even more dramatic change in women's lives than had marriage. Admitting that one missed life before children amounted to a major gender transgression. After her first child was born, Cynthia Thornton confessed, "I had kind of a drop in morale. I was ashamed that I, somehow, didn't find it altogether exciting to be tied down with [the baby], whom I had wanted, but I missed the social contacts of my job." Because her husband was in school, Patricia James continued to work after the birth of her first child. She experienced a similar emotional slump only after the birth of her second child when she did stop working. The transition to a home-based, child-centered mode of life frustrated young women.[69]

During the baby boom, parents spaced their children close together. Because of this childbearing pattern, many women cared for two to three tots in diapers at the same time. This pattern concentrated the demands of motherhood into a limited period of time and left young mothers overwhelmed. Marcia Sloan thought that perhaps she had borne her children too close together: "They were all little at once and I about went crazy. I just couldn't cope." Mothering was hectic if you had "one barely walking, and one barely talking, and a brand new baby," as did Irene Lawrence, who had several in about as many years.[70]

Young mothers experienced very little time away from their children. In 1957, May Perkins confessed, "Sometimes I feel that I just have to get out of the house I guess." She often felt isolated, alone all day with the children. Evelyn Mitchell pinpointed her problems on the unadulterated blocks of time she spent with her children. "I feel sure, too, that if I didn't have such long hours with them and didn't feel so inadequate I would do a much better job." Of course, childrearing experts in the 1950s recommended precisely that young mothers spend long uninterrupted hours with their children.[71]

For these women who felt trapped by motherhood, depression could be the result. Rose Little said she often broke down in tears when everything piled up with the kids and she fell behind in housework. On these occasions, "every couple of weeks I go on a crying jag for a whole day." Janice Rogers thought she was "successfully hiding" her feelings of depression from her children but decided to go "right to a psychiatrist" when her children told her they were afraid to leave her alone.

These problems went beyond occasional bad moods. Sandra Thomas, who spaced her children close, remembered that in the 1950s, she had difficulty leaving the house even to go grocery shopping: "I'd try to go but sometimes I just had to say I'm leaving and I went home again." She had the problem for "couple of years." Keeping up with several active children brought one woman to her wits' end. In 1959, Ruth Wright said she disliked getting mad. The depths of her frustration come through: "I don't like to hit 'em. Well, I'm afraid that if I keep on, I just won't be able to stop, that I'll go on until I could physically kill 'em."[72]

Once children arrived, the fundamental division of parenting chores within these homes was set. At least ten hours a day when dad was gone, the tasks and workload of parenting fell to mom. Despite the difficulties these couples encountered, few questioned the basic organization of their lives. With bills to be paid and a house full of children to be nurtured, few doubted the necessity of performing their assumed responsibilities. The legacy of traditional gender roles competed with evolving equalitarian norms. In a study of postwar parenthood, psychologist Ruth Tasch observed, "Failure to recognize the variety of functions which the spouse can perform suggests that role-typing may tend to be restrictive of the fullest potential of the person so typed. Either parent may have greater versatility in more functions of parenthood than the other parent's expectation will allow."[73]

While role typing according to traditional norms governed couples' patterns, postwar studies showed that, outside of child care and providing, who should do what remained unclear. In William Dyer and Dick Urban's study of marital equality, couples reported equality of activity in childrearing, with the glaring exception of "taking care of children's physical needs," which remained women's responsibility. When it came to household tasks, they found a much stricter division of labor, reporting, "In this area as in no other does the hypothesis of equalitarianism of activity break down." Men's responsibilities revolved around odd jobs, women's around household and family maintenance. There was evidence, however, that grocery shopping, yard and garden work, and household repairs and painting were less strictly defined by sex than in the past. With the exception of marketing, this would indicate that women expanded their activities in the family and household and stepped into previously male domains more than men experimented in female domains. An Omaha, Nebraska, study confirmed these findings, noting that middle-class marriages showed the most conformity to the "companionship ideal of husband and wife sharing of home responsibilities," but that husbands' participation was "most noticeable in tasks usually considered to be man's work and is largely absent in traditionally feminine tasks." Eight IHD couples attempted to work out greater flexibility in household responsibilities in the first decade of marriage and wives instigated those changes.[74]

Shifting codes of marital behavior and responsibility were not the only signs of conflict over the transforming topography of postwar marriage. Couples also had difficulty navigating the fault lines of marital authority, just as experts predicted they would. Companionship was predicated on mutuality of affection and satisfaction; surely shared decision making was part of the postwar companionate marriage. But concern about changing sex roles could just as easily lead to a reassertion of the masculine prerogative. Couples were left to write their own scripts. Marriage advice literature called for shared authority but reassured readers that in the case of conflict, wives preferred a take-charge mate. This duality translated into conflict as couples struggled to work out marital roles.[75]

Although 5 percent of wives had a dominant role in important family decisions, most IHD couples aspired to mutual decision making, but found expectations for masculine authority difficult to shake. Martha Bentley endorsed male authority. She said she was surprised that her husband was "so dominant and firm." When she married him she "somehow assumed that he would eat out of my hand." Yet, she insisted she was pleased: "I prefer him the way he is." Gail Henderson described how she worked out for herself the blend of democracy and dictatorship in her marriage. She said, "On the big decisions we talk them over together very often, but the big decisions are really made by Herbert. I prefer it that way myself. I like to have someone who is stronger." Dennis Perkins asked for his wife's input on household matters but rarely got it. He said, "I'll ask her about her own feelings about something or other, like the house. I'll say that it's her house as much as mine, then she says, 'You'll handle it ok.'" These women thought it right to defer to their husbands, at least in the early years of their marriages. Twenty percent of the families reported male-dominated decision making, with finances being a particularly male domain.[76]

Not all wives acceded easily to a lesser voice in marital matters. Mary Smith explained away her "bossy" behavior by saying that her husband always had the last word. "Oh, I'm bossier," she stated, "but he's the one who's really in charge. . . . If I get my way it's because he decides it." Although she expressed her opinions, Mary justified this by showing that if and when they conflicted with her husband's they did not count, saying, "We don't do anything that he doesn't want us to do. I get mad about it, but I'm really glad." Her willingness to let her husband overrule her seems forced and barely masked her genuine frustration with the situation. The little instances of giving in made her angry, but, she insisted, she really liked the setup.[77]

Married women in the 1950s, may have been members of a team, but their husbands called the plays. Wives were in the peculiar situation of being equal, but less than equal. Doris Jenkins said her husband Kevin made the decisions with her input. She said, "He has my preferences. We discuss pro and con. I give one way or the other." Joint decision making, then, contained an escape clause. Couples made decisions jointly unless they encountered disagreement, in which case veto power went to husbands. Jenkins explained why she left larger decisions to her husband: "He's the wage-earner and has the right to say about what goes on in his home." Economic power and the legacy of male privilege held sway, but not without cost.

For women, coping with a subordinate voice in family affairs required more than meek acceptance. Jenkins revealed her method of coping when she disagreed with her husband. She said, "I work by the iron hand in the velvet glove. He never knows." She went on to describe the elaborate lengths to which she went to change his mind without openly confronting him. One year she wanted a coffee table that he did not think they needed. Her scheme involved hot coffee and biscuits warm from the oven and comically collapsing portable TV tables—Doris's description rivals any episode of *I Love Lucy*. Nevertheless, she got her coffee table, and it was his decision. Malcom McKee's comment sheds light on the male perspective. "I have the impression she lets me make the final decision, but I think we men are fooling ourselves, often. The women make many decisions that they let us think [we] make."[78]

Other women objected to their husbands' unilateral rule of the roost. Leonard Stone admitted his wife was not completely happy with his attitudes. Not only did she feel he tried to "tell her how to run things," but she accused him of talking to her "more like I talk to the Mexicans who work for me." This comment is as revelatory of the racial hierarchy at Leonard Stone's business as it was of the gender hierarchy in his home. In his estimation, she would not think him bossy if only she were "more dominant." Miriam Stone would complain to Leonard about his authoritative behavior, unbecoming of a democratic modern husband, but was unwilling to take a more assertive stance of the running of the household. A minority, five couples, mentioned conflict resulting from male authority when asked about decision making.[79]

While couples disagreed over how much authority men should wield in their homes, few endorsed female authority. To some, sharing seemed perilously close to tipping the balance of power in an "unhealthy" direction. Tom Cole said he and his wife shared authority at home but was quick to add, "She certainly doesn't want to dominate our family. It's half and half responsibility. She doesn't want to step aside and let me make all the decisions." Nancy would not bow out; yet Tom wanted it clear that she did not overrule him. Trying to explain the way he and his wife worked things out, Adam Walker said, "I'm not henpecked, but still my wife has certain rights, too," revealing both his acceptance of and his deep discomfort with new definitions of shared marital authority. Middle-class married women expressed concern with wielding too much family authority, and yet they appear to have exercised a measure of influence alongside their husbands.[80]

But Leonard Stone had difficulty accepting his wife's request for more cooperation and consideration. He explained, "I just had been used to the man making the major decisions and I believe homes are happier that way." Eventually the Stones worked out a compromise. Miriam took more responsibility for running the home, because, as Leonard put it, "That's her job." By dividing authority into spheres, couples could affirm that they made decisions equitably, but major decisions remained the masculine prerogative.[81]

Thus, one way couples solved the marital authority problem was by ceding spheres of influence to one spouse or the other, meaning women took responsibility for daily decisions around the home and men took responsibility for larger family decisions. Nearly 10 percent of couples described their division of authority in this manner. Spheres of influence meant that small decisions, which men often viewed as inconsequential, fell to wives and major ones to husbands. Thomas Williams said that while he preferred to steer clear of home furnishing choices, his wife encouraged his involvement. He affirmed his hands off approach, however, saying: "I figure that she has the say in things around the home." That this was a common modus operandi is indicated by a study of more than one thousand Florida families with teenagers in the home (couples slightly older than those in this case study). Theodore B. Johannis Jr. questioned teens about economic activity in their home. Household purchasing of everything from furniture and appliances to groceries was seen as mothers' purview in over 84 percent of the families while car purchase, doling out allowances, and paying bills fell to fathers for over 76 percent. In general, the bigger ticket the item, the more likely men were to take charge.[82]

Dean Lawrence endorsed the masculine prerogative. He said, "I expect my wife to be subject to her husband's statements and I don't expect her to defy them." He asserted a gradually vanishing viewpoint. Howard Sims's comments reflect both his investment in the traditional male role and his understanding of new expectations for mutuality. He said, "It isn't that I think I'm king, and the king does no wrong. I think she realized that if there's a domineering one, I'm the domineering one. She kind of lets me have my way a lot of the time."[83]

Nearly a third of these couples adopted a democratic approach. James and Sharon Richards worked at sharing family decision making. James said, "It's always 50–50, at least we've attempted it, as far as economics goes, on major purchases. . . . I respect her opinions and she respects mine." James said the Richards went "back and forth" on some issues, implying a habitual give and take in their decision-making process. The Mannings also worked at an equitable decision-making process. Claire said, "We make decisions jointly. Nick has interests in things around the house as well as in the major things such as buying the car. He's interested in the little things too. It's a pretty mutual kind of thing between us."[84]

Competing modes of behavior coexisted within marriages. Alice Bremmer made key decisions about purchases, decisions which her husband disputed. She said, "When I bought the dining room set, he got stinking about it. He had to go out and look at it and made me feel like he has no faith in what I would buy. I bought a sewing machine once and he never let me forget it." They were "a bit on the old-fashioned side, where the man is the head of the family. He wears the pants but I don't feel left out." She went ahead with her own plans and ideas, incurring her husband's irritation when she did so but persisting nonetheless, even as she asserted he "wore the pants." The adjustments made to accommodate husbands' authority were wives' to make. And men tended to favor their prerogative to have the final say. Still many of these men made conscious attempts to fashion collective decision making and to make the interviewer aware of their modern sensibilities regarding their wives' right to input in marriage.[85]

The marital standoff of the 1950s is probably best summed up by the conclusions of two sociologists, Theodore Johannis Jr. and James M. Rollins. Their survey showed that "majority agreement of all groups was that the husband should be the head of the family" but also that "all groups distinguished between 'head of the family' and 'boss of the family.'" When it came to the concept of boss, "the majority in each group felt that no one person should be boss." Americans tended to express support for egalitarian notions of marriage in theory but in reality reverted to customary spheres of influence and responsibility. There was no place for a "boss" in postwar democratic family life but every family needed a "head," generally defined as male. When the sociologists asked the Florida teenagers they studied about family decision making, 63 percent of the teens perceived their parents as a "joint decision making team." But when the researchers asked for reports on who actually made decisions about the performance of various chores at home, they found that decision making was "more frequently shared in activities which traditionally may have been participated in by both fathers and mothers . . . least frequently shared in activities which have been the bailiwick of one parent." The researchers had uncovered a clash of "expectancy with observed role performance." Similarly, compromise and experimentation between egalitarian ideals and traditional customs characterized early marriage. The contrast between ideal and reality created contradiction and thus fodder for further change, especially once the demanding years of early childrearing had passed.[86]

Young couples upheld a shifting code of behavior that was both spouse- and self-enforced. In the process of complex negotiations over who did what in the home, the baby boom's parents created a transitional marital pattern, based on the outline of traditional gender roles and a built-in flexibility. This pattern featured shared or female breadwinning in the early years of marriage, conflict over household roles, negotiated decision-making patterns, and calls for active male parenting once children arrived. Dyer and Urban, in their study of young married couples found that there had been a partial "institution of equalitarian family norms" in three main arenas of family life: childrearing, decision making, and recreation. Equalitarianism broke down, however, when it came to household tasks. Both men and women reported expecting and practicing the equal sharing of financial decisions, but married women desired more equality than they experienced in practice when it came to child-rearing tasks. Middle-class women had more to gain from the new ethos of sharing popularized in family magazines in the 1950s, yet many continued at least to profess a belief in a man's right to rule and rest in his own home. These are the confusing strands of gender role change.[87]

Many youthful marriages benefited from wives' financial contributions before children arrived. The marked rise in family income associated with fifties affluence resulted in part from the contributions of married women workers. Middle-class wives worked so that their families could afford the accoutrements of a middle-class lifestyle—big ticket consumer items like household appliances and cars—a new definition of need based on postwar standards of living and consumption. Material aspirations transformed middle-class notions of need and young married women's definition of their role.

Youthful marriage conjured up images of brash experimentation. But ad hoc innovation battled with conventional expectation. Modern egalitarian expectations met with traditional ones and the latter often won out, at least initially. Conforming to marital roles was an uneasy process that mixed conflict into the relationship. And young couples clearly suffered emotionally as a result. Weary, overworked breadwinners were met at the door by teary, tired homemakers in suburban homes. Marriage may not have trapped these couples but the power of traditional gender roles and the pressure to mature and shoulder their responsibilities could. Yet to stop the story here and portray men as victims of the rat race outside the home and oppressors or alternatively "poor put-upon dad" swallowed up by the female world within it and women as fully trapped by domesticity and motherhood is to miss an important plot line. This was the early period of the family cycle, and, most important, these men and women were young, with many years of marriage ahead of them. Misery could lead to resignation or prompt a renegotiation of roles. The division of family labor and the distribution of economic power were the real barriers to postwar egalitarian hopes. It was exactly in these two areas that baby boom parents began to chip away at tradition.[88]

One cannot escape, however, a sense of egalitarian potential thwarted by the division of labor that accompanied the transition to parenthood. Emerging norms competed with traditional ones, and often the much-hailed experimentation of modern marriage reverted back to strict notions of male and female responsibility. And while fulfilling adult gender roles in their families gave couples satisfaction, it was also fodder for their discontent. The battles over clean laundry and checkbook balancing, frustrating and sad though they may have been to experience, could lead to compromise as well as conformity. But the issues postwar couples of the baby boom years dealt with prior to feminism still plague couples today, in the movement's wake. It is both fascinating and sobering to uncover the early history of this long process of gender role change.

Allegiance to traditional sex roles limited the scope of gender role transformation in the 1950s but did not preclude it. In fact, this very allegiance generated much of the difficulty couples experienced early in marriage, a factor that those who celebrate "traditional families" ignore. While childrearing and home-centered leisure did focus individuals on the family, this experience was not necessarily a conservative one. As couples struggled to fulfill the demands placed upon them, they also negotiated with one another and began a process of marital redefinition still in progress today. Sociologist Robert O. Blood Jr. saw psychological pressure, primarily originating with women, as a key force in role evolution. He surmised,

the TV-watching husband reclines within sight and hearing of his table-setting wife. And as she goes about the dinner preparations, she is visually reminded not only of her husband's ease but of the other chores which need doing; the dusting . . . baby tending, garbage emptying. . . . The existence of so much work to be done and of a man so potentially available to do it seems likely to create . . . a tendency to invite her husband's participation in these chores.[89]

And men responded to such invitations. "It's the late 1950s, and the kids are all under ten," a *Ms.* magazine reader recalled. "When my husband washes the dishes and puts the kids to bed two nights a week so I can take math courses to keep my brain from turning to Jell-O, is he doing a job or helping me with my job?" The cooperative efforts of couples in the fifties may not have redefined roles but did set precedents and expand them. Here, for example, baby-tending is shared. More significant is the implication that the home was less a trap than a crucible for a more egalitarian marriage pattern still being shaped today. In 1982, Gail Henderson recalled that she felt stuck in the early years of her marriage, which she described as conflicted. In the decades that followed, as they argued over and experimented with roles and responsibilities, this couple remade their marriage, until it became close and equitable. By rejecting tradition-bound notions of proper male and female behavior with which they had grappled unsuccessfully in the 1950s, they "made the most" of their marriage.[90]

As we shall see, women did more than invite men to take up the occasional household chore: they insisted men take a hand in parenting. But first, we turn to fundamental changes in the scope of women's family roles. By beginning family at young ages and, for the most part, completing childbearing in their early thirties, this generation of women found themselves freed of the more demanding aspects of homemaking by their mid-thirties. What they chose to do with the time that they had formerly devoted to full-time childrearing profoundly changed family and marriage. A period of shared breadwinning, albeit brief, in early marriage was a key component of the fifties contested egalitarian marriage pattern and set a precedent for future female contributions to the family bank account.

"Teacher feels she is a better mother": In 1953, Life *magazine featured a laudatory article about mothers who worked to improve family life materially. Here one mother is shown at home, with the appliances her salary has provided arrayed around her. Married women's employment created much of the affluence postwar families enjoyed.* NINA LEEN, © LIFE MAGAZINE.

To Row Your Own Boat

The Impact and Meaning of Employment for the Mothers of the Baby Boom

In 1963, Betty Friedan published *The Feminine Mystique*, an unmistakable clarion call to women to step beyond the bounds of the home for meaningful work. That same year *The Employed Mother in America*, a less popular academic book, also appeared. While it did not meet with the same reception, its soothing findings about mothers and work soon filtered through to popular literature in the 1960s. Also in 1963, the President's Commission on the Status of Women submitted its report to Congress and the president. The fanfare over Friedan's book overshadowed the other two, but together the three reflected changes in women's lives in the decade and a half after World War II. The timing of popular, academic, and government attention to married women's new role is no coincidence. That year the women in this study and their cohort nationally were between the ages of thirty-five and forty-two and their younger children had reached school age. Thus, while it passed much like any other year, 1963 signifies a turning point for American women and their role in the family and society. These publications hint at the transformations already underway by the early 1960s.[1]

Middle-class American women in the 1950s, 1960s, and 1970s turned to wage earning as an additional contribution to family life. By 1963, 41 percent of American women 25 to 44 years old were in the labor force. American women at all stages of the life cycle, but especially mothers of school-age children, were reshaping the American family, the labor force, and American society.[2] Women's labor-force participation was linked to the family cycle and increased with age, a pattern that becomes apparent when we follow cohort-based participation statistics. In 1960, over a third of American women ages 25–34 worked. In 1968, approximately half of all women ages 35–54 worked. And in 1982, 62 percent of women between the ages of 45 and 54 were in the labor force. Their taste for work continued to increase while the next older cohort was still going strong: 42 percent of those aged 55–64 were employed. Not only did more and more American women enter the workforce each postwar decade, but as women moved through the life cycle until they reached their late fifties, they were more and more likely to be employed. Postwar married women's increasing taste for employment is reflected in the labor-force participation of the IHD women over the life course.[3]

In the 1950s, a third of the women in my IHD sample worked between marriage and childbearing. As a group, these women worked a mean of 2.3 years before the birth of their first child, even at a time when young married women's rate of employment was diminishing in comparison to that of other age groups. One-fifth remained in the labor force after their children were born. Even early marriage did not entirely preclude employment for young women after the war.

As IHD women moved through the family cycle, they were increasingly likely to work. Sociologist John Clausen and political scientist Martin Gilens found that the average age at reentry to the workforce for IHD women as a whole was 36.3. Thus they were likely to return to work between the years 1957 and 1964, when they had school-age children and were free, at least part of the day, to pursue employment. While many worked once their children reached school age, by 1969, their children had left home and the percentage of mothers employed jumped even more, to 43 percent.

In my smaller sample, the employment rate was even higher. More than half of those women worked in the late 1960s and early 1970s. In 1982, even when these women were over 54 and thus potential retirees, nearly 40 percent were still working. Clearly, despite early marriage, high fertility, and stay-at-home expectations while their children were young, the women in this study integrated a role outside the home into their family lives.[4]

In 1963, the mothers of the baby boom proved a ready audience for publications on women and work. They were either already at work, contemplating entry into employment, or poised to send their youngest child off to school and thinking about what they would do next. Homemakers who made the transition to part- and full-time employment in the 1960s and 1970s undertook work in the name of family need. Women's historians have tended to dismiss the importance of this development because of the rationale behind it. But while couched in "traditional" rationale, middle-class women's employment had important ramifications for the family, the workplace, and American society as a whole.

The employment patterns of postwar women rested on precedents set in the 1940s. Changes in the nature of the labor market before and after World War II made the choice to seek employment at midlife possible for the mothers of the baby boom. The massive mobilization of the home front during the war opened unprecedented economic and employment opportunities: married women and mothers of young children in particular went to work in greater numbers than ever before. In addition to opening comparatively better-paid industrial positions to women, wartime hiring loosened cultural barriers against married women employees. Americans accepted married women's work as an exigency of the war.[5]

Yet temporary necessity brought no enduring elevation of the status of women workers. Inroads into occupations traditionally defined as male did little to dismantle sex-based occupational segregation and pay scales in or outside war industries. Women's employment advances during the war did not improve women's actual economic or social status as workers in the long run. Nor did it result in any lasting government or corporate commitment to solving working mothers' child-care dilemmas.[6]

Still, the wartime mobilization of the female labor force signaled an irreversible transformation in the makeup of that labor force. Contrary to government propaganda about Rosie the Riveter, which portrayed her as young and single, the real-life Rosie was a Mrs. and likely as not over thirty-five years old. By 1950, 52 percent of all working women were married, more than twice the figure in 1945. Beginning during World War II, married women became an ever increasing presence in the workforce and this presence would continue to grow each decade.[7]

Three important factors contributed to the expansion in older and married women's work in the 1950s. First, responding to the labor squeeze brought on by the coming of age of a small cohort of women following World War II, the falling age of marriage, and the rising marriage rate, employers reconsidered their longstanding prejudice against married women workers for the simple reason that they could no longer rely on a steady supply of single women. Marriage bars—state laws and corporate rules that banned the hire of married women and ended the careers of single women who wed—disappeared once the steady supply of single female workers evaporated. Second, for the same reason, employers made part-time work available for the first time. Part-time work met the needs of mothers and wives, encouraging women who would have otherwise rejected full-time employment. Third, through the 1950s and 1960s, the tertiary labor sector expanded, creating increased opportunities for women. Women's educational histories both prepared them for these largely clerical jobs and whetted their appetite for more demanding jobs commensurate with their educational background and developing skills.[8]

Paradoxically, married women's share of the labor market increased in the same decade that family incomes rose and family size grew. One would expect that with more children at home and higher salaries for their husbands, married women in the 1950s would feel less need to seek paid work outside the home and more need to perform essential unpaid labor at home. But focus on fifties family size obscures the actual ability of women to enter the labor force at different stages in the family cycle. First, the biggest expansion in married women's work in the 1950s was with women over 35, those whose children were in school or grown, while the number of employed mothers with young children increased much more slowly. Second, middle-class women in this decade reduced the number of years they spent occupied with full-time childrearing by clustering births close together. In this way the stage was set for a takeoff in married women's work in the 1960s, when the baby boomers reached school age.[9]

Economy and demography also contributed to women's greater labor-force participation. As the requirements of financing the Great Society escalated and the costs of the Vietnam War grew, the nation's households faced new economic limits, especially as compared with the relative prosperity of the 1950s. Inflation, the energy crisis, and the recessions of 1968–69 and 1974–75 all took their toll on American families. To continue to meet aspirations or to maintain a comfortable standard of living in the face of a changing national economy, wives and mothers marched off to work. Finally, by midcentury, women's life spans had lengthened, and many women realized that they faced a significant period of adulthood before old age without the responsibility of full-time motherhood. Thus, the baby-boom childbearing pattern created availability and demand for mothers' employment within the family. Both new freedom and family need opened employment possibilities for homemakers eager to earn extra income, get out of the house, and, increasingly, to seek personal fulfillment. By 1972, the typical middle-class family could no longer be described as headed by a male breadwinner and a full-time, stay-at-home wife. Instead, the typical American wife worked.[10]

Despite this steady growth in married women's employment since 1945, Americans persist in viewing changes in women's work and family patterns as new. Feminism, as some conservatives would have it, dragged women kicking and screaming out of the home, or at the very least bamboozled them into thinking they were dissatisfied there. Feminists and historians have contributed to this perception by painting a portrait of American women around midcentury as placidly contained in suburban middle-class homes. The stifled middle-class housewife completely devoted to family on the surface, bedeviled with discontent deep within, has in fact become a trope in the history of the revival of feminism. Daughters of the 1950s, we read in one account after another, rejected the homeward focus of the female life course largely in reaction to the dissatisfied, repressed lives their mothers led in the 1950s and 1960s.[11]

Betty Friedan first packaged the image of domestic discontent of the 1950s and its repressive impact on middle-class women in her 1963 bestseller, *The Feminine Mystique*. According to Friedan, an array of cultural authorities from advertisers to magazine editors to psychoanalysts conspired to convince women that female happiness was to be found only through marriage and family. But this cultural onslaught of fulfillment through brighter whites, fluffier cakes, and sparkling linoleum hid a darker side of discontent. Women's dissatisfaction Friedan dubbed "the problem that had no name." But Friedan named the problem and called the ruse, proposing an alternative life plan for women, based heavily on her belief in full human potential. *The Feminine Mystique* blew the lid off female dissatisfaction, and homemakers answered Friedan's beckoning call to careers. This version of postwar women's history has come to be widely accepted and only recently questioned and broadened.[12]

Friedan oversimplified middle-class women's predicament in the 1950s, overstated the all-consuming quality of the domestic ethos of the decade, and hid the vast diversity of women's experiences behind the full skirts of the bored middle-class homemaker. The picture is much more complicated. Historian Joanne Meyerowitz's survey of a wider selection of mass culture magazines than the women's magazines that Friedan examined reveals a broader spectrum of opinion about women's roles during the 1950s. In mainstream magazines, Meyerowitz discovered "a celebration of nondomestic as well as domestic pursuits and a tension between individual achievement and domestic ideals." Not only did Friedan gloss over the alternative expressions of gender beliefs, but she also ignored a significant theme of acknowledged discontent present in fifties women's magazines, according to historian Eva Moskowitz. This theme, expressed in marital advice columns, articles, and quizzes, "contributed to a discourse of discontent," about the domestic sphere while it affirmed a right to personal happiness, helping to set the stage for the feminist revival. As new research shows, despite its importance as a historical document, *The Feminine Mystique* serves poorly as an historical account of the 1950s. Not the beacon that Friedan and historians have portrayed it, her book instead echoed the thinking of countless suburban women like its author. The real power of *The Feminine Mystique* lies in its timely resonance for middle-class mothers who had reached midlife by the early 1960s and wanted, in Friedan's words, "something more," outside the domestic sphere.[13]

Friedan's version of the immediate postwar years and women's work posits a sudden shift from propaganda recruiting Rosie to the factory to propaganda returning her to the kitchen; yet popular views about women's work during the 1950s were actually more diverse than Americans have assumed, reflecting the irreducible impact of the wartime experience. Meyerowitz has amply documented the diversity of opinion in mass circulation magazines with regard to women's achievement and gender roles in the 1950s. Here, I discuss magazine articles that specifically referred, by title or subject matter, to women's work between 1950 and 1972. I include in this sample 34 articles from magazines that run the gamut from *Better Homes and Gardens* to *America*, a Catholic monthly, from women's magazines to what Meyerowitz dubbed "high brow" magazines such as *Harpers* and the *New Yorker;* and more mainstream, news-oriented magazines, such as the *New York Times Magazine* and *Time*, with the goal of uncovering the nuances of opinion and poles of concern about working women in the postwar years.[14]

Popular magazine articles supported and even advocated part-time and sometimes full-time jobs for women, even those with children. These views in both women's and general audience magazines reveal the wide-spread ambivalence concerning women's roles in American life during the 1950s. Writer Gerry Murray Engel pinpointed the nation's postwar ambiguity when she wrote, "For I am that contemporary question mark, a working mother." Reluctant acceptance of working mothers in prescriptive literature depended on the willingness of married women to work the double shift of paid labor outside the home and unpaid domestic labor within it and to work only once children were of school age. Detractors worried about the harm even women who met all those conditions might do to the nation's families.[15]

A 1953 *Life* photo essay focused on the "novel" phenomenon of the working wife. The editors highlighted working wives' commitment to bettering family life materially in order to derail critics who accused mothers with careers of individualist, ambitious aims. The text accompanying the photo spread compared the "strident suffragettes" who worked "to prove their equality with men" to "the typical working wife of 1953 [who] works for the double paycheck that makes it possible to buy a tv set, a car—or in many cases simply to make ends meet." Wives who worked to achieve family financial goals won acceptance by not working for individualist goals. The authors of the 1957 Ford Foundation study *Womanpower* noted this popular approval: "The desire to achieve a richer life for the family has such widespread approval that it provides a generally acceptable reason for married women whose responsibilities at home do not absorb all their time and energy to go to work." When mothers worked to meet needs at home, Americans condoned and even commended their jobs outside it.[16]

Supporters of married women's work pointed to the qualitative improvements for families that mothers with jobs provided. Writer Bernice Fitz-Gibbon, in an impassioned argument in favor of working wives, noted that they could improve their own as well as their families' lives. Women's wages brought material improvements and enhanced the quality of family life: "Electric dryers and dishwashers and a second vacuum cleaner upstairs and three telephone extensions do cut down on the household drudgery." To those who worried that working women might ignore their biological potential as mothers, David Yellin, in "I'm Married to a Working Mother," argued that his wife's job had in fact enabled them to attain their desired family size. He asserted, "Our two salaries have provided economic sanction for having children sooner and oftener." Far from detracting from family life, employed wives made it possible or enriched it, these writers suggested.[17]

The *New York Times* family columnist, Dorothy Barclay, reported on experts who agreed "if for her own morale, a mother feels she must have a job, it is better for her to do so than to fret and strain at the tasks of full-time homemaker to the detriment of her disposition and ultimately her family's happiness." As early as 1948, marriage advisor Frances Strain wrote in support of women "whose kitchens have so recently been mechanized, [who] love their homes and their children, but . . . need challenging occupations and need them beyond their own doorsteps." These writers recognized a rising desire among homemakers to earn money outside the home but, perhaps more important, contribute more than mothering skills to society. Full-time homemaking might not be for everyone and a job might be the best alternative, they acknowledged.[18]

Employment also won praise because of its long-term benefit for the working woman: it prepared her for life after childrearing. Yellin wrote "My wife's career is the best of all insurance policies for her future." By doubling up on career and motherhood, Mrs. Yellin would maintain her skills, always be able to support herself and the children, and be assured of an interesting occupation later in life. Postwar commentators recognized that childrearing occupied a briefer stage in women's lives, a theme Friedan expanded on seven years later.[19]

In contrast to sanction and acceptance, opposition to mothers and wives working centered on the maintenance of proper gender roles. Robert Coughlan told readers of *Life* that although a working mother might think she worked in the interest of the family, deep down, he suspected, another factor lurked. His list of the few acceptable reasons for wives to work ended with a warning: "a large number of young mothers work, not because they really have to but because in fact they are rejecting the role of wife and mother." Doubtful of the family need excuse, he urged women to put their children's moral and emotional well-being over their material well-being and reconsider employment. Signs of outside interest, he hinted, indicated psychological problems. He voiced the notions that Friedan called the "feminine mystique."[20]

According to critics like Coughlan, working wives imperiled the foundation of American family life, sex roles themselves. If American women en masse rejected the role of wife and mother by taking up careers, what might become of American men? Novelist Sloan Wilson posed a topsy-turvy scenario of gray-flannel clad *women* dashing off each day "while the men are left behind to loll around the house in kimonos, smoking cigars and cussing as they do the dishes." To prevent men from becoming "more motherly," Wilson concluded, "maybe even in 1950, the place for women is in the home."[21]

Why was it so important to Sloan Wilson and others in the 1950s that women remain at home? For Wilson it was simple. Modern corporations demanded so much of their male executives that many "have almost no time for anything but work." And it was up to executives' wives to "take up the slack at home." According to Wilson, "Modern man needs an old-fashioned woman around the house." Keeping a home for a young executive was enough job for any wife, in Wilson's estimation. Clifford Adams, marriage columnist for *Ladies' Home Journal*, agreed. In 1954, he told readers to "Fulfill duties to husband, home and marriage ahead of all other, discontinue activities that interfere. Marriage is a career itself, a job does not relieve a wife of household responsibilities." For the sake of husband, marriage, and society, commentators urged women to forsake outside careers, for the acceptable "career" of mother and wife.[22]

Well-known pediatrician Benjamin Spock also argued against mother working—this time for the sake of her child. He, like Coughlan, found little to praise in the reasons mothers gave for working. Mothers of infants, toddlers, and small children belonged at home caring for them, Spock advised. Money and personal satisfaction paled in comparison to the needs of a growing child. Spock wrote, "If a mother realizes clearly how vital this kind of care is to a small child, it may make it easier for her to decide that the extra money she might earn, or the satisfaction she might receive from an outside job, is not so important, after all." Spock urged women to renounce the potential gains of employment and played on the limited occupational horizon married women faced, in comparison to the joys of motherhood: "It doesn't make sense to let mothers go to work making dresses in a factory or tapping typewriters in an office, and have them pay other people to do a poorer job of bringing up their children." When the most popular purveyor of childrearing expertise denigrated mothers' employment, his words doubtless carried great weight. Yet, the attention he gave to the matter signaled that regardless of expert opinion, American mothers opted for employment. Interestingly, instead of offering fulfillment through staying at home, these authors stressed responsibility and sacrifice for the good of the family and society.[23]

Critics and supporters alike worried about family upkeep in homes where mothers worked. Writer David Yellin carefully demonstrated that his wife's job in no way turned him into a housekeeper. He had never even made his own breakfast. Mrs. Yellin's paycheck provided not only every modern appliance but also a "combination housekeeper nursemaid." Journalist Dorothy Thompson joined in recommending that working mothers hire household help, for, she warned, a woman could not work two jobs for long. These advisors placed household responsibility squarely in mother's lap and proposed individual solutions, available only to families who could afford to pay household help.[24]

Another journalist did propose public solutions to the problems of working mothers. Writing in 1951, Gertrude Samuels argued for childcare facilities and convenient transportation. Granted, a working mother led a double life by choice. Nonetheless, she suggested, "since production is linked directly to morale, it would seem both realistic and profitable to guard her health, psychologically as well as physically, to understand her family as well as factory needs." Yet, at the end of the decade the practical assistance and consideration of family needs that Samuels had proposed in 1951 remained unavailable, and these issues draw only inadequate attention today. In *Womanpower*, the nation's experts on woman's labor could not decide how to create these services for women workers or who should provide them. "Responsibility for developing and maintaining services needed by women as wives, mothers, and workers," they wrote, "does not rest on any single element in the complex structure of private and public agencies, citizen and professional groups, or levels of government." Household help was out of reach for most middle-class families, and social services for working mothers appeared at the bottom of the national agenda. Solutions to the dilemma of household work in prescription and reality fell to the individual working mother to devise.[25]

In fact, marriage experts cautioned wives with jobs about the size of the task they undertook, because in the notion of the "two-job" marriage in the 1950s, the wife had two jobs and the husband one. Author Edmund Bergler warned, "Successfully to combine the roles of wife-mother-career woman, however, the wife must accept the fact that usually it means double work for her; the husband's working day ends at five, his wife's task is only half done at the time." Helping with the dishes, which any fair-minded husband might do, he pointed out, made only a small dent in the long list of tasks most housewives performed. Frances Strain, author of *Marriage Is for Two*, concurred that some married women could and should have a career. But she warned that husbands would protest unless the wife was "one of those wives who are able to dismiss their business interests and become all wife during home hours." The burdens of the double day fell to the working wife in a pattern that would continue throughout the postwar era.[26]

Deeply held beliefs about men's and women's roles and concern to protect the sexual division of labor in the American home united the two sides of opinion on the issue of women's work. Both joined in locating responsibility for household maintenance and child care with the working mother or the woman whom she hired as her substitute. No one proposed anything beyond the most modest role-sharing. Sanction for women's work rested on the smooth running of the home, leading to the double day. While working-class and African-American women had been juggling these roles for decades, the middle-class working mother was news in the 1950s, and again twenty years later. Public concern over the "two-job wife" in the 1950s foreshadowed the "superwoman" discussion of the 1970s.

Although Betty Friedan painted a monochromatic picture of wholesale media condemnation of working motherhood and nondomestic womanhood in the 1950s, complex popular attitudes toward employed mothers vied with the Feminine Mystique and paved the way for later acceptance. A full decade before Friedan published her incisive survey of women's magazines, writers countenanced work for married women and mothers, suggesting that domesticity was not enough for many American women. Advocates emphasized the benefits to families of mothers' paychecks and of homemakers challenged by outside work. Opponents of women's work harped on the damage to marriages, developing children, and sex roles that a woman's job could cause.

In the 1950s, a third of the women in my sample were employed before their first child was born. Twenty percent were working mothers with small children. Their work was usually part-time or intermittent, as the only way they could fit work around childrearing. Working mothers with young children at home in the 1950s relied on individual solutions for child care, turning to flexible work shifts, parents, neighbors, and babysitters to work out child-care arrangements. When child-care arrangements fell through, it was the working mother's dilemma. This was the bargain women in the 1950s accepted when they went to work. So Ava Michaels said, with conviction, "If I thought for a minute it would interfere with taking care of my kids I would quit."[27]

For the majority of full-time homemakers work had to fit in around family life. Thirteen percent of IHD women anticipated an end to intensive mothering and planned to seek work. Their long-term plans to engage in work outside the home lend credence to demographer Susan Van Horn's assumption that the concentrated childbearing pattern of the baby boom was not accidental but instead an intentional clustering of births that enabled women to complete childbearing early in life. Janice Rogers, for example, intended to take classes while her children were small to prepare for employment when they were older. She wanted to work so that she could "pay her own way" and because she believed she would find satisfaction working. Alice Bremmer, a full-time mother in the 1950s, predicted that she would have "lots of energy when the children are grown and I'm not going to spend it keeping the house clean." In 1958 she already had nascent plans to go into business for herself, a goal she achieved in the 1970s. Men, too, saw work as an increasingly important part of women's lives. In 1958 James Richards said that he hoped his wife would seek out a half-time job once the children were of age. It wasn't the money, he said, "But I hope she does something that adds to the richness of her life and gives her a sense of contribution, something aside from that she gives to our family." The mothers of the baby boom consciously ended childbearing at young ages, and many expected to make use of their later years for careers.[28]

Other women had a difficult time justifying their desire to go to work. Katie Ryder said that "as the children get older I feel I have to do something and I don't know what it is." But her family was not supportive of her new idea: "I talked about going back to work for a while and everyone laughed at me, but I think it would be fun to work just part-time." The paradigm set up in the 1950s that legitimized married middle-class women's work for the sake of family need could render other reasons for work superfluous or even worthy of ridicule.[29]

In the midst of mixed messages from the media, warnings of the extra work involved, and limited options for child care, mothers in the 1950s did return to work and by the 1960s the media's message had changed. Arguments in favor of women's work diffused throughout the media. Magazines with national readerships affirmed the growing consensus of the 1950s that once a woman's children no longer required full-time nurture and supervision, it was permissible, in fact desirable, that she go to work. In 1961, the editors of *Life* called on women to jump on the bandwagon to help "further American progress in education and business." Women's labor, not their leisure, added a new weapon to America's Cold War arsenal. Comparing women's share of the workforce in the United States and the Soviet Union, they determined that Soviet women "outscored" American women: "Most U.S. women call themselves 'housewives,' and the country is incalculably in their debt. But the term also covers a great pool of idleness and futility in the civilized world." In this view, midlife mothers were both an untapped national resource and an inactive leisure class.[30]

Betty Friedan amplified these views and provided a cogent analysis of the problem of the "trapped" housewife. She expanded women's place in

American society without reworking it. *How* to go back to work, not whether to, became the problem to be solved. Friedan preached to the converted when the *Feminine Mystique* appeared in 1963. She found that the middle-class American woman yearned for more than marriage and motherhood, often to her own surprise and shame. But, "each suburban wife struggled with it alone." As the typical woman went about her daily routine of sandwiches, carpools, slipcovers, and Scouts, "She was afraid to ask even of herself the silent question—'is this all?'"[31]

In *The Feminine Mystique* and other writings in the early 1960s, Friedan highlighted both dissatisfaction with homemaking and personal fulfillment in the world of work. She based her argument in part on the life stage that many mothers of the baby boom entered just as Friedan's book hit the bestseller list, the empty nest. She criticized the women of her generation's mistaken choice:

> They all thought all they had to do was get that man at nineteen and that would take care of the rest of their life, and then they woke up at twenty-five or thirty-five or forty-five with four children, the house, and the husband, and realized they had to face a future ahead in which they would not be able to live through others.

To fill the years of a woman's life after family demands receded, Friedan proposed the "fourth dimension," employment, to supplement wifehood, motherhood, and housekeeping.[32]

Friedan suggested women find "creative work" outside the family. She warned them not to make the mistake of leaving the unfulfilling home for an equally unfulfilling job, cautioning,

> But a job, any job, is not the answer—in fact, it can be part of the trap. Women who do not look for jobs equal to their capacity, who do not let themselves develop the lifetime interests and goals which require serious education and training, who take a job at twenty or forty to "help out at home" or just to kill extra time, are walking almost surely as the ones who stay inside the housewife trap, to a nonexistent future.[33]

But part-time jobs, even supposedly unfulfilling ones, contrary to Friedan's predictions, had an important impact on families, society, and women themselves.

Friedan's was only one of the publications that explored the topic of women and employment in 1963. Social scientists F. Ivan Nye and Lois Wladis Hoffman, in *The Employed Mother in America*, quieted persistent assumptions about the negative impact of women's work on American family life by assembling a compendium of careful studies. Working mothers were happy mothers, they found. The study showed no negative psychological differences between children of employed and stay-at-home mothers. Contributor Elizabeth Douvan even made the astonishing discovery that adolescent daughters of working mothers were, in fact, more mature and confident than daughters of nonworking mothers. The third publication of 1963, the report of the President's Commission on the Status of Women, highlighted the problems working women faced. The remedies that it proposed included tax breaks for child care, a government role in ending job discrimination, and equal pay. The report called attention to the changing role of women and precipitated the first piece of ameliorative legislation, the Equal Pay Act.[34]

Building on Friedan's lead and the results of these studies, writers in the 1960s operated from the assumption that "motherhood as a career no longer lasts a life time." Author Hilda Sidney Krech, herself the daughter of a working mother, focused on the problems women faced when they did return to work. A full-time mother at 40 was unprepared for employment. Krech suggested, "If it is assumed mothers, at some point, will become participating members of society, society should provide ways to help them."[35]

The difficulty of reentering the work world after decades spent mothering became the focus of late-sixties articles on working women. In 1966, *Ladies' Home Journal* printed an excerpt of Lois Benjamin's *How to Be a Working Mother without Really Crying*. Benjamin assured women that job and family could "all be made to work beautifully." She prescribed adaptability, creativity, and the "other woman"—a "mother substitute" during the day. Interestingly, Benjamin targeted mothers with young children still at home during the day, a fact which was sure to comfort mothers of older children returning to work. In 1968, Nannette Scofield, author of *So You Want to Go Back to Work*, wrote, "These days when the youngest child turns six and marches off to first grade, a mother has two alternatives: either she wipes a tear and goes to the kitchen for a second cup of coffee or she wipes that tear and marches off to work." Both writers assumed this transition was a natural, expected event in every woman's life.[36]

In 1972, *Time* magazine told the story of a 42-year-old suburban housewife who took a job when her youngest child turned five, under the headline, "The Reentry Problem": "After years of confident supremacy in the kitchen, they find themselves in a new and often hostile world, like a nun who has recently left the convent." Older women had difficulty because, according to *Time*, their skills and educations had become obsolete in the intervening years spent childrearing. The authors of this article failed to note that significant numbers of women surmounted the problems of reentry each year. In fact, in that very issue, *Time* announced the publication of three advice books to target the flood of reentry women. The list included the *How to Go to Work When Your Husband Is Against It, Your Children Aren't Old Enough and There's Nothing You Can Do Anyhow*. These three themes, of life stage, of personal fulfillment, and of adding outside jobs to women's labor in the home characterized the popular and scholarly approach to women's work in the 1960s and early 1970s. And approving attitudes toward married women's work became the norm. In 1967, 44 percent of Americans polled approved and women were more likely to approve than men. By 1976 approval had increased to 68 percent and women's approval topped men's 70 percent to 65 percent.[37]

With or without family encouragement the first task midlife women faced was job search. They had to convince themselves and prospective employers that they had skills of value in the marketplace. From the late 1950s to the mid-1960s, on average at the age of 36, women in this study went or returned to work. They faced the challenge of returning to a world from which they had been absent many years. In addition to prejudice against untrained homemakers in the workplace they battled their own lack of confidence. Mary Smith recalled taking the first steps toward employment: "That was the hard part, because I felt, you know, totally incompetent from being home doing diapers." Women who looked for work after years of homemaking also confronted their fears of failure. Betty Morris said before she had even made plans to go back to work, "I think after not working so many years, it's really frightening—the thought of going out and getting a job, you know . . . I'm really not that qualified." Homemaking did little to foster confidence in nonhousehold skills. These homemakers expressed pessimism about the options open to women with little work experience. Everything from pink-collar clerical work to sales positions seemed out of reach to homemakers after twenty years devoted solely to the home.[38]

Marriage orientation in their teen years and family focus in their twenties and early thirties made finding employment later in life difficult for the mothers of the baby boom, but they rose to the challenge. Women mentioned their lack of experience and their ten- to twenty-year hiatus from working as considerations in the decision to go back to work. Blanche Warner said she "thought about it a good long time before she found the nerve" to return to work. Evelyn Mitchell had experience in office work; she put her husband through school and worked when he was laid off in the mid-1950s. Still, when she was working in 1970, she commented, "It's ludicrous for a woman to be as unprepared for life as I am. I'm just skimming by by the skin of my teeth, you know. Every woman should have a profession or at least be very well qualified in clerical work." Mitchell and women like her recognized that women were increasingly likely to interweave employment with their family lives, whether by choice or necessity.[39]

Work they did before or during the early years of marriage aided the employment transition and influenced the types of jobs middle-aged women considered. Women's choices in midlife reflected not only the current openings in the labor market but also the options available to young women in the 1940s and early 1950s. Drawing on this prior work experience gave homemakers skills to build on when they reentered the labor market. For example, Meg Fisher thought she would apply at the same company in which she had started out; "I used to work there before we were married and I thought I'd just like to see if I could do it again." Sylvia Gould kept working part-time throughout the years when she was primarily a homemaker in order to stay in touch with new developments in her field. She said, "It was sort of really like an insurance policy because these things do change so rapidly. . . . I did feel that I wanted to keep my finger in." Her "insurance policy" not only helped finance her husband's professional degree but also enabled her to assume the role of family breadwinner after his death. Both prior experience and contemporary choices were shaped by occupational segregation. As of 1977 over two-thirds of American working women worked in the female sector of the labor market. Midlife women sought jobs in that sector of the workforce—office, health care, and retail environments—where they had first gained work experience as young women.[40]

Many women, however, had not planned beyond the years they focused on maternity and had a difficult time gaining a foothold in the world of work. For these women, temporary work experience often opened the door to permanent part- or full-time work. A temporary job gave them a chance to try out working and improve skills. Ruth Wright recalled that her job, which was just supposed to help make some payments on a new house, evolved. Wright recalled, "It all happened very strangely. I had no intention of going to work. . . . [My sister-in-law] said they were hiring part-time help just for the opening and why didn't I apply." In this case a family connection and the promise of temporary work paved the way to work commitment. Wright worked long past the opening and ultimately left that job to become a manager. In addition, temporary work eased the transition to the working world because by definition it implied little commitment, thus minimal deliberation. Nevertheless, for many women it began a long-term involvement in the labor force.[41]

Similarly convenient, flexible jobs—for example, home cosmetic sales—provided contacts and confidence that led to other work. Martha Bentley found her permanent job by selling that way. She recommended to "anyone starting out in the world that that's one way of getting out." Betty Morris's experience in sales led to a job offer as Christmas help in retail which itself developed into a permanent part-time position. She remembered, "It was kind of a fluke that I went to work. Well, the girls called me before Christmas and they needed somebody. . . . So I said, 'Sure, I'll come down. I'll work through Christmas.'" Christmas lasted ten years. These informal jobs were stepping stones to better opportunities for housewives, expanding their skills, experiences, and contacts; they eased women back into the work world, and led to long-term involvement in the labor market.[42]

Maureen Gordon worked for several years in an office until the arrival of the Gordons' first child. While she, as many women in the IHD, did not believe in a mother working when there were young children in the home, she drew on this experience from time to time as she raised her children. Like other women in the study, she took occasional temporary part-time jobs, at holiday times, for example, if there was "something special" the family wanted. But her work experience shaped her plans in other ways as well. Maureen did not like clerical work, so, in the late 1960s she returned to school to earn a bachelor's degree in her field of interest, something she could pursue while her children were in school.[43]

Many women already agreed with Friedan that full-time homemaking was unfulfilling but, unlike Friedan, saw part-time work as a real solution. Friedan warned that taking just any job meant falling only further into the "housewife trap"; yet "just a job" fit many women's expectations and needs or was a nonthreatening beginning to greater work commitment. The mothers of the baby boom took the jobs Friedan frowned upon but, as surely as Friedan, created changes in American women's lives. Part-time work would begin the transformation of family life.

Friedan asserted that housekeeping was no longer enough and suggested work as the source of self-fulfillment. But self-fulfillment at work was purchased at the price of a woman's willingness, through her flexibility, ingenuity, and diligence, to balance her new job with her old, to add in Friedan's fourth dimension without disrupting responsibility to children, husband, and house. Despite the difficulties, that is just what the IHD women began to do. The subtle shifts in public opinion in the 1960s were in fact outpaced by the sweeping impact of behavioral change.[44]

At first, couples interpreted married women's employment as furthering family aims and thus as an extension of the conventional female role, which tended to brake the potential of women's employment to bring about concrete change. If family propelled women into employment, it could also pull them right back out because the job had to fit in with their preordained responsibilities. The ideology that supported maternal employment in the cause of family need cut in two directions, then. On the one hand it legitimated wage earning; on the other, it meant delaying or short circuiting a return to work because of familial circumstances. Meg Fisher preferred part-time work to full-time because of the double day: "It takes too much out of you. . . . I enjoy working but not when you've got a home and family. . . . There are just too many things to do." Homemakers who went to work in the 1950s and 1960s rarely questioned the boundaries of sex roles in their homes. When the strains of the double shift pulled in opposite directions, the balance shifted in favor of housework. If they continued working outside the home, they remained responsible for "maintain[ing] a serene atmosphere at home."[45]

For most, part-time work was the only way to balance employment and motherhood. Being with the family and doing for the family remained of prime importance—leading to the exhaustion of mothers when they met the demands of both home and work and to feelings of guilt when they did not. Working outside the home made Judy Kent feel as though she led a split life. Not only did it mean cramming laundry, shopping, and cooking along with family fun all in on weekends, but in addition to the extra work, she missed her children. This was Judy's "big reservation" about combining employment with family. A famous working mother, columnist Erma Bombeck experienced this extra work when she began to write her column in the mid-1960s. For the first several years, she remembered, "As long as my husband smelled his bath towel and looked like he had just seen God, I felt I was allowed to pursue a career for another week." Bombeck wrote, "As the decade wore on, guilt was headed for glut proportions. More men would come home to cold stoves. Children would have their own keys to open the door to an empty house. . . . And it would all be my fault." When the towels lacked a fresh scent, when housekeeping standards slipped, women accepted the blame. As Bombeck's personal anecdote reveals, employed mothers of the 1960s worked double days. They won the right to work outside the home by continuing to fulfill their domestic responsibilities diligently within it.[46]

Thus, although the middle-class baby-boom daughters popularized the superwoman image of the American working wife and mother, their mothers, working full- or part-time, tackled the double shift—a job at home keeping house in addition to paid work outside the home—a decade ahead of them. Through the 1960s, when the mothers of the baby boom experienced the strain of working two shifts, these women questioned, not the division of labor in the middle-class nuclear family, but their jobs instead. Working meant they led "split lives." "Somebody" had to keep the home in order—mothers retained that responsibility. As their dual role endured, a minority would rethink the division of household labor. Yet by upholding nearly full responsibility for sustaining the household, women cushioned the impact of their employment on husbands and children. Indeed, by absorbing the repercussions of their employment and responding flexibly to family needs, they integrated paid work into middle-class women's life course, making it an anticipated part of married middle-class women's roles.[47]

Postwar women's employment provided concrete economic gains to families. In fact, the attraction of an additional paycheck motivated 69 percent of working wives in a 1963 survey. Second or larger homes, children's college educations, and inadequate husbands' salaries all prompted homemakers to seek remunerative work outside the home. The definition of need varied from family to family. Some mothers went to work in response to financial crises, while others took jobs so that the family could afford extras. Although an initial short-term financial need often inspired a woman to get a job, families came to count on that additional wage and mothers remained employed. Thus, traditional justification for women's employment often had unintended results. Indeed, despite citing financial need as the motivation for working, one half of employed women polled in the 1963 study said they would continue to work if they did not need the money.[48]

Often home purchases began a woman's employment odyssey. Three women who worked significant portions of their adult lives cited purchasing a home as motivating them to return to work. Ruth Wright recalled that she went to work because their new house had put the Wrights in "completely over our heads." Karen Lewis, who went to work once her children were of school age, "hated to leave the children," but she returned to work in order to make mortgage payments. For these baby-boom families, women's wages made home ownership possible.[49]

The cost of college tuition for baby boomers was another financial pressure that launched married middle-class women out into the work world at midlife. Because they had spaced their children so close together, the two to four children all reached college age at roughly the same time. In 1971, Judy Kent remembered that she had planned to work only temporarily through a tight period surrounding the purchase of their home, but "We have [one] in college and [another] starts in the fall." So, she continued to work. Lois Dyer recalled her first employment venture when her child went off to a school "which was much more expensive than we could afford." She worked in order "to pay for it." By the 1980s, Maureen Gordon's youngest child was enrolled at an Ivy League school. Gordon, who earned a bachelor's degree in the mid-1970s and a master's soon after, worked full-time and reported that most of her daughter's tuition came from her earnings. Wages of working wives enabled middle-class families to achieve family goals, goals that often included college education for their children.[50]

When husbands' incomes could not be counted on, wives went to work. Harriet Pollard got a job when her husband left a large firm to go into business for himself. Harriet said in 1970, "He just didn't have any work at all. Just nothing coming [in] so I went to work. . . . I needed a job right then and there." When her husband went to work for himself and the children were in school, Marlene Hill resumed the career she had stopped at pregnancy. Not only did these working wives get their families through rough financial periods, by their willingness to take up wage earning, they also provided their husbands with the opportunity to attain their occupational ambitions including further education and independent businesses.[51]

It was not always monetary need that channeled women into part- or full-time work. Many worked because of the extras they could then afford. By adding to the luxuries a family could enjoy, women provided a noticeable, desirable difference in the family standard of living even though she earned a supplementary salary. Unlike homemaking, employment evidenced concrete value in a paycheck. That paycheck, no matter how small, offered a more tangible contribution to family well-being than the unpaid and often unnoticed housework women performed day after day. Furthermore, work taken in the cause of family need also fed a desire for women's personal satisfaction as providers, shifting self-perceptions as well as family perceptions of mothers' roles.

On average, by the 1970s, married women's earnings amounted to one-third of their family income. Women valued their ability to contribute weekend trips and new clothes to the family standard of living. Sharon Richards explained, "Well, I don't need to work, but it is very handy for paying for the Christmas gifts, and the taxes and the trips, vacations, whatever." Gene Lewis appreciated the money his wife Karen brought in. In 1982 he said, "Well, it makes it easier for the family to obtain things. The kids have no problem on clothing, shoes, whatever their needs are." When the kids' athletic season rolled around, Karen's paycheck paid for shoes and uniforms for them. She, along with her husband, was an important provider for their children. Families came to rely on these "extras." This increasingly common contribution to family life empowered women, expanding their view of their role to include financing recreation, vacations, and enhancing middle-class lifestyles. The IHD asked Ruth Wright about her job's impact on family life. She replied adamantly, "It's improved [it]. I tell you. If I didn't work . . . well, we'd get by with no extras, no nothing." Supplementing their husbands' incomes, breadwinning wives claimed credit as providers, and took pride in filling this nondomestic family role.[52]

As wage earners these wives became breadwinners, some for the second time in marriage. Lorraine Sherwood was proud that she contributed to the family sustenance: "Well, it's enabled them to eat pretty well." Caroline Wood wanted to help her husband Walter provide for their children. She said, "I thought it was time that I brought in a little cash to keep it going." It was not just working women who perceived themselves as important, if supplementary breadwinners. Ava Michaels's husband Floyd, when asked to describe his wife, remarked immediately, "She's a good provider."[53]

Working outside the home, initially taken on in the cause of family need, further unraveled notions that narrowly confined motherhood to children and housework. Wage earning became an acceptable extension of that role. Once in the workplace, new financial needs replaced those that had triggered entry. In this way family need and aspirations for a more comfortable standard of living fostered work commitment. Just as in the early years of marriage, working wives' wages permitted the achievement of evolving family goals. Their salaries contributed to the attainment of comfortable, commodious suburban homes, male occupational independence, and college educations for the children. Without homemakers' willingness to define their roles to include paid employment, the economic status of two generations, one of which came of age during and after World War II and the other that came of age in the 1960s and 1970s, would not have been possible.

Certainly married women's wage work materially improved baby-boom family life. But employment had other, more individual meanings, working a transformation on the mindset of this generation of women. As they came to define their jobs differently, these women subtly contradicted the messages that they had been raised to believe. For example, Anne Matthews's employment contained different meanings, depending on her family's situation. She described a progression of reasons for her continued employment. "At first," she said, "it was to have extra money, you know, to do things, and then it was to help to support us. And now I want to make my life more meaningful."[54]

Sociability was one important aspect of work that made it meaningful to women. Jobs provided social outlets for women whose husbands were at work and whose children were at school during the day. Their appreciation of the friendly contacts they made on the job is testimony to the isolation many experienced as full-time homemakers. Ruth Wright considered her friends from work "more like a family, I'd say." At work, women created a sense of community and combatted the loneliness of the suburban middle-class home. In 1970, May Perkins said, "I hadn't been out of the house for a hundred years. And that is not good. Gee, you forget what makes the world go around."[55]

Part and full-time work functioned as an antidote to days dominated by the concerns of childrearing and running a household. After retiring from a decade-long part-time career, Irene Lawrence concluded: "Without that, I think I would have gone out of my mind. The housework was not challenging for me." Nina Harris thought that "probably, working was the only thing to preserve my sanity when I had teenagers at home." Getting out of the house, away from the housewife role was important to these married women workers. Like Friedan, they, too, wanted a "fourth dimension" in their lives.[56]

Working outside the home, women gained even more appreciation from family members for the labor they performed at home. Paid employment also identified personal needs and interests beyond the circumscribed world of the family, enabling an assertion of individual identity after decades in the service of others in the family. May Perkins insisted on working for one personal goal, a design certificate, but she struggled to communicate her commitment to her husband and children. She recalled, "So I was always, constantly, trying, trying, to make them realize that—Look

I've got something else to do and [I] want to do it." She opened a small business and ran it for a few months and was pleased with the results. She said, "I did it just long enough to have some fun, then came back home. They had all pretty much found out that I did contribute something, you know." Even if what they appreciated when she returned home was "that their laundry was done, and their meals," May now felt validated. She continued, long after her brief experiment as a shop owner, to pursue her calling on an informal free-lance basis.[57]

Working wives also valued their paychecks for conveying greater financial independence within marriage. In the late 1960s and early 1970s, they responded to the growing impermanence of American marriage and their own economic vulnerability as their husbands advanced in age. But more important, they valued the authority a paycheck conferred. Marlene Hill put in over a decade in a skilled trade. In the 1980s, she took early retirement but was still coming up with entrepreneurial possibilities for herself, when she commented, "Working, of course, gives you independence. It gives you a great deal of independence." Alice Bremmer, who did not work for pay in 1958, wanted a job so that she could "buy crazy things that I want to." In 1982, when she was running her own firm, Alice said, "to earn your own money means something. . . . [I] needed to know that I can row my own boat."[58]

Working provided rewards homemaking could not. First among those rewards was remuneration for one's efforts. In 1958, Gail Henderson, who later realized these goals, stated, "I'd like the feeling of making my own money and doing what I want to do with it." Employed women could set aside a portion of their hard-earned money as their very own. She remarked in 1982, "It is very important to me to be able to earn my own way and support myself after being dependent on my husband while the children were growing up." Independence gained when wives earned money at a part- or full-time job contrasted sharply with the financial dependence they had experienced as stay-at-home moms, leading them to feel less dependent on marriage itself for financial support. Anne Matthews credited her job for helping "me to know that I can do a job and am self-sufficient and can take care of myself. I don't have to lean on somebody else." These working women vehemently rejected prescribed female financial dependence, while demonstrating that lifetime homemaking was no longer fulfilling to growing numbers of women.[59]

Wage-earning wives referred directly to their fears of being left without support, usually in reference to widowhood. One reason Ava Michaels was happy to be hard at work in 1958 was "If any thing happened to my husband, I could support my children this way." Her husband Floyd was a policeman, and she confronted this risk sooner in marriage than other women might have, but she knew she could fully support herself if she was widowed. Thelma Morton decided with her husband Albert that, "with the world we're living in today, it's pretty darned important for a woman to be able to take care of herself financially." Working assuaged married women's sense of economic vulnerability. The increasing probability that a woman would face divorce, not widowhood, no doubt encouraged many married women to consider or take up paid employment as well.[60]

By 1982 many women could look back on years of experience in the workforce. Several had moved from the initial jobs that got them out from under housework to full-fledged careers. In the years since they started working, the number of women in the workforce had continued to expand. As older women without responsibilities for growing children, they could more freely express the personal as opposed to familial meaning of employment.[61]

Working transformed women's sense of themselves. Devoting years to the care of others took its toll on homemakers in loss of self-esteem. Working for pay outside the home remedied this lack for many women who had spent between five and twenty years concentrating on raising their children. Middle-aged married women who worked attributed the sense of self-worth they gained in later life to their employment.[62]

Earning money in itself provided an enormous boost to self-esteem. If a woman entered the labor force, she was no longer "just a housewife." Looking back over her nearly forty-year career, in 1982 Ava Michaels commented that her job gave her confidence in herself because "[I] knew I was capable of doing something other than being a housewife." Worthy of a paycheck, working wives felt better about themselves. In 1982 Barbara Spalding remarked, "It has given me self-esteem." In fact Spalding chose to be self-supporting and divorced her husband. Through employment, women learned about abilities that they were previously unaware they possessed. They may have been excellent mothers, gourmet cooks, creative interior decorators—homemakers skilled in innumerable ways—but just as housework went uncompensated, the skills it took to manage a home and family went unacknowledged. In offices, stores, hospitals, and classrooms, women discovered or applied previously hidden talents. Anne Matthews found her job satisfying because "I'm doing things [I] never thought I could do." Women who as homemakers did not feel "capable of much" learned otherwise at work. In the process of working, these women transformed their sense of themselves: their abilities, skills, and contributions to the family and society. Evelyn Mitchell, who a decade earlier stated that she was just barely scraping by at the office, said emphatically, "I found out I'm one hell of a business woman."[63]

Married women who went to work after their children were grown sought fulfillment or found it on the job. These women did not find home-making a wholly fulfilling career on its own. Although they continued to fill their roles as homemakers, they discovered important satisfactions working outside the home. In 1970, Martha Bentley said that since going to work, "I am a better person because I'm doing something interesting." While Maureen Gordon placed marriage and children first on her list of influences on her identity, her job was second. On the job, she not only put in a full work week, sometimes rising at 5 o'clock in the morning to finish everything, but also gained "self-confidence, compassion," and a sense that "I can do what I set out to do."[64]

Looking back, Judy Kent said, "I finally felt in my life that I was doing something worthwhile. There was a reason for my existence. That I could work in an area few people could." Raising a large family gave her a pur-pose, but her job conveyed a sense of self-worth. Blanche Warner said her job "has made me feel like I'm not just a wife, but more [Blanche]." Mary Smith, who went back to work when her children were midway through elementary school, credited her job with helping her as a parent. In addi-tion, she located it "at the core" of her identity, helping her to "know who I am and where I am." Wage work had personally gratifying and important meanings, including a feeling of economic autonomy and even self-sufficiency. When these women married, popular wisdom held that wom-en's fulfillment and identity lay in the home. They contradicted and trans-formed this ideology based on their experiences as full-time homemakers who made the transition to part or full time workers. They found enjoy-ment, purpose and fulfillment in their work.[65]

Employment transformed marriages as well as working women. Those men initially hostile to female employment came to appreciate their wives' economic participation in the family and the importance of occupations to their wives. In the memoir of her marriage, Erma Bombeck tells how her job ultimately revolutionized her relationship to her husband. When she started working she effectively doused husband Bill's objections to her job when she told him she made three dollars a column. But struggling to meet deadlines and still perform like a model homemaker, Bombeck became a self-described exhausted supermom. After "running on empty" for several years, she called a caucus announcing, "Everyone is welcome to pitch in," and summoned her family to help run the household. It did not happen over night and she did not always agree with her husband's version of his new job description, but their marriage, the work they each did at home, and his attitude toward her career shifted dramatically. Bombeck's fame worked in her favor, while other women's family contributions remained more obscure, providing varying degrees of leverage.[66]

Men's attitudes toward women's wage earning could also work to keep its role subordinate or its value hidden. Men objected because a wage-earning wife reflected poorly on a husband's ability to support his family and they disliked their wives' jobs because their values dictated that women belonged at home. Men with reservations about their wives' paid employment wanted to maintain the household arrangements celebrated, not necessarily lived, in the 1950s.

Nearly 10 percent of the men in this case study expressed their assumption that whether or not a wife worked was a decision for the husband to make. John Anderson remembered that when he was newly married to his first wife, she did not work, because he "didn't allow it." But his second wife worked throughout their marriage. As husbands and fathers, these men felt it was their duty to see to it that their wives fulfilled their roles as mothers. In 1982, Glen Dyer reported that "I wouldn't let [Lois] work for a long time. She had kids to raise."[67]

A wife's significant salary was a direct challenge to a husband's status as breadwinner and power in the family—both of which men felt were worth maintaining. Sometimes husbands objected to the amount a woman earned, not her job as such. Female wage earning was acceptable to husbands so long as it was clearly supplemental. Betty Morris worked briefly after marriage and before her children were born, but she soon quit. David Morris recalled, "She was still working at the lab and she was making more than I was so I made her quit." Rick Snyder, too, was bothered by his wife's high salary, although she continued to work until the arrival of their first child. In 1960 he complained, "She . . . makes good money—almost as much as I. It's a source of some conflict for us." In 1959, Joan Sinclair said flatly, "Andrew made it quite clear that as long as he was able to work that I was not going to work and that was it." If she were to work, it would reflect poorly on his breadwinning abilities. She agreed with Andrew that this was his decision to make. If breadwinning gave men the authority to decide whether their wives performed wage work, it was often their status as breadwinners that they sought to protect when they objected to their wives' jobs. In this way, they shored up both men's and women's traditional roles. In the 1950s with young children at home they felt confident in these assertions.[68]

If it fell to some husbands to make decisions about their wives' wage earning, few women argued if their husbands insisted that their first duty was to the home and children. Betsy Downs did not work outside the home, partly because of her husband Steven's attitude. He recounted, "I told her well, if you want to go to work you got to make more money than I do and if you do that, I'll stay home and raise the kids, but somebody gonna be raisin' the kids. I'm not gonna kick 'em out in some nursery school or something or day care." Throughout his marriage Steven played off his superior earning power and Betsy's similar values to preserve his position as breadwinner. Americans agreed in the postwar era that child care should be performed in the home by the mother of the children. While some women disputed this contemporary wisdom, others agreed with their husbands that at least while the children were small, they should stay home to raise them. This generation of middle-class Americans could afford to implement these values. But these views crumbled as couples began to enjoy the supplemental income women's wages provided or when childrearing ceased to be a relevant obstacle to employment.[69]

Still, many men supported their wives' working only so long as it did not impinge on their comforts at home. When former full-time homemakers did go to work, they could no longer devote the attention to household tasks that their families expected. May Perkins, during her brief excursion in the business world, battled her family's indifference and complaints. Working against the wishes of husband and children weakened May's job commitment. Dennis missed the benefits of having his wife homemaking full-time. After three months, "It was getting to me to fight that all the time, of coming home and having him grumpy." Dale George lent grudging support to his wife June's ambitions. "It's fine with me, providing that she can still do the things that I would like to see in terms of keeping the home and dinner and this sort of thing." Family's support for work outside the home was contingent on an efficiently run household.[70]

The male response to female employment shaped the duration and degree of women's job commitments, braking social change. Those husbands who upheld traditional gender roles based their right to do so on male cultural authority in the home. In these cases, they could count on their wives' acquiescence. But that could change. Alice Bremmer went back to full-time work in the 1970s over her husband's earlier objections.[71]

Across all three interviews 23 men expressed unequivocal support for their wives' employment. Gordon James, whose wife Patricia put him through his last years of college and then quit for a few years to be with their infant children, disposed of his initial opposition to her working while the children were young. According to both Gordon and Patricia, he talked her into her three-day-a-week job in 1957. He said matter-of-factly, "She likes to work because she likes to work." Rosalyn Nichols worked throughout her marriage, including the time when her children were growing up. So when the IHD asked her husband David how he felt about his wife working, he replied, "She was working when I met her. I never knew anything else." For the Nichols, Rosalyn's job was not an issue. Most IHD men married to working women supported their wives' employment although 20 percent reported mixed feelings.[72]

When husbands supported their wives' employment, they did so for three main reasons. One approach interpreted work as therapeutic tonic to the difficulties of full-time housework. Others appreciated the extra money working wives brought in. Still others came to support their wives' individual goals and felt that wives who acted on what they needed made better partners. And, often, it was their wives who brought on this transformation of opinion.

Middle-class husbands of wage-earning wives, following popular trends, eventually endorsed their wives' jobs but as a solution to the idleness of the empty-nest homemaker. Employment found favor as a replacement occupation when the children no longer demanded full-time attention. Thus, Ken Harris could sanction his wife Nina's job without calling into question his own wage-earning abilities or position of authority in the marriage. Her job, he said, "is fine with me. She needs something to do since the children are grown." His attitude was more complex than that comment reveals. He also was glad to be able to put his wife through school since she had put him through school early in their marriage. Seen as an antidote to a void in their lives, midlife employment posed no threat to husbands as breadwinners.[73]

Back in 1963, Betty Friedan had insisted that what American housewives needed was jobs, not more tranquilizers or psychiatrists. These ideas made their way from the level of "popular discourse" to the kitchens and dens of suburban homes. Because Elaine's job gave her something useful to do, Edward Martin thought it had "therapeutic value" for her. The alternative to paid work outside the home, it seems, was a visit to the psychologist. Eager to point out that at work Katie made only just enough to cover clothing and transportation costs, Frank Ryder also surmised, "I think it was psychological therapy for her. I think it saved her from the couch, really." Diane Key believed she had her husband's full support for her career. Not only did she say he "encouraged me right along," but she added,

"He feels that I really need it. He insists that I would drive myself crazy without it." Work and careers were accepted solutions to homemaking dissatisfaction, and increasingly an option for more and more women.[74]

This male view contained innovation—legitimizing the expansion of women's sphere—while maintaining the importance of the traditional male and female roles. It was preferable, it seems, to undermine the doctrine of female fulfillment solely through motherhood and wifehood by linking this total focus with mental instability at worst and unhappiness at least, than to question the male role as breadwinner. These men chose to identify, not the money their wives brought in, but rather the money the women saved on therapists' bills by working. Working wives remained nonthreatening to the male position of breadwinner, if they were working to maintain their sanity.

But men of this generation did come to accept married women's work for what it was and did so because of their wives' jobs. It was difficult to argue with the benefits a second income bestowed on a couple. Simply by working, middle-class women swayed the opinions of their husbands. In 1982, Glen Dyer attributed his evolving attitude to economic setbacks and aspirations. He remarked that although his wife worked now, there was a time when he "wouldn't let her." He went on, "Then inflation started coming. It helped. . . . But we wanted some extra and I never thought we'd be a two-check family, but now here we are and it doesn't seem to go very far." Although, as his wife Lois said, Glen was "of the old school" that did not believe wives should work, Glen was a student of his times and adjusted to the social change largely because it was happening in his family and benefited its bank account. Not only that, he fixed dinner now too. Lois was the catalyst for his adaptation.[75]

Women's labor-force participation, often undertaken despite the objections of their husbands, was another way in which the mothers of the baby boom contributed to the beginnings of a gender role revolution. Other husbands reported changes of heart similar to Glen Dyer's, although much less half-hearted. These two quotes from Dean Lawrence's interviews, while not coterminous, reflect the ideological distance that he traversed as a result of Irene's work. In 1982, he remembered his first reaction: "I felt a little embarrassed that I was the man of the house, that somebody wouldn't be totally satisfied waiting for me, bare foot, and pregnant at home." But in 1970, when Irene had been working for a time, he was already reflecting on his shift in attitudes. He "had to recognize and accept that she's too vital and alive a person not to want to do something . . . and to make some contribution." Regardless of her husband's embarrassment, Irene Lawrence persisted in her work, retiring only when the last of her many children left home, to recreation and relaxation after years of juggling family and work demands.[76]

However the alteration occurred, whether a woman discussed or argued with her husband, or simply got up each morning and went to work, acceptance of married women's work spread. When Harriet Pollard went to work, Philip, too, had to let go of traditional views. In 1970, he described his aboutface: "That's the way I felt too: wives don't work. I mean this pride thing. I make money and you're the mother." Talking with Harriet, seeing her work changed his mind: "But I realize that women need . . . the fulfillment. It's not just women having children. It is much more than that. . . . she needs a profession. She needs other people." Dan Bentley became convinced of the benefits of Martha's job and understood why she had gone to work, commenting, "She feels more of a part of the outside world that wasn't available to her when she was raising a family." Whether it was economics, equality in marriage, or personal fulfillment, husbands began to echo the arguments their wives espoused in favor of married women's work. They learned through their wives that home life alone was not enough and endorsed their wives' attempts to find fulfillment outside of it. And, at least from their perspective, one adjustment a third of the husbands of working wives had made was to perform more household tasks.[77]

Alice Bremmer acknowledged the rationale behind her husband's original negative response to her job—she cut down her hours in the 1960s to placate him—but pursued her own ambitions in any case. In 1982, she said, "It insulted his masculinity, because he was supposed to be the breadwinner. . . . But, once I went back to work, . . . that was it. Never would I stay home again." Therefore, while men may have upheld traditional gender roles, they could only uphold them with the cooperation of their wives. Those wives who overruled their husbands' objections in spite of the extra responsibilities this added to their roles contributed significantly to the expansion of those roles. And by working, women enhanced their power in marriage, particularly with regard to financial decisions.[78]

Herbert Henderson fully endorsed his wife's career path, which took her from homemaking to working for him, then back to school, and finally a professional practice, because "I was even more dedicated to her doing what she wanted to because of help I got, the support she gave me when I wanted to do what I wanted." Gail's career was important to Herbert. He believed it had a positive impact on their marriage. Herbert said,

I've always wanted her success and wanted her growth. . . . I felt it was worth a gamble to me. It would be much better for me to risk having her independence then to object to it and not have a happy relationship. I was completely willing to gamble that if she were happy, we'd both be happy. At any rate, I think maybe my total support of what she's doing—maybe it was a factor in our becoming closer.[79]

Although the real story of both middle-class domesticity and cultural attitudes toward women's employment was more complex than Friedan portrayed it, her message, nonetheless, struck a chord with American women in the 1960s. The popularity of *The Feminine Mystique* cannot be denied. In 1963 Friedan's bestseller joined scholarly and government attention to women's employment—in response to the ever expanding presence of married women and mothers in the workforce—and its burgeoning social acceptance that began in the 1950s. At the same time, social science studies diminished the fears that employed mothers harmed home life. By the mid-1960s, a shift in coverage of the issue of mothers' working occurred in response to the influx of thousands of women into the workforce; articles focused on *how to* combine work and family successfully, rather than *whether to.*

At a key moment in the life cycle of mothers of the baby boom, Friedan stepped in to provide a timely new justification for seeking employment beyond family necessity; a career or part-time job could become a means of self-definition and fulfillment. Yet, Friedan was no revolutionary. Indeed, her views echoed a significant strain of positive opinion about women and work that developed in the 1950s and that she ignored in her research. Like those in this study, American women in general knew already the limitations and frustrations of homemaking and full-time childrearing. Without perceiving themselves as revolutionary, this generation of women transformed both American family life and the makeup of the American workforce. Often viewed as the keepers of tradition, women who gave birth to the baby boom fostered changes, undermining the traditions that they are credited with maintaining.

Postwar women integrated paid employment into middle-class marriage without overturning the sexual division of labor. Yet through their behavioral change, mothers of the baby boom were ultimately able to begin a shift in ideological norms. Wives who worked in the 1950s, 1960s, and 1970s made significant contributions to their families' comfort and finances under circumstances that did little to foster career commitment, and yet they persisted. At great cost to themselves, but little cost to their families, millions of middle-class women made paid employment a part of married life in the early decades following World War II. Part-time employment transformed women's lives, their view of themselves, and ultimately their families. The move into part-time work, set in motion prior to the presence of a mainstream feminist movement, gathered further momentum once the movement took off.

Postwar women's excursions outside the domestic realm were not limited to consumption and carpooling as central as these two functions were to postwar middle-class culture. Just as recent research in the history of masculinity in the 1950s calls attention to the ways men became more domestic, middle-class women took on the less domestic role of the breadwinning mother in the decades following World War II. Whether they worked to combat boredom, meet the mortgage, or to find fulfillment, working mothers found satisfaction in the paychecks they brought home. More important, outside the home, at work, these women found arenas for self-expression and self-development, altering the female life course by weaving paid employment throughout.

In reshaping the adult female role, these women gained a sense of self beyond domesticity. Self-definition that incorporated labor-force participation was the first step toward feminist consciousness, even for this generation of American women.[80]

Carving an indelible place for women as breadwinners in the middle-class family, the mothers of the baby boom, before their daughters' more publicized dual lives, struggled to balance the demands of both family and workplace. They also worked within the home to make their employment outside of it acceptable, altering the status quo in the process. Part-time work, the double shift, and the subtle determination to expand the definition of motherhood were their tools. This now common dual focus of American women's lives, often fingered as something imposed on them by feminism, is the result of a combination of historical factors including demographics, economics, and volition that launched postwar women out of the home and began changes still in progress within it.

There is another lesson here, however, and that is the power of traditional gender roles to contain the potential of change, often at great personal cost. Individual women responding to life course changes, family needs, and the desire for fulfillment could only do so much on their own. Only organized feminism could provide a collective political response to women's double days, occupational segregation, and pay disparity. But women's increasing employment was a major factor in changing American attitudes not only toward sex roles, but toward sex equality, laying the groundwork for the women's movement. As we shall see, work experience combined with family commitment to shape this generation's response to the solutions feminists posed.[81]

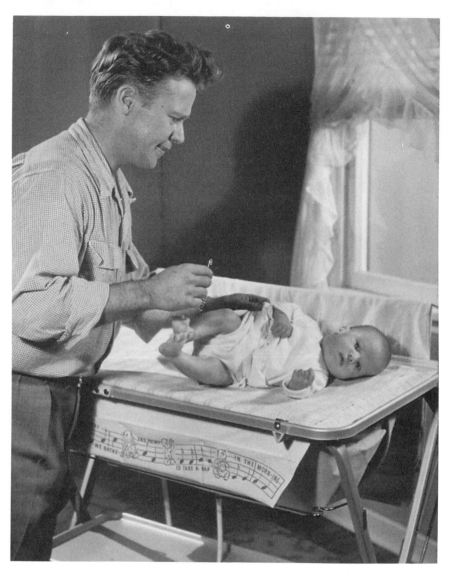

In the 1950s, fathers grappled with new expectations that they care for their children, often right from the start. ARCHIVE PHOTOS

⟨3⟩

Making Room for Fathers

Fatherhood and Family Life

On the long-running series *Father Knows Best*, Robert Young's Jim Anderson returned from work, stashed his briefcase and suit jacket in the hall closet, and donned a corduroy blazer for the evening, thereby signaling his complete switch from breadwinner to family man. Jim provided financial security for his family and was by turn companion, advisor, and disciplinarian to his children. Somehow his job as an insurance salesman enabled him to support his wife and three children in comfort and yet intruded little on his duties as a father. When he was not at work, this dad was home and available to the family.[1]

Situation comedies like *Father Knows Best* reflected the postwar emphasis on men's family role. Historians have studied women's rush back into the home following World War II but, until recently, have overlooked that the call for domesticity extended to fathers as well as mothers. The postwar trends of early marriage and childbearing directed attention to parenthood—fathering in particular—and set the stage for the reformulation and elaboration of prewar trends in fatherhood. After World War II psychologists, "family living experts," and journalists preached a doctrine of domestic fatherhood, one that reverberated through middle-class homes, provoking resistance, negotiation, and change.

This discussion of men's role in family life took place beyond the pages of magazines and advice books in homes across the United States as youthful couples set out to raise the baby boom generation. Moreover, women became key participants in the dialogue about fathering that ensued, one that ultimately extended beyond the 1950s over the entire family cycle. When Jim Anderson confidently posed yet another simplistic solution to a childrearing crisis, his wife responded with exasperation. Margaret Anderson, played by Jane Wyatt, vacuumed, dusted, cooked, and cleaned her way through episodes of *Father Knows Best.* Margaret consistently performed the domestic tasks required to keep the Anderson family fed, clothed, and happy. Her household chores continued after Jim Anderson had eased himself into the armchair to read the evening paper. When Margaret told Jim, "I'm the one who has to put up with it—you're at the office all day," her complaint echoed in many middle-class homes. Postwar women joined experts in beckoning men to partake more fully in parenting and domesticity. Mothers expected and demanded help with parenting from their husbands who, in turn, began to redefine what fathering would mean in their lives.

As Margaret's exasperated aside showed, even the fictional Jim Anderson did not successfully meet the competing demands postwar masculine domesticity placed on them in the eyes of family members. Young fathers in the 1950s were hard pressed to meet their competing commitments. Parenting vied with breadwinning for men's time, energy, and loyalty. Prescriptions for better fathering left unaltered the sexual division of labor. Even as they urged fathers to become more engaged in family life, experts never doubted that men would remain full-time providers and women full-time child rearers. The built-in limitations to their prescriptions and the demands that breadwinning placed on them circumscribed the degree to which men became involved in family life in the decades following World War II. Middle-class men struggled to conform to the ethos of participatory fatherhood, often coming up short; yet family life was still transformed by the process, beginning with negotiations between spouses over men's roles.

While proponents of active fathering in the 1950s haled contemporary changes in the family as novel, in fact, family experts had been calling for similar changes for decades. Fifties experts, who ran the gamut from academic sociologists and psychologists to pediatricians, home economists, and journalists or free lance writers, did not invent the "new" fatherhood; rather, they inherited a half-century-long trend. This attention to fathers' family function represented what historian Margaret Marsh has dubbed "masculine domesticity"—the focus of male leisure time on family and domestic pursuits, beginning at the turn of the century—in its postwar form. The work of historian Robert Griswold and historical sociologist Ralph La Rossa indicates that this trend accelerated prior to World War II.[2]

Questions surrounding father's role in a changing family arose in response to turn-of-the-century patterns of work and residence. Declining family size, suburbanization, and a shrinking work week redefined family life for Americans. Increased income and leisure made family time a realistic goal for middle-class men. Social scientists, worried that men's daily absence from the home harmed family life, called for more male involvement in childrearing. By the twenties, psychologists linked fathers to the appropriate sex role development of their offspring, adding greater urgency to earlier concerns about men's role in rearing children. Yet, by defining fatherhood as guidance and companionship, Jazz Age experts only cemented the association of motherhood with the actual labor of childrearing. Despite such limitations, however, men expressed a yearning for greater competence as parents and longed for stronger connections with their children in the 1920s.[3]

The Depression heightened anxiety about the male position as father and breadwinner as male unemployment became increasingly common. When women's efforts at getting by went beyond "making do" to include taking full-time jobs outside the home, the nation viewed them negatively. Indeed, New Deal policies focusing on getting men back to work discriminated against women, particularly married women. Thus, the economic crisis that disrupted so many American families enhanced the cultural importance of breadwinning for men. The onset of World War II restored American men's status as breadwinners, but it also raised new questions about the psychological and social ramifications of their absence from the home. With so many men serving in the armed forces, Americans wondered about the impact on children of separation from their fathers.[4]

After the war, two decades of crisis and family disruption came to an end. And, in the family-oriented atmosphere of the 1950s, parenting experts reemphasized the importance of father-child relationships—for the good of children, family, and American society. Family advisors preaching a doctrine of domestic fatherhood found a ready audience among the youthful and prolific parents of the baby boom.[5]

The middle-class family was perhaps at its most "nuclear" at the dawn of the atomic age. Suburban developments proliferated in the 1950s and young couples bid farewell to the crowded urban housing of the war years, leaving behind an extended family that had long been a source of advice and support. Thus isolated from traditional forms of family wisdom on childrearing, young parents sought alternative sources of authority and advice. An army of experts clamored for their attention, and chief among these was the calming voice of pediatrician Dr. Benjamin Spock. Spock's *Common Sense Book of Baby and Child Care* appeared in 1946 to spectacular popularity; it was revised the first of five times in 1957. His advice generated letters of thanks from suburban parents, one of whom demonstrated both her considerable affluence and a substantial appetite for expert advice: "I've got a copy in the living room, a copy in the bedroom, a copy in the kitchen, a copy in the bathroom." Spock's was only one volley in a barrage of childrearing advice that confronted young and insecure baby boom parents, who were an eager audience for the advice manuals and parenting articles that proliferated in both mainstream and women's magazines.[6]

Family advisors writing in popular magazines in the 1950s urged their readers to adopt some flexibility within the boundaries of traditional gender roles at home. Modern grooms and brides were not to be constrained by the rigid sex roles of the past, they proclaimed. Young wives might supplement their husbands' earnings in the first years of marriage, and in return young husbands might perfect a special meal and share the washing and drying of dishes with their wives. In 1952, O. Spurgeon English, a professor of psychiatry at Temple University Medical School, and Constance J. Foster, his co-author, noted changes in postwar lifestyles including high wages and labor shortages, which prompted young couples to "do things for themselves or go without." They concluded that a "sharp dividing line" between the sex roles no longer existed. "Mom still has the babies and Pop still does most of the supporting," they noted. "Otherwise it has become a fairly fifty-fifty design for living." Accordingly, they and other writers urged couples to view parenting as a shared endeavor.[7]

As the postwar baby boom began, scholars noted developments in postwar life that opened opportunities for men in the home. In 1947, Margaret Mead suggested that a few extra hours of free time a week would revolutionize the family. She wrote, "Free Saturday mornings are appearing all over the country, un-preempted by church or state or golf club." If men would just spend their Saturday mornings, a mere "one fourteenth" of the week, with their children, she proclaimed, "the American family would present a very different picture from what we have now." Mead's prescription for Saturday mornings demonstrated both the heady aspiration and built-in limitations of postwar plans for fathers. She asked for a minimal amount of time of busy middle-class fathers and yet predicted vast changes as a result, as did most postwar experts.[8] "With the rise of automatic machinery," Robert Coughlan wrote, "The father's working day grows shorter, and he is physically present in the home a good deal more. . . . And he is present in the flesh, at least, as a male image for his children." The change most writers noticed had, they hoped, as much to do with spirit as with flesh. Edward Streeter, author of the novel *Father of the Bride*, commented, "Father is much more a member of the family and his position in the group is much more real that it has ever been before." Reduced work weeks, suburban lifestyles, and new ideas brought fathers the opportunity for entry into the family circle. Dad's increased presence alone merited comment, but exactly what fathers would do once present remained unclear.[9]

Once they had entered the family circle, fathers joined their wives in the duties of parenthood. M. Robert Gomberg, executive director of Jewish Family Services and a guest columnist for the *New York Times Magazine*, wrote, "Advised, often demanded by experts in the field of family living, the change for the most part has been a healthy one, based on father's more mature willingness to share more of family life, including routine chores and day-to-day details of child-rearing." Gomberg urged dads to turn their attention to childrearing and shake off the image of the stern, distant father. "Today Dad finds families function best on a partnership basis," Ruth Newburn Sedam, another writer for the *New York Times*, noted. "He shares in the daily care and companionship of small fry—all sizes."[10]

One father mused enthusiastically about the satisfactions of parenthood in "It's a Man's Job, Too!" "I couldn't be satisfied to be home and not enjoy our daughter's company part of the time, whether it's listening to her coo, giving her the two A.M. bottle or, yes, even changing her diapers," he wrote. Experts invited fathers into the nursery to take part in the tasks of child care. If dads wanted good relationships with their kids, they were advised to participate during nightly feedings and bedtime stories. English and Foster wrote, "Early-fathered children will be better companions to Dad when they enter their teens because they learned to be pals on the night shift over a midnight bottle or a colic pain." These writers portrayed fathers as beneficiaries of their efforts at childrearing. It was through "the homely routines of early childhood, from reading a bed-time story to pulling down training panties for the toddler" that a father "earned his right to be warmly regarded by his growing sons and daughters." Daily tasks would reap immediate emotional rewards for dads. Loyd W. Rowland, director of the Louisiana Society for Mental Health and guest columnist for the *New York Times Magazine*, argued, "The father who is in there pitching from day to day, who will take his full share of responsibility for the training of the children," would win friendship with his children.[11]

The message was clear: if a man expected a good relationship with his children once they were young adults, he had to look after them during infancy and childhood. For men the work of childrearing fostered companionship, both in the present and the future. Mothers did the work because it had to be done; for fathers, child care developed friendship.

Dr. Benjamin Spock joined the call for early fatherly involvement with children, advising, "We know that the father's closeness and friendliness to his children will have a vital effect on their spirits and characters for the rest of their lives. So the time for him to begin being a real father is right at the start." Spock did not advocate that husbands and wives tally equal numbers of bottles heated and diapers changed; he suggested instead that a father could do these chores occasionally. The real danger was that men who avoided contributing to care during the first two years would lose out permanently: "He'll feel more bashful about pushing his way into the picture later." Spock predicted early involvement would lead to continued involvement in childrearing for fathers. The prescriptions for fathers incorporated the routine chores of feeding, tidying, and changing, but only as a means to an end—friendship—and never questioned the sexual division of labor in the middle-class family.[12]

One impulse behind the call for participatory fatherhood stemmed from a fear of the consequences for children raised almost entirely by mothers. Spock warned that unless dad got involved in their rearing, the children would view mom as the boss. According to experts, paternal involvement that did not supplant woman's role as primary caretaker would solve a fundamental problem in American homes. Family advisors did not call it "momism," but, like Philip Wylie, they warned that too much mother and too little father might warp American children. "Psychiatrists agree," wrote two fatherhood advocates, "that most children between six and twelve are too exclusively subjected to feminine influence." They wanted both parents in charge of the home, not mother alone.[13]

Casting contemporary family life in psychoanalytic terms, English and Foster viewed father as a key player in "the early family romance." Dads had a special influence over young daughters, "For it is only as he becomes her first boyfriend that she can experience the *feel* of being feminine and later make a happy marriage herself." For little boys, fathers not only supplied a "real man as an ideal toward which [they] can strive" but, if he was careful not to act jealous when "the boy seems to prefer his mother, as he is bound to at this age," paved the way for a son's future happiness (and heterosexuality). Fathers, the experts emphasized, were key if children were going to learn appropriate sex roles and grow up to marry happily.[14]

Men contributed factors to their children's upbringing that women could not provide, the advisors attested, emphasizing the very fact that fathers spent most of their time away from their families. Occupation outside the household almost wholly defined masculinity, even as it prevented adequate male contact with children. Yet, masculinity and the male role model had to be imparted to youngsters, and that meant dad belonged at home. Parenting professionals instructed fathers to spend more time there and insisted that they could do so without losing the masculine edge provided by separation from the home.

"As for discipline, he's replaced the 'woodshed' with a do-it-yourself workshop where everyone has fun," Newburn Sedam wrote. In addition to discarding fathers' authoritarian image, the new conception of modern fatherhood centered on friendship and fun—distinguished as the masculine domain of domesticity. Fun—hobbies, recreation, do-it-yourself activities, and vacations—was unsullied by onerous home-based duties with feminine connotations.[15]

Eager for men to model the proper male role, experts rushed to reassure new dads that it was masculine to participate in parenting, betraying deep-seated anxieties about sex roles. Spock wrote, "A man can be a warm father and a real man at the same time." English and Foster criticized the mistaken patterns of the past wherein men deemed infants' care as solely "woman's department." Changing a diaper no longer detracted from a father's manliness.[16]

Moreover, the parenting authorities appreciated the masculine qualities that fathers brought to care-giving tasks. English and Foster urged men to comfort colicky babies since "a little midnight floor walking . . . has more than comic strip value. Father's arms are strong and the child who experiences the security they give him grows up with a warm regard for some of the best qualities of masculinity—tenderness, protection, and strength." Dad's strength would counterbalance mom's gentleness, which they saw as inadequate on its own. Father, as the more "resolute" parent taught self-control, disciplined, and exercised a firm hand, leaving "mother free to play her protective role properly." If fathers failed to fulfill their responsibilities to their children and mothers picked up the slack, this would "throw the proper balance of family life off center." Men would complement and balance out women's influence over children.[17]

Ideally, augmenting fathers' childrearing activities assured children's sex-role development, countered the ultra-feminine influence in the American home, and in no way impinged on breadwinning responsibilities or a father's intrinsic manliness. In fact, experts sought to capitalize on men's daily absence from the home for eight or more hours a day. If fathers shared their experiences at work with their children, they could become "the exciting courier from the outside world of affairs when he comes home at night bringing with him news of what is going on in the larger universe." Mother could supply young minds with gentleness and comforts, but "they need stimulation and enthusiasm too, and father is the logical person to provide" this. *New York Times Magazine* columnist Dorothy Barclay told fathers who fed and bathed their infants, "Father almost from the start stands for 'man,' for 'competence,' and for 'the outside world' in youngsters' eyes." Seeking greater male involvement in childrearing, experts further delineated gender distinctions in parenting styles.[18]

Away from the home all day, and relieved of most of its daily maintenance, dad, the experts speculated, would bring to family life fresh ideas and zest mom might lack. Loyd Rowland wrote, "Adventure is a father's meat. Poor mother is so loaded down with seeing that clothes are clean and food is cooked, she doesn't have much head for thinking up exciting things for the family to do. Here's where father can be of help." In defense of fathers who were devoted to their jobs, the writer Edward Streeter proclaimed, "Indeed the very fact that he is away from home so much of the time gives him an edge on mother, who must spend so much of hers doing slave labor under the noses of her offspring that she tends to lose caste." Parenting remained heavily gendered and dads connoted fun, adventure, and excitement in contrast to the more mundane work of motherhood.[19]

The gendered separation between home and work was thus both problem and solution in these formulations. Experts cast the time men spent away from home in a positive light. Problems arose only when they spent too much time away from home, as men had in the past. Providing connection with the world outside the home partly defined fatherhood for the experts; yet, fathers needed to make the time to connect inside the home with their children in order to pass on their knowledge and experience. Postwar conditions seemed well-suited to permitting men more time at home—in theory, at least.

In practice, however, work competed with the aim of involved fathering. Consequently experts focused on helping dad get the most out of the few hours he had available for parenting after he had fulfilled his work obligations. No longer was it enough for "a father to be just a breadwinner in the family." Although he complained of fatigue after a full day at the office,

Willard D. Lewis wrote, "Being of sound mind, I realize that for the sire of this home kindergarten, there can be no easy chair and slippers waiting." Participatory fatherhood was an additional responsibility men shouldered after a day at the office. "Only at the price of your own convenience," Andrew Takas admonished his fellow fathers, "can you give your child what he needs." Fatherhood experts instructed men to set down the evening paper and play with their youngsters.[20]

Not every childrearing expert hailed the new role fathers played in family life. Fathers, according to some, had become too much like mothers. M. Robert Gomberg cautioned, "The pendulum in some families has swung—or been pushed—too far and father has moved with it from one incorrect position to an opposite, but equally false one." These nay-sayers concerned themselves less with the time fathers spent with children and more with the way children perceived them. Bruno Bettelheim, writing in *Parents Magazine*, bemoaned the blurring of the sexual division of labor that shared care could lead to. Children needed to observe and experience the distinction between male and female roles. New ideas about fathering threatened this distinction. "No longer," he wrote, "is there one central figure in the home—the mother—whose sole or at least major function is to provide physical, physiological, emotionally intimate satisfactions to the members of the family and another equally important person—the father—whose role is clearly to protect against the outside world and to teach how to meet this world successfully." He feared that fathers, in trying to find satisfaction in fatherhood through "womanly" care-giving tasks, suffered confusion when they found their status waning in their children's eyes. Women could find satisfaction in the home, but, according to Bettelheim, "fulfillment of manhood is not achieved largely through fatherhood. The fulfillment of manhood is achieved by making a contribution to society as a whole." Bettelheim sanctioned men's devotion to occupation and success outside of the home. Mistaken attempts to find fulfillment through actual child care led to the "utter bafflement which the modern father feels." Attempts to reshape fatherly behavior, Bettelheim implied, harmed both developing children and fathers. His concerns only highlighted the assumptions beneath all calls for enhanced fathering roles; he applied the brakes to a station wagon that coasted safely in the middle of the road. No fatherhood expert advocated revolutionary changes in the middle-class home. Above all else, the division of labor within it would remain unchanged.[21]

Revealingly, most prescriptive literature about fatherhood targeted women. Mothers facilitated fathering fashion, according to experts. Bashful fathers, Dr. Spock suggested, "just need encouragement" from their wives. If men were not participating enough in parenting, writers hinted, women should make sure that they allowed them to try. Mothers, Selma Lentz Morrison maintained, influenced the tenor of a father-child relationship; they could "foster it, stunt its growth or completely destroy it." When fathers did not pitch in as they should, advisors instructed mothers to examine their own behavior to see how they might be shutting their husbands out, fearing that mothers failed to include their husbands in the joint venture of parenthood. They advised wives to support and guide fatherly interest in children. If a husband was not measuring up to new standards, English and Foster insisted, "It will pay you to do a little soul-searching, and see whether, without realizing it, you have been doing some of the things that make a man retire behind his newspaper or play golf instead of enjoying his youngsters and taking a sharp interest in home and all of its doings." Women observed and adjusted family interactions, drawing hesitant fathers into the home.[22]

The concerns experts raised about paternal behavior and maternal monopoly reveal a discomfort with the organization of American domestic life. Rather than reorganize American domestic relations, family-living professionals sought to temper what they saw as their most grievous excess—nearly complete female control over childrearing and male distance from the domestic world. Bettelheim's concern with the flip-side of the coin—men feminized by too much participation in child care—serves to highlight the anxious attention focused on the organization of American family life in the 1950s and the fact that American couples demonstrated a new potential for flexibility in parenting tasks. Yet giving only the vaguest instructions for postwar fathers and upholding the primacy of traditional gender roles, professionals created complicated expectations for postwar parents.

Despite widespread expert attention, the cultural reconfiguration of fatherhood in the 1950s remained limited. In contrast to the many articles on fatherhood in popular magazines, in one of the most influential books on childrearing, Dr. Spock's 1957 revised edition of *The Common Sense Book of Baby and Child Care*, a mere 13 pages out of over 300 specifically addressed fatherhood. The postwar formulation of father's place in the home contained unchanged assumptions about male characteristics and male gender roles. What family experts envisioned was the injection of male presence into the family, not a fundamental reassessment of male and female gender roles. Father still represented the family to the outside world and spent the majority of his time outside the home. In the new framework, it was manly to parent but fatherhood remained only a supplement to motherhood.

As important as fathers were to the fifties conception of family life, then, women were still assumed to modulate the emotional content of the home and regulate the ability of men to father. Experts communicated to female readers that "enjoying his youngsters" was not just a requirement for fathers, it was in fact part of the rejuvenation men derived from the suburban middle-class home, preparing them to reenter the work world each weekday. Women's hold on family life potentially erased men entirely from the family picture, but it could also be used to bring him back in. Female readers funneled advice from women's and family magazines into the suburban den.[23]

Couples interpreted and implemented advice, shaping it to meet their own expectations and needs. Turning to the words and experiences of men and women who had children in the 1940s and early 1950s, we find, first, men aware of cultural mandates to spend time with children; second, men divided between occupational and familial pulls; and, third, women fully attentive to postwar expectations for partnership in parenthood and seeking to implement them. In practice, middle-class men and women negotiated within the new parameters of fathering. But women took charge of change.

Women instigated the transformation in paternal habits with demands that cut deeper than the palliatives offered by advice columnists. Humorist Erma Bombeck described the deal she struck with her husband while their children were infants. At first, her husband's only role was to ensure that there was "strained squash" on the table by bringing home a paycheck. Annoyed by his leisure at home, while she labored on, Bombeck recalled that, "My hours were getting longer and my job description kept growing." To save herself from exhaustion, she divided the tasks, delegating feeding and bathing their child to her husband—allocating to him the "top half" while she continued to handle the "bottom half"—messy diaper duty. Bombeck's anecdote illustrates the role women played in redefining fatherhood, insisting that men take a hand in infant and toddler care. Yet she also reveals the obstacles women faced in their efforts to share the burden of parenting. The messier, less rewarding jobs remained women's. As the demands of infancy abated, so did Bombeck's claim on her husband's time. Once their children were out of diapers, his role devolved to "tossing them in the air until they threw up from laughter." Play had triumphed again.[24]

Like the Bombecks, the parents of the baby boom debated the proper responsibilities of fathers. Young men felt torn between their dual roles as breadwinners and parents. Most fathers who felt the tension between their breadwinning and fathering responsibilities chose to be good providers rather than good pals for their youngsters. They could make this choice because their wives were full-time homemakers. Yet, many men absorbed at least the assumption that they should be more actively involved in family life.[25]

In the 1950s, eight men in the IHD study indicated involvement in their children's development that included companionship, affection, and effort. Ernest Johnson said, "I do definitely take an interest in the children and what they are doing. I'm available to them all the time." They conveyed a companionship model of father-child relationships. "I like to give my boy as much time as I can," Howard Sims said. "He figures me a playmate." These men consciously adapted their inherited definition of fatherhood to include greater involvement in their children's lives. For example, Adam Walker declared, "My daughter isn't going to grow up with a father who is a stranger." IHD men shared this conception of fatherhood with their contemporaries. Sixty-two percent of the fathers in one study ranked companionship high as a function of fatherhood. Young fathers aimed for friendly relationships with sons and daughters. Yet they expressed confusion as to how to carry out this new ideal.[26]

Men's plaintive "I don't spend enough time with the children" from the 1950s interviews and later ones as well indicates that middle-class fathers recognized the cultural imperative to parent their children more enthusiastically. The parents who turned to Spock's *Common Sense Book of Baby and Child Care* when their children were infants could continue to read about parenting in women's and family magazines, and in the *New York Times Magazine*, which ran a weekly column on "parent and child." Parenting prescriptions became an external reference by which to measure one's performance. Often, fathers found that they did not measure up. Scott Parker confessed, "I don't do enough romping or playing with them, that you read about in those books about happy, happy homes."[27]

Fourteen men in my sample specifically mentioned in 1950s interviews that they didn't spend enough time or wanted or planned to spend more time with their children. They acknowledged that they were supposed to invest time and effort in their relationships with their children, but they had not succeeded in doing so. John Thompkins tried to adopt new ways but, "I don't spend as much time with the kids as I'd like to. I'm understanding and easy going with them, but we're not together a lot." The fine line between not spending enough time and poor fathering was difficult for some to gauge. Malcom McKee said, "I feel [if] I'm not with them all the time that that's not enough. Sometimes, I feel I neglect them. The old style of father is what I am." Knowing what one should do and enacting those changes were two different things. Dale George indicated that despite his wish to be with his children, "at the same time I don't make the effort. I don't go out to play with them." The belief that they should spend more time with their children was a trait that IHD fathers shared with other men surveyed in the 1950s. In a study by Robert Sears at Stanford University cited in Griswold participants expressed a desire to spend time with their children. Another study of American men published in 1960 found that "highly educated fathers were more likely to include 'not seeing his children enough' as part of their feelings of inadequacy." Middle-class men heard the admonitions to embrace a new style of fatherhood, but often still behaved as "old-style" fathers.[28]

Regardless of how well they measured up to contemporary standards of fathering, 10 percent of the IHD men mentioned that when they compared themselves to their fathers' generation, they spent more time with their children and one woman compared her husband favorably to her own father. Dean Lawrence said, "I'm taking a more active part in their training when I'm at home. My father left it all in my mother's hands." Dennis Perkins reported, "I'm less aloof with my children than he, although I don't spend as much time or play with them as much as she [his wife May] thinks I should. . . . Although I'm better than my father was, I get home all in from my straining job and want to relax. I'm learning, but my parents were not playful." Having experienced aloof fathering as children, these men set out to distance themselves from the patterns of their fathers.[29]

Baby boom fathers internalized new expectations without effecting them and felt guilty as a result. Leonard Stone admitted his fatherly failings. He said, "I don't spend enough time with the children and I guess if I actually made a good, honest try, a real stab at it, I could spend more time with them." For Gordon James, the fact that he didn't "show much attention to the children" was a lapse for which he "punished" himself, but one he did not redress. James pointed out the peculiar impact of new expectations on fathers. He ranked his own effort at fatherhood somewhere between the less-involved men he knew and an ideal father: "I don't do as much as I should. Oh, lots of husbands don't feel they should do as much as I do. That's half the fun of bringing up kids. It's part of your responsibility." He expressed the notion of fatherly sociability and rationalized his own limited contributions to childrearing by creating a continuum between what he should be doing and the way "lots of husbands" fathered. Regret and feelings of inadequacy accompanied expectations for enhanced fatherhood, emotions that could become further stumbling blocks to active fathering.[30]

A sense of fair play set Robert Mitchell apart from his contemporaries.

He hoped to share in parenthood as much as his schedule would allow. His wife, he said, "has the load all day. As soon as I get home at night I try to take over and take care of both children and put them to bed, and on weekends I see to it that she gets out and I stay home." When the IHD interviewer questioned whether this schedule was not too demanding for someone who had been at work all day he responded, "My gosh, she's had 'em all day, she's worn out, and the least I can do is to take over both of them for her." More than an obligation to himself and his children, Mitchell expressed an obligation to share parenthood with his wife. His was a unique voice.[31]

But like Mitchell, men added the responsibility to be more involved fathers to their duty of providing for their families. For 85 New York City fathers queried in 1943, the role of "economic provider" ranked number one in their concept of the paternal role. This was a generation of middle-class men who, if not the stereotypical "organization man" of William Whyte's description, gave much of themselves to the task of earning a living. For many, fatherhood and providing went hand in hand. One study found that men ranked companionship and providing equally high on the lists of "greatest satisfaction of being a father." But providing was simpler to excel at. Corporate careers demanded extensive time commitment from employees. For young executives, the years of heaviest demand from the job often coincided with the early years of parenthood, when children required twenty-four-hour care. Because of job demands, young fathers missed out on parenting.[32]

In addition to work commitments, a suburban middle-class lifestyle left little time available to spend with children. Most men commuted from suburban homes to offices in the city. Many were gone from home from 7:00 to 7:00 weekdays and junior executives and small businessmen devoted Saturdays to work as well. It is not clear where the extra time would come from. Gordon James, who repeatedly bemoaned the dearth of time he had with his children, added, "I do play with them during the evening after supper. On weekends, too." With a 40-plus hour work week, evenings and weekends were the available times fathers could offer children.[33]

Family-living professionals may have railed against men who thought that their paychecks alone made a fitting fatherly contribution to raising a family, but earning the family living remained inextricably bound to being a father. Dean Lawrence defined his primary role as breadwinner when an IHD interviewer asked him to rank his "virtues" as a parent: "Well, I think being a good provider and eager to have children and very happy we have a family and for the most part anxious to help them and play with them." First and foremost, Lawrence saw himself as a breadwinner and secondarily as guide and playmate. At another point he revealed his interpretation of the calls for more fatherly involvement and parental role flexibility. He said, "I think it's better for the children to have two parents; to say nothing of the relief to my wife. When I take over the discipline, she's the comforter—when she does, I'm the comforter. . . . We think it's unwise for one parent to have exclusively one role and the other to have the other. It's not fair to the parents or wise for the children. They need to know both parents are understanding and both expect [things of kids]." He expressed the desire to share the responsibilities of parenthood and sanctioned a diminution of heavily gendered emotional roles but left actual child care to his wife.[34]

Men could, they hoped, be fuller partners in parenthood and still succeed as breadwinners. Leonard Stone remarked on how satisfying he found it "to do a creative and honest job . . . to earn a good living for my family while I have them near me so I can take an equal part with my wife in training the children." His nearby business allowed proximity to his young children. Yet, for at least forty hours a week, work prevented most men from taking an "equal part" in parenthood, and Stone himself, at least according to his wife, didn't take much part at all, despite his ambitions.[35]

The gospel of expanded fatherhood did not reach all ears. Instead of viewing the labor of caring for children as the building blocks of close companionship, some men persisted in seeing it as an unpleasant task with little to redeem it. Sam Arthur confessed that not only did he not devote enough personal attention to his children but, "I don't honestly enjoy spending great amounts of time with them." Joseph Maxwell said, "I am of the opinion women should generally take over the problem of raising children." Sold as leisure and companionship, if fathering proved unsatisfying, men had a ready excuse for withdrawing their efforts. Milly Benson complained that her husband Dick left the "child direction" to her since he believed that a mother's influence was "all important." Traditional assumptions about parenthood coexisted with the innovations the experts encouraged. The reformulation of fatherhood as play left comfortable room for men to leave care for children to their wives but still find satisfaction as companions to their youngsters.[36]

In spite of attempts to participate more actively in parenting, men in the 1950s still viewed the work of parenthood as primarily women's responsibility. Grant Thornton told his wife, "God created mothers because men just couldn't stand it." Implicit in statements about fatherhood was the idea that women had special tolerance for the routine, less pleasant tasks of child care. Tom Cole said, "I don't really enjoy changing diapers and such." Thus fathering, unlike mothering, was an activity to be enjoyed. And this criterion governed participation. Even simply spending time with children could be a challenge for men, while their wives did so unquestioningly.

Admiring his wife's calm, Scott Parker said, "They would drive me crazy if I had to stay home all day." These men had a choice about how much effort they put into childrearing. They did not have to change diapers or mind children consistently as their wives did. If fathering was to be fun, that meant opting out of the work.[37]

Not only did they express relief that they escaped the tasks their wives performed regularly, they viewed these aspects of parenting quite negatively. "I give them all the affection I can stand giving," James Evans commented, "until I'm exhausted." He viewed postwar fatherhood as a burden. Showing affection or creating companionship with their children was difficult and tiresome for some fathers. Here, too, the IHD patterns of fatherhood matched with those of their peers across the nation. Sociologists William G. Dyer and Dick Urban's 1958 study of one hundred couples showed similar apportioning of parental responsibility. Couples reported equal involvement in childrearing activities such as discipline and decision-making, but not when it came to "taking care of children's physical needs." A majority said that these tasks were performed by the "wife mostly." The men in Tasch's New York City study ranked "problems arising from routine daily care" as their "number one headache."[38]

While their husbands waffled between old and new modes of fatherhood, women read the advice books and articles in *Parents* and other magazines, bringing the professionals' advice into their homes to support their requests for more help from their mates. In baby boom households where there might be three or four children under the age of six, there were simply too many meals, baths, and diapers for one parent to handle alone. Young wives who persuaded their husbands to join in child care responded to another impulse. Necessity convinced mothers of the need for an additional pair of hands at midnight feedings and evening bathings more effectively than the urgings of experts could have done on their own. While experts and dads were no doubt satisfied that postwar fathers played more with their children, mothers, clearly, were not. Dad's new playtime with his youngsters only highlighted the difference between men's and women's parenting experiences.[39]

Wives praised husbands who participated in childrearing, speaking proudly of their efforts. Meg Fisher reported that her husband and son built things together, and Tom also "helps out with the cub scouts." This, she said, made him "just nice to be married to." Women valued their husbands' contributions to their children's upbringing, whether that meant excursions, homework help, or actual care. Based on such activities, Judy Kent noted that her husband was "one of the dearest fathers."[40]

But when expectations for greater involvement went unmet, wives openly criticized their husbands. Claudine Parker told the IHD, "I gripe that Scott doesn't do more with the kids. . . . All he does now is that he comes home and sits down and eats. He does get [child] ready for bed, but that's about the extent of it." May Perkins complained that her husband Dennis "barricades himself in the garage, and counts nails out there. He doesn't have to take care of the kids." She added, "Dennis is tired at night, and he doesn't want to deal with the kids. He only thinks of himself." On weekdays, Claudine Parker resented being responsible for enforcing the discipline her husband instigated on weekends, "His strictness can go too far. He sometimes starts something that I have to finish all week long." He was out of touch with the day-to-day realities of childrearing. Thirteen percent of the women interviewed in the 1950s criticized their husbands' lack of involvement in childrearing. Professionals romanticized the meaning and influence of 15 minute doses of fathering. In ordinary American homes, women rejected the fatherhood romance and complained about the more limited reality.[41]

Women increased expectations not just for more time but for more emotional involvement in childrearing from fathers. Claudine Parker reported that she would not mind the weekends Scott spent out of town if "when he is home he was more interested in us and the children—if he gave more of himself when he is at home." Wives, who still maintained primary responsibility for childrearing, added their voices to the clamor for more paternal involvement, hoping for companionship, discipline, and emotional engagement between their husbands and children.[42]

The discrepancy in time and effort devoted to childrearing fostered fatigue in women. They resented their husbands' leeway in parenting. Janice Rogers described her husband George's relationship with their children: "I think he gets more pure enjoyment than I do. I have more of the detail work." Fathers were parent-playmates while mothers were often too busy to join in games with their youngsters. Milly Benson, whose husband Dick felt their children were her responsibility, wanted to "dump it all on someone else for a while, but he won't accept it." Georgeanne Gaynor said, "For a period of four or five years . . . he hardly saw anything of his children, and after spending 14 unadulterated hours with the children, I envied him very much." She wanted more help with the children but Richard's work was an obstacle to this hope. Wives envied husbands who could practice weekend parenthood and schedule their childrearing for week nights between 7:30 and 9:00.[43]

In fact making space for dad to spend quality time required effort from women. Play rooms had to be picked up, children's faces and fingernails scrubbed, and evening meals prepared, so that all would be peaceful when father arrived. May Perkins recounted that "I try to feed the kids before he gets home at 7:00 in the evening. I want [them] to be with their father some time during the evening. [They] . . . should go to bed then, but I keep [them] up so Dennis can play with [them]." Despite her efforts to present Dennis with fed, bathed, and quiet children, she noted that he did not want to "deal with the kids." She went on, "It's really a problem. He's a good father, but he's not sympathetic. Sometimes he acts kind of guilty at ten at night. He felt he should have been with the kids more."[44]

Women performed the physical work to neaten up kids for dad's arrival at the end of the day, prepping them for "quality time," and performed additional emotional labor as well. Dorothy Simon internalized the role of tutor to her husband's neophyte status as a parent. She used several tactics to increase his interaction with their children. She did not take as much responsibility for the children "as I would if I didn't know so fully that what he needs is an opportunity to function with his kids. Every time I've said that I was tired, desperate and needed some rest, I wish he'd take the kids out, he has come back home worn out but looking fine and comfortable with himself." The problem was "He just never sees the things to do that he would be so happy in doing." Thus it was always, "old pedestrian me who had to plan the picnics, the ski parties, tracking in the snow, etc."[45]

But wives also catered to their exhausted providers' needs for succor and relaxation at home, a goal that conflicted with their hopes for shared parenting. Janice Rogers said, "I do try to get them to bed before George comes home. He's really too beat to put forth much when he comes now." He was too tired to exercise patience with their children, and a noisy family room full of children would distract him from his rest. Postwar fathering exacted a toll on mothers as well, for they sought to buffer men from the more demanding aspects of parenting and demanded help from them at the same time.[46]

While experts wrote of the importance of fathers in their children's development, these men seemed removed from most of the actual childrearing in their homes. Because the time fathers spent with children was limited to a few hours a day and on weekends, men observed that they had a different relationship with their children than their wives did. Dean Lawrence said, "I'm told that the children are more independent and self-sufficient and better children when I'm not home. My wife means that the children crawl all over me when I try to read the paper. Sometimes I play with them or throw them on the floor." Tom Cole reported that "I'm inclined to let them get away with more than my wife is. I only see them for a couple of hours." Since he only saw them for short periods of time, Tom did not want to spoil the brief interludes of fun by disciplining his children. Mothers also noted the differences that their full-time motherhood made. Cynthia Thornton's husband Grant was "not around" and "couldn't get the total picture." Fathers' absence from the home meant mothers were "more involved with the children." Claudine Parker defined her virtue as a parent as, "I'm willing to do all the work."[47]

The contributions men made to their children's upbringing appeared minor or supplementary to their wives' efforts. Gordon James said, "I read to the kids once in a while, but she does most of that, too. . . . Oh, I'll see that they get their teeth brushed." Gordon acknowledged that his wife did the bulk of the parenting and felt peripheral as a result. Lloyd Andrews told the IHD, "Beth and I get a lot of satisfaction out of the children. In certain ways I think she's better with them, possibly because she's with them more and understands them better." Lloyd did not feel he knew his children as well as his wife did. Gary Simon said, "Dorothy, because she's home, obviously does more of the training, although I'm learning to do more and more." He accepted that his wife was the influential parent even as he attempted to conform to new standards of fatherhood. Mothers disciplined more, read to the children more, understood the children better, and directly oversaw their development. These dads played and supervised tooth brushing.[48]

With fatherhood in flux, men wondered what impact a few hours of play had on their children. Dale George worried that because he did not spend time with his youngsters, he wouldn't be "much of an influence on their lives." Ronald Chase voiced this concern, saying, "My effect as a parent to the kids is not too awfully strong because I'm not around them as much as my wife." Participatory fatherhood could only supplement the mothering children received. Trying to squeeze into family life revealed for some men their true distance from it. Yet, while they admired the close relationships their wives created with their children and regretted their distance, these young fathers did little to change their paternal patterns. A decade later the same issues surfaced and the consequences of male distance were not as easy to ignore.[49]

In the late 1960s and 1970s, as midlife couples flipped through women's magazines and even news magazines, they perused yet another round of renewed attention to fathers. More involvement from fathers was a consistent refrain. One note remained unchanged: the task of socializing fathers continued to fall to mothers. The experts still puzzled over fathers' role and continued to assign blame for the problem of fathers' absence to women who drove men out of the family. Dr. Spock remarked on the continued problem of fatherly abdication: "Many American mothers themselves complain bitterly to their husbands because husbands decline to take responsibility for the children's management—even at those times when the mothers urge them to do so." But Spock went on to intone ominously, "The most important and frequent cause of the shirking of discipline by fathers in America: the disposition of some men here to be passive or submissive toward their wives and the tendency of a number of women to be too bossy toward husbands." Now it seemed the prodding that women had practiced to engage their husbands in paternal endeavors had left them open to even more criticism. They were at fault for men's removal from family involvement.[50]

The focus in late sixties articles was on the parents of infants and very young children, reflecting the targeted readership of magazines like *Redbook* and *Parenting*. But such articles offered little consolation to women with adolescent children and middle-aged husbands who hoped to help forge closer ties between them. The significant opportunity had been missed. The time to hook men on parenthood was during pregnancy, at the birth, and in the crucial early months afterwards, professionals advised. Pediatrician T. Berry Brazelton admonished, "Creating this sense of family may not be easy for a new mother during the first weeks after her baby's birth, but if she doesn't begin to involve her husband with the child at this time, it may become more and more difficult." Mothers of the baby boom, by giving birth at a time when it was unfashionable for fathers to be present in the delivery room, had missed the boat of shared parenting. Such admonitions could only enhance women's sense of responsibility for the family patterns their husbands and children now lived out. Yet, despite the chorus of criticism directed at women, as the family cycle wound down, baby boom mothers voiced their views on where the responsibility for male distance from the family lay.[51]

For older parents, both mothers and fathers could take the blame for the problems of the "hippie generation." Again, the complaint was that work commitment produced "father absence," "leaving mothers to raise sons with insufficient fatherly support." These were the homes from which flower children fled. One essayist suggested, "Many 80-hour-a-week executives might try something else: rejoining their families. In recasting themselves as fathers, they might recast their values and change their lives. Making a living is important, but selling more soap should not destroy the process of raising sons." From the 1950s through the 1960s, postwar concerns about fatherhood centered around gender role socialization in homes without male role models.[52]

The tensions and conflicting pulls men felt between family and occupation in the 1950s had not been resolved by the 1960s. Rather, men resigned themselves to the necessity of choosing one demand over the other, accepting that to be successful occupationally, they would have to withdraw from the family circle. This, it seemed to them, was men's lot. These choices were also clear to wives and children. Many of the subjects' children surveyed by the IHD in 1970 perceived "their fathers as overinvolved in their jobs" and "relatively unhappy." The material benefits that their jobs extended to their families would, dads hoped, make their sacrifice worthwhile.[53]

And work they did. The IHD asked male participants how many hours a week they worked in the 1969–71 interviews. Of the 72 men from my sample who responded to this question, 34, or 47 percent, reported working between 40 and 50 hours a week. Eighteen fathers, or 25 percent, worked between 50 and 60 hours a week. Just over 20 percent worked more than 60 hours a week. Only four men reported working fewer than 40 hours a week. Added to commuting time, the 40-plus hour work week left little time even for "quality" time at home.[54]

Undeniably, the work men did outside the home was crucial to family survival and to maintaining a middle-class standard of living. For many men, providing well for their families was part and parcel of fatherhood, if not, in fact, its primary responsibility. Several men ranked breadwinning as their key contribution to family life; and wives, too, noted "good provider" as central to what they found satisfying in their husbands. Norman Smith said, "It's important to me to have made enough money to build a home that would be comfortable for the family." Edward Martin commented, "Really, my most important function as a father is to earn the money the family needs." Providing for a family, lambasted by the experts in the 1950s as not being enough, remained fundamental to paternal identity for this generation.[55]

The irony was that providing interfered with the more direct emotional satisfactions of parenting. Dean Lawrence mused, "I don't contribute to the home development . . . I'm the classical provider. I think I've been a good provider." Having chosen to devote time and energy to work, men discovered they had missed out on their offsprings' childhood. Time devoted to work subtracted from family time, and distance between father and child ensued. Scott Clinton commented, "That is the crime of the age, that is the trouble with my generation, they've been too busy to take care of their own kids."[56]

It was a crime that pricked men's consciences. In 1969, Russell Weber said, "This is a gap I have with my children. I don't feel that I really know my children. I never spent a great deal of time . . . " Being busy with work often meant being too busy to father. Malcom McKee admitted that he had not devoted the time he "should have" to his children, but this realization came after the youngest child had reached adolescence, when there was little hope for paternal renewal. Responding to a prompt from the IHD, Bill Mills explained, "I'm probably one of those guys you read about all the time, away from home. . . . That's right—the absentee father." He went on to describe a busy work schedule that required that he leave before the children awoke in the morning and often kept him away three or four days a week: "Working six or seven days a week you just don't have time for your . . . family." He recognized the emotional costs of his lifestyle, realizing that "I'm perpetrating the same crimes as I used to accuse my father of, you know, of neglect and, oh, temper and that type of thing. Maybe," he surmised, "that's just a masculine way to go."[57]

While these men regretted the consequences of the masculine way, for others, the time they devoted to their careers was simply a fact of life. In 1971, Leonard Stone said, "I didn't have much time for children when I was a young man. My wife kind of took over the burden, did the bulk of the family raising, and I was really deeply involved in the doing of business." Happy to be a father and proud of his children, nonetheless, he accepted that being involved in business meant less time for family concerns. He explained, "I think if you're very successful [at] something . . . you have to take it from some place, so you take it from family life." He recalled that his commitment to his business hadn't always been accepted: "When we were first married, why my wife just couldn't get it through her head, you know, why I didn't come home till after dark. And I left just about the time the sun came up. Had to boot her out of bed to fix breakfast for me. And get going. But she finally accepted the routine." Richard Gaynor admitted, "I don't know at the time whether I really wanted to spend any more time 'cause I was really wrapped up in a number of things. And I was interested in what I was doing. I did what I felt I had to do." Success as breadwinners had eclipsed the other family goals that these men expressed in the 1950s. Work was often more compelling to these breadwinners than the daily lives of their wives and children.[58]

The payoff for these men and their families was the economic advantages they received. Ken Harris admitted, "I would like to spend more time with my kids I guess, yea. But I like my work. . . . And I feel that I must do that in order to in the long run help them and in the short run help myself." Fathers derived satisfaction from the economic comfort their efforts offered their children. Yet, even focusing on the long-term benefits of occupational success could not completely make up for a lack of involvement in family life for Harris. He said, "I probably don't spend enough time with them. That's the thing, I think, that probably bothers me more than anything. I'm one of those guys who's pretty well married to his work." Still, Harris was not bothered enough to change his work habits and continued to work from early in the morning to late into the evening and weekends, too. In his view, missing out on his children's early lives was regrettable but inevitable. Providing well for a family and achieving occupational success remained a primary goal for men of this generation.[59]

A few others saw the same options that Leonard Stone and Ken Harris did—success in business or time devoted to family life—but thought they chose family over work. It is not clear that these men spent more time with their children than those who saw themselves as choosing work, but what comes through is their sense that they sacrificed greater success because they were unwilling to let work encroach on family life. Clay Kent said, "My business has been good enough, but I won't sacrifice family because of it. I could do much better and I don't really work all that hard, but I spend more time with the family." Dean Lawrence maintained that, "If I had a smaller family or no family, I would be more work-centered . . . and perhaps I would be a greater personal success . . . but as a result they bring me closer to family and they keep me poorer and they keep me interested in simple pleasures." Wealthy in-laws permitted Gary Simon to choose his family over work. He realized that if he had not had that cushion, "Maybe the kids wouldn't have turned out as well and the marriage wouldn't have lasted because I would have been spending a lot of time at the office and some of the jobs that pay well require an awful lot of time." Whichever side of the work-family equation men chose—and most chose work—they viewed family and work as competing spheres that siphoned off energy from each other.[60]

Despite the demands of work, some middle-class men in this sample did convey a sense of participation in childrearing. Glen Dyer said, "I did all the normal things and, you know, played ball with 'em, involved with them." For Dyer, scouting was one way he contributed as a father, serving on committees and going on occasional camp-outs. Dyer emphasized sociability and community service as key ingredients of good parenting, not ongoing daily care. George Rogers reported, "I'm very attentive to the family. And as a father, by that I mean I'm home . . . most of the time, except when I work. But I mean . . . I don't go on trips," indicating that his leisure focus was his home and the children in it. Still, how much participation in childrearing was enough remained in question. If there were problems, especially with sons, not enough fathering was to blame. Carl

Gordon guessed his son's difficulties at school developed because he "wasn't spending enough time on him."[61]

Regrets mingled with confidence that their wives had shouldered capably the burden of childrearing. Men who chose work also expressed the emotional distance they felt from family activity. Hal Powell summed up his feelings, "I've always felt that I'm at somewhat of a disadvantage. . . . In the earlier years she had so much greater an exposure than I and I felt essentially I couldn't do anything." Peter Wood attested, "No, I definitely don't pay enough attention to the children. I've had to work very hard for the last couple of years and have simply not had the attention that I should have had for the children. But she's done the best she can to correct that." Men lacked exposure and, therefore, influence; women compensated for the lack.[62]

Men agreed that their wives were the primary parent in the family. Thomas Williams said, "Any success we've had in the family is to her credit. I'm just along for the ride." He had, he said, "taken little or no interest in the total family growth and development picture." Philip Pollard noted that his wife Harriet was "the one to raise the children. Well, we thought we were all doing it together, but the children have really been all of Harriet's life." Burt Hill described himself as a "stranger in the midst" of his growing family, and thus artificially the "center of attention" when he was around. Charles Bremmer was satisfied that he and Alice, "always went on a partnership" when it came to parenting. But then he went on to describe the division of labor between himself and Alice: "She's left the discipline up to me and I've left the education and rearing up to her." Theirs, it seems, was a limited partnership, with traditionally defined roles.[63]

Herbert Henderson said, "I'm not very happy about the fact that I did not give my time and attention and love to" his oldest children. He felt shut out of family affairs but not wholly responsible: "As I see it, Gail should recognize my role in these things and the fact that they mean a lot to me, too." Herbert relied on Gail to acknowledge his interest and arrange for its expression, even as he desired more involvement. The demands and responsibilities of earning a living removed these men from daily family activity, leaving them removed emotionally from childrearing and, often, their children.[64]

Women, too, responded to the division of family labor with resignation. But they expressed disappointment and anger along with their grudging acceptance of male involvement outside the home. While men were more likely to characterize their job as a fact of life, their wives saw some degree of choice when their husbands did not participate in the home as much as they might have hoped. Miriam Stone complained of Leonard, "but he's always been too busy, from the time we were married, no matter what it was: 'I can't do that. Don't bother me with details. I'm too busy.'" She also expressed her wish that he had given their children more time. Lois Dyer told the institute, "Oh, I've told [Glen] a couple of times if he doesn't stay home and raise kids that I'd probably leave." May Perkins, whose husband used to spend his evenings puttering in the garage complained, "He doesn't have to take care of the kids. I secretly resent his freedom." Mary Smith complained that Norman wanted little to do with the discipline. She recounted, "I used to get really mad and accuse him of being an uncle instead of a father. A drop-in catering job." The few hours Norman spent with his kids seemed more like friendly visits than parenting to Mary. In all, fifteen wives interviewed in 1970 were openly critical of their husbands' contribution to childrearing. Such criticism was common in other studies of family life; one 1972 study found wives disdainful of their husbands' abilities in interpersonal relationships.[65]

These women noted how much closer they were to the children than were their husbands. Patricia James said, "I am, of course, much more available—he is home almost only in the evenings and one day on the weekend." In the 1950s, Marie Weber had complained strenuously about her husband's working on weekends and reported eleven years later that he had a difficult time communicating with his children. Women saw themselves as more involved with, more available, and, thus, closer to their children than their husbands.[66]

Wives continued to urge their husbands to devote time to their maturing sons and daughters hoping to help bridge the emotional distance. In 1970 Fred Adams told interviewers, "[My wife] tells me that she doesn't think I spend enough time with the kids, and I don't really know what that means ... when it gets right down to it, they don't want you around it seems." When Fred expressed interest in his children, he found they themselves had other interests. Wives worked to strengthen ties between their husbands and children.[67]

One popular song from the 1970s captured this sense of distance between fathers and their children, especially as the decade wore on and the baby boomers left home, leaving their parents to face the empty nest. The father in singer Harry Chapin's song, "Cats in the Cradle," laments,

> I've long since retired and my son's moved away.
> I called him up just the other day.
> I said, "I'd like to see you if you don't mind."
> He said, "I'd love to, dad, if I could find the time."

The lonely, workaholic father realizes as he hangs up the phone, "My boy was just like me." Here was a postwar father who had placed business success above family concerns and now could claim only the most tenuous of relationships with his grown son. Chapin's lyric harmonized with the often painful emotions of the baby boom's fathers as they reached retirement age.[68]

The media had long supported the notion that both fathers and children suffered from the ailing American pattern of paternity. In 1972 *McCall's* reported on a survey that asked American children about their dads: "Almost every answer described a grim, harried man who works hard, yet has no fun, feels no joy and shares no love: Father." But now feminist critiques of family life lambasted the inequity of American gender roles— criticism that finally questioned a division of labor that experts had long accepted. Throughout the 1970s, feminist theory and psychological research brought a greater emphasis on male effort. By the 1980s coverage of "the new fatherhood" included a fresh element that had only been an undercurrent in previous decades when advice bombarded mostly mothers. Men now bore responsibility for their position in the family. "Fathers," one writer concluded, "you have an important role to play in raising your infant. You are needed and are as capable as your wife of performing this function. Besides, active involvement will be a source of great support to your wife and baby as well as emotional fulfillment to you. Don't miss it." Such advice received support from psychological research that found men perfectly capable of nurturing and not precluded from it by their sex.[69]

By the early 1980s the day-to-day sharing of parenting tasks no longer occupied the couples in this study, now in their fifties and sixties; yet, the problems of unequal parenting still felt current. In fact disagreement often focused on the "matter of [male] unavailability and its consequences." Couples may have disagreed, but no one could dispute that unavailability was a problem. According to sociologist John Clausen, in 1982 interviews with all IHD subjects, 60 percent of the men interviewed said that they "had not been as available to their families as would have been desirable." And among wives, 60 percent "reported that their husbands' lack of availability had been a problem for them." This seems a stunning failure at attaining even fifties fathering objectives.[70]

Wives of "absent" fathers begrudged the hard work of childrearing that they had undertaken almost without help. Jane Mills said, "I would have liked someone to take more interest in the, you know, the raising of the family. . . . I've had to do all that myself." Claire Manning thought, "so far as I've had basic good children, I've always had a husband that's been wrapped up in his work. . . . He's never had time for his children, sit down and help them with the home work." She could take the credit for raising children of whom she was proud but would have preferred to share both the task and the pride with her husband. Nina Harris commented that she was disturbed that her husband "wasn't more intimately involved with the children and other members of the family. He was content to have me do most of that, or just not particularly interested." According to Dina Powell, her husband Hal "never saw the kids." He worked "six days a week, 12 hours a day, and Sunday we sleep." These wives believed they had essentially parented on their own and that their husbands' commitment to career indicated a lack of interest in family life.[71]

Even advocates for more male involvement in day-to-day aspects of parenting never suggested supplanting traditional assumptions about female responsibility for maintaining emotional relationships in the family. Nevertheless, Nina Harris wished that Ken "was a little more caring about his children and his family. That he would just pick up a phone and say 'Hi, how are you doing?' or 'What's happening?' but he just, again, relies on me to do it. And I'm not sure that he would do it if I wasn't there. They'd probably have to come to him." Thus, long after the children were grown, when childrearing no longer defined their roles, middle-class women continued to be the primary communicators, providing connection between fathers and kids, performing the role even as they questioned the exclusive responsibility.[72]

Women felt confident that they had closer relationships with the children than their husbands did. Janice Rogers said, "Until recently, the children did not feel they knew George very well; he was not heavily involved in their lives." Irene Lawrence believed her close contact enabled her to relate better to their children and their views: "I don't know whether Dean's that easy. He wasn't around them that much." Marlene Hill, whose husband traveled frequently throughout his career, remarked simply, "They're my kids and they're not very fond of their father."[73]

In the 1980s, facing retirement, the fathers of the baby boom assessed their parenting contributions in response to questions from the IHD. Their paternal participation had fallen short of even their own expectations. According to sociologist John Clausen, men questioned by the IHD in 1982 "often deplored that they had missed seeing their children grow up." They laced their responses to questions about the effects of work on family with regret. Louis Miller said, "I don't contribute a great deal as 'husband-father.' As a matter of social and physical circumstance I qualify for both, but I don't feel that I've fulfilled the function of either to more than the marginal, minimal need or requirement." Of his wife Lillian, Greg Fox said, "She probably had too much of a burden of raising the boys. I would think that's probably where I fell down most." Hal Powell concluded, "I guess you've got to say that if I abdicated that's what I did." According to Clausen, for those who remarked on their unavailability, 25 percent admitted "that there had been serious problems for their wives and children" as a result.[74]

Retrospectively, baby boom fathers saw themselves as having chosen commitment to job over family. Bill Mills said, "I made a choice: the job. I'm sure they were shorted on the thing." Ken Harris reported using his work as a respite from the complicated emotions and stresses of nuclear family life. He said, "I tended to walk away from it. I didn't like it and I used the fact that I had work to do and I would walk away and not face the music so my wife suffered more than I." As the full-time parent, Nina Harris could not walk away from the emotional difficulties of raising teenagers in the turbulent 1960s and 1970s. Sam Arthur spent lengthy months of travel for more than a decade and felt that "Consequently my father-child relationships were nebulous at best." Working, which these men had set out as their duty to their families, actually distanced them from their families: "I've been just as affectionate and close to my daughters as my business or my time would allow." With these words, John Thompkins expressed the central dilemma for men who started families after World War II.[75]

Despite the material rewards and occupational success work-oriented men had achieved, they regretted and indeed reassessed the familial ramifications of their career commitments. Twenty-two fathers said that if they had to do it again, they would have spent more time with their children. Grant Thornton expressed it poignantly, "But when I was young and started out, I presumed that my work was essentially more important than that of my wife who would shape our children and act as the primary parent in order to develop them. I have subsequently concluded that, in terms of my satisfactions, that hers is a more lasting and useful and meaningful job than was mine."[76]

Plans for retirement offered men in their fifties and sixties relief from the pressures and responsibilities of breadwinning. Men expressed the hope for more time devoted to wives and children. As their work lives wound down and their children formed families of their own, they sought, some for the first time, personal involvement in family life. Ken Harris assumed his distance from the family would "work out and change once I retire." Placed on hold for over three decades, interest in family life rekindled as occupational demands waned and the family nest emptied. Perhaps, formerly absent fathers would forge with their grandchildren the close companionship their careers had denied their children.[77]

The irony of the male life course was not lost on the men of this generation. Looking back in his early sixties, Andrew Sinclair observed, "I don't think any father is as close as they should be. . . . the span of our life is upside down. . . . It should absolutely be reversed. When you're young and you're raising a family, you're so intent on making ends meet at whatever social level, that takes priority." Working hard for the sake of the family, many of the men who dedicated their lives to creating and supporting families in the 1950s discovered in later decades that they sacrificed deep involvement in family life in the end.[78]

In the decades following World War II, as young American couples made the headlines and surprised demographers by producing the baby boom, prewar pleas for improved fatherhood revived. Experts' calls for participatory fatherhood echoed in suburban middle-class homes in the requests of women for more help from their spouses and men's poignant sense that they were not doing enough for or with their children.

Problems with and limitations of the fifties definition of fatherhood wound through fathering in practice. Men took on duties and joys of fatherhood in addition to the responsibilities and satisfactions of breadwinning. Advisors embellished father's role but proposed no other adjustments in the organization of the home. Wives would continue to be homemakers and men would continue to be providers. The years when young children demanded most of paternal time and energy coincided with the years young executives devoted to career-building. The writers of fathering advice never pinpointed exactly what it was fathers did beyond providing companionship with children. Articles and books on parenting left men with the sense that they should spend time with their children and develop companionship with them. But experts did not portray fathering as work. Instead, fathering was an inconvenient frolic or a bedtime story at the end of a hard day. Except for advising a fifteen minute breather before plunging into hectic family life after work, the professionals offered little advice on how to combine these two important roles. In making room for fathers in the family, experts shaped the beginnings of a male double day—one at the office and another at home, leaving men ill-equipped to balance the competing demands.

The gospel of involved fatherhood percolated through and about middle-class ideas about family life in the 1950s and continued to do so as couples moved through the family cycle. The postwar ethos of fathering made most men conscious of themselves as fathers and of the mandate to spend time with their children. For families in this study, over the thirty-year interview period, forty IHD fathers mentioned to the IHD that they did not spend enough time, devote enough attention, or do enough for or with their children. Over that same time period, almost the same number of IHD women criticized their husbands for those faults. Half as many, twenty-one women, said they were satisfied with the care or companionship that their husbands provided their children. Spending time with the youngsters remained what men knew they should be doing, not what they did.[79]

Consequently, tensions over fathering ran through middle-class homes during the postwar years. Two themes recur throughout these sources: regret and resignation. Men held themselves to standards of parenting that they could not or did not wish to achieve. Their wives hoped for parenting partners, but resignedly accomplished the day-to-day work of childrearing. Both husbands and wives recognized that mothers were the primary parent. Men conveyed feelings of regret about the emotional distance between themselves and their children and women felt satisfaction with the closeness they had achieved with their children. Nevertheless, women expressed bitterness over husbands who rarely forayed into the sometimes frenetic work of parenting. Both unrealized expectations and the actual experience of family and childrearing fostered familial conflict across the cycle of baby boom family life. Baby boom era homes were permeated with a dual consciousness—on one level what men should be doing and on the other what they clearly were not—a consciousness that ran throughout the family cycle. But the harm—to themselves, their children, and their wives—of what men were not doing, only barely visible in the 1950s, was glaringly apparent in the 1980s. Baby boom homes haunted by father absence helped to foster the recent renewed focus on fathering.[80]

Historian John Gillis has distinguished between the families we live with and the family we live by: the reality of the people with whom we live out our lives and the symbolic family that lives in family photographs, family gatherings, and the other cultural practices with which Americans celebrate the idea of family. He also has noted, building on recent contributions of women's history and feminist scholarship, that the family Americans "live by" falls to women to create. Just as Sunday dinners and Christmas celebrations have been the pleasure of members of both sexes to enjoy, but the burden of women to prepare, so too the enactment of involved fatherhood required women's orchestration.[81]

On the surface, the ideal of quality time for dads seems a neutral, if new, family practice. But middle-class couples experienced a conflict between culturally mandated expectations and expert prescriptions for their family behavior *and* their own lived experiences with the pressures falling differently on men and women. High expectations without structural support to aid their implementation led directly to disappointment.[82]

As couples pioneered the baby boom family form, they hoped to reinvigorate fatherhood and with it American family life. When the aspirations of experts and ordinary middle-class men and women proved unattainable largely because this reformulation of fatherhood left traditional gender roles unchanged, resentment and regret resulted. And yet the expectations and the variety of efforts to fulfill them had an important transformative impact on the middle-class family. Postwar couples, through their desire, negotiation, and disappointment, created a significant emotional space for men in family life. Couples since then have attempted to fill that space left largely vacant by their parents. Indeed, distance from fathers was a central theme of the evolving men's movement of the 1970s and 1980s.[83]

Contemporary commentators attribute the "new," enlightened father of the 1980s and 1990s, more active in his children's nurture and care, to the feminist critiques of gender roles and family dynamics, which brought long-held notions of father- and motherhood into question, and to the increasing labor-force participation of married women and mothers in the 1970s. The baby boom generation is accustomed to reading about their novel attempts to refashion the family, shape egalitarian marriages, and create new patterns of childrearing. Certainly, the tenor and tone of fathering advice had shifted by the 1970s to reflect these changes with calls to incorporate fathers from conception on and demands that they participate in routine care after birth. The roots of involved fatherhood, however, predate second-wave feminism and accompanied rather than followed postwar shifts in American family life. Women's efforts to incorporate men into childrearing predate feminism. The baby boom era families of the 1950s, building on the prewar legacy of masculine domesticity, laid the foundations for today's pattern of daddy tracking and co-parenting. And this pattern, still very much under construction, remains predominated more by desire for than by equality of effort between men and women.[84]

Fathering was one of many facets of family life affected by the developing democratic ethos of marriage and parenthood during the baby boom. Togetherness, to which we turn in the next chapter, set new standards of emotional engagement in marriage which, like those for fatherhood, played out over the family cycle.

Togetherness ideology favored activities that involved the whole family but ignored the fact that this family style fit only a temporary stage of the family cycle. ARCHIVE PHOTOS

The Quest for Togetherness

Companionship, Childrearing, and Marriage

In May 1954, *McCall's* magazine invited its readers to "live the life of McCall's" and announced the dawning of the era of "together"-ness. Explicitly contrasting postwar affluence with the struggles of decades past, editor Otis Stiese glowingly described advances in family life. According to Stiese, what set the good life in the 1950s apart was that "men, women, and children are achieving it *together*. They are drafting this new and warmer way of life, not as women *alone* or men *alone* isolated from one another but as a *family* sharing a common experience." With togetherness, Stiese grounded the couple firmly in the context of the family.[1]

McCall's coined the term to characterize the focus on the family that swept the nation and to sell advertising space, by selling their readers—

baby boom parents—to American business. Stiese heralded a family style that included youthful marriage, an egalitarian ethos, and the increased sharing of parental and breadwinning tasks. Since that time the phrase has evoked powerful images of fifties family life, conjuring up soft focus visions of emotionally satisfying family life in almost total isolation from extended family, neighbors, and community. But the meaning of togetherness has rarely been explored. In the 1950s, a decades-long trend toward heightened ideological emphasis on the couple reversed in favor of the family as a whole. The revived focus on parenthood in marriage that accompanied the baby boom required a new set of expectations and adjustments of couples. Middle-class marriage had a dual emphasis in the postwar years: the couple and the children. Togetherness redefined both the meaning of marriage and the position of the married couple with respect to the outside world.

These ideals set standards few couples could uphold. In the early stages of the family cycle couples concentrated almost wholly on parenting. Togetherness family style required the presence of children. But where did children fit in a romantic marriage? And what would happen when the children left home? As their children matured, the parents of the baby boom struggled to balance the often conflicting aspirations of parenthood—family togetherness—and marriage—couple companionship. Of course, these were not mutually exclusive categories; still, the romantic and reproductive aims of family life clashed.

Children provided the purpose and sometimes the problems of middle-class marriage. Togetherness encapsulated both the comforts and conflicts of baby boom family life. As an ideology, it provided a solution to the dilemma couples with large young families faced by combining family time and couple time. But togetherness turned out to be a leaky vessel on which to navigate through the family cycle. By isolating the family unit and glossing over the family division of labor, it created more tensions than it resolved.

The ideology of "togetherness" sprang out of a century-long dichotomy in prescriptions for American middle-class marriage. Historians identify two conflicting patterns that emerged during the nineteenth century— "separate spheres" and companionate marriage. Separate spheres was the middle-class, Victorian-era notion that men and women inhabited distinct worlds. Industrialization removed productive labor and men from the home, leaving reproductive labor in the home as the purview and specialization of women. According to historian Carroll Smith-Rosenberg, women's world existed almost wholly on its own, punctuated by female rituals and woven together by intimacy and friendship. Men lived in the competitive public world of politics and commerce, although historians of masculinity have recently begun to explore the close qualities of male friendship and the meaning of masculine sociability. In contrast to this polarized description, recent research has called into question the ideology of gender division, showing that in reality stark distinction between spheres was never wholly practiced. Similarity marked male and female experiences more than nineteenth-century prescriptions reveal. Women shaped the public sphere and men could be warm and engaged participants in the private sphere. In a contradictory trend, companionate marriage evolved within the rubric of separate spheres ideology.[2]

By "companionate," historians mean the increasing emphasis on love and mutuality and the heightened value Americans placed on the affective qualities of middle-class marriage that emerged in the nineteenth century and came into full flower by the early twentieth. With the rise of companionate marriage, husbands and wives expected love and companionship to characterize their marriages. Both "separate spheres" and "companionate marriage" provide historians with reductive descriptions of marital ideals rather than an accurate portrayal of married life for most middle-class Americans in the past. Nevertheless, these concepts reflected certain basic facets of middle-class marriage by the turn of the century—the sexual division of labor and an increasing emphasis on romance and affection in marriage.[3]

Between 1900 and 1930, the parameters of the sexual division of labor in marriage remained for the most part unchanged, but the romantic ideal of marriage was greatly enhanced. Contraceptive use began to increase among the middle class. Sexual expression without fear of conception shaped expectations for a new sphere of intimacy for middle-class couples. Increased leisure also created space for communication and companionship in marriage. As the home became the focus of recreation and relaxation, Americans' expectations for happiness in marriage heightened. These hopes for satisfaction and fulfillment contributed to an increasing divorce rate as Americans sacrificed unsatisfactory matches in search of unions closer to the promised romantic ideal.[4]

The American divorce rate in the roaring twenties is testimony not only to the high hopes for marriage but also to the new pressures that consumer-oriented companionship put on husbands and wives in addition to their traditional roles. Twenties leisure culture, based on consumption and entertainment, placed a greater burden on men's financial abilities. And, middle-class women now faced, in addition to their duties as housewives and mothers, the challenge of being fun-filled pals to their husbands. Americans in the 1920s celebrated the image of the fun-loving, romantic couple. After their wedding vows, smaller families and the fun and amusement available outside the home encouraged couples to continue habits of companionship formed while dating. With more time and energy and higher expectations for marriage Americans looked to it as a means of personal fulfillment and companionship.[5]

Throughout the first three decades of the twentieth century, the middle-class family remained small. During the 1930s, economics combined with the long-term trend of small families to limit the number of children couples chose to have. The birth rate reached a low of 18.7 percent in 1935. However, with the onset of World War II, and particularly after the war, four decades of declining family size and increasing marital focus on the couple came to a close. Eager couples responded to two decades of postponed childbearing with the baby boom. Significant numbers of Americans aimed for and surpassed the 3.4 children per family that was the national average in the 1950s. Three-quarters of the couples in my sample had two to four children and there were several families with five or more children.[6]

The boom in births shifted the ideological emphasis in American marriage from the couple to the children. The family ideal was now a companionate one that united parents with children. Fulfillment and satisfaction dominated more functional family goals. "Togetherness" with its emphasis on family-based activity, fun, and fulfillment attempted to refashion the romantic marital ideal around the seeming obstacle of large families. The couple orbited the family. Husbands and wives desired companionship—as families and as couples—from their marriages but also knew it was prescribed for them. In a 1966 Roper poll published in the *Saturday Evening Post,* 71 percent of respondents answered "companionship" to the question "what love means to you now." Companionship and mutual understanding also ranked high in IHD couples' expectations for marriage.[7]

In theory togetherness would preserve the couple in the face of heavier family demands brought on by the baby boom. It bridged the potential gender divide of the postwar, middle-class nuclear family. A "whole-family" lifestyle distinguished postwar families from families of the past, according to the experts on marriage whose articles filled the pages of women's magazines.[8]

A key feature of togetherness, as proposed by *McCall's,* was that men partook of family life in a new way, as "friends and companions." In the togetherness family, exemplified by Ed and Carol Richtscheidt of New Jersey in the special May 1954 issue of the magazine, life was centered "almost completely around their children and their home." Bringing both parents into the family fold meant that each had to disengage from the outside world. Politics, the bar, the golf course, charity societies, and women's clubs—all detracted from family life. Togetherness's heterosexual emphasis directed the attention of a couple away from homosocial interactions. Yet, as with parenting, most of the work involved in achieving togetherness fell to women. Often, men's main contribution was to participate in activities their wives organized.[9]

Family togetherness, as women's magazines presented it, underpinned both family unity and marital harmony. But more was at stake than the simple enjoyment of family activity. When parents followed the formula correctly, "the children leave off their tussling, whining and bickering and grin. The mantle of togetherness of spirit between Mr. and Mrs. K settles down over them and they glow and relax in the warmth of the moment." The image was of harmonious family companionship that wove a couple together, preserving both happiness and marriage.

Experts warned flagging couples of the dangers of ignoring their mandates. With an atom-friendly nuclear analogy, writer Helen P. Glenn predicted what would happen to the unwary, unprepared couple after they had children: "Exclusive concern with each other is bound to fly out the window when the stork flies in but the natural and inevitable separation of interest and concerns at this stage of a marriage can lead as the years pass *without* recognition into the habit of fission—or as the years pass *with* recognition to fusion" (emphasis in the original). Togetherness, then, counteracted the otherwise inevitable separation of roles once children entered the middle-class family.[10]

If they failed to emphasize togetherness, experts feared that the worrisome routines of everyday modern life would drive couples apart. In *Better Homes and Gardens*, writer Marjorie Holmes prophesied this troubling scenario should couples neglect togetherness. "Business, parties . . . bills . . . repairs, worries about the children," whittled away at marriage, "until it's as if the man who pleaded, 'I can't live without you' and the woman who whispered, 'We'll always think of each other,' are practically yelling 'Yoo Hoo!' across the cluttered canyon." Togetherness was the spiritual bridge that would join and support families in both happiness and common purpose. Experts hoped it would connect a couple across the "cluttered canyon" of family life.[11]

Advisors in the family field did ultimately step back to rethink the infatuation with togetherness. In 1956, the *New York Times Magazine*'s family columnist Dorothy Barclay noted, "Emphasis on family members' sharing every aspect of one another's lives has risen to an extraordinary pitch in the past year or so." Her article, entitled "Family Palship—with an Escape Clause," argued for moderating the all-encompassing ethos. *Parents Magazine* contributor Jean Komaiko called for moderation, saying, "We do many things together: swim, barbecue, give parties, take vacations, read. Our table is always ready for an 'extra' child, and we picnic at the drop of a hat. But Chuck and I have lives apart from our children." These writers pinpointed the internal contradiction contained in togetherness. It was meant to counter the division of roles in marriages wherein wives devoted themselves to home and children, and men through work, to their upkeep. Yet, joining all family members together left little time for husbands and wives apart from their children. It is significant that Komaiko asserted their autonomy as a couple only after first establishing the couple's credentials as "togetherness" parents.[12]

Outside of the fabled family world of fifties magazines, togetherness was not so easily achieved; nor was the dilemma between couple autonomy and family demands as easily resolved. Couples in the 1950s valued marriage for its contributions to individual well-being. They expected emotional satisfaction along with economic support and parenthood. In reality, however, marriage did not meet the high demands middle-class couples placed on it. Analysis of a 1957 study of Americans showed that aspirations for "affiliation" could not be met wholly by marriage. "The expectations for companionship that characterize modern marital role," the social scientists Joseph Veroff and Sheila Feld concluded, "are not easily translated into gratification." But that translation was, the voices of postwar couples show, an ongoing effort across the family cycle.[13]

Another challenge for couples arose from the fact that husbands and wives shared ideas about mutuality and cooperation in marriage that coexisted with an enduring attachment to fulfilling prescribed marital roles. As much as the roles of breadwinning and homemaking divided them, and as much as they searched for flexibility within them, men and women relied on them as organizing features of their identities and lives, providing important clues to the longevity of traditional norms.

Togetherness prescriptions fit only the early stages of family life when children were young and families socialized as a group. But as an ideal, it cast a long shadow over baby boom era marriages. The tension between a romantic desire for a couple-focused marriage and the reality of child-focused marriage, the sexual division of labor, and the changes over the family cycle challenged couples to measure up to their individual version of the togetherness ideal.

At the early stages of the family cycle, while the ideal posed cheerful couples orienting their energy and themselves around family by choice, for young parents of growing children, togetherness was often the only option. The backyard barbecue had a practical component. Entertaining at home found popularity with young families because it meant not hiring a baby sitter. Romantic evenings on the town remained a luxury of time and expense in which few couples could indulge. Maureen Gordon noted how much more social the Gordons had been before they had children. Parenthood changed their lifestyle: "You won't go out as much because you think of baby sitting and some places you can't take the children, so a parent changes."[14]

Actually finding time for "togetherness" was difficult. In addition to work and household chores, community activities beckoned parents away from family-centered fun, despite prescriptions to the contrary. Referring to scouts and other organizations, Judy Kent said, "We both enjoy an active social life and yet we feel that our children deserve our time too. We've tried to keep Sunday as a family day, although that's not easy since we've been working on the house." Couples set aside the weekend for family activity, but often outside commitments, household chores, and do-it-yourself home repairs supplanted family fun.[15]

With so much of the week experienced apart, for many couples, togetherness was only a weekend activity. On Saturday and Sunday couples created togetherness with a vengeance. Philip Pollard bent over backwards to keep his weekends free to spend with his wife and family. He said, "I do my darndest to work late on other nights so I'll have my Saturdays and Sundays off with the family." His pursuit of weekend leisure time with the other Pollards restricted his availability to them during the week, no doubt enhancing his wife's sense of isolation. Nevertheless, like many young men, his commitment to provide for his family superseded and underwrote notions of togetherness. Indeed, social scientists examining data from the 1950s posited that dual role expectations on men for success at work and involvement via togetherness and fatherhood at home contributed to the problem of "role overload" in young men.[16]

In the 1950s, when most baby boom families had several children under age ten at home, the lives of middle-class mothers revolved for the most part around home and family. In contrast, most men's lives had two loci, home and work. This discrepancy even appeared in *McCall's* flagship article. After dressing and feeding the children with his wife in the morning, Ed Richtscheidt, the man *McCall's* chose to exemplify the modern, togetherness male, joined the car pool, leaving the family for the office. Ed's eight-to-ten-hour absence each day placed a limit on his full participation in family life. Indeed, at home, Ed severely circumscribed his commitment to complete togetherness. He helped alleviate the burdens childrearing placed on his wife, but he did so only as his schedule permitted and according to his preference for various chores. Family togetherness for men was a leisure-time pursuit, secondary in importance to their main role. Under togetherness, couples shared family work but did not share it equally, despite the egalitarian hyperbole.[17]

Middle-class women, too, played new roles in family life, according to *McCall's* editors. From its inception togetherness was linked to a new role for "modern women." Even though it required father's participation, its achievement fell to mother. One month after the special issue, the editors of *McCall's* wrote, "For quite a while now families have been living a new kind of life. It's more casual, easy going, and home is its pivot. And it takes a certain knack to get the most of it. This life calls for a very special sort of woman, a 1954 model." That year's "model" of womanhood had expanded duties in the home.[18]

Togetherness placed additional demands on homemakers. Women emphasized family activities and fostered them. In part they responded to prescriptive edicts. But mothers in the 1950s had a greater stake in family togetherness than simply fulfilling prescribed social roles. By engineering shared family time, they involved their husbands more directly in childrearing and enjoyed more adult companionship. IHD records reveal women as initiators of togetherness. For example, George Rogers said his wife shaped family recreation: "Janice is a great believer in the family doing things together. She keeps me on a narrow path, too." Wives tutored their mates in the habits of familythink. While new prescriptions for married life required extra effort on the part of wives, women benefited from this culturally sanctioned sharing of care-giving tasks.[19]

Not surprisingly, given what they had to gain—a partner in the duties and delights of childrearing—women expressed a greater interest in family fun than did their husbands. They mastered the language of togetherness. Gail Henderson set out to create a different family style from the one she had grown up with: "Herbert and I really enjoy our children. We would never take vacations without them. . . . Although the notion of togetherness is a trite one, I would say that it's in that the two families really differ." Trite or not, Gail Henderson wanted to create it in her home. Togetherness was one way for the parents of the baby boom to distinguish themselves from their parents' generation, but women effected the change.[20]

Judy Kent summed up the importance of a family-centered social life, saying, "We love the togetherness of our family. Clay and I feel happy as a unit with just the family, without having other people around. We seek our entertainment as a family. We'd just as soon go on a picnic or go some-where. We don't feel any necessity for getting away from the family." Family fun isolated the nuclear family from the outside world. Judy's words imply that there was something wrong with feeling the need to escape the confines of the family. The family was not just enough; it was everything. Her husband Clay had a different view of why the Kents spent their time the way they did. In 1958, an interviewer asked whether or not the home was "child-centered." He answered, "Well, it has to be around the children. There are so many of them." The Kents had all but one of their several children by then. While for Judy togetherness was an aim, for Clay it was a result. Large families in effect necessitated family-oriented activities, but for many women togetherness was both a goal and proof that they were successful mothers and wives.[21]

What did togetherness mean on a daily basis? It meant excursions to parks and the zoo—even trips to the dump—meals, backyard barbecues, and vacations that included the children—anything that incorporated children and adults, cost little, and was informal. David Morris thought baby sitters cost too much so he and his wife Betty shaped their social life around neighborhood gatherings. Affording a sitter for the occasional evening out was not the only issue for young couples with children. Leonard Stone said, "My wife and I don't go very many places without them. I feel rather guilty about leaving the children at home." Clearly, couples were aware of the cultural injunctions to create entertainment that involved the kids but also fit their budgetary and child-care needs.[22]

Meeting expectations for togetherness and family companionship brought couples a sense of satisfaction. Desires for a family-based lifestyle were not solely the product of ideology nor simply a pragmatic response to the circumstances of baby boom family life. Gail Henderson remarked, "We both enjoy doing things with the whole group and life looks good." Twenty-three couples volunteered descriptions of their families that echoed togetherness ideology. They spoke of having fun "in the family as a unit," having "family days," doing things "together," "as a whole family," "all with the kids." Couples found joy, comfort, and pride in accomplishment when they watched the family play together and they enthusiastically joined their children in activities. As Hank Jones summed it up, "There should be some sort of family enjoyment together during the leisure hours, not as individuals, but as a family." Togetherness appeared to be a national phenomenon. When 1000 families of Tampa, Florida, high school students were studied, togetherness characterized their family social activity. Family outings topped the list as a shared activity for 94 percent of the families.[23]

Yet, togetherness had a hitch; family activity prevented a couple from

spending time together without the children. Connie Small found it difficult to strike a balance between having family togetherness and setting
time aside for herself and her husband. She did not want her children to
feel that their parents sacrificed too much for them or, on the other hand,
that they were not getting enough time or attention from their parents.
She wondered where parental devotion blurred into parental martyrdom.
Was it selfish for parents to devote some time solely to each other?[24]

Women with little choice but to be with their children on a daily basis
longed for time alone with their mates. Judy Kent insisted that her husband stay up late at night with her after the children were in bed: "The
only time that I have without the children and that we can have together
is at night. . . . I really need some time without the children." On the one
hand, she protested that there was no need for activities that did not include the whole family, almost to the exclusion of the outside world. Yet,
on the other, she craved time alone with her husband. Claire Manning
found a solution: "We all do things together. But then my husband and I
have a social life that does not include the children. My husband and I
don't want to lose contact with each other. If we do, life becomes just more
of an existence."[25]

Men expressed frustration with the perceived burdens of constant togetherness. Dean Lawrence said, "I wish she would take steps so that she
and I could spend more time together. I wish she would declare some more
independence of the children occasionally. I wish she could locate baby
sitters and take care of this aspect of it." Wives carried responsibility not
only for creating togetherness but also for providing respite from it. They
arranged both family time and couple time. Both men and women perceived their children as cutting in on the husband-wife relationship.[26]

These couples brought up the flip side of the togetherness ethic. Experts' injunctions for large families in the 1950s conjured up harmonious
images of husbands and wives united by joint childrearing. Raising children, however, many found, did not always bring couples together. On
balance, mothers did the bulk of the rearing of baby boomers, while fathers
provided most of the financial support. This split in roles shifted the emphasis in middle-class marriages away from the couple dyad during the
1950s and 1960s. Early in marriage, the division of labor exposed the contradictions of togetherness on the one hand and the tensions between family togetherness and couple companionship on the other.

Having children so early in marriage, couples fell into dissimilar daily
existences, despite efforts to the contrary. Young men at the beginning of
their careers found themselves with growing families to support. They
worked long hours to earn more, gain promotions and thus assure their

families financial security. Meanwhile, young women with two or three children under ten to care for spent the majority of their time attending to the needs of household and family. Two sociologists who studied marriage in the late 1950s observed, "But for American marriages as a whole, the trend is unmistakable: during the child rearing years, husbands and wives often cease doing things together and grow apart from each other."[27]

The division of family labor distinguished the days as well as the duties of husbands and wives. Couples may have disagreed over contracting and expanding definitions of men's and women's roles in marriage and, in the case of fatherhood, may have attempted to bring men into the family circle; yet, once they began childrearing a basic division of labor within the family was set. Life in the suburbs was sex-segregated, a factor for which couples struggled to compensate.

Long hours for husbands in the office meant long hours for wives at work in the home. Janice Rogers complained of how little she saw of her husband. George stayed late at the office and she put the three children to bed before he came home. So, he rarely saw the children during the week. Once he was home, Janice commented, "He's really too beat to put forth much." She herself was "very tired and strained." Wives spent most of their days at home with their children and without their husbands, who, in turn, missed out on both wives and children most of the week.[28]

The separate lives spouses led meant differing sets of concerns. Dennis Perkins relayed this when he said, "We certainly do have our modes of expression, though on different matters. My work upsets me but not her. May is depressed more about the home. It's not that important to me." Husbands and wives centered their energies in different areas. James Evans, a construction engineer, described his wife as a woman who made mothering her profession by keeping abreast on the latest information in manuals and magazines. "With myself it's sewers," he explained, "and it's children with my wife." There was, apparently, little crossover in these fields of expertise. In postwar marriages, spouses specialized. With distinct worries and priorities, it became difficult to remember the common goals of family life.[29]

Companionship as a couple, nevertheless, remained a major goal. Togetherness might have been fun, but few couples found family picnics and touch football romantic. The child-centered trend contradicted a continued expectation for romantic companionship. Family unity and couple unity clashed; couples did not resolve the conflict until the children grew up, when they could focus on one another once again, but for many, by the empty nest, it was too late.[30]

Patterns put in place while children were small continued to steer marriages as the years passed. Recalling the early years of her marriage, feminist Betty Friedan described the prototypical togetherness tableau. "We bought barbecue grills and made dips out of sour cream and onion soup to serve with potato chips, while our husbands made the martinis . . . and cooked hamburgers on the charcoal, and we sat in the canvas chairs on our terrace and thought how beautiful our children looked, playing in the twilight, and how lucky we all were and that it would last forever." Yet, that stage of the family cycle did not last forever, and toddlers grew into teenagers. The desire for couple togetherness still presented challenges as adolescent children readied for adulthood and men and women confronted the consequences of the different family roles each had taken on.[31]

Distinct responsibilities in the household led to different experiences and interactions within the family that continued as children approached high school and college age. In 1969, Meg Fisher described a typical evening at the Fisher home: "He doesn't want to be interrupted when he comes home. Just wants to come in and change his clothes and read the paper and eat dinner and then after dinner then he can sit down and talk to me. As soon as I come in the kids are all over me and in and out of the bedroom and I'm telling everybody what to do and listening to all their problems and fixing dinner and changing clothes." Responsibility for the care of the children involved Meg (who worked) in their children's accomplishments and failures each day in a way that Tom Fisher, exhausted at the end of his day away, could not handle. Her engagement with and his disengagement from their three children worked to limit their joint experiences.[32]

Family activities and concerns also overshadowed the Arthurs' interactions as a couple. Sam Arthur said, "So what we do together other than the normal things, play bridge on occasion and go to school functions and maintain a home and raise children, I have to say that it's pretty limited. We really haven't done much together." The effects of this de facto separation lingered. Twelve years later he described himself and Liz as still estranged, because "she developed her own life and I developed my own life and consequently, even to this day, we're not as close as many other people that have been married as long as we are. Because by necessity, for 12 or 14 years she went her way and I went my way. And now it's very difficult to meld back into a togetherness sort of a thing." Years spent devoted to their different roles led, it seems, inevitably to a sense of separation, the "fission" about which experts warned in the 1950s.[33]

Ernest Johnson complained about the consequences of leading separate lives, particularly the division between homemaking and breadwinning. As a result, he and his wife shared few common interests. He said, "I find it hard to become interested in sewing, and cooking, and flower decorating," naming the creative tasks and diversions that had occupied much of his wife's time. This was a gulf Ernest found difficult to cross.[34]

Home was the prescribed site for both family fun and romance. While earning a living removed the husband from the home, and raising children focused women within it, because home was where couples could be together, they noticed that childrearing came between a couple, but more rarely leveled any criticism on a man's full-time job and even less so the gendered division of labor. Couples perceived childrearing as taxing to a marriage.[35]

Wives worried it drew them away from their husbands. Amy Chase thought that she was "too involved with the girls." The fact that she worked hard as a mother meant, she feared, that "I'm not as good a wife as I should be." Childrearing, largely seen as women's work, separated couples physically and emotionally. Helen Evans found it difficult to balance her roles in the family. She said she felt torn between the demands placed on her as a mother and also a wife. Helen, thinking of all her efforts mothering their children, concluded, "I didn't put my husband first. In fact, he ended up low man on the totem pole." Togetherness made men better husbands because they pitched in to help their wives, but women worried togetherness ultimately might make them better mothers but worse wives.[36]

A large family, many fifties couples' goal, shifted a couple's emphasis away from each other. Meg Fisher observed the redirection of energy that occurred with raising children. She said, "Then when you have children . . . as your children are growing up you sort of sometimes forget why you're married because you have too many problems with work and school and everything. Then as your children get out on their own, then you can get more together again." While children were the key to the original vision of togetherness, comments from the 1970s and 1980s reveal that the baby boom's parents held fast to a competing marital ideal that they thought their children prevented them from attaining. Tom Fisher recalled the time and attention he and Meg devoted to their children until "Eventually it dawned on both of us that we needed more time to ourselves." Neither the fun of togetherness nor the joys and sacrifices of childrearing supplanted belief in a romantic marital ideal.[37]

The Ameses had several children, and in 1970 the youngest was in elementary school. By then their older children could take care of the younger ones, much to their parents' relief. Max Ames said, "Sometimes I think we felt straddled by the children." While Max was relieved when some of his children reached teen years, Patricia James found herself frustrated with her teenagers because, "the kids are up as late as we are unless we stay up too late and to just have an hour or so of quiet and relaxation is impossible." Many wondered how to be a couple with a house full of children.[38]

These gripes about the sacrifices made for children were all voiced in relation to marriage. Instead of being the fulfillment of marriage as they had hoped, the parents of the baby boomers found raising children often conflicted with their expectations for romantic marriage. Ken Harris presented the problems he saw his children causing:

> We both resent, in a way, the children because of the drain in our emotions . . . I have to take a job that I didn't especially like but that paid good because I recognized the fact that I had a family to support. Nina has done much the same thing, worked very hard physically for the family, for the children. . . . If we could just live through this until the time when they leave home, why, we could get back to the relationship we used to have, which was more of a carefree, light-hearted, enjoyable sort of thing—tender.

In his opinion, "The children are secondary. And yet right now they have to come first. So, we put off our relationship." Harris expressed more bitterness than most, but his comment reveals the costs of raising children at which many hinted. The conflicts inherent in the original ideal of togetherness made themselves felt over time.[39]

In addition to distracting spouses from one another, children could become the focus of conflict in some baby boom era marriages. Lisa Sims analyzed her marriage and gauged that while, she loved her children, "a lot of conflicts in my marriage revolve around them. And the jealousy. So I can look back and say that if we had never had children we probably would have had a better relationship." She and her husband disagreed over disciplining the children. As a result, her husband Howard complained, "I'm the Simon Legree and Mommy is Miss Goodshoes." Their longstanding disagreements created a rift in the marriage. Resentment over the strain of raising children and its effects on marriage cropped up in the commentary of parents of the baby boom. Many couples voiced this idea that their separate lives were both necessary and temporary. Yet, they underestimated the force of habit and lingering legacy of distinct complementary roles.[40]

Couple companionship as distinct from family companionship remained an important goal from the 1950s to the 1980s; it was not wholly subsumed under the rubric of family togetherness. But, even as baby boom children matured, the achievement of the close companionship about which parents dreamed, remained elusive for many. Twenty-six couples described gendered family responsibilities as dividing husbands and wives. Husbands and wives strove to overcome the gap their differing roles within the family created, even, as we have seen, as they worked to modify those roles. The discrepancy between expectations for couple companionship and family togetherness was a widespread experience, but, the accommodations and negotiations couples came up with remained highly individual.

One response to the dual demands of marriage was to elevate companionship as a marital goal. Some couples worked at maintaining companionship, specifically setting aside time for it. Grant and Cynthia Thornton reserved an evening a week for themselves throughout their marriage. In 1970 Grant said, "We make it a practice, and have since marriage, almost every week, to go out alone without the children. And I still try to romance my wife when we go out. And we still hold hands when we are out in public." In 1982, Cynthia described their dates and said with satisfaction, "So we've kept our courtship going all of our life." By "courting" one another throughout their marriage, the Thorntons carved out a marital relationship distinct from their parental roles. Another couple set aside time each day apart from their children. May Perkins and her husband Dennis spent an hour each evening together when he got home from work. Dennis proposed it as a partial solution to the time he spent working and commuting each day. May described how he came home one night and announced to her, "'Well, I think I've found the answer.' And he made martinis." Dennis said, "We're going to have a martini every night. . . . The kids are staying in there, and we're going to have cocktail hour." As he explained their ritual, "It's a matter of just being together."[41]

Not all baby boom parents sought to spend couple time. More than fifteen couples grew to like the freedom to pursue independent interests their relationships provided. The Gordons eased into a compromise as their children grew older. He liked to fish, while she preferred the theater; these interests they pursued separately. Maureen commented, "I've always been an independent person, so the things that we like to do together we do together." Roberta Johnson discussed the evolution of her attitude toward companionship: "I guess I used to feel as though if we didn't do it together, the relationship wasn't good. I've found from years that the relationship is still good, but you don't necessarily have to do things together all the time." She relinquished her hold on the companionate ideal, but found a satisfactory compromise.[42]

When James and Helen Evans could not find shared interests, they too gave in and followed their personal pursuits independently, rather than conform to the companionate ideal. James found it exciting when they returned from a weekend apart eager to share: "We compete over who tells the other their experiences first. It's sort of lively. . . . It's better than each of us forcing ourself to do something we think is proper." They only occasionally made plans for a shared activity such as a movie. As James became more and more active, however, leaving for weeklong athletic adventures, he worried that his wife became more sedentary, concentrating on her studies, distancing them even more. This couple broke from injunctions for constant couple togetherness to work out a satisfying compromise in their marriage, thriving on their independent interests. Nevertheless, they worried that their individual activities could further separate them.[43]

Joint activity was an expectation women brought to marriage. Connie Douglas could not "think of anything that I'm doing now that I wouldn't be happier doing with my husband. I mean the things that I do myself now, it's only because he's not available." For her marriage meant a companion, a buddy to do things with. Aileen Ross complained that her husband spent too much time by himself reading. She got "steamed up" about this: "It's insulting not to have him show some companionship." One reason Karen Lewis decided to rate her marriage as a three on a scale of one to ten was because, "As far as doing things with a companion we just don't do it. If we do things companionably, it's because I will play golf with him. But he doesn't [do] things that I like to do." Husbands, it seems, set the terms of companionship, defining which activities couples could share, and their wives adapted, but continued to yearn for greater intimacy. Husbands and wives defined companionship differently. While Nina Harris wanted sharing, for Ken companionship meant shared activities. He was pleased because he "wanted to do more with my wife than I saw my mother and father doing together. They did less and less together as they got older." Surpassing the companionship his parents had achieved satisfied him, while his wife hoped for more intimacy. To wives devolved the responsibility to shape both family and couple togetherness, across the entire family cycle.[44]

Although Don Baldwin felt he had learned the importance of companionship when his first marriage broke up, there was still a gap between what he should be doing and what he did. He said, "I learned to take an interest in my wife more. But right now I feel that I still sometimes lack these qualifications whereas I come home and I'm tired and eat, read the paper, and I fall asleep. My wife feels at that present time that she's there by herself, living by herself and this isn't right on my part because we gotta have companionship." These men struggled to meet expectations for marital companionship—their own as well as their wives'.[45]

When the companion-spouse model worked for couples, it provided a great deal of satisfaction. Rodney Scott complimented his wife, saying, "I would say that she's been a really good, steadying influence in my life, provided me with a lot of wonderful companionship—a real good friend as well as wife and mother." This couple managed to balance the demands of being parents and spouses across the family cycle. His wife thought the secret was their willingness to both acknowledge individual pursuits and spend time together.[46]

Often the companionship couples dreamed of only became possible after their children left home or husbands retired. With their children grown and work life winding down, they had the opportunity at last to create companionship. After retirement, Didi and Hank Jones "made it a point" to do things together, from vacations to weekend drives. Hank said, "I've always felt that if I couldn't do it with my wife, I just don't do it."[47]

The late 1970s and early 1980s marked a new stage in the life course for the parents of the baby boom. By then their youngest children had entered high school or left home, and after twenty-five to thirty-five years in the workforce, baby boom fathers looked forward to retirement. For such role-based marriages, these two events, the empty nest and retirement, meant disruption of entrenched marital patterns. The empty nest removed from women who had devoted their lives to homemaking and raising children their primary occupation. Retirement brought husbands back into the home, from which they had, except on weekends and evenings, been largely absent for nearly three decades. Many men saw retiring as a chance to rearrange priorities and to focus on their wives and children. Both spouses looked at this period as an opportunity for marital renewal, the first time since they were newlyweds that they were just a couple. One quarter of the couples greeted or looked forward to greeting the empty nest as a chance to build companionship. Another fifteen IHD couples described their partnership as companionate, best friends, or as an ongoing experience of couple togetherness.

Once their children left home, couples who had grown accustomed to grappling with competing demands on their time found themselves on new terrain. As one scholar summarized this period, in a review of research on midlife, "The middle-aged couple may come to the realization that their energies as a couple have been totally on child-rearing, and not on the maintenance of a vital marital relationship." Baby boom parents looked forward to the empty nest. Eugene Good described, "a period of some 30 years or so, where your time is spoken for when you're raising the kids. And you really don't have time for the 'marriage.' You're so busy with the kids. But when the kids are gone . . . you have parent liberation. And, boy, I'm all for it. It's really great stuff."[48]

One problem the empty nest raised, however, was that when children took wing, the baby boom era couple lost its primary purpose. As his youngest approached adulthood, Edward Martin observed, "I guess the thing we devoted most of our lives to up until this point [was] the kids, and now it sort of leaves a vacuum." Raising children united a couple, despite their distinct roles, in a common purpose. When their children reached maturity, parents faced uncertainty. If they had separate hobbies and pursuits, without the children around what did unite them? Thirteen couples expressed worries of this nature.

"When my wife and I were raising the kids we were pretty much a team. Now we don't have that so our relationship is new and different. I guess we're still groping a little bit as to which way we're going, what is there to do." That is how James Evans described the new dynamics of his marriage now that the children were on their own. While childrearing united a couple, each partner played a very different role on the "team." Blanche Warner pondered the shift in emotional focus away from the kids to the couple—specifically whether her husband could shift back from being a parent to being a partner. She thought it would be harder for Keith "to make an adjustment to going back to being more of a husband to me, you know. He seems to have so much importance on being the provider and the father and everything." The "groping" Evans observed was a common experience as baby boom era couples adjusted to the empty nest.[49]

Couples faced the empty nest with more than worry or trepidation. The significant change it meant for couples could reach crisis proportions. The Williamses had a large family. When they had been married over two decades and their youngest child started school, Sally hoped that she and Tom would start to do things together again as the children matured. If this did not occur, she said, "The marriage may break up after all the children have left." She went on to say that she would never seriously consider divorce; nonetheless, her comment serves to highlight how couples viewed the next stage in the family cycle. As the youngest of his children neared high school graduation, Dale George joked with his wife, "Why don't we adopt another one?" But, he told the IHD, "I don't want to be alone. I don't want it to be just us. I want another young one around." This couple parted in the early 1970s.[50]

Women felt the empty nest particularly poignantly since they had made raising children a focus of their lives. When her youngest reached high school age and her oldest child got married, May Perkins realized, "I better get out here and get going. And I did. I got real involved in my own life." Mary Smith described the empty nest as the only real crisis she'd faced in her life. She recalled, "I had a big adjustment when they left. I really sweated. It was a good thing I was working. I knew they were leaving, and I read all the crap. . . . I talked to other people whose kids left. But that doesn't change it. When your house is empty, it's empty." On the other hand, when Olivia Adams had a few more years before her last child moved out, she predicted, "It'll be kind of a feeling of relief." Similarly, having raised a small army of children and worked part-time while they were in school, Irene Lawrence said, "Oh boy, I'm really going to be on my own. Then I'll have no one to bug me. I'll do what we want to do." When her youngest reached high school, Lawrence figured she had earned her retirement. She joined a country club and began playing sports four days a week. She said, "I've done my job, this is my time now." The empty nest significantly changed family life for women reorienting their focus toward their husbands, or often their own pursuits.[51]

Men also looked forward to the end of full-time parenthood. When the youngest of the many McKee children left home, Malcom felt a sense of accomplishment as well as relief. He said, "It was now the two of us and we can do what we want and do things together." Scott Clinton shared his ambivalence in 1970 when the youngest of the Clinton children was college age, "Frankly I was sort of sorry to see them go . . . but basically I was glad to see them go. Because, let's face it. My wife and I were with [them] for [many] years and we gave a lot of our life and . . . we're together now. I mean we have our own life to lead, and basically our life is better with them gone than with them there." The empty nest signaled a new post-childrearing lifestyle.[52]

For some, then, the empty nest was an eagerly embraced release from the day-to-day obligations and tensions of parenthood. Sociological research in the early 1970s confirmed that "renewing marital satisfaction" was a frequent empty nest experience. It provided a new opportunity in marriage. In 1969, Nina Harris, dealing with children in the deep throes of adolescence, confessed, "At this point we're just about ready to get rid of them." Frank Ryder said that he and his wife Katie were more and more in agreement. There seemed to be "a coming together better and better all the time. And I think it's because we don't have the influence of the kids. . . . When you're raising kids you do have to consider them." Katie Ryder agreed with this assessment. She said, "I had always thought that when they got older and moved or weren't living home all the time, it would be difficult. But instead, it's been keen, which is a terrible thing to say. But it's kind of nice being alone again."[53]

For men, retirement meant a chance to focus on and spend time with their families. Since their children were often out on their own, they had high hopes for improving their marriages. Hank Jones welcomed retirement and the empty nest. This lull in their lives, which had been spent working and rearing children, meant the Joneses had time for "togetherness," finally. In response to the interviewer's query he rated this the best period of his marriage. With more time together, he and his wife had more in common, he explained. This arrangement probably pleased Didi, who in 1970 had worried that Hank's upcoming retirement might cause their marriage to go "downhill." John Thompkins was glad to be done with the "toughest part of life—work." Retired, he rediscovered his children, and spent time with grandchildren in addition to "getting a little closer" to his wife. Men greeted retirement with hopes for more family and marital fulfillment.[54]

Nevertheless, retirement required readjusting habits of thirty years or more. Hal Powell had not yet retired in 1982, but he was already anticipating the changes it might bring to his marriage. Over the years, while he worked, Dina had adjusted to doing things on her own. They had organized separate leisure activities. After he cut down on work, he hoped, "Then we're probably going to have to hammer out a little different detente there and hopefully make it better." Yet, while retirement came as a relief to their husbands, many wives expressed worry over this major change in their lives. Dina Powell had already warned him, "I don't want you underfoot all the time." Accustomed to separate activities and lives, spouses wondered how to accommodate one another. May Perkins confessed, "One thing I'm not looking forward to is when Dennis retires. That I can have nightmares over." She was enjoying her independence for eight hours every day while her husband was at work and the children off on their own. A number of women expressed concern for the adjustments they faced when their husbands retired. One 1970s study of wives of soon-to-be retirees found "pessimists" who, feeling quite territorial over their household independence as well as their responsibilities, dreaded their husbands' retirement.[55]

Wives wondered what their formerly work-absorbed husbands would do after retirement, and how this would affect their days. Roberta Johnson said, "I don't know what he'd do if he retired. I'm always busy doing something, but he plays golf and he plays tennis. He can't do that every day of the week." Georgeanne Gaynor echoed this sentiment, "From my point of view it's a real problem. Because . . . within limits, I'm very independent and do exactly as I please. And . . . if Rich were home 24 hours a day, I'm sure that at a certain point we're gonna start getting on each other's nerves." This new stage in the life course required giving up some of the unspoken benefits of "separate spheres." Sociologists and psychologists noted what amounted to a conflict in the "life-course trajectories of males and females" at midlife and retirement when a woman's moved "outward, away from dependency on her husband, away from providing nurturance and support to him, so that the source of his recognition, affection and sense of value becomes precarious and threatens to disappear."[56]

On the other hand, many wives did look forward to the opportunity to spend more time with their husbands and pursue long-awaited goals, such as joint travel. For Kay Patterson, her husband's retirement simply meant "more time we can play." She said she "bristled" when her friends suggested she might be getting sick of having her husband around all the time. The stage of the life course governed by childrearing was over; perhaps now couples would realize their aspirations for marital companionship.[57]

With the advent of the empty nest, Joe Maxwell anticipated his wife's restoring him to a central place in the marriage. "I suppose I'd like to have her spend more time with me—put me number one on the list. That's a selfish thing, I suppose, that she should place the children in a more subordinate position, that we would be closer together." Interestingly, his wife hoped he might make some close male friends so that she wouldn't feel guilty for spending time with her women friends. Used to having his wife there for him when he was home, another man was miffed when his wife did not change her schedule to match his. Gordon James was "putting in a lot less time in the office" than he had most of his working life. He was home more, but his wife was "getting out more and doing more things. I've been jealous. Not of her doing something with another man. . . . I mean I'm jealous that she's not there when I call. I'm not used to this after 35 years." Ready to refocus their lives on the family, these men realized some of the costs of "separate spheres" in marriage, issues their wives had dealt with throughout marriage.[58]

In contrast to their husbands, housewives never really retired. They continued to carry out their lifelong homemaking tasks while their husbands puttered in workshops or putted on the golf course. Milly Benson realized, "The beds still have to be made, the vacuuming has to be done, the dishes, the cooking." She resented her husband's new free time.[59]

By returning men to the home, however, retirement might also bring about another sort of togetherness, in addition to companionship—help with those dishes and household tasks. Among eleven couples, many in which wives worked after their husbands retired, men increased their household responsibilities. This resulted in the greatest degree of role symmetry a couple had experienced. Meg Fisher pronounced her husband's retirement "perfect . . . [because] he does all the cooking . . . the house work. . . . We just switched roles." Studies showed men increasing their interest and attention to the home after retirement although in gendered ways. They tended to focus on the male role in the home—outdoor and repair work. But retired men did help out with tasks gendered female on an occasional basis. Studies showed that wives tended to focus on the benefits of increased couple time during retirement, while men focused positively on increased household responsibilities.

The empty nest did fulfill hopes of togetherness for the McKees. Having survived the stage where "she goes this way, I'll go that way," Malcom described them as "very close today. . . . There is no question in [my mind] I won't even go any place anymore without saying 'why don't you come with me.'"[60]

One couple's experience serves to highlight the importance Americans placed on companionship in marriage, while also highlighting the other bonds that kept marriages together, even those not characterized by togetherness. The wife wanted companionship. She felt this was lacking in her marriage. Her solution was, "If your husband doesn't give you all that you're searching for, where do you find it? With somebody else." The early years of the marriage had been rife with conflict. The couple grew apart. Then she found someone who was companionable. She was very clear about what needs the other man met. "[He's] a fine man as far as making love is concerned," she explained. "So it wasn't that I went away for. Somebody to talk to, and somebody to listen, and somebody to know how I feel." Finding companionship elsewhere enabled her to remain married. In fact neither she nor her lover would divorce their respective spouses. The idea of togetherness still brought this couple together for family gatherings, even if the marriage itself lacked companionship. If she did not share feelings or interests with her husband, they shared children and a history together.[61]

So togetherness was no guarantor of marital happiness. The ethos had an even darker side. A focus on family to the exclusion of all else isolated couples, leaving spouses few outside resources when conflict erupted, as it did consistently throughout the twenty-odd years of one very troubled marriage. The wife described the first few weeks of their marriage as a "good time," until "our problems really began." Her husband abused their children, a problem she sought to solve wholly on her own—she said that she "raised Cain." And as the beatings worsened, she threw herself between her husband and the children taking the brunt of the violence herself. She reported to the IHD, "when [he] gets mad at them I can sidetrack it to me and I can take it much easier than the kids can."[62]

Through the two decades of her marriage, she limited her activities to the nuclear family, largely because he insisted she do so. She confessed, "I would like to be more social than I am except my husband doesn't allow me." She also focused on her family so much because she viewed her own mother as overly socially active outside the home. So she participated only rarely in the PTA, "leery" of overcommitment since as a child she felt neglected. Gradually, she revealed to the IHD that she stayed home for another reason. She said, "I never leave the children alone with him," fearing what bruises she might find upon her return.[63]

This woman feared her husband and his rages but addressed his brutality and violence only within the confines of the togetherness marriage. "We're really not as happy as we should be," she stated. She also saw companionship with his children as having an ameliorative impact on her husband. While she acknowledged that it was "very hard for the children to live with him," still she couldn't "bring herself to leave [him]." Instead, she focused on his "good intentions," following the now well-known patterns of a battered spouse. "When he's not torn apart, he tries to be kind," she explained. "He does things that are very nice for the kids. More and more he is getting so he can play with them. He is improving." Togetherness left her stranded trying to make a "happy" home and raise children in between the rages and beatings that she could neither prevent nor stop. Those around this battered wife preserved the fiction of togetherness, bolstering the entity of the nuclear family. Later, after the marriage ended, she recalled sending her child off to school with blackened eyes, thinking, "God, I hope the teacher notices and does something about it. Because I'm so frightened of him that I don't have the willpower to do anything about it." When her children fled the house to summon help, they were disappointed. She remembered, "I can't say I blame the neighbors. They wouldn't come. They didn't want to get involved." Much to her distress, she had no friends to call on for emotional support, since her husband objected to those outside contacts as well.[64]

Violent conflict in the family is a vivid expression of the underlying structural inequalities within it. Male authority backed up by force and abetted by female economic dependence preserved a violent status quo. Before we too quickly mourn the "loss" of family commitment and willingness to sacrifice personal goals for the good of the family in contemporary settings, it is worth remembering the family members who suffered in isolation under the auspices of togetherness.

The overwhelming cultural emphasis on "togetherness" existed in the context of suburbanization, male careerism, and the changing role of women inside and outside the family. Like historian Elaine Tyler May's description of "domestic containment," togetherness beckoned both men and women back to the home. It served as counterweight to pressures on men and women that threatened to disrupt not only individual marriages but American families as a whole. Ideally, "togetherness" brought men and women's experiences closer together; in practice, men's continuing option to share home labor cast the disparities in starker relief. Achieving togetherness added to pressures on both sexes, but in particular on women to orchestrate it. For experts and ordinary couples the concept provided a means of ameliorating the problems of the traditional gender division of labor, but without questioning its primacy. With a new culturally and maritally important duty to perform, perhaps the other roles women were taking on—wage earning, for example—would remain subordinate. As postwar couples discovered, it was an inadequate prescription.[65]

Young spouses in the 1950s attempted to live the new ethos of "togetherness." Magazine articles and advertisements overflowed with images of and exhortations for family fun. Exploring the reality across the family cycle complicates the sunny image that togetherness summons to mind. In the early years of the baby boom, it was much more than a cultural ideal; it derived from necessity. Several small children required that most recreation centered around the home. But often, togetherness meant couples devoted time to the family as a whole and not to each other.

In addition, men only participated in the child-centered home for a portion of the week, despite women's concerted efforts to involve them more. In the 1950s and early 1960s, togetherness, if couples achieved it at all, remained a weekend activity. During the week, husbands and wives led discrete lives in distinct environments. Not only did the disjunction between cultural expectations for togetherness and the reality of suburban life discourage couples, but the strains of this version of the division of family labor troubled many of them.

Companionship, contrary to the prescriptions for togetherness, continued to mean time spent as a couple, without the children; this baby boom parents found difficult to achieve in the 1950s, 1960s, and 1970s. The differing demands of mothering and fathering, and the manner in which the parents of the baby boom divided their roles, made companionship almost nonexistent in the childrearing years. Couples shared joint long-term goals but not daily experiences. Husbands communicated little of their work worries with their wives, who in turn kept mum about the frustrations of homemaking, childrearing, or working. Further complicating these aspirations, they nurtured differing conceptions of companionship. Shared activity satisfied most men, while their wives sighed for deeper emotional intimacy and communication.

Not until the late 1970s and early 1980s could parents of the baby boom again focus energy and attention on their marriages. For couples who had centered their lives around their children, the empty nest pointed out a void in their own relationship that led them to greet this new stage in the family cycle with anxiety. But others welcomed the post-childrearing stage of marriage as a new lease on the relationship, or in the words of one study member, a chance for a "second honeymoon." They felt "released," "relieved," and "liberated," after devoting two decades to their offspring. This was their turn to experience togetherness—as a couple they hoped, without the family.

Rita Frank's hopes for her children's marriages betray the lack she felt in her own. She wished for them, "to have the closeness I'm trying to find, a real friendship where you could confide a lot of your innermost thoughts, and you wouldn't have to go to another friend to do that. You would have your own spouse to do that with." But her children's generation inherited many of the same pressures as well as ideals, with the added complication of women's growing work commitment.[66]

Surveying middle-class marriage over the twentieth century, the 1950s stands out again as an anomaly—refocusing the ideological emphasis in marriage to the family as a whole after four decades of increasing focus on the couple. Fifties "togetherness" attempted to weave both goals, the romantic couple and the child-centered home, within the web of fulfilling family life. It was the dual focus of the baby boom era marriages that created most of their satisfactions and dissatisfactions. After thirty years of marriage, couples still struggled to achieve their versions of togetherness. Given couples' experiences with companionship, it should not be surprising that when it came to sexuality, the intimacy and satisfaction they yearned for could prove elusive as well.

"I'm beginning to think everybody in the whole world is preoccupied with sex except Henry and me."

Top, The public discussion of sexuality convinced Americans that everyone else was having more plentiful and better sex.

Middle, Through best-selling books and magazine articles, middle-aged Americans kept abreast of the latest marital and sexual advice.

Bottom, Parents confronted the sexual revolution when the baby boomers brought it home.

"Bertha, will you do me a favor and stop reading those damn 'How to Save Your Marriage' articles?"

"Your friend is more than welcome, dear, but we just want you to know that your father and I didn't do anything funny till after we were married."

You Can't Really Believe the Magazines

Prescription and Reality in the Middle-Class Bedroom

In a drawing from the 1970s by *New Yorker* cartoonist Saxon, two staid middle-aged couples chat during a theater intermission. While her husband averts his eyes, one woman addresses the group: "I'm beginning to think everybody in the whole world is preoccupied with sex except Henry and me." This cartoon conveys the popular view of middle-class, middle-aged, married couples as the United States reverberated with the seemingly cataclysmic transformations of the sexual revolution. At first glance the suburban bedroom appears far from the hot spots of the sexual revolution.

And in many ways it was. The generation gap, to some extent, was sensual as well as social. Bachelor pads, fern bars, and college campuses were the sites of heterosexual erotic rebellion. In them, the baby boomers championed free love, challenged morality, and questioned sexual differences to their parents' supposed dismay.[1]

Nonetheless, as cartoonist Stevenson depicts in another sketch, wherein a workaday, middle-aged husband greets his modishly dressed middle-aged wife with a gruff "Bertha, will you do me a favor and stop reading those damn 'How to Save Your Marriage' articles," changing ideas about sex and relationships penetrated middle-class marriage through the popular media. Whether they embraced or evaded the shifting sexual ethos of the 1960s and 1970s, to ignore the older generation's response to the sexual revolution is to miss an important part of the story. What was the impact of the sexual revolution among those "over thirty"? The parents of the baby boom imbibed key tenets of the sexual revolution and their responses to it reveal a great deal, not only about the uneven progress of the sexual revolution but also about middle-class marriage in the postwar years.[2]

A brief survey of the historical transformation of twentieth-century sexuality and gender relations places the developments of the 1960s and 1970s in context. Between 1890 and 1930, American sexual mores shifted. Urbanization, the blossoming of a consumer economy, and changes in women's lives produced new social relations, and unease about them. At the turn of the century working-class young people abandoned the homosocial recreational patterns of their parents—the saloon for men, tenement stoops for women—and, at dance halls, movie theaters, and amusement parks they shaped a new heterosocial environment. Here, the sexual economy of treating evolved, whereby young men, privileged economically by their gender, "treated" young women to meals, drinks, and shows and expected in return female companionship, romance, and sexual favors.[3]

By the 1920s, treating emerged as dating, and middle-class courtship followed working-class courtship out of the home and into the marketplace, moving, in historian Beth Bailey's words, "from front porch to back seat." In high schools and colleges peers, not parents, supervised dating and the boundaries of permissible sexual behavior expanded for middle-class young people. Youths engaged in petting and the betrothed might engage in premarital intercourse all in line with the evolving middle-class moral code.[4]

In the 1920s expectations for American marriage and the good life included the ability to participate fully in consumer culture, which meant, according to the new institutions of mass culture, everything from new appliances—that promised, if they did not provide, more free time to women—to clothing and make-up that supplied sexual allure and new forms of commercial entertainment that offered amusement and relaxation. Just as in dating, leisure and recreation remained primary components of male-female relationships once across the threshold as well. In tune with the Jazz Age, experts advocated companionate marriage built around consumption, companionship, and sex.[5]

Companionate, sexualized marriage, in particular, eased anxieties over women's role in the 1920s. The vote, employment before and after marriage, and the potential for independence these implied: the horizon open to women at the dawn of the Jazz Age seemed newly limitless. Companionate marriage, by accommodating women's increased autonomy, might also control it. The same went for the new public quality of women's sexuality embodied by the flapper: within marriage the sexualized woman was appropriate; outside the bounds of matrimony, she remained a threat. Even former sex radical and birth control advocate Margaret Sanger couched her contraceptive lessons safely between the conservative covers of her advice manual, *Happiness in Marriage*, where she insisted on the "complete fulfillment of love through the expression of sex" in marriage.[6]

Talk of an American sexual revolution dates back to this period when in addition to the increasing premarital exploration of American youth, marriage advisors mandated sexual pleasure for both husbands and wives as the key to successful marriage. These ideas stemmed from the work of sexologist Havelock Ellis and drew support from Sigmund Freud's emphasis on sexual impulses in the makeup of the human psyche. Through the first half of the twentieth century, marriage experts and writers of advice manuals like Sanger emphasized the role of sexuality in love and marriage. Victorian Americans had divorced the notions of sexuality and love. But beginning in the early 1900s, Americans began to "sexualize love," weighting it with the emotional power to secure happy marriages and express loving feelings. With good sex deemed essential to good marriages, the experts advocated increased accessibility to birth control in the guise of family planning. The emphasis now was on marital sexuality, not sexual freedom. Over the next four decades the increasing sexualization of American culture, approval of contraceptive measures within marriage, and the freeing of sex from procreative constraints combined to create a collection of values that historians Estelle Freedman and John D'Emilio label "sexual liberalism," fully ascendant by the mid-1960s. In the 1950s, it was legal for doctors in most states to prescribe contraceptives to their married patients, although the remaining barriers would not fall until 1965, when, with the Griswold case, the Supreme Court overturned a Connecticut law that had restricted access. The third development in the ongoing sexual revolution gathered steam among single men and women, detaching sex not only from reproduction, but also from marriage, opening the way for gay liberation.[7]

According to the data contained in biologist-turned-sexologist Alfred Kinsey's ground-breaking studies of male and female sexuality released in 1948 and 1953, respectively, behavior as well as law and ideology had changed in the interwar period. Among American teens, petting was practically universal and fully half of the women surveyed engaged in premarital intercourse; a quarter even indulged in extramarital relations. Kinsey found evidence of increasing contraceptive use. Of women in the Kinsey study who were born at the end of the last century, slightly less than a third relied on the diaphragm. Nearly two-thirds of those born in the 1910s, however, had used the device. Kinsey's data also showed that increasing with each generation was the possibility that married women reached orgasm during intercourse, particularly those born after 1920. Sexual liberalism had a behavioral component, preparing the way for postwar changes.[8]

Developments associated with the sexual revolution of the 1960s especially the eroticization of love and liberalization of legal codes represented the acceleration of prewar social trends. As the Kinsey reports demonstrated, higher rates of premarital sex predated the sexual revolution. Having already eroticized love and construed it as a site of pleasure and fulfillment and the centerpiece of marriage, in the 1960s, Americans divorced the goals of pleasure and fulfillment through sex from both marriage and love. These became fitting ends in and of themselves without the trappings of legality or even the sanction of romance. Finally, one new significant postwar development identified with the sexual revolution was the relative decline of the sexual double standard. Women, in increasing numbers, now adopted the behaviors formerly permitted to and practiced by men.

As feminist author Barbara Ehrenreich has argued, young women's sexual behavior was perhaps the most revolutionary development of the 1960s. Single women, even as they struggled with a lingering sexual double standard, claimed sexual autonomy, a right young men had taken for granted for decades. Indeed, for men, the sexual revolution did little more, at first, than increase the availability of female partners of the same social status. Until feminism. The young radical feminists who emerged in the late 1960s highlighted the differences between men's and women's experiences of sexual "revolution," questioning the possibility of sexual liberation without women's liberation. For these women, the quality of sexual encounters was as much at issue as the quantity, although that might increase as well. Male sexual liberation, they insisted, furthered female sexual exploitation. Yet these outspoken feminists, in their critique of sexism, missed the extent to which ordinary women had shaped the sexual revolution they attacked. Not only did young women begin to shake off the stigma of premarital sex, but, with the help of the popularization of 1960s sex research, the spread of consciousness-raising, and radical feminist theory, they challenged the very nature of heterosexual sex. They insisted on female pleasure; expanding the standard sexual repertoire for American couples, they radicalized the sexual revolution. But what about the men and women who came of age prior to the liberated sixties and seventies: did the ideas of the sexual revolution alter the gender dynamics as well as the sexual relationships of married midlife couples?[9]

Middle-class married Americans did embrace postwar ideals of sexual pleasure, but many were unable or unwilling to put accompanying prescriptions for emotional intimacy into practice. Psychologists designated honest discussion of sexual complaints and desires as the pathway to mutual satisfaction and happy marriage. Communication about sexuality, perhaps the least shocking item on the "sexpert" agenda, proved the most difficult to accomplish. Instead, suburban couples absorbed the heightening standards of sexual satisfaction that accompanied the sexual revolution, standards they often felt neither they nor their partners met. This gap raises questions about both the historical timing and extent of the sexual revolution. Even willingness to communicate about sexuality with IHD staff was not a given. In many cases interviewers received cursory one word replies to their questions. Answers such as, "Satisfactory, I think," reveal information, but little about internal thoughts. As historian Beth Bailey aptly reminds us, there were plural sexual revolutions, not one single transformation.[10]

In the postwar years, the most glaring evidence of sexual revolution, the increasing public display and discussion of sex, accelerated a twentieth-century trend. And it is with the public quality of the sexual revolution that its deepest contradictions lie. As we shall see in the following pages, the chasm between public prescription and private practices, at least for the affluent couples of the postwar middle class, remained deep and wide.[11]

Sexual prescription focused on marriage in the early postwar years. The conventional goal of improving marriage encouraged innovation, particularly when it came to the public and private discussion of sexuality. In the

1950s, marriage experts deemed sexual education essential to successful marriages because, they assumed, it eradicated confusion and ignorance. According to experts and marriage advisors, ignorance bedeviled American marriages, trapping couples in unhappy relationships. Even the iconoclastic Kinsey prophesied that the dissemination of scientific research would shore up the stability of American marriages by diminishing sexual dissatisfaction. The ways in which Kinsey couched his arguments about the place of sexuality in American culture hold as much interest for historians of sexuality and marriage as his findings regarding Americans' sexual behavior. Kinsey deplored the "remoteness" of Americans' sexual mores from the "actual behavior of the average citizen." He peeked into American boudoirs and back seats and revealed the stark contrast between professed standards and actual sexual behavior, exposing the hypocrisy of America's moral code. Yet Kinsey, the public spokesperson, fit his survey findings squarely within the twentieth-century faith in scientific knowledge and education as solutions to human problems. Objective research would lead to the acceptance of such "universal" behavior as petting and to the rejection of moral condemnation, he hoped. Thus freed, married couples would experience healthy sexual adjustment without any guilt or inhibitions. And publicly, Kinsey, as he sought to promote his data, championed pleasurable *marital* sexuality, even as he showed that Americans indulged in a variety of erotic practices both in and outside the institution. Americans' prudish mores resulted in sexual inhibition in young people—a prescription for sexual disappointment in marriage, Kinsey declared. Awareness of objective behavioral or physical facts would stabilize American marriages and eliminate infidelity, he wrote. Kinsey's justification for his findings landed squarely within the domain of sexual liberalism, supporting the eroticization of the married couple in the context of the Cold War and the baby boom.[12]

Pursuing similar ends, Paul Landis, the author of the college textbook *Making the Most of Marriage*, defended the "sensible" discussion of sexuality in college marriage courses, offering the reassurance that education conferred healthy attitudes, thereby preserving marriages: "It is unlikely that anyone who was happy and contented with his or her sex life would be interested in experimenting outside of marriage." In addition, he urged young couples hoping for happy sex lives to avail themselves of the latest contraceptive information: "The ability to control conception is at the very heart of the companionship marriage and is a prerequisite to the maximum happiness of the romantic marriage." Marriage educators encouraged both the use of contraceptives and high expectations for sexual satisfaction in marriage. Constant excitement apparently awaited the educated, and therefore sexually "well-adjusted," couple. Landis's textbook and Kinsey's research embodied the contradiction that ran through the prescriptive advice of the sexual revolution. They posed scientific information as the pathway to sexual satisfaction.[13]

But how were readers to determine their sexual adjustment? The answers marital advisors dispensed were shaped by the cultural construction of gender in the 1950s. To what degree men and women differed sexually became a key question. Kinsey began the decade by attempting to overturn cultural conceptions of gender difference. *Ladies' Home Journal* popularized this finding in its preview of *Sexual Behavior and the American Female*, emphasizing that there was "no basic difference" in the "pattern of sexual response of male and female"; conditioning, not biology, caused misunderstandings between men and women. This message of similarity, however, remained muted, drowned out by experts who—in an attempt to overcome the potential for conflict they assumed resulted from deep differences in both arousal and climax—classified women's sexual responses as more emotional than physical and slower to develop than men's. Landis's *Making the Most of Marriage*, for example, failed to pick up Kinsey's iconoclastic message, continuing to insist that "Sex feeling is much more diffused throughout the body of the female and more closely related to affection and general emotional satisfaction."[14]

Popular conceptions of gender difference permeated the advice of experts even as they claimed the position of objective observers. Thus while they professed a disinterested stance, sexperts injected their advice with the view that women were inherently less sexual than men. Clifford Adams, who wrote the "Making Marriage Work" column for *Ladies' Home Journal* in the 1950s, defined the "sexually responsive wife." Sexual responsiveness, according to Adams, included such attributes as "strength of sex desire, ease of arousal and ability to reach climax," a gender neutral description. Yet he warned against placing too much emphasis on a woman's physical response: "Even some well-adjusted wives sometimes fail to experience climax and they do not renounce sex or their husbands." For women, "adjustment" connoted adaptation, not necessarily satisfaction. He counseled that the female orgasm was an entirely "different phenomenon" from that of the male. He then discounted not just orgasms but even the importance of female arousal in the creation of a good sexual relationship. "As long as she can respond to her husband's advances without feeling frustrated, and if neither is upset by absence of climax, sexual activity can be rewarding and gratifying for her in the same way as a loving embrace." Marriage advisor and physician Abraham Stone also spoke to this issue. Acknowledging that the "husband ideally should employ in advance various forms of sex arousal" that would enable the wife to enjoy a "full response," he reminded couples that a woman may have "sufficient satisfaction from being desired, and sufficient pleasure from the act itself." This then was the extent of "sexual sharing" without which, Stone warned, marriages would be "always vulnerable to frustrations from within and to attack from without." Adams did not place climax last on his list of sexual response attributes for nothing. The sexually well-adjusted woman who populated the pages of women's magazines and marriage manuals found satisfaction in meeting her husband's needs. Female accommodation, not autonomy, defined adjustment for fifties experts. It would take the work of another set of pioneering researchers combined with feminism to upset the accommodationist consensus.[15]

Influenced by the double standard, experts assumed that sexually wives lagged behind husbands: not only did a woman enter marriage less informed, she developed sexually much more slowly than her mate and was by far the less adventurous member of the couple. Citing the Kinsey report as proof of the wide variety of sexual acts in which Americans indulged, Adams, a psychologist at Pennsylvania State University, admonished married women that "neither is a wife justified in assuming that her husband's behavior and preferences are unnatural simply because they are different from ideas of conduct she holds." She should be willing to learn from and with him—barring actual spousal compulsion, he added. If she still hesitated, he counseled a visit to a doctor. Advisors appointed husbands to be the sexually advanced, informed initiators of the marriage bed and classified resistant wives as potential patients.[16]

Marital experts suggested individual adjustments to sexual disappointments; and, as elsewhere in marriage, adjustment was a particularly feminine task. With marital stability still the ultimate goal, experts recommended the least disruptive solutions. Adams toted up the psychological features of the "sexually responsive woman" and then admonished the unsatisfied reader that "changes within herself are much more likely to bring about improvement than blaming her husband." These adjustments meant accepting the supposedly inherent limitations of women's sexuality.[17]

Women's magazines popularized the emphasis on sexual education as a panacea for American marriage, and, like the experts whose message they carried, they emphasized that women were the remedial pupils. Flipping through the May 1956 issue of *Ladies' Home Journal*, a young bride might spot the article "What Wives Don't Know about Sex," by Abraham Stone.

There, she read, "Knowledge of the processes of sex makes for a better physical adjustment in marriage. It makes a couple more aware of each other's needs and desires." Such knowledge was no longer the exclusive purview of men. Stone and other sex experts of the 1950s expanded the requirements of the good wife in the name of sexual awareness: "'a woman of valor' . . . wants to be a good companion, a good homemaker, a good mother. She should also educate herself, and this applies to her husband as well, to be a good sexual partner." For women, sex education meant catching up to their husbands in terms of attitudes, but not in terms of experience.[18]

That the *Journal*'s readers reacted to this advice with anger suggests that expert advice did not meet the challenge of addressing everyday experience. Stone's column on wives prompted a "flood" of letters to the *Journal* from women demanding an article on "What Husbands Don't Know about Sex." Apparently American women were not so passive as he had assumed, and they believed ignorance befell both sexes. In his response, Stone admitted that men, too, might suffer from repression or inhibitions and could also fall victim to "sexual illiteracy." But most important, according to Stone, men too little appreciated the "marked differences in the emotional attitude toward sex between men and women." He used this opportunity to emphasize once again the differing rates of arousal between men and women, reminding men not to be "perfunctory."

Even as he acknowledged that men might have something to learn and encouraged conscientious attention to female arousal, Stone recommended a solution that incorporated long-held notions about women's role as emotional facilitators, now expanding this responsibility to the sexual domain: it was women's responsibility to erode the edifice of male ignorance. The "best source" of such information, he argued, was the open and communicative wife. He encouraged women to subtly indicate their sexual interest to their husbands. Communication was a theme that wove through Adams's columns as well. Advisors linked verbal and physical intimacy: "Resolving a sexual problem in marriage, like any other, depends on the full and free communication between husband and wife. Indeed, the physical relationship is a profound and fundamental form of communication." Calls for greater communication would become a primary theme of the burgeoning sexual advice industry in the ensuing decades.[19]

Advisors waxed poetic over the bonding qualities of well-adjusted sexual relations. "Sex union," wrote Stone, "is outer expression of inner grace." It was a "spiritual" center of marriage where couples found "oneness." In the column "Tell Me, Doctor," physician Henry B. Safford reminded a couple who came to him for sex counsel, "A satisfying sexual relationship is an absolute necessity in any happy marriage." In contrast, writer Dorothy Thompson attempted to puncture what she saw as the ballooning romanticization of sex in marriage. "Even when this attraction is exceptionally mutual and keen, it does not . . . rule out other affinities and disaffinities. . . . No one is sexually enraptured twenty-four hours a day, and few if any, married couples are always sexually susceptible at the same time." But Thompson's deemphasis of the sexual side of marriage was the minority opinion; over the course of the 1950s the focus on sexuality continued to grow, as did the contradictions inherent in the advice.[20]

Sexual advice for married couples in the 1950s retained prewar patterns. This despite the incorporation, in a few postwar manuals at least, of Kinsey's findings. Uniting Kinsey and marital advisors was a faith in the power of education to eradicate sexual ignorance and the belief that education and sexual adjustment would spread in tandem. Nevertheless, while Kinsey's data might have been cited to allay fears of abnormality, his key points remained buried beneath the weight of statistics. His insistence on similarity between men and women was lost; instead, experts continued to emphasize differences between the sexes and to urge women to accept these differences. Finally, advisors did begin to suggest that women should be actors at least in shaping the quality of a sexual relationship, if not particularly during the act itself. But women, the experts advised, acted by learning, accommodating, and increasingly, communicating with their spouses—so long as they did not say too much. Men's responsibility continued to be gentlemanly attention to their wives' pleasure during at least the preliminaries of the sexual act.

Advice of this type created a conundrum for female readers. From the experts' perspective, sexual relationships were the glue of married life, but women must not expect more excitement than a tender embrace. Advisors instructed them to avoid resentment when they failed to reach climax and yet adjust themselves to being responsive, uninhibited, and communicative about sex with their husbands or risk harming the very foundation of their marriage. The fifties message was to adjust without rocking the marriage boat, a message in keeping with the values of middle-class men and women in the postwar era. Ironically, at the same time that the experts glorified satisfying sex's salutary effect on marriage, they also counseled women, to whom they imparted greater sexual responsibility, to sublimate their concerns about orgasm in favor of adapting to the erotic status quo of their marriages—a contradiction that could prove a recipe for disaster.[21]

With the stakes high for men and women when it came to marriage in the 1950s, and as sex played a more and more central role in experts' definitions of marriage, the ante was upped for the postwar husband and wife. According to experts, it was up to individuals to make up for parental ignorance, schoolyard misinformation, and personal inhibitions. They had simply to read the appropriate, up-to-date books that told them how to foster sexual adjustment and satisfying sexual relations would be theirs. In reality, of course, neither sexual education nor sexual adjustment was that simple. In addition to locating helpful information, couples faced the challenge of incorporating it into practice as they battled the obstacles of embarrassment, habit, and upbringing.

Despite prescriptive calls for greater access to information, secrecy and prohibition still denied access to that information to the young women and men who married in the late 1940s and early 1950s. Indeed, even the revolution detailed in Kinsey's massive studies of male and female sexuality had scattershot impact, passing many of these couples by. Many entered marriage without experience or education, unaware of both sexual and contraceptive techniques. "The adjustment we all feared and never talked about," wrote the syndicated columnist Erma Bombeck of her generation, "was sex." In haling the changes in sexual behavior indicated in the Kinsey reports, historians have tended to neglect the evidence of continuity, and have tended to ignore the difficulties of changing behavior, leaving a central experience of the sexual revolution unexplored.[22]

Couples who entered marriage as virgins complained about youthful inexperience and the ensuing awkwardness that accompanied it. Twenty-three couples reported problems of "sex adjustment" related to inexperience, ignorance, or misconceptions. First experiences might fail to meet romantic expectations, or if couples were lucky, far surpass them. Doris Jenkins commented that she "wondered what I saved everything for." She found sex a "painful procedure" and was "disappointed," sure only that the "rosy picture I had conjured up . . . wasn't right." But Joan Sinclair said, "All I can say is it was well worth waiting for." Sex adjustment, Judy Kent testified, in response to an IHD query, "was really quite difficult. I think our sex life was very slow getting going." Husbands, many inexperienced themselves, initiated their young brides. From her husband Clay she "learned more about sex than I've learned anywhere else." Another woman referred to her husband as a sexual tutor as well.[23]

Men internalized this responsibility. For several years after the wedding, Gary Simon "felt inadequate with Dorothy, I didn't know . . . how to be considerate about sex or anything else." Their sexual ignorance left men disappointed in themselves. Jack Stevens also felt bad over the way he had approached sex early in his marriage to Molly. He remembered, "I was pretty immature . . . not sensitive enough, or too sensitive to my own animal needs and not enough to her needs. It has scarred our relationship over a period of years."[24]

Couples, just as they sought childrearing advice from professionals, turned to expert advice in response to their sexual troubles. Janice Rogers pronounced a premarital visit with a marriage counselor a "godsend," saying, "It made a tremendous difference in our sex adjustment." Others found help in the pages of marriage manuals. The Lawrences "consulted a lover's handbook," when they became anxious about their sexual relationship. "I don't know if it's really any more exhilarating," Dean reported. The heights of passion touted in the advice books still seemed out of reach. But, he added, "I think I can consistently make my wife happier more." Kay Patterson received a "little blue book on marriage and sexual relations" from a friend and found it such an eye-opening read that she and her husband kept a similar book on hand to lend "to couples shortly after [they are] married." Patterson enthusiastically embraced sexual education, stating, "It's never too late to learn." Couples recognized an obligation to educate themselves and shared their new-found knowledge with their partners and friends.[25]

As they embraced expert advice and attempted to implement it, couples internalized idealized standards by which to measure their own sexual experiences. In Dennis Perkins's opinion he and his wife had "more problems than normal as far as our own sexual relations went." For the Simons, "It was two full years after our marriage before our sex adjustment became healthy." Newlyweds aspired to "healthy," "normal," and "satisfying" sexual adjustment, a set of goals increasingly defined by arbiters outside the marriage in question. New information circulated through the pages of marriage manuals, or among friends and spouses and disseminated knowledge, as well as norms and expectations of what sex should be. Implementing advice in ways that met high expectations proved to be the primary challenge of the sexual revolution.[26]

Many couples marveled at the changes in the sexual discourse that they witnessed in the 1950s. But while some, like the Pattersons welcomed access to information, others were less sure. Taken aback to be asked by the institute about such intimate details of private life, Didi Jones responded, "It embarrasses me to talk about it. I often wonder about Kinsey, how he gets people to say what they do." Not only were the behavioral disclosures of the Kinsey study a shock, so was the degree of exposure his studies attracted. Marie Weber chided, "Irrespective of how important the Kinsey report may be for scientific reasons, when it gets picked up and carried around by the newspapers, the important aspect gets lost." Some, apparently, resented the increased public discussion of previously private matters that preceded the sexual change of the postwar years.[27]

Even those who had premarital consultations with physicians or read books, manuals, and magazines found themselves confused by expectations, technique, or anatomy. That the new expert line placed responsibility for success squarely with the couple caused discomfort; sexual failure or disappointment now demanded rationalization. One man found an explanation in both puritanical upbringing and the togetherness of baby boom family life. Clay Kent explained that when he and his wife were growing up, sex was "really taboo" in both their families. Therefore, "sex," he said, "plays a relatively unimportant role in our lives. . . . I think sex in a physical sense is much more important in many families, more so than in our own. We have so many other ties." The Kents attempted to subordinate sexual expectations to togetherness and childrearing but did so unsuccessfully.[28]

Echoing those who insisted that it was the wife's role to adapt, couples who brought their grievances about sexual compatibility to the attention of the IHD also presumed the primacy of male desire. Clay complained, "I could go, go every night. She would rather go about once a year. I get upset every six months and raise a scene." Claire Manning assumed that she had "more sex drive," than her husband but felt that she had "learned to adapt" to his "needs without strain." She attributed their differences in desire to her wish for more children (which contradicted his) and accepted experts' insistence that to women fell the task of accepting their husband's sexual status quo. Nan Meeker described sex as a "huge problem." The problem was "I don't know if he wants more or less, and it's all a terrible mix-up."[29]

And, despite the much-vaunted emphasis on pleasure, the procreative and recreative or pleasurable aspects of sex confused some couples. Only after the Thorntons began hoping for children could Cynthia embrace her sexuality without guilt. She recalled, "Somehow planning to have a child and starting a child removed the guilt of sex for pleasure." Dorothy Simon also recounted feeling guilty over having sex when an additional child was not intended. Shedding prior beliefs in favor of the experts' ethos of satisfaction could be a difficult, gradual, and incomplete process. New information about sex helped some, even several years into a relationship; but in other cases it came too late. This generation found it easier to adopt principles and standards in theory than to put them into practice.[30]

While procreative and eroticized marriage was the pinnacle to which baby boom era couples aspired, recreative sex faced two obstacles to widespread acceptance. For one thing, religious and other traditions frowned on selfish, frivolous sexuality. For another, given the contraceptive methods available in the 1950s, and sometimes their limited acceptance, the problem of unplanned conception loomed over ostensibly recreational sex. Apparently, as with the idea of sex for pleasure, expert sanction of contraceptives did not necessarily translate into universal practice. Contraceptive ignorance characterized the educated, middle-class couples in this study. At her premarital medical examination Judy Kent was "absolutely disillusioned," to find out how babies were born. Of course, in the early years of marriage, most couples aimed for conception. For them, as for Kent, contraceptives were not an issue—they wanted large families with children spaced close together. Their procreative enthusiasm set this generation apart from their parents. Kent's mother had been active in her local family planning organization; her grown children teased her "for years" about the contradiction they created for her: she had nearly twenty grandchildren. For many like Kent and her siblings family planning was at best a theoretical concept, especially in the first years of marriage.[31]

Although she chose not to act on the information, Kent at least learned something from her visit to a doctor. Betsy Downs used her diaphragm incorrectly because shyness prevented her from seeking further instruction. She recalled, "The doctor, he explained, 'Betsy, this is a diaphragm, and this is the way you put it in.' I'd say, 'Yes, doctor. Oh yeah, I understand. That's fine.'" Once home, however, Betsy could not make sense of the contraceptive's workings, and disliked the mess of contraceptive jelly. She went on, "And I found out I was using it upside down and backwards. So it's no wonder I had three." Despite the experts' advice on openness, her reticence began at the doctor's office and continued after each contraceptive failure, helped along by what historian Elaine Tyler May calls the "reproductive consensus" of the baby boom.[32]

For a significant minority of the parents of the baby boom, reproductive consensus seems to have been a more convincing ideology than sexual liberalism. Despite the national figures indicating the proliferation of contraception in the 1950s, and regardless of the stamp of approval their already large families gave couples to employ family planning methods, worry over contraceptive failure or refusal to use them was still a problem even later in marriage. Catholicism governed several couples' attitudes toward birth control. The Mannings, like other Catholic couples in the 1950s, relied on a combination of abstention and withdrawal, which left Claire wondering aloud about the validity of her husband's claim that "withdrawal does reduce satisfaction." In 1958, Dean Lawrence stated that he and his wife "adhered strictly to our faith's teaching as far as contraceptives go." But more than just religious teaching affected Lawrence's thinking. "I can't see how other people put up with them," he told the IHD. The couple began to see concern over conception as "a definite problem" in the mid-1960s when they "thought we had enough children." They hoped that the Pope would approve oral contraceptives, but when he did not, continued to abide by the Church's teachings. Religious scruples, contraceptives' inconvenience, and clumsy interruptions of passion combined to produce the Lawrences' distaste for birth control.[33]

Among Catholics and non-Catholics, in fact, IHD records reveal surprising nonchalance toward family planning and negative attitudes toward the existing methods, given what coterminous statistics say about Americans' increasing use of contraceptives. Eighteen couples told the IHD they had unplanned children—sometimes more than one—and used birth control infrequently or refrained entirely. Eleanor Maxwell recalled that she became pregnant for the first time "very early on" in marriage. She "couldn't handle" the diaphragm and had tried douching "which didn't do the trick." Her ineptitude persisted; later, she attributed the birth of her youngest daughter to "sloppy preventative measures." Crystal Robertson "never really used birth control seriously." The diaphragm "seemed too artificial . . . and it was such a hassle and by the time I'd get out of bed and get the diaphragm in and get back into bed I was out of the mood." So after her first few babies she "just decided to bag it," and relied on the rhythm method and "of course that doesn't work." The Robertsons ultimately had quite a large family. Sandra Thomas called herself and her husband "careless Protestants." She said, "It was not my choice to have a large family. . . . In my opinion I took very good care but it was still not enough." She viewed all her children as unplanned but when asked about contraception related, "I don't trust anything. I just rely on abstinence," a tactic that obviously did not serve her very well at all. Sally Williams professed to be "very much interested in family planning or birth control," yet dubbed her many children her "darling little surprises."[34]

The postwar circumstances of those who made it to the middle-class made these nonchalant attitudes possible. A buffer of economic affluence underwrote such casual approaches to birth control. In addition to affluence and ignorance, a strong belief that marriage and children were

inextricably connected and that, for women, sexuality and motherhood remained strongly linked abetted the arrival of baby boomer "surprises" well
into the 1960s. The contraceptive habits of the IHD couples do not seem
too far removed from those of American couples nationwide. For married
white women under 45 years of age who had borne a child in 1965, 31
percent reported using no contraception and 13 percent relied on either
withdrawal or rhythm. In contrast, pill users constituted 28 percent. A significant percentage of Americans risked conception rather than employ
birth control in the 1950s and 1960s, even as usage increased overall.[35]

Once they achieved desired family size, however, couples did seek to
limit births. They did so in a decade of expanded options for contraceptive
techniques. The pill hit the market in 1960 and non-Catholic clergy
approved the use of devices to prevent conception in 1961. Sterilization
was also an option. Couples navigated their way through these emerging
choices. One couple moved from "Vatican roulette," to the pill, and finally
to vasectomy in 1971.[36]

Walter Small recalled, "The first few years we had the . . . children and
then after that it was rather difficult and we didn't want any more children
and she got pregnant very easily." For the Smalls the pill put an end to
years of worry. Once it "came along, well then it was . . . relaxed and comfortable and so forth." After decades of anxiety over pregnancy, others
turned to sterilization. Claudine Parker had a tubal ligation in the late
1960s, her husband Scott reported. "And I might add," he said, "that's been
quite a source of great satisfaction and lack of worry is a better way to put
it." For one couple the prospect of sterilization confronted them with value
differences. May wanted Dennis Perkins to have a vasectomy and he refused. He said, "I feel that whoever created us created us in a certain way,
and I do not believe in changing any of this. . . . I just don't think it is
proper to have this operation." Dennis's hesitancy was apparently not uncommon. Studies in the 1960s showed that women were more likely than
men to undergo sterilization.[37]

These examples of contraceptive sloppiness point to isolated pockets
within the American middle-class who rejected a major tenet of sexual liberalism: use of birth control. They declined the methods modern technology offered, refused to fuss with the inconveniences or side effects of the
available methods or implemented them lackadaisically. For others, given
the available options, vasectomy and tubal ligation could be attractive simply because they were supremely effective. For baby boom parents who
already had a sizable family, effectiveness might be of paramount concern.
In fact, demographers have found that factors linked with the baby boom

family patterns are heavy predictors for sterilization: for example, long marriages, and a high number of births during the first five years of marriage. But the context of sexual reserve indicated by IHD interviews provides a potentially more persuasive explanation. Once couples made the initial decision, which could indeed be contentious, there was little need for further communication about the subject of contraception, nor a need for further anatomical instructions, or even coital interruptions.[38]

While private conversation about sex remained limited, the public discussion accelerated as the 1950s drew to a close. This trend did not go unquestioned. In 1959 *Newsweek* ran a piece called "Sex in the Magazines," noting that issues that "once were discreetly raised in the privacy of a doctor's office" now had very public coverage in everything from *McCall's* to *Reader's Digest*. Such articles lauded "some mysterious state of sexual glory a la D. H. Lawrence" that prompted heightened performance anxiety in readers, according to *Newsweek*.[39]

While education and marital sexual satisfaction were the watchwords of the fifties public discourse, a move was already afoot to expand the territory of sexual pleasure beyond marriage, spearheaded by publishing impresario Hugh Hefner and his *Playboy* magazine and network of clubs. In the early 1960s, writer turned editor Helen Gurley Brown asserted a similar theme for women. Marriage might or might not be in a young career woman's plans, but sex certainly should be, she argued in *Sex and the Single Girl*. Sex apart from the trappings of marriage became the sine qua non of those who trumpeted revolution. Lawrence Lipton, chronicler of the "erotic revolution" reversed the edicts of the fifties experts. They had called for improvements in marital sex, to save marriage. In Lipton's opinion, it was marriage that endangered sex. He wrote, "The vital question for millions of Americans today is not 'Can this marriage be saved?' but 'Can these people be saved from the ruinous consequences of conventional monogamic marriage?'" The sexual liberation of the 1960s posed an enticing sexual smorgasbord for the young, hip, unwed, or swinging. Still, ordinary Americans remained wary of the utopian promise attributed to sex. In a 1966 poll, over half of the respondents picked the statement "enjoyable and important—but other things are just as important" in answer to the question "How important is sex to a marriage?" In contrast, 16 percent replied that it was "the main thing around which a good marriage is built."[40]

The sexual revolution seemed to threaten marriage from the outside while sexual ignorance and dissatisfaction bore away at it from the inside. But if some preached free love and proclaimed the end of marriage, most

implored Americans not to forsake the marriage bed, but instead to reinvigorate it. Sex researchers William Masters and Virginia Johnson, whose
subjects included both the married and the unmarried set out to reconsti-
tute the sexual side of conventional monogamous marriage. Like their pre-
decessor, Kinsey, they packaged the import of their findings as needed
tonic for American couples. Good sex would be their salvation. In "objective" laboratory conditions, Masters and Johnson and their research staff
witnessed hundreds of couples and individuals engaged in a variety of sexual acts. They left nothing to the imagination, recording and charting every possible physical response. Accused by critics of denuding sex of all
emotional and spiritual attributes, for the most part the St. Louis research
team attracted the interest of the American public. While they encouraged
communication, as had their less clinical forbears, Masters and Johnson
went back to the drawing board to discover what merited discussion.[41]

They focused on what they dubbed the "sexual response" cycle. Like
Kinsey, Masters and Johnson interpreted the preponderance of their data
on heart rate and other signs of arousal to rule unequivocally that men and
women were more similar than they were different when it came to physical responses to sexual stimuli. But their finding on female orgasmic potential constituted the biggest news to emerge from their research into human
sexuality and overturned the verities of postwar marriage manuals. Their
observations showed women to be fully orgasmic and, in fact, able to surpass men in orgasmic potential, blatantly contradicting the assumptions
governing medical discussion and diagnosis of "frigidity." After exploding
the shibboleth of female sexual infacility, Masters and Johnson took their
findings a step further. Precise clinical measurements showed that psychoanalytic distinctions between "immature" clitoral orgasm and "mature" vaginal orgasm had no grounding in physical reality. The only orgasm origi-
nated in the clitoris, and traditional heterosexual intercourse was not the
best route to achieving it, they discovered. Masters and Johnson saw their
findings as contributing to the expansion of sexual understanding, linked
to the service of sex education. And they concentrated their efforts on sex
in marriage. With their findings on women's sexuality, they created the
potential for a transformation in gender dynamics within the institution.[42]

By the 1970s, few would contest that Americans' public culture had become highly sexualized; the publicity surrounding Masters and Johnson
was just one indicator. Sexual advice books topped the best-seller lists. Dr.
David Reuben's *Everything You Always Wanted to Know about Sex (But Were
Afraid to Ask)* maintained 30 weeks on the best-seller list and sold 700,000
copies; *The Sensuous Woman* by J, or Joan Garrity, sold 250,000. *Human*

Sexual Inadequacy, Masters and Johnson's less accessible follow up to their first blockbuster, joined these titillating books on the best-seller list that year.[43]

Seventies experts incorporated the ethos of openness voiced in the 1950s but added to it more technical and physical information. Women's magazines now included a host of explicit articles on sexuality in their pages. Words like orgasm, masturbation, and fellatio entered the women's magazines' lexicon and presumably the vocabulary—if not the experience—of their readers as well. *Ladies' Home Journal* ran a regular feature by Dr. Theodore Rubin entitled "What Women Ask about Sex," that purported to answer readers' "most intimate questions." Rubin's column of March 1975 promoted openness of two sorts. He encouraged one writer to broaden her definition of normal sexual practices and not "automatically" reject her husband's sexual requests and another to abandon her "old-fashioned idea," advice that resembled that dispensed almost twenty years earlier by Clifford Adams. In another article, William Masters advised that an experimental approach to sex could "open up an incredible spectrum of sexual responsiveness." Experimentation joined accommodation as the watchword for women.

In addition to promoting open-mindedness, Rubin and others also stressed open communication. He suggested that one couple would find "great relief" if they talked out their sexual relationship and advocated "open discussion of likes, dislikes and preferences" so long as the chat did not occur "during love-making." The editors of *Ladies' Home Journal* took it upon themselves to encourage such open discussion with the ubiquitous feature of women's magazines, the quiz. One entitled, "The Intimate Hours," included the challenging subtitle, "Do you Dare to Ask Your Mate These 50 Questions?"[44] When *Redbook* sponsored a forum of young couples who met with the sex researchers Virginia Johnson and William Masters, Johnson promised that communication was a "word we'll be using often this afternoon." The calls to "talk about it" had their origins in earlier advice during the 1950s. What had changed by the 1970s was the "menu" of options to discuss and the emphasis not only on understanding, but on honest disclosure. And, now featured on the list of topics was women's pleasure, not just accommodation.[45]

The ideas of postwar psychology, sexual liberation, new research, and women's liberation combined to direct special attention to women's sexuality. One magazine ran an article entitled, "How to Say No to Your Husband," intoning, "It's a sexual lesson we can learn and share with the men we love: When we are free to say 'No' to them without hurt, we are also free to say 'Yes' with all our hearts." Here the author argued against sexual "capitulation," redefining women's sexuality from a female point of view. She asserted the right of women to set the terms of married sexuality, rather than merely respond.[46]

Along with its imprimatur for discussion then, the advice industry touted the possibilities of pleasure, with a renewed focus on women. *Newsweek* covered the "Battle of the Sexes" supposedly going on in America's bedrooms: "The message of female pleasure . . . is constantly hammered home." With alarm, the magazine reported a new study that revealed a "startling reversal"—sexually interested wives and sexually inactive husbands.[47]

Advisors repackaged the sexual revolution's notions of sexual liberation and personal choice, shaping them into tools to secure the institution of marriage. The implication was that by following this advice couples would achieve "mutual pleasure," and remain both sexually satisfied and married. Yet critics sounded warnings that the search for sexual satisfaction might destroy as well as enhance marriages. Adelaide Bry, a therapist, cautioned of the "catastrophic" consequences when "the sexual revolution, particularly the increasingly graphic books and movies that preach the gospel of a perfect sex life, is sending both men and women out in search of a perfect union."[48] Other advisors joined the fray, blaming precisely the cultural expectations that many of their colleagues had helped to create for Americans' sexual dissatisfaction. "Many of the problems of sexual adjustment that occur in marriage from the wedding night on actually result from little more than ignorance or misconceptions that lead the newly married couple to expect too much from their sexual relationship."[49]

In *The Sexual Wilderness*, social critic Vance Packard warned of the threats that the new developments in sexual openness posed to marriage. The "sensual content" of American life, he argued, approached saturation. And he cast a skeptical eye at seeming advances in sexual knowledge. He wrote, "From Freud to Kinsey to Masters, the emphasis of the research moved ever further away from the quality of sexual relationships (with their components of affection, love, and fidelity) to emphasis upon the nature of the physiological release." Packard pointed to contraceptive advances and improvements in women's status as factors altering the sexual dynamics of American marriage. But he reserved special criticism for the advice industry: "Typically, the manuals prescribe how to squeeze the last bit of erotic feeling out of the sexual encounter, and devote a good deal of the tract to techniques and descriptions of anatomical acrobatics." Rather than promoting sexual satisfaction, such advice created extreme self-consciousness, something Packard thought "particularly disconcerting to the male." By championing the "earthshaking simultaneous orgasm" the experts only enhanced the possibility that couples would feel inadequate, Packard wrote, reserving his greatest sympathy for men. In addition to the jarring openness and endless discussion of technique and clinical findings, the recent acknowledgment of women's pleasure and potential sexual assertion irked Packard. But Packard noted an important problem—translating prescription into practice.[50]

Always countering such warnings was the basic faith that satisfactory sexual relations built on effective communication made or broke a marriage. Virginia Johnson told her seminar of young couples, "Without the ability to communicate sexually, the marital relationship has a wide gap in it, and most often this gap contributes to the breakdown of other kinds of communication. It's that simple." And it was that complicated.[51]

Critics of the sex advice industry were right to worry. High expectations for satisfying sexual relationships did reach American marriages in the 1970s. While most American couples appeared to be satisfied with their sexual relationships, they still worried about frequency, climax, and technique. In *Redbook*'s report on female sexuality, 85 percent of women married more than 10 years rated their sex lives "Very good/good," and only 15 percent marked "Poor/very poor." However, among couples seeking advice for marital troubles, sex problems figured in the requests of 40 percent of the husbands and 20 percent of the wives. Endowed with expert endorsement of erotic bliss within marriage and the tantalizing knowledge that outside of marriage countless couples experienced sexual ecstasy, spouses looked to one another for fulfillment, and felt cheated when they found only disappointment. Thanks to endless press coverage, for baby boom parents there was an ever present awareness that they could only play catch up or reject the younger generation's innovations.[52]

Men communicated these expectations to the IHD, at least. Rick Snyder shared his complaint: "Well let's just say my wife doesn't completely have an open mind about sex. Let's just say that she was shy." In part, he attempted to justify a recent affair by indicating that his wife lagged behind the times. Clay Kent, disappointed in the outcome of a marriage counseling session, revealed that sexual incompatibility remained a long simmering marital conflict. He griped, "I wanted the counselor to say, 'Mr. Kent, we think that you are an exceptionally wonderful, splendid individual, and it's this no good wife that you've got that won't give you enough sex.'" He was baffled when "none of this came out." The messages from the expert community bolstered men's expectations for enthusiastic sexual partners in their wives.[53]

Women also agreed that their spouses deserved an enthusiastic sexual partner, whether or not this reflected their actual experience. Martha Bentley followed fifties notions of women's responsiveness throughout her marriage, despite growing public protests of exactly that sort of subordination. She said with some pride, "I've never once ever said no to my husband. And I think this is sort of a kind of a secret of being successful in this area." The sharpened focus on sex put pressure on women to measure up to external standards. Michelle Anderson said, "I think if there's any problem in our marriage it's probably sex, because I'm just not very very sexy. And I have to continually work on this problem." She concluded, "I know that a lot of times I have to force myself when probably other people don't have to." Aware of increased expectations, she could not extend her candor to her husband. "John, right now is impotent," she revealed, but added hastily, "I don't think it was anything I did, because if anybody should have an academy award, I should have had one . . . I don't think he's ever realized that I didn't care for it." This woman felt left by the wayside; she had never felt "sexy." Yet, she preferred to act the part of passionate partner rather than initiate a discussion of the matter with her husband. Anderson absorbed only half the injunctions of the sexual revolution, ignoring feminist messages that would have liberated her at least from faking orgasms and expert advice that advocated the sharing of sexual feelings. Her experience also reveals the continuing pressure women felt to please their partners over and above themselves.[54]

With the proliferation of explicit sexual advice, medical and psychological jargon entered couples' vocabulary. New requirements to discuss sex spurred partners' efforts to diagnose themselves and each other. When the Jenkins's sexual relationship deteriorated, Doris recalled her husband saying, "Well I think this is rather frigid, because you were by nature very passionate but because it was the right thing to do, you held yourself back all these years, and then suddenly it's very difficult to let yourself go." Here Jenkins spouted a common expert explanation for women's supposedly inhibited sexual response popularized by Kinsey and Masters and Johnson. First Kinsey, anecdotally, and then Masters and Johnson, with electrodes and cameras, had demonstrated women's orgasmic potential. This left experts with the quandary of explaining why, for so many women, that potential went unfulfilled. They scientifically expanded the scope of women's sexuality, but maintained the ideologically rigid category of frigidity. But frigidity as an all-purpose label for women's sexual behavior was falling out of favor. As Alex Comfort wrote in *The Joy of Sex*, frigidity "does not mean failure to enjoy sex when one is dead with fatigue, when children are hammering on the door, in the middle of Union Square, or, generally, with the wrong man at the wrong time, all of the time every time, or with the wrong vibrations." Despite this couple's emotional difficulties over issues that included his devotion to career and hypercritical stance toward his wife, when it came to analyzing their sexual relationship, the medical explanation of frigidity, so popular in the 1950s became the explanation for the problems they were having two decades later.[55]

Doris offered a different interpretation of their dissatisfaction—one that suggests an interesting insight into the relationship between information in principle and passion in practice. When they were first married, she explained, her husband turned to marriage manuals to learn about sex. "There isn't a thing we couldn't do by books," she recalled. "But honestly, I could see him turning the pages. I could see it all on page 46. Everything is going according to rote. It wasn't from the heart. . . . And if that doesn't take the romance out of life." Kevin took responsibility as the family expert for their sexual success, judged, no doubt, by the fifties standard of mutual satisfaction. Doris, meanwhile, felt as if clinicians had invaded her bedroom. She held high romantic hopes and kept mum about her disappointment. In spite of such expectations and efforts or perhaps because of them, Doris confessed, "I have never known . . . well, any gratification. I've never known any in my life. I've often wondered what it would be like. I guess every woman does." Technique overwhelmed feeling in this case. Doris longed for both romance and gratification but withdrew from sex almost entirely when she was disappointed. Both fell back on clinical definitions of women's sexuality when their attempts failed. Doris wanted romance. Her husband, she said, did "his best." But as a man, she thought, "his sexual appetites are like all his appetites. When he's hungry he dives in and he eats and he's through and that's it." Going by the book meant to Doris that Kevin was insincere. But as much as she wondered about her own satisfaction, she gave up hope of experiencing it. Discussion and marriage manuals failed this couple. Instead they each held fast to cultural assumptions about male and female sexuality, which appeared to them to be insurmountably different.[56]

Spouses turned to convenient gender stereotypes to explain away the sexual differences that complicated their relationships. Virginia Walker mentioned that while sex for her was "second hand" for her husband "it's always uppermost." "I don't know," she concluded, "maybe most men are like that." Her husband, who hastily admitted that Virginia was "not nearly as big an old maid as I make her out to be," nonetheless said, "She doesn't have the desire that I, as a man, have." These stereotypes were convenient explanations for what amounted to sexual impasse. They relieved a couple of further need to discuss their problem. Male and female sexual differences were simply an immutable given. That couples resorted to formulaic explanations reveals that, contrary to expert assumptions, sexual differences in marriage were not necessarily resolvable. For the middle class, communication, the palliative that the advice industry had been dispensing for decades, remained a huge stumbling block to intimacy, whether physical or emotional. The intimacy gulf could be wide indeed.[57]

Just as sexual dysfunction was often a symptom of poor communication, conflict over sexuality became one more factor distancing spouses from one another. One couple experienced years of sexual unhappiness, and each sought independently to understand the other's motivations and point of view. Malcom McKee claimed his wife was "quite frigid," a condition he attributed to menopause. But then he suggested that he might have exacerbated their sexual problems because his job had been so all-consuming. He surmised, "I think you lose sight of what the woman you married really is and so I think there's a tendency when it gets down to . . . the sex part of it, that a lot of people probably including myself, it became more of a physical process." The subtext of his comment reveals a conversant familiarity with the gender differences in sexual style that the advisors discussed. Like "most men" Malcom assumed he had neglected the romantic niceties that the experts said women appreciated.[58]

His wife also wondered if her feelings about sex were related to menopause, but her comment revealed the lack of intimacy in their marriage. Celia confessed that she might "make him a little unhappy," by rejecting his advances. Although he had never complained to her, still she suspected a problem. "I'm much slower . . . in accepting anything like that right now. I don't know whether it's change of life or what it is, but I'd just as soon not have any relationships. I won't always cooperate in that. But it's not been an argument." Speaking specifically about sexuality was difficult for Celia, who referred to it obliquely as "there" and "that." Moreover, as difficult as it was to discuss with the interviewer, Celia found it even tougher to talk intimately with her husband about their differing desires.[59]

The sexual revolution, defined in terms of frankness and pleasurable experience, then, made only erratic inroads into these midlife marriages. And IHD couples who felt this way, although a vocal minority, were not alone, as a national survey of 3,880 married men and women found that 11 percent termed their sex lives "significantly unhappy" and another 11 percent labeled them "variable." Variable probably described the sex lives of many couples. But according to the benchmarks of the sexual revolution, variable was no longer good enough.

Paul Meeker stated that he and his wife adhered to "high ideals" and hinted that these required some accommodation when it came to sex. That their "interests have never totally" meshed had not, he said, been a problem. His wife told a different story, showing that she had absorbed high expectations for satisfaction but stopped well short of communicating her dissatisfactions directly. He rarely made advances and after feeling rebuffed, she eventually decided against "forcing" herself on him. At issue was not so much rejection as what she saw as a lack of consideration on his part. Despite the efforts of sexual edifiers, the message regarding female pleasure did not necessarily hit home among the middle class. "In about ten minutes he was through," she complained, "And I cried myself to sleep so many times." Nan envisioned tender and climactic sex, but her husband's morals, ignorance, or insensitivity left her unsatisfied. She had absorbed the belief that women could initiate sex and expect orgasm, but her husband had not yet caught up. And, she could or would not broach the subject.[60]

Another couple also felt sexually stymied. The Arthurs, recounted Liz, had "more or less drawn a blank," when it came to their sexual relationship. Neither she nor Sam were "real affectionate." Each waited for the other to make the first move, to the point that Liz said, "sometimes I feel like a piece of furniture in the house." She attributed this to any number of factors: her not being "the world's most sexiest woman," or, perhaps his insistence on twin beds when she would have preferred a "big king size bed." Nonetheless, Sam "keeps saying I should be the aggressor once and a while." This was a wish she found difficult to implement. The Arthurs became another case of crossed signals. She hankered for more open display of affection and consideration and her husband for her greater expression of sexual interest, along the lines of the new equality the sexual revolution offered women. These examples show that new avowals of women's sexual rights could, in the bedroom, or at least up to the bedroom door, translate into new expectations for performance, and additional fodder for disappointment.[61]

Still, this generation did see sexual openness as an improvement, especially when it came to alleviating the ignorance that they had experienced as youths. Liz Arthur remembered her mother had not told her "one damn thing." Her mother's generation was "hush hush, no discussion about it.

And I think it makes it much harder in marriage." While not exactly loquacious on the subject herself, Arthur approved the greater discussion of sexuality she encountered in public life, even if it highlighted her own dissatisfaction.[62]

Awash in advice, warnings, and recommendations, couples found it difficult to determine realistic possibilities for sexual pleasure given the central status to which experts had elevated sex. Mary Smith responded to a question about sex from the IHD with, "Oh, hot and cold. It's hard to compare with other peoples. You can't really believe the magazines, I don't think." Yet, magazines did serve as disseminators of the supposedly new sexual age, keeping middle-aged couples abreast of changing ways and mores. Often one spouse imported the ideas of the sexual revolution directly. These changes proved frustrating for some, liberating for others, sometimes within the same marriage. In 1982, 21 percent of the couples interviewed reported consistently satisfying sexual relationships over the course of their marriages. Sixteen percent said their satisfaction had increased. The younger Berkeley cohort were more likely to report satisfaction and increased satisfaction, suggesting that these couples had greater success incorporating the lessons of the sex experts. New attitudes filtered unevenly throughout American society, passing some families by, uniting others, and dividing still more. And new attitudes and new information might be accepted in theory but never incorporated in practice.[63]

For one couple, a painful but sexually liberating awakening left a shipwrecked nuclear family in its wake. The husband had denied his sexual orientation in the 1950s when the stigma and risk of homosexuality were high. He married and had children without revealing any inkling of an inner conflict. His wife noted that early in marriage, he had believed that sex was only for procreation, that he had been surprised to learn it was pleasurable; she took some pride in imparting that lesson. But in 1971, he observed that while he enjoyed sex, "many times she had to be sort of the one to nudge me in to it." The reasons behind his hesitancy soon became apparent. In the late 1960s he began to explore his sexuality, visiting gay bars then gaining public notice. "It was a great relief to get that all out about homosexuality and everything, because I had lived with that ever since I could remember. I experimented with the life of a homosexual for a while and I was able to accept it more," he said. The relief was his to revel in. His wife became distraught when he began to stay out all night while making up his mind about his sexuality. He eventually decided to divorce after over two decades of marriage and acknowledge his homosexuality. She remained behind to contend with the pain of rejection, as well as the initial shock of learning his sexual orientation, which the sexual revolution enabled him to express. By the 1970s, homosexuality was no longer a characteristic one hid; it was instead a core identity, which for this man superseded other attributes—husband, father—that had buried what he gradually came to see as his true self.[64]

While gay liberation dramatically changed this marriage, the ideas of women's liberation, even if diluted through articles in women's magazines, initiated more subtle changes in bedroom behavior in others. Prior to Crystal Robertson's exposure to feminism she usually gave in and waited "until it was over. Not really enjoying it. Thinking of it as a sort of duty type thing." Crystal thought, "That's another thing that the feminist movement has taught women—that they're not just little vessels waiting to be filled. You have a right to say no. I wish I had known that earlier." Crystal's realization does not exactly read like a women's manual for sexual liberation but is significant nonetheless. She may or may not have been able to speak to her husband about her bodily pleasures. Her interview does not address that.[65]

But she could, apparently, quite effectively speak one important word, "No." Beth Andrews reported in 1970 that she had recently become more vocal with her husband as well. What she was willing to say more frequently was "Not now, I'm tired." Perhaps as the mother of adolescents and a devoted volunteer for charitable organizations, Andrews was often exhausted. But the point is that when she was she spoke up. Celia McKee and Doris Jenkins also successfully communicated a refusal to engage in unwanted sexual relations with their husbands. While they did not use words to reshape their sex lives satisfactorily, these women did use them to reject the continuation of unsatisfactory ones. For marriage advisors, such stagnant standoffs indicated sexual dysfunction and threatened to destroy marriage—these couples had failed. But the marriages survived. And while the refusal to participate in sex that they did not enjoy certainly fails to qualify as sexual liberation, popularly defined, it was no small assertion of female autonomy in marriage and offers clear evidence of gender change.

Men, too, reported a learning curve when it came to the new approaches, including greater understanding of their wives' perspectives. Lloyd Andrews confessed, "I think I honestly felt until about five years ago that sex between me and Beth was more for my benefit than hers. I think I've finally come to realize that it's beneficial for both of us." We can only wonder if Beth's more vocal refusals prompted Lloyd's awakening; while his earlier attitudes may have prompted her fatigue. Yet, his enlightenment extended to higher performance requirements for himself: "I'm becoming a little dissatisfied that I can't be such a partner to my wife that she's left panting for the next time." The sexual revolution could bring couples one step forward and two steps back. Andrews's attentions to mutuality improved his relationship with his wife on the one hand, while on the other, his greater awareness of the potential for pleasure left him feeling inadequate if he did not fully provide or achieve it.[66]

Nan and Paul Meeker had completely different readings of the tenor of their sexual relationship. The two had gone their "separate ways;" Nan reported, "Maybe I didn't satisfy him or something. . . . He just sort of ignored me. . . . So after crying my heart out for quite a while, I just gave the whole thing up." She described their relationship as "sort of pals." His emotional distance during their physically intimate moments upset Nan. She puzzled out the reasons on her own and chose avoidance over the hurt of rejection or being ignored. Paul had a very different take on their sexual relationship. In response to the question "Is sex more important for one partner?" Paul answered that he was unaware of any discrepancies and he went on to say that the couple dealt with sexual problems "by openly talking about them." Communication breakdown characterized the relationship to the point that they held entirely different views. Without putting the expert advice into practice, however, Paul knew that the only acceptable response to questions about sexual problems was "open discussion."[67]

Barbara Clinton engaged in wishful thinking and 20/20 hindsight when it came to intimate communication. She believed that it might have alleviated some of the dilemmas she and her husband faced. If she had to do it all over again, she commented, "I would have discussed even more than I did, or than we did together—sexual problems." *Redbook* magazine's 1974 survey of women's sexuality showed that discussing sex was least common among women over thirty-five, like Clinton. The survey also resoundingly confirmed marriage counselors' insistence on full disclosure. Forty-seven percent of the women who responded to the survey said they "always" or "often" "discuss sex with husband." The authors concluded, "The more they talk, the better they rate their sex lives, their marriages, and their overall happiness.[68]

A few spouses did attempt to bring expert advice into the bedroom and start conversations about desire and dissatisfaction. Once they had, however, they found their mates unready for these unfamiliar interactions. Kevin Jenkins knew he and his wife were both unhappy. "But," he said, "I've found that talking about it makes it worse. And every book that you read, everybody says, 'Get together and talk about it.'" But he broached the topic, with what delicacy we cannot know, and his wife became defensive, driving them farther apart.[69]

Raising the topic of unmet sexual needs had particular meaning for women who married in the 1950s. Marie Weber described an upbringing that encouraged her to protect the male ego, and so was silent about her sexuality for years. It had never occurred to her to make a suggestion: "I just thought you just didn't do that to men and that I was just being marvelous because I was so understanding." In her desire to be a good wife, Marie felt constrained to protect her husband despite the personal costs of silence. Emboldened by the ethos of communication and by the social acceptance of women's sexuality that accompanied the sexual revolution, she finally ended her longstanding silence: "I tried to talk about our sex life, and the fact that these were the things that were wrong and I tried to be tactful . . . but I hurt him dreadfully. So that there's been no relationship at all." The experts promised that honesty led to intimacy, but Marie found herself further estranged from her husband instead of closer as a result of her attempt at intimate discussion. In speaking up, she met not only a therapeutic injunction for honesty but a feminist insistence that no longer privileged male ego over women's selfhood or sexuality. Unfortunately for Marie, her husband still expected silence and protection from his wife.[70]

Aging, marital conflict, and inability to communicate about sexuality took their toll on sexual relationships in the midst of the sexual revolution. As the years passed, many couples downplayed the physical side of their relationship, contrary to expert axioms about sex among the middle aged. Thelma Morton reported that her husband had become impotent, but "we decided that there is so much in our life that's wonderful, and we do have a very loving relationship, that this is minor compared to when we were younger." Despite the exhaustive discussion of impotence in sexpert literature and Masters' and Johnson's finding that it was quite treatable, couples who experienced impotence did not seek professional help and struggled, often independent of one another to cope with the problem themselves. In 1982, Alice Bremmer reported that the sexual dimension of her marriage ceased years before. She said, "I can't figure it out." Neither therapeutic intervention or sharing of feelings were options for this couple. Grace Owens recounted that her sexual relationship with her husband had "petered out" despite "great efforts" on their parts. But her husband Jim refused to seek medical advice for his impotence, figuring the couple could "work it out" themselves. For her part, Grace had "great feelings" about it, assuming "it was all my fault." New research about the treatability of impotence and the glories of sex after fifty could stimulate further feelings of inadequacy instead of hope for a solution.[71]

What couples found was that, in fact, the experts could be wrong. Sex did not play the all-consuming role in marriage that advisors touted. Kevin Jenkins put it this way: "I've heard somebody say if you don't have sex in your marriage, it's a little like rearranging the chairs on the Titanic before it goes down or something. Well, that's not really true." Love and interdependence, commitment to marriage, these superseded sex for couples like the Jenkins. In fact, one study showed that over time, married couples ranked sexual activity lower and lower as a preferred leisure activity. Other joint or independent activities had superseded sex for older married couples in the 1970s.[72]

Even when the idea of sex remained important to one partner, commonly, couples lived with the problem, rather than work it out. Looking back on his first marriage Leonard Stone was bitter. He recalled that his first wife was "unimaginative." The problem, he disclosed, was that she did not initiate sex. "In 28 years you'd expect some kind of come-on from the woman you were married to. . . . she never said to me, 'Hey, let's go to bed early.' I resented that." He felt resentment but appears to have suffered in relative silence. It was his wife who finally instigated, not sex, but a divorce.[73]

Even younger couples in the 1970s had come to terms with the mandates of sexual liberation, failing at sexual communication, satisfaction, and desiring or seeking help. In a 1976 *Psychology Today* survey of people in their twenties and thirties—a younger and supposedly more liberated cohort—24 percent reported "lack of communication about sexual preferences" and "lack of interest in sex" as psychological problems that they had experienced. Furthermore, over half of the men and a third of women reported dissatisfaction with their sex lives. And in a sample that was overwhelmingly self-identified as politically moderate or liberal, over two-thirds had no experience with therapy whatsoever.[74]

If the sexual revolution had raised expectations for younger Americans, it had also shifted their attitudes in the direction of sexual permissiveness. The generation gap was most noticeable over the value differences between youths and their parents with regard to premarital sex. In August 1975 First Lady Betty Ford appeared on the television news program *Sixty Minutes.* Morley Safer broached a topic presumably bubbling in many middle-class homes. "What," he asked the forthright Mrs. Ford, "if Susan Ford came to you and said, 'Mother, I'm having an affair'?" Ford responded, "Well, I wouldn't be surprised. I think she's a perfectly normal human being like all young girls. If she wanted to continue . . . and I would certainly counsel and advise her on the subject." Ford added that the young man in question would be of interest to her and that Susan's intentions for the affair would be an important consideration. Apparently Ford's answer to a hypothetical question set off somewhat of a national commotion. In response, *Ladies' Home Journal* polled 200 readers for their take on "Mrs. Ford and the Affair of the Daughter." A majority of the readers, 53 percent, approved of her candor and response. The *Journal* reported, however, that "acknowledgement of changing standards is not the same as acceptance of them. Many women, our survey would indicate, feel trapped in a gray, no-woman's land—in between the morality of their mothers and the very different standards of their daughters."[75]

Clearly, the sexual revolution did not just affect relationships between husbands and wives. And what Betty Ford faced hypothetically on camera, thousands of American parents confronted in reality. It was often as parents of baby boomers that this generation encountered the changes and challenges of sexual liberation—particularly sexual permissiveness. General Social Survey data gathered in the 1970s showed that while premarital sexual behavior was increasingly common, "restrictive" attitudes still characterized 41 percent of the respondents. The generation gap, when it came to premarital sexual relations, thrived. Only 14 percent of those between the ages of 30 and 49 in 1975 expressed permissive responses. The younger generation lived with partners outside of marriage and embraced, at least superficially, sexual liberation much more wholeheartedly than their parents did, occasionally changing their parents' minds in the process. Mary Smith said her daughter "got liberated," and therefore Mary followed along, accepting at least that for her daughter "what you do with boyfriends" included sexual intercourse. Other parents proved more difficult to win over. When George Rogers's college-aged child moved in with a lover, George drew the line and stopped financial support. Some parents simply threw up their hands. Rita Frank said of live-in boyfriends and girlfriends, "You don't approve . . . but what can you say?" Betty Morris hoped for a wedding when a pregnancy was announced, but soon learned to "just lean back and enjoy" being a grandparent. While they might not have approved of their children's choices at first, as Dean Lawrence found, "I guess I am more broadminded about it when my own children do it." Twelve couples told the IHD that their children's choices changed their minds.[76]

A few even saw much to admire in the more relaxed attitudes about sex and marriage their children lived or espoused. One element Connie Small approved of was that sex "doesn't have the stigma and all the things that it meant" when she came of age. Gail Henderson appreciated that young people were "free" about sex and that girls had access to contraception. She was happy to see "these old horrible attitudes about how wrong it is . . . changing for the better."[77]

Others hung on to their stricter moral stances. Keith Warner maintained firmly, "We believe in marriage." Anne Matthews could not understand the popular aversion to marriage: "The only thing I can think of is that it's easier to escape responsibility." Ava Michaels disapproved of the dispensation of contraception to young people: "Now they give the children instructions. . . . We're telling them it's okay to go ahead and do it and I don't believe in it."[78]

A *New Yorker* cartoon portrayed what amounted to the permissiveness gap in the following manner: A middle-aged couple greets their daughter and her long-haired boyfriend at the door with the following salutation, "Your friend is more than welcome, dear, but we just want you to know that your father and I didn't do anything funny till *after* we married." For the older generation, marriage remained paramount, for most at least, and living together remained unacceptable. Mom might admit to engaging in "funny stuff"—but only after marriage, and one could hardly rest the survival of a marriage on "funny stuff."[79]

What do these intimate revelations of ignorance, high expectations followed by lowered ones, disappointment, and conflict have to tell us about the sexual revolution? They remind us of the uneven pace of social change, the gulf between prescription and reality, and the mixed ramifications of what have for the most part been perceived as positive advances in American sexual culture. Postwar experts and their prewar counterparts, by advocating a level of intimate conversation and sexual exhilaration most Americans could not put into practice, remained out of sync with their intended audience. Calls for communication fell on deaf ears, or at least inept interpreters. As humorist Erma Bombeck put it, "I dreaded the day when our children asked us what we did to aid in the advancement of sexual freedom. Somehow I had the feeling that 'I tried to give at the office' wouldn't win me a place in history."[80]

Postwar couples picked and chose from the gamut of sexual advice, often in self-serving ways. They saw what changes their partners could make to conform but perceived few of their own flaws. Who would measure up to whose standards remained undecided. Stand off was often the result. Nonetheless, the bedroom, or more broadly, the sexual relationship, was one more site of negotiation, conflict, and change in postwar marriage.[81]

A strong strain of sexual conservatism thrived in the midst of the heyday of sexual liberalism and sexual liberation. Some couples did turn to the pill and sterilization, finding freedom from worry for the first time in their marriages, but others sought to abide by the religious or cultural precepts that frowned on contraceptive measures. Still others struggled to employ various barrier methods with a striking lack of success, prevented by modesty, embarrassment, even carelessness from learning or practicing effective birth control.[82]

Historians observe that early twentieth-century standards for male conduct and female satisfaction in marriage added new burdens for both partners. Similarly, as a result of postwar advice, men and women felt both constrained and freed by the postwar sexual ethos: free to say no, on the one hand; free to feel cheated by a partner's sexual unresponsiveness on the other. Recrimination, both self and spousal, followed as expectations were dashed. Men felt bad when they did not provide essential ecstasy for their partners every time. Women felt bad when they could not be sexually more assertive as their husbands desired.[83]

As historian Stephanie Coontz notes, "the most striking aspect of the sexual revolution is its unevenness." Despite the experts' insistence on the centrality of sex in marriage, few couples elevated it to a similar position in their own lives. Not only did the ideas of the not-so-revolutionary sex revolution progress unevenly through the postwar population, midlife couples made mixed uses of its messages. And the values it promoted, which contemporary Americans take for granted as liberating, did not necessarily free those who adopted them. Honesty about sexual disappointments often was more wounding than bonding for a couple. And most had difficulty putting experts' instructions into practice.[84]

Feminists had first demanded the right both of refusal and of pleasure for women at the turn of the century. Then marriage advisors instructed men in the "art of love," for decades viewing them as the primary sexual actors in marriage, responsible for their wives' pleasure. After the war, experts began to enjoin wives to take more sexual responsibility in marriage. Yet throughout the twentieth century the distribution of pleasure and power in the marriage bed remained inequitable. In the late sixties, feminists once again raised the issue of female sexual autonomy. They built on the findings of a few sex experts and the fruitful discoveries of consciousness raising and attacked longstanding injunctions regarding women's sexuality. Turning a critical eye to male-female power imbalances, they called attention to the presence of power in sexual and marital relationships.

While few of the women in this study would have agreed with the more radical feminists that men were immaterial to women's sexual pleasure, they did begin to assert, if not their right to sexual satisfaction, at least the right to decline unpleasurable sex.[85]

The perceived gap between high expectations and the more prosaic reality of sexuality in marriage is a twentieth-century concern. What distinguishes this concern in the postwar era is the seemingly irrefutable evidence demonstrated by numerous scientific studies, youthful changes in behavior and attitudes, and the media coverage of both that worked to convince Americans that everyone else was having great sex and plenty of it. The baby boom's parents felt sidelined or eclipsed by the new heterosexual consensus toward nonmarital sexual expression or heightened marital sexual expression at a point when they were deeply ensconced in marriages and had been for decades. Meanwhile they were tempted by the atmosphere of erotic plenty just out of reach or seduced by the promise of pleasure to reinvigorate their marriages. In their disappointment, however, as the plethora of self-help books and obsession with expanding definitions of sexual dysfunction in the 1990s indicate, they share more with younger generations than the idea of the sexual revolution has allowed us to acknowledge.

When experts published detailed anatomical diagrams in manuals and textbooks for marriage, when they rhapsodized on the transportive potential of sexual pleasure, they hoped to secure the institution of marriage by infusing it with passion. And yet as the critics pointed out, tomes on tumescence—with their step-by-step instructions—made sex clinical, technical, not romantic. As couples experienced, studying new techniques produced sex by the numbers rather than paroxysms of passion. The hopes of advisors and the experiences of ordinary couples have never seemed farther apart. But the well-intentioned solemnizing of the expert and the well-meaning bumbling of a husband or wife seeking to satisfy their partner shared an optimistic take on American marriage as both mutable and perfectible—at the very least worth working on, and this says a great deal. While so much of the advice seemed unworkable, the fact that couples sought it out and sought to apply it, trying so hard in the process, meant that the goals, if not the methods, that experts touted resonated deeply with the couples who read them. Armed with explicit sex manuals and guides to intimate communication, many couples felt they had been provided with a faulty road map to sexual satisfaction—a geography that remained in many ways alien and unknown.[86]

When compromise failed and settling seemed like second best, dissatisfied couples questioned their marriages. Nearly a quarter would find that the answer lay with divorce. As with sexuality, public attitudes toward divorce permeated private marriages, and American family life was transformed in the process.

When a divorce did come to the Mary Tyler Moore Show, *it was middle-aged Mr. Grant and his wife Edie whose empty-nest marriage dissolved.* CBS PHOTO ARCHIVE

6

This Is the Time to Fly

Divorce and the Generation That Gave Birth to the Baby Boom

In the early 1970s, divorce caught the eye everywhere Americans looked: on television, in magazines, at the movies, and down the street. Mounting divorce rates and new no-fault divorce laws captured national attention. Not only did divorce dominate the headlines, but one aspect of the divorce phenomenon garnered particular interest: the new trend of middle-aged divorce. At the same time, the members of this study reached a new stage in the family cycle, the empty nest. With the changing cultural and legal climate, divorce was one possible consequence of this new family stage.[1]

Two popular television shows illustrate the national concern with divorce. In 1970, MTM productions went to CBS with an idea for a sitcom. The star would play a newly divorced woman who takes a job in a TV newsroom and struggles with a career and the single life. Gags revolved around the workplace and the friendships of this modern young woman. When *The Mary Tyler Moore Show* debuted, however, Mary Richards moved to Minneapolis because of a broken engagement, not a divorce. The producers deemed the television audience unready for a divorcee as a main character. The network feared viewers would think Mary had divorced the fictional Rob Petrie of the "Dick Van Dyke Show," in which Moore gained fame as Laura Petrie, and reject the new show.[2]

This television anecdote brings out three important aspects of divorce in the late 1960s and early 1970s. In their original conception, the show's creators responded to the increasing prevalence of divorce in American society. In their trepidation, the network executives revealed the continued discomfort with divorce many Americans still felt. Most significant, however, is that when a divorce did actually occur later in the series, it was Mary's boss, Lou Grant, who divorced, after more than twenty years of marriage, three children, and three grandchildren. And it was Lou's wife Edie who demanded it.

The Grants' marriage ends when Edie, having raised their children, decides she needs to do something for herself. Their divorce was portrayed as her response to the empty nest. It came after her struggle to return to school and Lou's difficulty adjusting to her new self-interest at what he saw as his expense. The Grants' empty-nest marital troubles rang true in the homes of many parents of the baby boom, as did Edie Grant's declaration of independence.

Another divorce demanded by a former mother of the 1950s took place on television in the early 1970s. This one was not fictional, however. In a sidebar to a cover story about divorce, *Newsweek* discussed one of the best-known families in the nation in 1973, the Louds of California. The Louds, a "typical" middle-class family of five, had agreed to have a documentary filmmaker follow their daily lives for a year. And what a year! In the course of the filming of *An American Family*, the Louds' son declared his homosexuality on national TV, and, perhaps equally shocking, Mrs. Loud announced her intention to file for divorce to an audience of millions. This was, as *Newsweek* proclaimed, "The Divorce of the Year." Reflecting on a tumultuous experience and the very public airing of private troubles, Pat Loud told *Newsweek*, "If we've done any good . . . we've demonstrated that divorce is not a tragic failure." Perhaps more surprising to readers was Pat's statement that if not happier, she was at least "more comfortable" after divorce. Even if they had not initiated the divorce, women, it seems got on quite well outside of marriage.[3]

Twenty-four percent of the couples in this study divorced, many going on to remarry and several to divorce again. Most of these marriages ended after decades of marriage, at a time when more and more Americans were turning to divorce. The older members of the IHD Study, those born in the early 1920s, tended to divorce in their late teens and early twenties, during the chaotic years spanning World War II. Only three couples divorced in the 1960s, 1970s, and 1980s. Once the first difficult years of marriage had passed, this cohort eschewed divorce. In contrast, for the younger cohort, born at the end of the 1920s and married in the late 1940s and early 1950s, divorce was scattered over the family cycle. Whereas only four divorces occurred within the first five years of marriage, ten occurred after a minimum of 15 years of marriage. Most remarried. More than a quarter of those divorced went on to marry and divorce at least once more. It is significant that the clusters of divorce in this study fell during periods of enhanced economic opportunity for women: during World War II and after 1965.[4]

The timing of these divorces coincided with national patterns in the twentieth century, occurring during peak periods of divorce. After a high of eight divorces per 1,000 married females in 1929, divorce rates in the United States took a downturn during the Great Depression. During and after World War II divorce rates increased markedly, reaching a high of 17.9 divorces per 1000 married women in 1946, a number not surpassed until the 1980s. Beginning in 1947, the year the baby boom began, divorce rates declined precipitously, not to reach attention-getting highs for another twenty-five years.[5]

The postwar divorce rate decline reversed the prewar pattern. Divorce statistics alone mark the 1950s as an aberrant decade. But the divorce slowdown lasted barely ten years; by the 1960s, many couples who had assumed after the war that marriage and children were the answer to the problems of life reconsidered. The contours of what has come to be known as the divorce revolution become apparent when we examine the numbers of divorces registered. In 1958, when divorces reached a postwar low, there were 368,000 divorces. The number of divorces increased in the 1960s to 708,000 in 1970. Divorces continued to rise and by 1981, 1,036,000 divorces occurred. Put another way, the divorce rate leapt from a low of 8.9 divorces per 1,000 married women in 1958 to nearly 15 in 1970. Divorce rates accelerated in the late 1960s and continued to climb until they peaked in 1979.[6]

The so-called stable marriages of the 1950s were part of this increase. Even members of the generation that embraced marriage most heartily in the twentieth century—the parents of the baby boom—divorced. The cohort that married between 1945 and the late 1950s, according to sociologist Andrew Cherlin, have lower levels of divorce based on projections of twentieth-century trends; however, for this cohort as well, "a greater proportion of them will divorce than was the case for previous marriage cohorts." In other words the long-term trend of increasing divorce rates slowed but did not cease or reverse for Americans married in the early postwar years. Cherlin explains, "Those who married in the decade or so following the war were the only cohorts in the last hundred years to show a substantial, sustained shortfall in their lifetime levels of divorce." While they may have eschewed divorce as compared to other cohorts, Americans married in the early postwar years did not necessarily refrain from it entirely. Lifetime projections are that 31 percent of American women born between 1928 and 1932—the cohort of the Berkeley Guidance Study— married and will divorce.[7]

What impact did an increasing divorce rate and changes in social attitudes about divorce have on marriage in the postwar era, particularly marriages made in the nuptially oriented 1950s? What happened when these changes coincided with the later stages of the family cycle? To address these issues we turn first to coverage of divorce in popular magazines and then to the first-person evidence from IHD case files.

In the course of the lifetime of this generation, consciousness of divorce became part of being married. American opinion about divorce shifted and divorce rates climbed in the postwar era. More and more Americans accepted divorce among their friends and themselves turning to it as a solution to marital or personal dissatisfaction, in keeping with American tradition.

Both divorce and increasing divorce rates have a long history in this country. In the nineteenth century growing numbers of Americans viewed their marriages as "dissolvable contract[s]." Divorce patterns in eighteenth- and nineteenth-century America reflected "the growing importance of three qualities in marriage: respect, reciprocity and romance."[8]

Romantic aspirations for marriage triggered increasing divorce rates in the 1920s as well. In the "roaring twenties" the heightened pursuit of happiness and fulfillment in marriage contributed to an increase in the divorce rate. The Depression temporarily stanched the divorce trend in part because few couples could afford to part legally. The marriage rate also slowed, as couples postponed weddings. The wartime return to prosperity spurred a new peak in both the marriage and divorce rates.[9]

Americans carried with them over the threshold high hopes for happiness in marriage through the big band era and into the early years of rock and roll, just as they had in the Jazz Age. While aspirations for marriage contributed to divorces in the 1920s, in the 1950s, Americans, like the members of the Kelly Longitudinal Study on which historian Elaine Tyler May bases *Homeward Bound: American Families in the Cold War,* rejected divorce when faced with marital disappointment. Rather than divorce, couples lowered expectations and compromised. Heavy normative injunctions discouraging divorce, the isolated suburban nuclear family, and the comparative compensations the married state afforded men and women, particularly when they had children: these factors combined to lower divorce rates. Nevertheless, public opinion about divorce was by no means monolithic in the 1950s. Changes in marital behavior as a result of World War II sparked the beginnings of calls for a new approach to divorce.[10]

Two strains of opinion characterized popular attitudes toward divorce from the 1950s through the 1970s. Both toleration and denunciation of divorce wove their way through popular magazines. The tolerant articles were most often written by judges, marriage counselors, and lawyers, and the now familiar family experts and advocated legal reform combined with counseling to help avert divorce. Critics' backgrounds were more difficult to identify; their criticism took the form of personal testimonial or social observation. The debate about divorce both reflected and contributed to revised opinions on divorce at midcentury.

In the late 1940s the American divorce rate was front-page news. Marital advisors lent their expertise to the matter. The immediate postwar rise in divorces forced the reassessment of traditional assumptions about divorce. The divorce rate skyrocketed to 17.9 divorces per 1,000 married women in 1946. The flurry of divorces in the late 1940s could have set off hand-wringing and warnings from the body of experts who studied marriage and family, but, for the most part, did not, for two reasons. First, wartime divorcees quickly remarried, calming popular fears about social and sexual disruption. Second, the complementary peak in marriage rates also helped to deflate concern about divorce. In view of the rate of remarriage and the convenient explanation the war provided, commentators concluded that impulsive wartime marriages, not disturbed or immoral people were the explanation for a high divorce rate.[11]

In response to the postwar explosion in the divorce rate, calls for a new understanding of divorce emerged. The problem, according to commentators who included doctors, lawyers, judges and clergymen, was that statutes lagged behind behavior. This movement toward legal reform reveals the first signs of a growing American acceptance of divorce as a fact of American life.[12]

Legal critics in the 1950s complained that divorce laws in the United States composed a crazy quilt of differing requirements and grounds for marital dissolution. Couples from states with only limited grounds for divorce flocked to Nevada or Florida to sever marital ties. Worse still, according to critics, in states like New York, which allowed divorce only in the case of infidelity, couples committed perjury in order to obtain divorces. Such articles grimly listed divorce statistics and relayed horror stories of couples victimized by an archaic court system. Divorce, the reformers insisted, was not a moral failing that called for restriction and censure; rather, it was an unfortunate event in the lives of men and women unlucky enough to have chosen the wrong partners. Reformers believed that already unhappy couples should not be made to suffer unnecessarily. They urged Americans to work to reduce divorces from a position of acceptance, not condemnation.[13]

Legal reformers insisted that they did not advocate changes so that Americans would divorce more frequently. Rather, relaxed divorce codes would allow those who admitted marital failure to end their unions with less difficulty. Divorce law, they believed, should accommodate divorce practice. Reformers suggested that statutes granting divorces based on marital fault did not address the situation of couples who had agreed that they could no longer sustain their marriages. Their reasoning widened the dialogue about divorce, even as some legal reformers hoped their proposals would limit the number of divorces.[14]

The fight to replace old-fashioned statutes with more modern ones played out on the printed page alongside a broader debate about divorce in American society. Division plagued expert and popular opinion. Although divorce rates declined in the 1950s, high divorce rates in the United States as compared to other countries continued to garner coverage in the popular press. Articles coolly outlining the necessity for new divorce laws shared pages with articles passionately condemning divorce and divorcees.

Throughout the 1950s, experts continued to criticize the prevalence of divorce. For psychiatrist Edmund Bergler, writing in 1949, divorce was an ugly manifestation of Americans' poor psychological welfare. Divorce, he wrote, was futile. "Instead of taking a trip to Reno," he recommended a trip to the psychiatrist. He condemned what he called "the divorcee's senseless hunt for the compatible mate," arguing that psychological flaws, not incompatibility, caused divorce. A writer for *Reader's Digest* took an extreme view, proclaiming that, "divorce is failure. . . . It is family bank-ruptcy." If divorce meant private bankruptcy to some, to others it indicated public default as well. A *Saturday Evening Post* writer, in the conclusion of his four-part study of divorce, quoted a judge as saying, "Divorce is a pub-lic disgrace. . . . America is the most divorced and delinquent country in the world." In this view, divorce signaled grave deficiency at the private and public levels.[15]

Others addressed the problem with more sympathy for the divorced and referred positively to the process of divorce and remarriage. Frances Strain, author of the 1955 marital advice manual *Marriage Is for Two*, advised read-ers, "Human life is too short, happiness too rare, unhappiness too destruc-tive in this troubled world to ask any man or woman to live out together an empty and unproductive existence." From this perspective, divorce was preferable to an unhappy marriage. By the 1960s, more and more Ameri-cans agreed with Strain and other advisors.[16]

Regardless of expert criticism or support, divorce became a prominent feature in magazines targeting the middle class. By the early 1960s it was common to assert, as novelist Herbert Gold first articulated in 1957, that "every marriage is a potential divorce." In 1962 *Harper's* devoted an entire issue to the topic. Divorce, one writer proclaimed, was all too prevalent. "However shocking the figure one in four may be, it is a respectable one. Divorce is now openly offered as a solution to the malaise of life."[17]

Marital dissolution may have offered an answer to the malaise of matri-mony, but in the 1960s, it was still not deemed fully respectable. Moreover, the stigma of divorce lingered long after it had become common practice. Even as it became "a familiar fact of life," as anthropologist Margaret Mead pointed out in 1968, Americans did not treat divorce "as the recognition of a failed marriage which it is wise to leave." Instead they continued to consider it a "sign of disgrace." Mead called for an end to what she termed America's "double talk" about the practice. That is, Americans acknowl-edged that unhappy marriages were best ended but persisted in snubbing those who followed through on that sentiment and divorced.[18]

Despite the support of legal minds across the country in the 1950s and 1960s, states moved slowly to change their laws. Not until 1966 did New York, for example, add grounds besides infidelity to its divorce code. But, in 1970 California pioneered "no-fault" divorce, and other states quickly followed.

For good or ill, the successful campaign to reduce the legal obstacles to divorce by removing statutes that encoded marital fault came at the ex-pense of divorce reformers' other goals. While reducing the complications and adversarial nature of divorce proceedings might put some derailed marriages back on track, advocates of fairer divorce statutes usually included formal proposals for "reconciliation" courts and court-appointed marriage counselors to patch up "broken marriages." In other words, reformers wanted to reduce the legal trauma of divorce and weed out salvageable marriages before it was too late. Ultimately, however, compromise and political maneuvering overshadowed the complexities of mediation and reconciliation and legislatures adopted no-fault divorce without the accompanying programs for ameliorating troubled marriages.[19]

Against a backdrop of easier access to divorce and contested expert opinions about the meaning and consequences of it, the American divorce rate gathered momentum in the 1960s and continued to increase after the no-fault revolution. The voices of members of the generation that gave birth to the baby boom suggest that divorce became, in the postwar years, a permanent part of middle-class consciousness. Even if individual couples rejected divorce, the baby boomers' parents considered it as an option right from the outset of the postwar era.

Indeed, many parents of the baby boom participated in the initial flurry of divorces surrounding World War II. This experience with ill-fated wartime marriages might have set precedent and eased the way for future divorces but did not. Nor did it signal a sustained increase in divorce rates. Rather, youthful divorces actually seemed to have made members of this generation more committed to marriage the second time around.

Wartime marriages often did not survive the exigencies of separation. Rodney Scott recalled spending a total of two weekends of army leave with his first wife before their divorce. In many cases, the veterans returning from overseas and the brides welcoming them home discovered that they had married veritable strangers and divorced.[20]

These brief, youthful unions ended with relative ease for, as Marlene Hill said of her first marriage, young couples had, "No children, no possessions, no nothing." Nevertheless, a divorce, no matter how short the marriage, was a troubling admission of a mistake or even failure. Marie Weber's first marriage was annulled within a year and she recalled, "Obviously it had been a failure and I didn't like that too much."[21]

IHD sociologist John Clausen has stated that youthful marriage was a strong indicator of a later divorce, but separation because of the war also led to divorce and it is difficult to determine which factor ultimately caused the breakups of those who divorced during the forties. The war disrupted many marriages in their infancy. On the other hand, those who divorced early in marriage complained about a wrong choice of mate, their partners' infidelity, and an unreadiness to settle down, all issues that may have related to their youthful unions. Yet, postwar divorcees quickly found new spouses. Believing their only mistake had been choosing the wrong partner the first time around, they held fast to their faith in marriage. The majority of these second marriages endured.[22]

The divorces of the 1940s occurred in the early stages of the family cycle, usually before children arrived. Because of the war and the subsequent expansion of the service sector labor market it was possible for young women without children to support themselves outside of marriage. Marlene Hill, who felt she quickly outgrew the young man she married at eighteen, secured a job apprenticing in a shipyard and she continued to work after her second marriage, until she was pregnant with her first child. Once a couple had children, it was much less likely that if faced with marital dissatisfaction a woman would choose to divorce.

As the years passed, and when the dissatisfactions of marriage obscured or outweighed the satisfactions, divorce became a factor in marriage. In times of trouble it was among the list of options couples considered, whether or not they actually divorced. Bluffing about divorce was perilous, but unhappy men and women played the divorce card in hopes of changing their spouses' behavior or to free themselves of unhappy unions. When couples had problems in the 1950s, they thought of divorce without necessarily acting on these thoughts. The prevalence of divorce discussion indicates that while the national divorce rate had slowed during this decade, acceptance of divorce continued to develop. Steven and Betsy Downs fought over his friendship with another woman. The issue for him was the "lack of freedom" her demands suggested. Steven said, "The way it is now, I feel too much confined." He insisted that were it not for the children, he "wouldn't take this from her," implying that troubled marriage would have ended without the need to consider what was best for the children. They fought and thought over divorce but stayed together.[23]

Karen Lewis discussed her marriage in 1959. "Can our marriage be saved?" she asked jokingly, repeating the title of the monthly feature in *Ladies' Home Journal*. She went on, "Really, we've thought we have so few things in common. I just don't see how we've lasted." Lewis acknowledged that her marriage could end in divorce. In the advice columns, marriages that could not be saved resulted in dissolution. Columnists began to view divorce as one possible solution to a severe problem in marriage, and so did their readers. Without choosing divorce, couples in the 1950s and 1960s introduced it as a possible resolution to marital conflict.[24]

Worry over a partner's potential to divorce shaped marital behavior.

Divorce came up in arguments between David and Rosalyn Nichols, and after one such instance, David quietly visited an attorney who told him to go home and "be the best husband you know how to be" and maybe his wife would "snap out of it." Chastened, he set out to alter his behavior, and Rosalyn's mind, with success. Another man experiencing marital difficulties in the early 1970s, Rick Snyder, also determined that his marriage would not "break up." To keep the relationship going, he said he had "killed everything that was irritating her. I'm trying to get her out more now and I'm spending more time with the children." Dread of divorce motivated nervous spouses to iron out difficulties.[25]

Once couples acknowledged divorce as a probable outcome of marital difficulty, the threat of divorce became part of disagreements. Divorce came up so often in arguments between Connie and Walter Small that their child told Connie, "Oh, threats, threats, threats, all you do is threaten to separate, threaten to break up our home." Nevertheless, within a year, Walter had acted on these threats and moved out. Rita Frank described an ultimatum she gave her husband. He was out of work and unwilling or unable to job hunt. Desperate, she circled a date on the calendar, telling him he had to move out if he did not have a job by then. She recalled, "He went out and searched and got something. It was like the greater fear. I realize now how much we meant to him. Because he went beyond his own fear to the worse fear of not having us." Threats of divorce had a double edge; they might act to bring a spouse back into the marital fold, or to expedite marital dissolution.[26]

Although the thought of divorce may have been a passing one, divorce became an expected solution to marital unhappiness. In many marriages the idea of divorce erupted in a heated argument and was quickly dismissed, or merely flitted across the mind of a frustrated spouse. Aileen Ross said she thought about divorce, but "never to the point" of actually getting one. "But I really don't think down in my heart I really meant it either. I just thought maybe it would be a little bit more of a threat." Malcom McKee, looking back at thirty-eight years of marriage said, "There were times that I'm surprised my wife never divorced me." When faced with marital disagreements, few could avoid at least considering the likelihood of divorce. This pattern of riffing on divorce without resorting to it changed American attitudes.[27]

In some cases the topic of divorce was not confined to isolated arguments but was woven into the fabric of married life. Hazel Drew described herself as "tempted a million times," to divorce her husband. As Sam Arthur put it in 1970, "I think anybody that says they've lived together for 23 years and never really seriously thought of getting out of it is lying through their teeth." He and his wife had serious discussions about divorce that they set aside until the children were grown. Only when they had another child late in life did they shelve those discussions for good. And Laura Gilbert's response to the question of whether she had ever contemplated divorce was a terse: "You betcha." These couples did not part, but their experiences show how pervasive the theme of divorce had become. Like a refrain, they returned to it again and again throughout married life, women more often than men.[28]

By 1966, half of those queried in a Roper poll supported the belief that "it is worse for children to live with parents whose marriage is very unhappy than it is to have their parents get a divorce." Compared to a 1937 poll, between 9 and 27 percent more believed divorce was permissible for such causes as "incompatibility, adultery, desertion, nonsupport, and mental or physical cruelty." Building on these changing attitudes, the divorce reformers triumphed in the effort to reshape the codes. The adoption of no-fault divorce in California in 1970 and the spread of divorce reform in the early and mid-1970s prompted a renewed national focus on divorce in the media. In particular, all eyes turned to California. How would modern, fault-free divorce unfold? Continued ambivalence greeted the changes wrought by no-fault divorce. Objectors questioned the new simplicity of marital dissolution long before the ramifications for children's and women's economic welfare became apparent. One critic wondered how to stop "the embalming of marriages prematurely," and the "mangling [of] the lives of so many children"—problems he blamed on no-fault divorce. But, that same year a publication celebrated the possibility of *Creative Divorce: A New Opportunity for Personal Growth.*[29]

One line in a *Newsweek* cover story on divorce, "The Broken Family: Divorce U.S. Style," summed up the irresolution with which Americans viewed divorce. Its author wrote, "the nation is producing more men and women . . . devastated by divorce but resilient enough . . . to fashion their own innovative solutions to the problems and the terrible loneliness of the single parent." *Newsweek's* reporter acknowledged new freedoms in American society that allowed those who divorced to make satisfactory lives for themselves after marriage as well as the continuing difficulties of divorce. In fact, the comment contains something for everyone: hints of the possibility of life outside of marriage for those truly miserable in it juxtaposed against the difficulties of divorce for those seeking comfort and solace in intact marriages.[30]

A consensus developed that while regrettable, divorce was not a tragedy.

Experience showed that men and women divorced, mourned, then picked up the pieces and built new, more satisfying lives, often including remarriage. One writer for the *Nation* proposed that while liberalization of divorce laws did increase the divorce rate, it also paved "the way for more satisfactory relationships in second marriages." As Margaret Mead observed, those who divorced recuperated soon enough and were more than likely to "try it again with someone new."[31]

The propensity for long-lasting marriages to break up also caught the nation's attention. One journalist warned, "Something malignant is happening to middle-aged marriage. All over the country . . . couples in their middle years are breaking up." Divorce was now not only possible but quite likely as well. Divorce happened everywhere, and not only to the members of the younger generation.[32]

News magazines trumpeted the surprising trend toward dissolution among marriages of long duration. Journalists offered personal testimonials and anecdotal evidence that middle-aged marriages were troubled. Feminist Betty Friedan noted in *McCall's*, "In suburb and in city, marriages are breaking apart like branches of dead trees that offer no resistance to a sudden storm—breaking apart after ten, twenty, even thirty years." She recalled that of six friendly couples that shared backyard barbecues in the early 1950s, three had divorced, including Betty and Carl Friedan.[33]

Two women, in different magazines, analyzed their marriages after divorce and came to similar conclusions: They warned of the dangers of the empty nest. Writer Mackey Brown cautioned *McCall's* readers not to let their marriages disintegrate as hers had. Everything in her marriage had been focused on the children. But, then the children "moved out and with them went the notions of the Family. We were left to stare astonished across the breakfast table, strangers in a strange land." Another woman told a familiar tale, sadly stating that after three children and "a quarter century, we were locked into a neurotic relationship that only divorce could break." Americans interpreted the completion of childrearing as a potential crisis in marriage, especially as it coincided with the loosening of divorce legislation.[34]

It was not just that middle-aged marriages were breaking up, but who instigated the changes which garnered notice. Women now left marriages that no longer met their needs. As the author of "End of a Marriage" wrote, a marriage "better than plenty isn't enough for me anymore." Apparently, numerous American women agreed with her.[35]

Particular attention focused on the "drop-out wife," as *Life* magazine dubbed the woman who left marriage and full-time homemaking behind.

Journalists and others noted that women could now leave marriages at will. *Newsweek* found the "phenomenon of runaway wives" a key symptom of troubled U.S. marriages. Many women, not just men, it seemed, answered the question, "Is a bad marriage better than none?" with a resounding "No."[36]

In the early 1970s, then, coverage of divorce had three poles of concern: the impact of no-fault divorce and the phenomenon of rising divorce rates, the new instability of long-term marriages, and women's rising ability and propensity to exit marriages. Divorce, just twenty-five years before, had been a sign of neuroticism; now divorce could be a sign of health and staying married a signal of neurosis. In an age of sexual freedom and new opportunities, marriage was no longer the inviolable institution it had once appeared to be. As journalist Richard Boeth concluded, "Women need no longer sell, and men need no longer buy, and the monkey of marriage is off our backs."[37]

No one had to read sensational magazine stories about divorce in the 1970s to be aware of the growing tendency of Americans to resolve marital dissatisfactions in the courtroom. Friends, neighbors, and prominent celebrities all divorced. Divorce seemed to many to be everywhere.

Couples who did not divorce felt fortunate to have escaped the conflicts and consequences experienced by their peers. In 1970, Ken Harris said, "We see a lot of our friends' marriages breaking up, so we're grateful to each other, isn't this nice it didn't happen to us? Aren't we lucky?" Nick Manning, married for thirty odd years, commented, "I really think it's incredible to stay married this long." The prevalence of divorce in the 1970s and 1980s set commitment to marriage in stark relief.[38]

Being surrounded by divorce led to a sense of vulnerability to it. While Nick Manning, noting the divorces in his social circle, gave himself a pat on the back for having an enduring marriage, this same observation made his wife feel anxious. Claire Manning said, "I have been around so many people who have been divorced that it does give me a feeling of insecurity to have witnessed it." Seeing neighbors and friends divorce brought the impermanence of marriage home, just about the time when a new stage of the family cycle altered family dynamics.[39]

The baby boomers grew up and left their parents' homes when they reached college age. Couples who had maintained marriages for the sake of the children reassessed their options when they faced an empty nest. Having married and borne children young, most parents of the baby boom were still in their forties or early fifties and felt young enough for a fresh start in life. For example Leonard Stone married Miriam, his high school sweetheart, within a year or two after graduation. Their marriage, he said, "Got worse as we grew up. And when finally the last child left the nest, why then she felt, 'Well this is the time to fly.'" The empty nest signaled the end to a specific period of family life, and for some the end to a marriage.[40]

Placing children at the fulcrum of marriage meant that as the baby boomers grew up, some of the purpose and meaning of their parents' marriages disappeared. In 1970, Clay Kent maintained that the "single most important thing in the whole thing are the kids . . . that has to be superior. And that's how I would end up by judging the whole relationship." When his youngest child reached high school age, he judged his marriage differently, and left his wife. Murray Borden recalled rather bitterly that he "stayed and raised my children, got 'em married off," and then left his wife after almost three decades. Emphasis on children in marriage, then, cut two ways. If children became a reason for staying together, once they were grown, divorce could be the result.[41]

What is most striking, perhaps, about the divorces of the parents of the baby boom is the longevity of the unions that did break up. Dale George divorced June after over three decades. Miriam Stone moved out and left a note on the table for her husband Leonard as they neared their thirtieth anniversary. Leonard observed, "But that's nothing. My friends are calling it quits after thirty-three years. Can you imagine?" Divorces after two or three decades of marriage seemed increasingly common. These late-in-life divorces are a testament to the high value placed on marriage by this generation, since many partners had harbored discontent for decades before deciding to make the break.[42]

With the empty nest, the responsibilities of marriage eased, children no longer were present to camouflage differences; some took this as an opportunity. Jack Stevens divorced his first wife in his forties. He said, "As you get older you realize that those years that you are giving away with a mild amount of happiness or unhappiness are too precious to be wasted any longer." Couples who had ignored incompatibility and individual needs for the sake of the children no longer had to do so. Evelyn Mitchell believed that as a result of her divorce, both she and her ex-husband were happier. The emphasis on happiness or fulfillment in marriage has a long history in the United States; by the 1970s and 1980s, more and more couples were acting on such expectations. Evelyn Mitchell's reasons for divorce also reflect postwar Americans' emphasis on not just romantic, but passionate love in marriage. Of her first marriage to Robert she said, "We had a wonderful working relation where we truly liked each other, truly, but it didn't have the passion it should have had . . . and that's what dissolved our marriage. We were doomed to be great friends from the beginning." Great friendship did not meet this woman's romantic hopes for marriage.[43]

Increasingly, men and women found their marriage vows less binding. Americans rejected the premise that marriage lasted forever, the family-oriented baby boom parents included. In 1982, Barbara Spalding remarked, "I see no reason why you should stay with someone if there's nothing holding you there, nothing whatsoever." This comment and others like it from interviews in the 1970s and 1980s reflect the widespread acceptance of new attitudes toward marriage and divorce. These men and women expressed the idea that there needed to be a good reason to stay married, rather than a justification for divorce. Couples ended marriages because the relationships lacked companionship, communication, or love. With their marriages lacking these ingredients, many thought they could find at least individual fulfillment and possibly better marriage if they divorced. This ideological shift, from justifying divorce to justifying remaining married marked the full-fledged acceptance, at least in practice, of divorce in American society.[44]

Yet for all its increasing frequency, divorce carried with it a heavy emotional toll. As Evelyn Mitchell put it, "Nothing's commonplace with yourself," and after her divorce in 1970, she found it difficult to meet new people and announce that she was divorced. For the parents of the baby boom, much of their adult identity was wrapped up in their family roles. Divorce forced a change in these roles. As liberating as divorce appeared, often participants interpreted the end of a marriage as a failure. Nancy Cole claimed as her responsibility what she called the "failure" of her marriage. Not only did she think her marriage a failure, but she felt herself to be one too, even though she had left the marriage in search of something more for herself. Without a successful marriage and family life to her credit, in her forties she said, "I'm not feeling that I've achieved anything in particular." Her husband, too, had focused his ambitions around family. He had a great deal invested in "making a woman happy and secure and sure that the children get a good start in life." When Nancy filed for divorce, he believed he could no longer claim those accomplishments.[45]

Divorcees experienced feelings of shame as well as failure. Barbara Spalding remembered the pressure she experienced from her social circle in the early 1960s during the year that she and her husband Harry were separated. Their friends wondered, "How could she do that with such a wonderful husband?" Social censure and concern for her children persuaded her to reconcile with a husband she considered far from wonderful and would divorce at a later date. Judy Kent recalled going to her class reunion a short time after her divorce: "We were given little booklets with our name and nickname, and after mine it said 'divorced.' I was humiliated." Through the 1950s, 1960s, and 1970s, divorcees continued to experience and to express embarrassment over the "failure" of their marriages.[46]

Despite growing acceptance and increased prevalence, then, the end of a marriage was a highly disruptive event in the lives of the parents of the baby boom. Divorce, couples had believed, happened only to other people. Men and women found their own unexpected divorces shattering. While Judy Kent's husband had been planning their divorce for a while, she and their children only learned of his intentions when he suddenly announced it and left the rest of them stunned, in the middle of a family gathering. She was, she recalled, "really devastated by this divorce. I didn't want to go anywhere, see anyone or do anything." When Harriet Pollard took the initiative and filed for divorce, her soon-to-be-ex-husband Philip found himself "in complete shock . . . completely disoriented by the whole concept." These men and women registered the deep surprise and challenge to their assumptions divorce represented.[47]

Divorcees also felt confused and adrift, even when they themselves had orchestrated the changes. Sue White said, "I've just come completely apart at the seams and got put back together. And I think I had to really almost revolutionize my soul in a way in order to divorce." Jack Stevens recalled the dramatic change divorce meant in his life after he chose to end his marriage of more than twenty years: "I dropped not only . . . children, a wife, a way of living, a community." He felt, he said, "Like a drowning man clutching for a straw."[48]

Historians, in our discussion of changing attitudes, have often overlooked that those who experience divorce do not always believe in it. Giving in to the desires of a persistent spouse did not mean that individuals relinquished long-held beliefs in the sanctity of marriage. Judy Kent remarried after her husband divorced her. Her new husband, himself a divorcee, relayed that neither of them would have broken up their first marriages and that both fully expected their new marriage to last.[49]

After divorce, former spouses found new freedom. But men and women had different experiences of divorce. Divorce freed men of many of the responsibilities of family life. Women could pursue their own goals and careers—a freedom they felt marriage had denied them. These freedoms had their price, one that fell more heavily on women with children still at home who faced trying economic circumstances without a steady income of their own to fall back on.

In the late 1960s, after the divorce his wife initiated, Philip Pollard linked up with the burgeoning singles scene. He said, "I'd never done anything reckless . . . and I was just letting . . . everything hang out." He stopped working, traveled, and started dating again. Following his divorce, also initiated by his wife, Stuart White quit his job and bought a van and a guitar. Robert Mitchell began a relationship with a much younger woman and contemplated quitting his job to live in the country. Divorce, in these cases, released these men from full-time breadwinning responsibilities at a time when "dropping out" was a possibility. They broke away from the work-a-day, nine-to-five lifestyles that had defined their identities since early adulthood.[50]

Women with children to raise and provide for could not tune in, turn on, or drop out. In her study of marriage in the late 1950s and early 1960s, Benita Eisler concluded that women rarely divorced without first masterminding what she called "the plan." By this she meant that women who had chosen marriage, homemaking, and childrearing, and the economic dependence that accompanied those choices first insured that they could support themselves after marriage before making the great leap of divorce. IHD evidence does not reveal any activity as explicit and conscious as Eisler's "plan," but does suggest that childrearing and economic dependence played a large role in women's attitudes toward divorce, as well as their options afterward. Once children were of school age or grown, women could begin to carve out economic support apart from their husbands.[51]

In the 1950s, economic dependence provided strong incentive to make marriage work. Hazel Drew separated from her husband temporarily. Their separation precipitated sessions with a marriage counselor, and the Drews reconciled. In 1970 she was still struggling with a marriage she did not find fully satisfying, although it had improved. She had not gone through with a divorce she said because, "I didn't understand about social welfare or I probably would have divorced him many years ago. And I guess the only reason I didn't go running home to my mother and daddy was because they were so far away and I couldn't afford to get there for one thing." She had no financial resources of her own and could not foresee supporting herself and the children.[52]

But once the children were in school, it became possible to conceive of survival without a male breadwinner. As a result, women could take advantage of new opportunities available to them in the 1960s. Nancy Cole opted for personal fulfillment over stability for her children, saying, "If I don't start feeling things that are important to me, I'm going to resent everything the children are feeling." Cole said she thought about her divorce for years before acting on the initial impulse. She left her husband, and continued to raise their children, but was now able to pursue her own goals freely.[53]

Barbara Spalding's story highlights the dilemmas women of this generation who were dissatisfied with marriage faced. She made it clear in numerous interviews over the years that she was unhappy with her choice of marital partner, while making it equally clear that because the children needed and loved her husband and he them, she would not leave him while they were at home. In 1970, she thought that if she waited until the children were grown, it would be in her words, "too late" for a divorce. Nevertheless, she put it off. In the ensuing years, when her children were teenagers she went back to school and then to work. After working for a few years, she filed for divorce, figuring the time was "now, Barbara. Or forever hold your peace." Without the children to worry about, she put her own satisfaction first.[54]

Women contemplating divorce strategized for economic self-sufficiency. Marlene Hill had once made all the arrangements to leave her husband, including getting a job in another state. But health problems influenced her decision to stay with her husband. Still, nearly four decades after her marriage, she made sure to have a savings account solely in her name just in case. Sue White went back to school for professional training after her divorce; her alimony payments bridged the gap until she was earning money on her own. Work and the empty nest enabled women dissatisfied with their marriages to opt out of them.[55]

Without young children demanding their full-time attention, women could act in their own interest. When Mabel Baldwin got a job, she decided she need not any longer overlook her husband's quick temper and "loud and aggressive" behavior just because he was a good provider and interested father. Women often experienced economic problems after divorce, but chose this form of constraint over that which they had known in marriage.[56]

In contrast, women whose identities were deeply connected with being wives, who did not make plans for economic self-sufficiency feared divorce and clung to marriage. Connie Small complained, "Every time we have a fight, all I can think of is oh, if I just had the money to leave, I'd leave!" But her marriage, she predicted, would go on forever unless she found a way to support herself. Much to her surprise, her husband moved out and ended the marriage. Years later she described herself as suicidal around the time of her divorce, unable to imagine supporting herself. Yet, after the divorce, she discovered talents and pursued new interests, working part-time into her second marriage. Keeping in mind her traumatic experience, she vowed, "Now, I would never let myself feel that I had to depend on somebody else."[57]

After divorce, women experienced a dramatic drop in income and change in lifestyle. Judy Kent was unaware of the financial plans her husband made for his divorce. He transferred ownership of family assets out of his wife's reach so that they would be untouched by a divorce settlement. She was working part time during the divorce and scraped by with her youngster on a small monthly salary combined with child support payments. She complained of the judicial inequity when it came to marital assets: "You have to split everything 50–50 even though he had this magnificent salary, and I had a small salary." Her situation highlights the way in which divorce reduced the incomes of middle-class women by not taking into account the economic disadvantages of women's family roles. Not all women shared in the benefits of a changing labor market and the legal system failed to acknowledge this. But clearly, greater labor-force participation, increased job opportunities, and the possibility of midlife employment for married women affected divorce patterns.[58]

It was not just economic dependency that tied women to marriages they found unsatisfying. Emotional dependency also figured into their commitment to their husbands. Many women could not imagine living on their own, particularly because they had married just as they entered adulthood. In 1971 Judy Kent said, "I think I would probably last the worst marriage in the world just because I didn't want to live alone." Betsy Downs thought, "I would be very lonely without him. . . . I mean I would be lonely without being married. I need to be married." When the thought of divorce occurred to Crystal Robertson, the experiences of other women quickly banished it. She mentioned love, dependency, and fear as factors keeping her marriage together; "I've seen other women who've done it and it's been rough." Married since their early twenties, these were women who could not imagine living on their own.[59]

Divorce's feared economic impact dissuaded others. Victor Gilbert said he had thought of, but dismissed divorce. His reasoning was, he said, "Selfish, I guess, from a financial standpoint. It certainly would cost you. Half of what we've generated plus whatever else the good judge. . . . So you make the best of a situation and try to be pleasant." Living alone cost too much, according to Claire Manning. She said, "I'm gonna stay. And

he'd better stay with me too. We kind of kid together—we better stay together. It's just more practical that way." The economics of married life and
anecdotal evidence of divorce's negative financial impact were an effective
deterrent to divorce.[60]

In considering what had held them together over the years and what
would continue to join them as they approached old age, some mentioned
financial constraints. Russell Weber said that among the rationales direct-
ing him away from divorce, one was economic, because, "If you have a lot,
you'd have to split [it] up. There's an economic strain." Russell viewed the
assets he and his wife had amassed during their marriage as a mutual accomplishment. One salary simply went farther in one household than it
would in two. It seemed better to keep the family fortunes, such as they
were, intact.[61]

These attitudes reveal the shaky premises of the postwar marital enter-
prise. What's mine is yours was the implicit and explicit marital bargain.
Men and women would each perform complementary roles for the good
of the family as a whole. Ideally, the male breadwinner worked for the family for pay outside the home and his wife worked for the family without
pay within it. Together, they shared the fruits of their labor—until divorce.
Leonard Stone was angry that his wife received what he considered more
than her share in the divorce settlement: "I had an awful lot to lose. I had
made my fortune and one day I woke up and it was gone along with my
ex-wife." Men feared an equal division of the assets they had worked so
hard to shore up. Women feared that their physical and emotional investment in homemaking during marriage would no longer be compensated
after divorce.[62]

The parents of the baby boom for the most part maintained their fierce
commitment to marriage. Aware that they could leave dissatisfying marriages, most baby boom parents chose not to. Rose Little had briefly separated from and reunited with her husband several times during their long
marriage, but in 1982 vowed that she would not do so again. "I have my
home and that's the way it is," she said. Herbert Henderson acknowledged
the importance of wanting to stay together in the new context, saying, "I
guess we were interested enough in each other to want it that way. There
were many opportunities to drop it." In 1982, Dan Bentley said, "I always
thought I would resist any temptation or impulse to get divorced." These
couples recognized divorce as an option for others but rejected it for themselves.[63]

At times, the commitment was to marriage as an institution, combined
with the specific relationship with the spouse. One quarter of the couples

in this sample said that they believed marriage was, as Lois Dyer put it, a "permanent commitment." Neither of the Chases believed in divorce and this pulled the couple through times Amy Chase described as "difficult as the dickens." Many couples expressed this belief in marriage and disapproval of divorce. Jane Mills said, "I just believe in marriage, good or bad; for better or for worse. I just wouldn't break that vow." This faith survived even when love did not. Catherine Hudson's unhappy abusive first marriage ended when her husband died. If her second marriage was not all she had hoped for, she intended to stick it out because "it boils down to the fact that my mother told me when I was married the first time that I made my bed and I could lay in it because that was the way it was going to be."[64]

Still, coupled with the commitment to marriage was a firm belief in the need for satisfaction and happiness therein. This duality is apparent in Patricia James's comment: "We're going to work our problems out and that's that. We do not get divorced after . . . years of marriage. . . . But in turn, I refuse to spend the rest of my life gritting my teeth and bearing with it." These two tenets—commitment to marriage and happiness in it—coexisted and often conflicted.[65]

The high premium these men and women placed on family life and children fostered their commitment to marriage. Although by the 1950s social workers, marriage counselors, and doctors conceded that when divorce put an end to conflict-ridden marriages, children might actually benefit from their parents' divorce, nineteen couples claimed that they stayed together for the sake of the children. Steven Downs said, "And if we didn't have a family we probably would have busted up. But all the responsibility and problems involved in breaking up—it just didn't seem worth it." His wife focused on the emotional effects of divorce on children, saying she believed "so strongly that you could really hurt your children very badly by disrupting what appears to them and to everybody else a very fine arrangement." The belief that divorce might harm children was a major consideration tempering decisions about dissolution.[66]

The joint mission of raising children cemented these relationships. Joseph Maxwell attributed his enduring marriage to the fact that he and Eleanor married "to raise a family, to work together." The Robertsons carried the baby boom ideal of a large family to what might be considered extremes, but Ben said proudly that in addition to genuinely loving each other, "I suppose having [all these] kids hasn't hurt. It's kind of hard to split the blanket." For these parents, childrearing forged a strong marital bond.[67]

Although recent generations have lessened commitment to the institution of marriage in favor of finding fulfillment in specific marriage relationships, overwhelmingly the parents of the baby boom prized commitment, stability, and security. This is not to say that they settled for unhappy marriages. This generation also emphasized other positive aspects of marriage when romantic love and companionship waned: shared history, goals, and family life. Patricia James concluded, "I don't think either of us would say that we're still married per se because of love. It's part of it but there's something much more important." They took pride in working together to raise a family.[68]

As Dan Bentley put it, "I've found that marriage is not this blinding pink cloud, glorious . . . all the time. It doesn't have to be that way." He loved and admired his wife, but marriage meant something more: "You [have] got a life of a family, it's not one person, it's a group." One factor that worked to foster Sam Arthur's commitment to his marriage was "It's difficult to break the norm. In many instances, it was felt to be easier to put up with adversities of marriage than to start all over again and do something different." These couples opted for the known, finding comfort in the familiar, and also, significantly, committed themselves to working to maintain it. For them marriage meant balancing both individual and family needs for the greater good. Rather than sacrificing marriage in pursuit of personal satisfaction, many concluded along with Kevin Jenkins, "Nobody's really going to get all their options satisfied."[69]

Echoing the language of advice literature on marriage, twenty committed couples emphasized the work necessary to sustain a marriage, attributing their success in marriage to that effort. Referring to the effort each partner should put into marriage, Frank Ryder said, "We realize that marriage is a 95–5 situation both ways, that you have to give more to make a marriage work." The energy one couple put into making their marriage work comes through in Gail Henderson's comment that the worst period of her marriage stretched through almost two decades: "It was a long time to have a terrible marriage." Effort and compromise characterized these enduring couples.[70]

Those who remained married saw their willingness to struggle through difficult times and to hammer out differences as distinguishing them from their children's generation. Ernest Johnson said, "Divorce is an easy way out of . . . trying to resolve these difficulties. People seem to be more interested in what they want individually rather than trying to keep the marriage together by talking it out and working out the differences. Whoever said, you know, you have to work at being married is entirely correct." In marriage, Barbara Clinton said, "You've got to give up some things. But they don't realize that it's for a better good. I feel that if they were willing to work more together toward a common goal, there would be fewer divorces." For the baby boom's parents, often, that common goal was maintaining marriage.[71]

More than just a willingness to work things out created the enduring unions that parents of the baby boom enjoyed. In fact, thirty couples listed love, deep caring, or belonging together as reasons they remained together. In interviews, baby boom parents paid tribute to the partners with whom they had spent nearly all their adult lives. Andrew Sinclair said of his marriage, "I would say that when we met, that was a start from nothing and today, it's just as strong as a piece of steel. . . . It's closer and closer. She's the greatest person that I've ever known."[72]

When reformers argued for kinder, gentler divorce laws in the 1950s, they envisioned a legal system that might save as well as sever marriages. When they advocated no-fault divorce, they planned a divorce procedure that limited rather than augmented the adversarial nature of divorce. Nevertheless, no-fault divorce hardly proved the panacea for the problems of divorce that early postwar reformers envisioned.

It is significant that divorce reforms did little to address the economic complications divorce creates and continue to do little to protect the economic interests of children or "displaced homemakers." Ever since, divorce has been pointed to as a key contributor to the impoverishment of women and children. While sociologists and some feminist scholars have been quick to zero in on divorce's harmful effects on the financial well-being of formerly middle-class women and children, the story of divorce since no-fault is more complicated than one of unmitigated unfairness and poverty for women. As feminist economist Heidi Hartmann suggests, divorce statistics, a changing world economy, and national labor market tell a different story. Certainly, especially in the early years after divorce, women suffer disproportionately the negative economic effects of divorce, as the experiences of women like Judy Kent attest. Nevertheless, since the 1970s, women have opted for divorce and they are *able* to leave unhappy or unsafe marriages with the knowledge that they can create viable, if financially strapped, lives for themselves outside of marriage.[73]

One woman's literal escape from her marriage dramatically illustrates this change. Battered physically and emotionally, she stuck with her husband for over two decades. At first she stayed to protect her children, but soon her dependence and the cycle of wooing and brutality entangled her. As her children grew, the roles reversed, and the children tried to protect her. Finally, they told her they could no longer be there to protect her from their father. Together with her children, she packed some belongings on a day her husband was not home and began her new life. It was an economic struggle, but she was safe from physical brutality. Her children stepped in and supported her while she went back to school. She recalled that one of them said, "'Ma, I'm going to leave and I want you to come with me.' I said, 'What am I going to do. I've spent twenty years raising you kids, I can't do anything. Where am I going to live?' [The reply was] 'Don't worry, I'm earning money, you've got time, you find something. I'll take care of you.'" In 1982 she was self-supporting and self-employed. Divorce reform and social changes that recognized the problem of domestic violence and provided educational access for older women made the new life she constructed for herself possible.[74]

Advocates of no-fault divorce failed to consider the unequal economic positions with which husbands and wives approach the bench, and women and children unquestionably suffered economically from this oversight. But in the ensuing decades, the changes in American society as a result of women's labor-force participation and feminist gains made life outside marriage possible for women with children. Mothers of the baby boom numbered among those women who took hold of these opportunities and divorced. Men responded to the reduced stigma, changing attitudes, and perhaps the knowledge that their wives had alternatives for self support. Both men and women left marriages that never had or no longer provided the satisfactions they had come to expect from the relationship.

Witnesses to the reform of divorce laws and their consequences, shifting American opinion about divorce, and the baby boomers' marital patterns, a majority of parents of the baby boom staunchly stood by their commitment to marriage. Evidence from the 1950s to the 1980s shows that marriage's comforts and advantages continued to balance marital discontent for most members of this generation. They shared habit and history. Marriage provided economic and emotional security. As these personal histories show, many spouses had ample excuse to divorce and chose instead to stay married. As often happens, looking at divorce reveals a great deal about marriage. Baby boom parents believed that in addition to love and despite the sacrifices the marriages demanded, these unions provided the best opportunity for satisfaction in life.

For those choosing dissolution, divorce caused a painful disruption. Divorcees left behind their long-term partners and part of their identities as husbands, fathers, and breadwinners, as wives and homemakers. The increasing prevalence of divorce failed to make the individual experience of divorce any less emotionally wrenching, despite the fact that divorcees left unhappy unions in search of future personal or marital contentment.

Mindful of the potential of the difficulties they might face, nearly a quarter of these couples ended unhappy marriages, testament to the painful problems with which they grappled and their optimism for life outside of one or in another marriage.

Even the parents of the baby boom could not entirely escape the divorce trend. The majority of these divorces occurred after fifteen, twenty, and even thirty years of marriage. The "empty nest," a term practically invented for baby boom families, always a time of transition in marriage, was particularly stressful for this generation. They concentrated childbearing in a youthful and brief stage in the family cycle. In so doing they focused much of themselves into raising children. When children left home both the purpose and the modus operandi of marriage disappeared. A marriage that was maintained "for the sake of the children" lost its stabilizing force.

Postwar couples' experiences reflect the increasing ubiquity of divorce in American life. Midlife divorce and the empty nest coincided with a particular historical moment. Beginning in the 1960s several historical changes paralleled the waning of baby boom child raising. The reform of divorce laws broadened access to divorce and made it front-page news. The stigma of divorce faded as practice increased and normative censure ebbed, making divorce a part of married life for most middle-class Americans, even if they did not, in fact, divorce. The therapeutic community of experts pushed the view that a strife-ridden home was perhaps more detrimental to children than divorce. Finally, the women's movement offered women dissatisfied with marriage the ideological justification to reject the injunctions of their youth and direct energy to their own pursuits instead of those of their husbands and children. Divorce was only one possible result. The empty nest and employment could prompt reconsideration of women's role. Experiences in the family and labor force shaped midlife women's responses to feminism.

Although the media portrayed feminists and homemakers as diametrically opposed to one another, middle-aged married women could find much to admire in the causes feminists espoused and the opportunities the movement opened for their daughters, even as they distanced themselves from women's liberation. ARCHIVE PHOTOS

7

Treated like a Lady

Feminism and the Family

Gail Henderson married in 1949 when she was 21. She and her husband raised a large family in the next decade and a half. In the early 1960s she began to help out at her husband's firm. She worked to help the family and to build the business until, worn out by the double duty of office and home, she quit. But accustomed to working outside the home, she disliked the isolation and boredom of full-time housework, especially once her youngest child was in school. In addition, a second income would ease the family through slow times. Gail soon resolved her dilemma by returning to school and later became a professional who was regarded, "somewhat as an expert" in her field. Gail Henderson's story illustrates the possibilities and yearnings of midlife women who tumbled head over heels into marriage and motherhood in the early 1950s and then, step by step, reshaped their own and their families' lives in the 1960s and 1970s. How did members of this generation respond to the feminist movement, which irrevocably changed so many younger women's lives in the 1960s and 1970s?

Judging from accounts in the popular press in the early 1970s, a deep divide separated homemakers and housewives from the controversial feminist movement. The "frustrated feminist"—young and active—and "the happy housewife"—middle-aged and quiescent—constituted convenient oppositional archetypes in the 1970s. A special issue of *Ladies' Home Journal* illustrates this supposed dichotomy. In August 1970, *Ladies' Home Journal* ran an eight-page women's liberation supplement entitled, "The New Feminism," produced by radical feminists in response to their sit-in at the *Journal*'s editorial office protesting sexist policies earlier that year. *Newsweek*'s blurb on the issue predicted that the *Journal*'s women's liberation supplement contained "acrimonious opinions" that might "shake up the normally sanguine *Journal* reader." With one brief sentence, *Newsweek* managed to pigeonhole both readers of women's magazines and the feminists who reached out to them.[1]

The invasion of the editorial offices of a major women's magazine was only one of numerous visible displays of feminist activism in the early 1970s. Speak-outs, hexes, and picket lines generated headlines and attracted interest to the women's movement. While marches like the Women's Strike for Equality—when thousands of women across the nation withheld their labor and took to the streets—brought new recruits flocking to NOW offices, they could also garner criticism. Few feminists would pay that criticism much mind. A tide of court decisions and legislation seemed to indicate that women's day had finally arrived. Abortion rights, recourse for employment discrimination, political clout, and even, as of 1972, an Equal Rights Amendment were all within sight. By the early 1980s, however, it appeared that the quiet housewives the *Journal* alluded to in 1970 held sway and ERA went down in defeat. According to the media this was largely because ordinary women rejected feminism.

That simple narrative belies the complexity of women's attitudes toward new gender roles and feminism. The media exaggerated the breadth of the chasm between feminists and homemakers, clouding the debate over women's roles in the 1970s. The oppositional portrayal of women in the 1970s and 1980s continues to distort the experiences of middle-class American women and their complicated relationship to the women's movement. Middle-class, midlife women felt threatened by critiques of marriage and motherhood, true. But if the beliefs of younger, radical feminists

frightened sympathetic older women, these women, nevertheless, remained unequivocal in their own belief that women should be granted
greater opportunity than they themselves had been granted early in life.
Regardless of feminist commitment, without outright activism, middle-
class midlife women who married and bore their children in the 1950s
and then went to work or school in the 1960s and 1970s changed their
families and society in the process. Based on their individual experiences,
the mothers of the baby boom responded supportively to key tenets of
feminism.[2]

The waning of childrearing demands inspired midlife women like Gail
Henderson to seek a new direction. Crystal Robertson lost her place at
school when she married and devoted the next two decades to bearing and
caring for her many children. She branched out of her family-centered life
as she entered middle age. Crystal's heavy commitment to motherhood,
and the long span of her childbearing would seem to indicate that this
mother of the baby boom, at least, had little time or inclination for activity
outside the home or feminist questioning of women's role within it.

In fact, of the women in the study, she became one of the most articulate
and outspoken on the women's movement. Crystal read Betty Friedan's *The
Feminine Mystique* for the first time in 1971. Crystal paraphrased the first
few pages of the book: "She was walking in the Berkeley Hills with a
boy.... She made a promise ... gave up a graduate assistantship. She
would have gotten to marry this fellow and have kids and do the Susie
homemaker bit and all that." She felt a special resonance with Friedan's
experience; "I thought to myself, 'Well you know, this is just like me.' Like
I was walking in the Heights above the Center and I made a promise to a
boy." Friedan's words reinforced many of Crystal Robertson's thoughts and
concerns about the next stage in her life, confirming her plans to pursue
her own interests once her youngest child was in school. She finished up a
bachelor's degree part-time in the early 1970s, and earned a masters after
that. Then in 1982, she was enrolled in a training program to achieve the
long-deferred goal put aside when she married. After decades devoted to
her family, Crystal dedicated the next stage in life to herself.[3]

Baby boom mothers like Crystal and Gail began their odysseys before
the feminist revival, but their return to work and school and the empty
nest coincided with its flowering. Interviews from 1958 to 1982 indicate
that in their late thirties and early forties, as they looked forward to the
end of intensive nurturing, women of this generation began to reconsider
the assumptions they had made about female identity as young women.
For example, Blanch Warner commented, "'Mother' is a fine thing but I

don't think it's a glamorous institution in itself." She objected to her husband seeing her only in that light. And she admired younger women because, "They're stressing more being an individual and a person who may have feelings and rights."[4]

Midlife women took on new roles or modified old ones as they responded to both their evolving position in life and new ideas about women's needs circulating throughout American society. Employment, the empty nest, and marital disruption increased the likelihood that baby boom mothers had experiences outside of marriage and domesticity in later life even though these themes had dominated their early adulthood. This broader base of experience in later stages of the family cycle contains clues to the complicated response of this generation to feminism.[5]

Mothers of the baby boomers contributed to social change early on by shaping their daughters' life plans. In their homes, they served as models, to adolescent and college-age daughters, of women who successfully combined work and children over the life course and juggled homemaking and jobs while they were employed. In addition, mothers of the baby boom consciously groomed their daughters to make choices different from those they themselves had made. They hoped their daughters would marry at later ages and form equitable partnerships when they did wed. Furthermore, they actively encouraged baby boom girls to pursue college educations, and after that, careers.[6]

They raised their daughters with broader opportunities in mind. Sally Williams guided hers to "expect to do anything that [they] wanted to do. I did not feel that because she was a woman she should have role limitations. . . . I really do feel that I did suffer from that." They refused to bequeath the constraints womanhood conferred on them to their daughters. Blanch Warner's ambitions for her daughters included hoping that "they can make some impression or contribution to the world. . . . I want them to have some goal in life besides being a housewife. I'd like to see them make a living so the house isn't the end of all things." Hopes for their daughters contradicted the expectations for women of this generation.[7]

For example, in 1958, Thelma Morton summed up her plans for her daughters—education, occupation, a family—but most important: "I want them to have something, to be more independent than I was." All she wanted for her daughters was a good deal more than had been available to Thelma herself. May Perkins, in 1957, said, "I sure don't want [her] to turn out to be just a housewife like myself." Their expectations for daughters still included family and motherhood, but with differing timetables and without the exclusivity of focus that had dominated the early years of their adulthood.[8]

Because many had aborted or rejected careers and education in order to marry young, mothers of the baby boom had not lived independently as adults. When Marlene Hill, whose first marriage had rapidly disintegrated, was asked what she hoped her children would avoid, she said, "An early marriage." In 1970 Crystal Robertson said, "I still would be disappointed if they got married the day they got out of high school and found themselves in the nest and [were] just a nice little housewife." When the female baby boomers delayed marriage, it was not just that they were rejecting the choices of their mothers, as so many historians have asserted, but they also acted out new life plans that their mothers fostered.[9]

One message midlife mothers conveyed by example was that work could be combined with family life. Yet they encouraged variations on their own sequential pattern for their daughters. Olivia Adams thought, "Every girl should have a period in her life where she can be independent and self-sufficient and make a contribution." Doris Jenkins explained, "We've discussed it and you can mix a marriage and a career, I think, very agreeably and wait to have your family because you're younger for a lot longer than you think." They urged that their daughters not start a family immediately after marrying. Sylvia Gould's aspirations for her daughters were, "I want them to have a life where they have an interesting job. I do think that women require a job outlet as well as a home and family." The mothers of the baby boom advocated a life plan for women that included a period of independence prior to marriage. The pattern they envisioned is one common today: work, then marriage and employment, followed by motherhood, then by employed motherhood.[10]

They expected their daughters to support themselves. They assumed, however, that employment would be secondary once their daughters began to raise children. Laura Gilbert worked before marriage and said in 1970 that she would not go back to work because she was "too lazy." Nevertheless, she wanted her daughters to have a skill and work experience that they could rely on, too. If a daughter were widowed she said, "She'd need something to fall back on, something she can do to support herself. . . . We call it an insurance policy."[11]

Relatively secure in marriage and supported by their husbands, mothers of the baby boom still felt economically dependent and hoped work experience or professional training would confer the independence that they had missed on their daughters. They spoke of jobs as "insurance" and "just in case" at the same time that work was becoming more and more a certainty in women's lives, and they were helping to make that so. Those who did not work conveyed their message to daughters with added urgency. Nina Harris stressed the importance of a career to her daughters. She said that she had worried because, "I couldn't run out and get a job if I had to, or a good paying one, one that would take care of the kids." In response, she stressed that her daughters "at least . . . get something behind them . . . if they ever have to work or wanted to work, which I think they should for a while anyway when they get out of school." Harris wanted her daughters to escape the dependency she had experienced as a full-time homemaker. She took her own advice and went to work.[12]

Mothers endorsed their daughters' opportunities for fulfillment outside the home—choices they themselves had only later in life. Barbara Spalding said that she was encouraging her daughter to have a career: "Because it's a full life." She contrasted this with her own experiences wherein, "You prime a girl for getting married because it's a happier situation, a more complete person. And once she gets married and has one or two children or three . . . there's sort of a let down. And she realizes that there's more to life than the wants of others. Just [to] dedicate herself to her children and her husband isn't enough. She has to be an individual herself."[13]

Connie Small used herself as a counterexample for her daughters. She didn't want them to "end up" like her: "I think everybody should have something besides another person. In other words, I made another person my career, which is very wrong. . . . I always should have had something that was just me and not completely wrapped my entire life up in a man." Connie and her husband were discussing divorce; this confronted her with her economic as well as her emotional vulnerability, a situation she hoped her daughters could avoid. Based on personal experience, mothers of the baby boom warned their daughters not to center their lives exclusively around husband and family.[14]

Their mothers' message did get through to the women of the baby boom. Crystal Robertson said of her daughter with pride, "I think she's just a super person because she's a woman I would have liked to have been, combining motherhood, being a wife and having a part-time career." After her daughter graduated from college May Perkins learned where the perseverance to finish that degree came from. Perkins recounted, "She told me after she graduated, that she many times wanted to give it up, but that I wanted it so badly that she went through it." Clearly mothers of the 1950s proved to be more than just counterexamples to the next generation of women.[15]

While they affirmed the plethora of opportunities opening for their daughters, many of them the result of feminist activism, they remained dubious of sweeping feminist reform. As we saw in chapter 2, even as they shaped the next generation of women, many women actively reshaped their own lives, often through employment. Mothers of the baby boom's most committed working years coincided with the peak years of the feminist movement, the late 1960s to the mid-1970s. Decades of intensive mothering and the increasingly empty nest meant these midlife women greeted mainstream feminist demands with mixed feelings in the 1970s. They approved calls for expanded roles outside the home and workplace equity. Yet they had strong reservations about the more "radical" ideas within the movement. While more egalitarian sex role attitudes had been evolving since the mid-1960s, the pace of change in attitudes accelerated after the 1970s, when feminism claimed center stage. IHD women joined women nationwide in supporting the notions of shared housework, working mothers, equal opportunity, and "the possibility of a full life for women outside of marriage." Nevertheless, American women reported a "continued predominance of support for the basic sex division of labor." Midlife women's objections were twofold: ideological and practical.[16]

On an ideological level, the "zap" tactics of radical feminist activists and their negative portrayal in the press stirred discomfort among women who identified heavily with their family roles. Demonstrations that poked fun at the trappings of femininity alienated these older women. Grace Owens could agree with feminist claims while distancing herself from the protesters. "Some of the exponents are rather weird themselves," she observed, but, she admitted, there was justification for their protests: "There probably isn't the equality and choice of careers and salary." Not only that, but she had read *The Feminine Mystique* and "got really kind of excited about it." The angry confrontation of protest, which they perceived as unfeminine, diminished a sense of connection with younger, more radical, feminist women but not with the basic justice of their message. It may also have been the collective protest itself, in addition to the confrontational form that radical feminist actions took that put off this generation. For example in a 1972 poll of the American electorate, 79 percent saw individual training and achievement as the best path to ending sexual inequality, while only 21 percent preferred the strategy of collective action. By 1972 most Americans were weary of disruptive demonstrations for equality, even for causes they considered just.[17]

Other women were far more hesitant than Owens to support the tenets of feminism apart from feminist demonstrations, although they expressed ideas in concert with new roles for women. Feminists, according to Doris Jenkins, were "out for a lot of attention." While she could encourage her daughters to pursue careers, from her perspective, "There shouldn't be equality. . . . This unisex business is not for me. I don't want equality. And I don't think any real female does. They want to be treated as a female, no matter how much they cry about equality." Jenkins interpreted calls for equality as a leveling of sexual differences. She did not want to be treated as a man. Her concerns echo in the interviews with other IHD women and men as well.[18]

Once the nation began to debate the ERA, the definition of equality was up for grabs. Both liberal and radical feminists failed to define it adequately for mainstream women. Opponents of the movement defined it for many when they argued: Feminism and equal rights unsexed women and denied motherhood. This generation feared equality meant not only disadvantage on an unequal playing field, but a loss of femininity. They approved feminist principles only so long as the practices of femininity escaped alteration.

Feminism struck at core fears. While feminists might promise a more equitable future to young women with education and ambition, financially dependent, midlife women with decades out of the labor force or part-time or pink-collar jobs behind them had much to lose. They feared economic ruin. Women who had married under one set of assumptions wondered if feminist reforms meant they would have to reconfigure their marriages. Connie Small, in the midst of marital strife and watching her daughters enter high school, continued to uphold the precepts of womanhood that had guided her since she was a girl. Asked about women's equality, she replied, "Well, wait till they get it. Wait till they find out, 'Oh yeah, I'll marry you but you still have to bring in just as much money as I do.'" She preferred to be supported by a breadwinning husband. In her estimation "what a woman's got to do" was "be [a] helpmate. If this is all going to leave now and every woman is going to have to make her own way and be completely independent and earn her own living and all this then I won't like being a woman." Connie's response was directly related to the precarious state of her marriage. She faced just such a transition, with or without feminism. Given their lack of training and female niche in the workforce, many women of this generation doubted that they could support themselves, let alone their children, if they had to. Their interpretation of feminism, shaped by the media, made their dependent positions seem all the more precarious, and they blamed the movement itself instead of the structural inequalities that feminists criticized. Their marriages had protected them from the worst of the inequalities outside the home, and in exchange they had accepted many of the inequalities within it.[19]

Harris polls of women's opinions in 1971 and 1972 showed that among women 40 to 49, the approximate age of IHD women in 1971, support for "efforts to strengthen or change women's status" was at 39 percent. While not a majority, the measure of support is higher than media coverage in the 1970s would lead one to expect. The very next year, that percentage had increased to 42 percent and to nearly half for women who were between the ages of 30 and 39. As sociologist Jessie Bernard concluded, "Although in cross-section, the older women were uniformly more conservative than the younger, they had changed in a modern, rather than in a traditional, direction." Still, it was women in the 40–49 age range in 1972 who had the greatest affinity for traditional marital roles. Sixty-one percent of those polled agreed with the phrase "Want husband to take care of me," compared to 50 percent of those aged 18–29. Midlife women were fence sitters. Public equality they could safely endorse, but they did so without rejecting traditional roles within the private sphere.[20]

Marriage, motherhood, homemaking, femininity—all appeared under attack. Negative media coverage of women's rights issues and antifeminists seeking to discredit the Equal Rights Amendment exacerbated their reservations. Practical concerns raised by feminism and its popular portrayal as antagonistic to family life lay behind their ambivalent response to the radical branch of the movement. They held no truck with what they saw as androgyny, worried that women would lose the privileges of protection, and voiced concern over their own economic survival. In the early 1970s then, feminism symbolized a threat to midlife women. Yet even as they dismissed that which threatened them, they embraced the new opportunities opening around them. The public-private split in views toward feminism exhibited by IHD women was consistent with a survey of women's attitudes. Karen Oppenheim Mason and Larry L. Bumpass found women's attitudes "to be partly organized according to a core ideology regarding the basic division of labor between women and men and a secondary ideology regarding women's labor market rights. As of 1970, most women lean toward the more traditional pole of the first dimension and toward the more egalitarian pole of the second."[21]

This generation continued to respond to the passage of time, feminist gains, and work experience through the 1970s. At the last interview, in 1982, the Institute of Human Development specifically asked participants for their views on, as they put it, "the movement to change women's roles." More than half were, at a minimum, in favor of equal pay for equal work, generally in favor of the woman's movement, or extremely supportive the movement. The answers reveal a continued ambivalence around the meaning of equality, concern over the issue of motherhood, and a stirring embrace of the new patterns their daughters created.

Let's pick up Connie Small's story. In 1970 she vehemently disavowed feminism, wanting no part of a movement that might deny her lifelong role as a "helpmate." But within a few months of that interview her husband filed for divorce, beating feminism to the chase; she was no longer his helpmate or dependent. Riddled with self-doubt, she feared having to become self-supporting when her identity as a homemaker went up in smoke. Someone suggested she find a consciousness-raising group. Connie followed this advice and joined "this group I just found in the paper. . . . We met every single week and everybody took turns sharing their thing. And they were the most supportive group I've ever been with. . . . Everybody gave love back to the others and made everyone feel 'you're all right . . . You're a fine person.'" In her consciousness-raising group, Connie found encouragement to transform her homemaking and home renovation skills into more than an avocation. In the early 1980s she led docent tours, became an expert in regional horticulture, and taught classes in design. Despite all her accumulated expertise, Connie had not completely revised her view of her family role. She struck a bargain with her second husband. In return for full financial support, she would keep her outside interests from impinging on the homemaking services she happily provided. But Connie had shifted in a very crucial way: "Now, I would never let myself feel that I had to depend on somebody else." She maintained an active role outside the home. She would not have called herself a feminist, but feminism, and, at a crucial juncture in her life, a supportive women's group, had contributed to her new identity. This divided response to feminism was not uncommon. While divorced women were "more likely to espouse equal rights in the labor market," they tended "to be more supportive of traditional roles" in marriage, according to one study.[22]

Two beliefs underwrote the ambivalent response of midlife women to the women's movement: a profound commitment to motherhood and an enduring faith in the ethic of individualism. When mothers of the baby boom expressed reservations about the gains of the women's movement, they worried about the place of childrearing in women's lives and what they perceived as a loss of femininity—concerns first raised in the 1970s. They remained unwilling to rethink gender identity despite their hopes for public equality. Pro- and anti-feminist women shared concern about childrearing. After her children were born Mary Smith earned a degree, then once her children were in school all day, worked full-time. She saw herself as an "aberration," someone who had "done it already," that is, been a liberated woman. Still, she concluded, "I think in some cases women are trying too hard to be both and they're going to lose their parenthood in the shuffle if they're not careful." These views speak to the way this generation organized their lives, making room for work as a family obligation, or after family obligations were fulfilled.[23]

Another concern was what one woman called "the little courtesies in life." Barbara Clinton, while believing in "equal pay for equal work," still liked "to have the feminine amenities that a man accords a woman." Feminism and employment opportunities offered women unprecedented options but with no guarantees. For this generation of women, the symbolic privileges that to younger feminists indicated women's inferior status continued to hold great meaning, connoting protection as well as respect.[24]

Yet several believed that in small but significant ways their lives and marriages had been transformed by the movement. Although Virginia Walker felt the movement came along "a little too late" to change her very much, and she characterized much of it as "a big mistake" largely because of her concern for childrearing, she did take one small step sanctioned by feminists. "I sign my name now Virginia instead of Mrs. Adam Walker." Roberta Johnson conceded the movement might have affected her marriage "a little bit." Now, she reported, "I'm not so meek. I just stand up for my rights." To Alice Bremmer it bequeathed "the courage to do what I want." Martha Bentley also attributed her burgeoning outspokenness to the movement, stating, "I can stand up and speak out and not be a dowdy little old housewife."[25]

"The women's movement," said Crystal Robertson, "made me see myself as an individual with capabilities. I've gone out, I've gone back to school. I've proved to myself I can do things." Robertson's life history brings up an aspect of postwar women's lives: the reentry education movement. For women like Crystal, it could be just as empowering as employment. For others it was a stepping-stone to employment. Approximately one quarter of the women in my sample went back to school between 1960 and 1980. For many of them it was a chance to do something for themselves after years of service to others. Rita Frank explained, "I thought you got married and lived happily ever after with your family. . . . then, you see other opportunities. I thought 'Hey.'" And she went back to school. As Helen Evans put it, "It all gets back to your basic housekeeping. I much prefer going to classes if the truth be known."[26]

While they may not have directly credited feminism with the change, the convergence of the movement and midlife allowed for new insights. Patricia James said, "I've been a superhuman therapeutic mommy to all my children, one of them my husband, and it's been terrible getting out of that. . . . I don't want to be a mommy to anybody anymore." Both Janice Rogers and May Perkins said that if they had to live their lives over again, they would incorporate "something" or "stimulation" outside of the family. At midlife, mothers of the baby boom challenged the life of total domesticity—responding to their own life history and the movement's ideological validation of the challenge.[27]

Even such seemingly infinitesimal changes in attitude could send shockwaves through marriage, and did. As they had throughout their marriages, couples drew and redrew gender rules as their lives evolved. Laura Gilbert believed the movement going on outside her marriage altered the dynamics within it. It "did something" to her husband, she said. "He keeps throwing at me, 'Ever since you've been on this ERA kick.'" But Laura felt that she had always carried herself the same way: "I support ERA but I haven't been throwing it around much. He feels it's threatening." And indeed women's new attitudes could threaten marriage relationships.[28]

Women who spoke out more questioned their husbands and asserted their own opinions. Opening the door to feminism meant opening a door to conflicts. Decisions, housework, women's employment were all up for discussion and argument now. Feminism initiated Crystal Robertson's "involvement in other interests," besides her husband and children. From there it was a short step to "physical" and "emotional" problems for her husband. She placed studying for her exams above cooking dinner, for one thing, which he found "an inconvenience." And in addition, accustomed to being the center of their wives' attention, husbands like Ben Robertson felt displaced when their wives turned their sights outward. Crystal related that "He's felt really unloved because I've been studying." While husbands could interpret such changes negatively, the net impact on the marriage was not necessarily deleterious. Blanche Warner reported that when she "got caught up with this women's rights thing," she became more conscious of how difficult her homemaking tasks were to accomplish. The resulting give and take made her marriage "more equal." Nor was Blanch "passive" any longer. She saw a net improvement when she got out and did "her own thing," a development she attributed to the women's movement.[29]

Men also acknowledged the women's movement's impact on their marriages. Leonard Stone believed his second marriage showed the effects of the movement. He described his new wife as "freer," saying, she "doesn't feel she has to cook meals every night." But Betty Stone did not see the freedom in her marriage as a done deal and instead depicted it as an ongoing problem. While he knew how important going back to school to earn her degree was, she still got "static" about it. In fact, she worked hard to "compensate for going to school," leaving "better" meals behind in the refrigerator on class nights. Leonard, apparently talked a good game and recognized the importance of increased latitude for women in marriage but had great difficulty relaxing his habits of entitlement and domination—habits his first wife had silently accommodated until she divorced him.[30]

Tom Fisher felt that the movement had a salutary impact on his marriage and those of his friends. Feminism had, he said, "Caused myself and the men that I know that are married . . . to realize that the woman has a lot more to offer than they thought. They're able to do just about anything a man can do, sometimes a lot better." This realization was important because "being more on an even status" brought them "closer together." For Norman Smith, the women's movement meant that while he did not do "a lot" around the house, he did "do more than I used to." And if not fully in practice, in principle, he agreed that "men should do some of the work" at home.[31]

Two men insisted that the reason the movement had not changed their marriages was that they had shaped egalitarian relationships with their wives from the beginning. Albert Morton asserted, "I married the original women's libber. . . . My wife is a very, not in a derogatory sense, but a very strong-willed person. She has her ideas of what her rights are, how she should be treated. . . . So I'm a very strong supporter of women's lib." Some elements of the movement seemed old hat to Hank Jones because "we've been practicing all the time . . . sharing the work. I never expected her to be a full-time housewife and mother." The IHD's question prompted him to think a bit more deeply about how much they shared the work. Although each pitched in, he admitted, it was along traditionally defined gender lines: "Definitely around our house we have different things that we each do. She never mows the lawn, for example, and I never cook dinner." As Hank acknowledged, the private implications of women's liberation were difficult to measure and to apply.[32]

In fact when it came to the private sphere, like the women of this generation, the men expressed concern for the preservation of gender difference, and even gender dominance. Gary Simon, who could affirm the justice behind feminist claims for change in the public sphere drew a line when it came to marriages. He said, "It's hard for me to see a marriage surviving when woman becomes the dominant force." Feminism implied a complete reversal rather than a redistribution of marital power from Simon's perspective. Similarly, Scott Clinton insisted that "someone has to be the head of any group of people" and it was more "healthful" if that someone was "the man." He objected to the private ramifications of feminism, saying, "If I were twenty years old, I wouldn't want to put on an apron and do the dishes . . . and raise the children . . . nor would my wife want to go out and bring in the money and fight all the stress that a man has."[33]

Nevertheless, in the same breath, Clinton could also say, "I'm very much for women's rights." What this translated to was "They should have equal pay for equal work and so on." "Equal pay for equal work," as Dennis Perkins put it, "Nobody will argue with that." Indeed, only a few men found much to quibble over when it came to rights and fairness-based arguments about opportunity and discrimination in the public sphere. Rodney Scott said, "I'm for ERA. I think women should be looked upon more as equals than they have been. I'm glad to see when a woman gets to a position in management on the same level with men." Like their wives, the challenge, as these men saw it, was how to provide equality of opportunity outside the home without impinging on traditional notions of masculinity and femininity within. They ignored the deep connections between cultural assumptions about gender and the division of labor in private life and structural inequalities in public life, which feminists strived to unravel and expose.[34]

While supporting public equality, men too remained invested in gendered notions of civility and protection. Victor Gilbert favored "anybody being compensated and rewarded and promoted on ability," and "the movement" but disliked "the loud ones" who agitated for more disruptive changes. From Murray Borden's perspective, in the quest for equality women had given up "an awful lot." He continued, "We used to open doors and carry them over the threshold. Now, they're equal so they open their own damned door or they walk across the threshold themselves." These men, like their wives held on to the "common courtesies." But they maintained that equality and gender distinctions could go hand in hand. Fred Adams averred, "Women don't want to be treated like men and men don't want to treat them like men. That doesn't mean they shouldn't be treated equally." Interestingly in the Harris polls from the early 1970s both men's support for changes in women's status and sympathy for women's liberation outweighed women's by as much as six percentage points.[35]

Whether they dismissed or affirmed the women's movement, the parents of the baby boom sided definitively with individualism. They believed firmly in the American ethic of equality of opportunity, an ideology they could support much more enthusiastically than the ERA, which they feared tampered too much with the equality of results. A blanket law, they feared, might sweep away individual choice. Diane Key, who nurtured her part-time career along with her growing children, distanced herself from the liberation movement: "I am a person. I'm accepted . . . at [work] or in my home as an individual who has ideas and yet she's a feminine individual." Irene Lawrence defined herself as an "independent woman" so much so that she had no need of an equal rights amendment. She insisted, "Everything I've ever wanted to do, it didn't make any difference whether I was male or female, I did what I wanted to do." Connie Douglas expressed similar sentiments. She believed in "equal treatment." She "came up when women were nothing." But on the other hand she said emphatically, "I don't think I need an edict that says I have equal opportunity. I think I have it and if I'm going to let somebody take it away from me maybe I shouldn't have it." This divided approach to feminist change is reflected in a 1972 poll of women's opinion. Women responded more favorably to the statement that they favored "efforts to strengthen women's status in society" than they did to the statement that they were "sympathetic with the efforts of women's liberation groups." Since the phrase women's liberation was associated with radical feminism, we can assume that even ten years later the threat to marriage symbolized by women's liberation limited support, while few questioned the more general principle of equality.[36]

A combination of work experience and belief in individualism spurred one woman to criticize the women's liberation movement, saying, "I don't really think they know what they're doing." Her skepticism stemmed from a recent experience during a temporary job where she observed women who had to lift heavy packages. When she asked why she was told, "We don't discriminate." Equality portended heavy physical labor from which women would be unable to claim exemption. She acknowledged that women faced inequality when it came to pay. Although a firm supporter of the social movement for civil rights, she did not think that a similar movement would benefit women. She fell back on individualism in her explanation. "I think it should be up to the woman because they might just throw everybody in one category and say, 'Okay, you're along with the men and go along and do it.'" Ten years later, after she had gone back to school and earned two degrees, she still mistrusted feminist demands. In fact, her work experience convinced her that women just should not perform certain tasks.[37]

Her detachment from the movement had much to do with both her class and race identity. As a member of a minority who alongside her husband, despite discrimination and racism, had obtained middle-class status, personal experience reaffirmed her faith in individualism. She also had a jaundiced view of feminists' demand for the "right" to work. She said, "The world of the [minority] woman has always been somewhat different, and so one of the things that they are striving for in coming into their own right, we've been there." She went on to elaborate, "We've never been put in the role of a nice little feminine woman who stayed home and took care of her kids and belonged to this or that organization." Perceptions of feminism as focused on the privileged complaints of middle-class women alienated her.[38]

On the whole, experience as working women made this cohort enthusiastic supporters of the feminist demand of equal pay for equal work. Marlene Hill said, "I want equal pay for equal work. Forget all the rest of the jazz." She had begun her career in an all-male field during World War II and faced sexism on the job. As she put it, "I had a man's job before Women's Lib." But in her opinion further changes both within and outside the workplace would take care of themselves. The successes these women had at crafting more equitable marriages, making their way into formerly male professions, or transforming themselves from housewives to part- or full-time workers, were, they believed, individual ones. The feminist movement helped make the changes these women effected possible in part by raising the nation's consciousness, and their own, of what women were capable of and entitled to. In this way, the movement's overall success dulled its ability to continue to attract an active constituency. From each individual woman's perspective these private improvements did not require their public activism to be achieved or maintained. Of course, without a large and vocal social movement for not just women's rights but more far-reaching gender reform, structural inequalities would remain intransigent.[39]

Yet a handful women of this generation felt that they had directly contributed to the women's movement or benefited from its advances. A few years younger than Betty Friedan, they charted similar life courses. Gail Henderson, who trained to become a professional in the mid-1960s, identified strongly with the women's movement. In 1982 she said, "I have been a part of the whole movement by moving out and becoming a part of the workforce. I am very conscious of any kind of sexism or discrimination against women, particularly when it affects me. I will often call my husband on it when he makes a sexist remark, whether it has to do with me or not." Alice Bremmer challenged the definition of a breadwinner when the state denied her unemployment compensation, assuming that as a woman she was not the provider in her family. In reality, her husband had long since sold his small business at the time of her layoff. She said, "So I got to thinking, I was a breadwinner. I was working full-time. My husband wasn't. He wasn't working at all. So I wrote back and told them that . . . so they had to give it to me." She also confronted prejudice as she ran her own small business. She said, "In the business I am in and dealing with men, you can feel a prejudice against older women and I feel it lots of times. I feel angry about it. It is like not giving someone a chance, prejudging." Vehemently she said, "I hate to feel the prejudice people have against older women, that an older woman has no brains." Working, midlife women became less likely to ignore obstacles and slights and more cognizant that the women's movement provided resources, support, and precedent for protest.[40]

From a temporary employee, Lois Dyer, whom we first met in the Introduction, had worked her way up to a position of authority in a large corporation, replacing her former supervisor: "Now I have his chair, his desk. I have his responsibility. I don't have his title. I don't have his money and I don't have a promotion." Working impressed women like Dyer with the fact that there were inequalities and discrimination to fight against. Struggling to achieve the title and salary, which she believed should accompany her new job responsibilities, Dyer felt very much a part of the movement. She described herself as "depressed" at the ways women were "underrated in corporate life." She said, "Women could move backward very easily. It's a very very important time for the women's movement. I recognize that, because I'm right in the middle of it." She set her sights on securing the new title and higher salary befitting her job description and sought out a professional women's support group where she could "talk about how upset I am about the women's movement with other people." Still fighting against persistent prejudice, Dyer feared the gains of the 1970s had stalled. But she was eager to respond to the problem with feminist activism. Dyer, like many of the women in this study, was drawn into employment by financial need, which fostered a long-term commitment to both employment and a career. Dyer's experience illustrates political scientist Ethel Klein's finding that once women "entered the labor force, they learned that they were capable workers who were not given the same opportunities as were men, and they embraced feminism." Dyer questioned domesticity, augmented it with employment, and became a feminist as a result.[41]

Dyer was correct; women were in danger of moving backward in the early 1980s. Ronald Reagan was swept into office on a sea of votes from the new and Christian right. And in 1982, the ERA, which so many of the parents of the baby boom endorsed in principle, went down in defeat. The amendment died in spite of support for the spirit of equality and in spite of the increasing employment of married women. This was so largely because the political right had successfully characterized ERA as destructive to both femininity and the family. ERA became a national referendum for responses to sweeping gender role change since the 1960s.[42]

In fact the most visible result of changes within the middle-class family, working mothers, came to symbolize what had gone wrong with the nation in the four decades since World War II. IHD participant Steven Downs hated "to see what's gonna happen in this country" because working mothers placed children in day-care centers. Ignoring structural explanations, he went on to blame economic difficulties and inflation on working mothers, "That's created . . . the high cost of living nowadays . . . this double income family, and banks loaning money because of two incomes, so that the whole price of housing has gone up." But as other baby boom families had found, two incomes had made surviving in an inflationary economy easier and this and other changes in gender roles had been permanently interwoven into middle-class life. Rick Snyder welcomed the changes in women's role, saying, "Today, it takes two people to work to survive. Women should be recognized as a force with independence." "I'm not a women's libber, but not a male chauvinist," he explained, "Women's lives have been ignored too long in [terms of] their desires."[43]

Assessing the world she'd helped reshape, Alice Bremmer felt lucky to live in an era "in this time when it is accepted that a woman has her life too, not just devote life to husband and family." Others celebrated new options that they themselves could not fully enjoy. Charlotte Thompkins appreciated the changes in women's lives since the 1940s. In 1982, she said, "When I got married . . . you lost all of your identity. But that's not true today. You're not a man's property because you got married." And Milly Benson said of the women's movement, "I'm all for it. Well . . . when you have daughters and you see them becoming independent and having lives of their own without needing a man to look after them, it's a good feeling." Lisa Sims summed up the viewpoint of many of her generational "sisters." She simultaneously affirmed the privileges of femininity, eschewed social activism, and yet enthusiastically condoned the changes in women's lives that feminism made possible. She said, "It's a great thing. I wish I were young now. I wouldn't be a demonstrator and I like having a door opened but to be able to do whatever you want would be fantastic." They admired younger women's self-sufficiency and envied their opportunities. But Crystal Robertson, an ardent supporter of women's liberation, did have one criticism of the next generation: She wished her daughters' age group were "a little bit more feminist."[44]

To the extent that feminist goals reflected their individual experiences, the parents of the baby boom responded supportively even as they defended their notions of femininity from what they perceived as attack. Michelle Anderson, who in the 1970s had her sights on a position no woman had ever filled at her company, nonetheless, said "I have a t-shirt that says, 'The best man for the job is a woman.' But I'm not a women's libber, okay? Some of the stuff they're going after, I just wish they'd leave it alone. I think that women are losing out a lot by trying to be macho. And I just don't go for that. I still like to be treated as a lady. I still like to have the door opened for me."[45]

A generation of "ladies" who preferred that gentlemen open doors for them themselves opened "doors" for women. Rejecting far-reaching transformation of gender roles, this generation of women nonetheless transformed both family life and the makeup of the workforce. They also passed on an important legacy to their daughters, helping to shape the younger generation's attitude toward work and marriage. Bothered by their own lack of financial independence during their childrearing years, and for the most part relegated to working in pink-collar positions, they encouraged their daughters to pursue careers and professional training, urging them to postpone marriage until later in life. Most historians have portrayed mothers of the 1950s as negative influences on their daughters, largely drawing on the impressionistic accounts of daughters who were attracted to feminism and wary of domesticity in the 1960s. Examining this older generation's voices reveals that the ambitious aspirations of baby boomer women had more complex roots: in both the discontent they observed *and* the encouragement they received from their mothers.[46]

The anti-feminist homemaker is as much a stereotype as the bra-burning women's libber. The "macho" media image of feminism's radical branch overshadowed the contributions that radicals actually made to the women's movement. For example, few thought to mention the women's health movement, abortion rights, or rape crisis centers—all contributions of the radical feminists that went mainstream—when they discussed the movement. Despite these oversights, there were generational and experiential ties in addition to the more obvious differences between young feminists and suburban housewives. Many a fifties housewife raised feminist daughters and supported rights-based arguments for reform.[47]

For women whose only access to movement thought was the media, what exactly the demand for equality meant remained unclear. It was one thing to demand equal opportunity and another entirely to proclaim the end of all gender difference. How much change would feminism entail? How would these changes affect them? Economic and structural discrimination outside the home, any grievous imbalances within the home, these mothers of the baby boom deemed appropriate targets for reform. But feminist critiques of marriage, gender roles, and sexual relationships coupled with the perception of militant feminism as unfeminine made them uncomfortable, and in some cases defensive. They did not wish to see femininity changed and worried that a brave new feminist world offered even fewer protections for mothers and children than the world that they had known. They lauded their own and their daughters' opportunities and life choices while remaining skeptical of more fundamental feminist change. Their response to feminism illustrates the irreversible social changes that spawned and supported the groundswell of feminism in the 1970s and raises key questions about the meaning of women's family roles and the value of childrearing to society that Americans still have not fully addressed and feminists still struggle to solve.

Epilogue

Today, the harmonious marriages of popular sitcoms of the fifties—*Father Knows Best, Ozzie and Harriet, Leave It to Beaver*—shape the image of the 1950s family. Thanks in part to endless reruns on nostalgia cable television channels, an idyllic model of family life based on a male breadwinner and a stay-at-home female homemaker and their two or three children has come to symbolize the decade and filter contemporary debate about family policy and family values. Conservative politicians and social critics harken back to an idealized time before the sexual and divorce revolutions and the women's movement, searching for a golden age of American family life. Although grounded in historical fact, stereotypical fifties characteristics— large families, lower divorce rates, and a strict division of family labor— have become the standards by which the "decline" of the American family since the sixties is measured. This politically convenient and nostalgic image obscures more than it illuminates about postwar family life and the changes that have occurred in the past 40 years. A closer look has shown that beneath the patina of fifties nostalgia lurks subterranean evidence of significant innovation. Even in the 1950s, saccharine sitcoms masked the dynamic quality of American families.[1]

The baby boomers' parents transformed American family life, playing a key role in postwar social change. They did not disrupt fundamental assumptions about the division of labor, but they did create a more egalitarian marriage pattern, pioneering changes in men's and women's family roles. Along the way, they struggled to come to terms with the increasing instability of American marriage exacerbated by the contradictory tensions of togetherness and the heightening expectations of the sexual revolution and feminism. They changed American family life incrementally and fundamentally.

As we have seen, the particular life course of the parents of the baby boom shaped the changes that they made. Youthful marriage and parenthood, novel in themselves, were responsible for many of the innovations I have pinpointed. By collapsing these experiences into a brief period in their early twenties, this generation created the preconditions for massive social change while simultaneously giving the outward appearance of a traditional family structure. Only by using a longitudinal, cohort-based analysis does this process of social change become apparent.

Youthful marriage and parenthood required economic cooperation between husbands and wives. The concentration of childbearing and raising into roughly a fifteen-year span placed demands on young parents that spawned collaboration. While women continued to contribute to the emotional content and physical upkeep of the American home, the economic contributions women made also altered family life. The exigencies of intense mothering set women's sights beyond the home as they looked forward to release from the requirements of full-time childrearing. Later in the family cycle, financial need reinforced their search for roles apart from motherhood. Women's work outside the home called into question their complete responsibility for the work inside the home and gave women a greater voice in families. It also dramatically altered what had been a truism of marriage—women's economic dependence. Their paychecks permitted more autonomy in marriage and the possibility of life outside of it. Feminism legitimated these pursuits and arose in part because of the transformation in the labor force and family life this generation of women helped enact. Postwar middle-class women initiated the expansion of both women's economic and men's parenting roles in the middle-class family.

Men, often at the urging of their wives, took greater part in raising children after World War II. Greater did not mean equal. Indeed, it might not necessarily mean enough, even judged by men's own expectations. Commitment to work, distaste for the messier aspects of child care, and faith in their wives' maternal capabilities all limited the extent of their participation. Yet, as experts enshrined the psychological and emotional importance of fathers to children, women imported these ideas to the family and mixed in some of their own. A generation of men who worked hard to support their families and who tried to be more involved with their children than their own fathers had been, later wondered if they had failed both their children and themselves by focusing so intently on work and careers. By inviting men to become part of childrearing, baby boom families grappled with work and family as a dilemma for men. Women proved instrumental in shaping the hopes and managing the disappointments of postwar fatherhood.

Hopes and disappointments also accompanied the postwar notion of togetherness. With this concept, Americans attempted to grapple with the challenges of large families that competed with the notion of companionable companionate marriages. This was a notion thoroughly grounded in the context of the Cold War, the baby boom, and the early stages of the family cycle. Encouraged to find satisfaction and fulfillment in activity with the whole family together, couples wondered first where the romance in marriage went and then how to get it back once the kids were gone. With their early marriages, this generation also spent a considerably longer portion of their lives together once their children were grown than previous generations of Americans had. Sustaining companionship in the context of child-centered demands of the youthful family-building years, the empty nest, lengthening life spans, and the divorce and sexual revolutions of the 1960s and 1970s proved difficult, especially as aging couples sought to balance interdependence and individual independence.

Autonomy in the bedroom was another matter, the postwar generation found. Often, burdensomely high expectations prompted sexual frustration. Certainly, as the private revelations from the 1950s make clear, the broader public revolution in sexual discourse of the 1960s did much to diminish the significant hangover of ignorance that plagued many couples. But the accelerating aspirations of sexual liberation attended the broadening of sexual knowledge. Once endowed with lofty erotic expectations, the baby boom's parents managed the resulting dissatisfactions with variable success. Most difficult of all the experts' edicts to adopt was the one demanding emotional intimacy. Accepting and accommodating disappointment appeared a safer route than exposing emotional vulnerability. But while couples may not have achieved the projected heights of erotic delight, many women at least did apply new sexual rights by ending sexual relationships they found dissatisfying while remaining committed to their marriages. And this is sobering evidence of increasing mutuality in marriage. Husbands and wives abided by their spouses' wishes to discontinue or diminish the sexual side of marriage. In so doing, this generation proved the "sexperts" wrong. Modern, sound marriages did not necessarily depend on great sex for survival. And saying too much was in some cases as damaging as saying too little.

Divorce, always a presence in American family life, was an increasing possibility as a result of the liberalization of divorce codes and married women's participation in the labor market. Its presence in the lives of this generation speaks to an increasing negotiability of marriage, probably symptomatic of the increasing negotiations going on within marriage. In such arguments marriage itself became a bargaining chip. Although 24 percent of the couples in this sample ultimately divorced, the majority found a way to "make marriage work." Those who divorced, a few more than once, for the most part, opted out of one marriage hoping for happiness in the next.

The timing of divorce in the lives of the parents of the baby boom speaks to the importance of cohort analysis. The baby boomers' parents encountered and participated in the divorce revolution at a crucial stage of the family cycle. Most couples divorced after the baby boomers reached the teen years. The empty nest also coincided with the feminist movement, married women's labor-force participation, and early seventies notions of personal growth. These offered a panoply of justifications as well as opportunities for those seeking a solution to marital distress.

Attuned to the importance of the family patterns of this cohort, we can see their indelible impact on our understanding of the postwar era. Patterns we associate with each decade since the war coincide with the family cycle of the parents of the baby boom. They shaped the postwar era. Fifties togetherness ideology evolved in part to suit the needs of young parents of the baby boomers. Millions of mothers of school-age children stirred to the words of Betty Friedan in 1963, not because what she voiced was new, but because she described their experiences. After intensive child-rearing, this generation gave meaning to the idea of the empty nest and defined the phenomena of middle-aged marital break-ups in the late 1960s and early 1970s. Finally, these couples, "over thirty" when the epicenter of social change shifted to American youth, were not as immune to the ideas of the sexual revolution and the women's movement as is often assumed. Only by following members of this generation over the family cycle do the connections between cohort, life course, and historical change become discernible.

Not only did families evolve over time, but so did American cultural ideals. Media images both reflected and shaped changes in the postwar family. Accompanying baby boom parents at every stage of the family cycle, a growing coterie of experts and professionals enjoined them to follow modern precepts for successful family life. Aware of such advice, postwar men and women made their own uses of prescriptions. They imbibed the recommendations that resonated and ignored those that did not. Advice could inspire action, or guilt over inaction, and could cause increased frustration as much as the intended satisfaction. Women carried experts' injunctions for fathering further than the advisors ever expected themselves. Couples made their own compromises with the prevailing beliefs about women's role in the workforce and sifted through the confusing definitions of feminism that barraged them, deciding for themselves what they would and would not imbibe. Cultural prescription added fodder for family conflict, joining with actual behavior as an ingredient in the transformation of gender roles. And what couples did with experts' edicts and their own expectations and experiences was experiment with them, argue over them, negotiating and debating their way to compromise and change.

This analysis places families at the center of historical shifts. As the site where gender gets created and lived, the family is also the site of continuous minor and major negotiations over roles and expectations. The differing expectations and resources men and women brought to such negotiations and the historical developments that affected them—the women's movement, the divorce and sexual revolutions—these are the elements around which postwar gender evolution hinged.

The differences of opinion between men and women—over parenting, homemaking, career commitment, sexuality—that come through so strongly in the IHD interviews should not be mistaken for ahistorical conflict symptomatic of married life. Rather, these arguments and negotiations were the tools of change. When women raged against bearing the heavy responsibility of rearing children, when men complained about the rat race and regretted their disengagement from the family, for example, the postwar generation chafed against traditional gender roles and their high emotional costs for both sexes. In their compromises, successes, and failures we find the roots of contemporary solutions and contemporary struggles.

Fatherhood, wage-earning, togetherness, sex: All demanded increased emotional and physical labor within the home. Women were charged with making men better parents, supplementing the family's income without disturbing its maintenance, facilitating family activities, and communicating clearly about sexuality. With the rewards for these new responsibilities—partners in parenthood and family companionship, the promise of fulfillment in a nondomestic pursuit, and better sexual relationships—in mind, it's easy to see why women shouldered these additional demands. For men, these new developments also demanded sacrifices. Gradually, in a process that continues today, male leisure at home was chipped away by requirements to participate more actively in child care and family activity. They were asked to learn to nurture and essay verbal intimacy. Togetherness and the new fatherhood began demanding double days of men. The sexual revolution heightened emphasis on male performance. Male prerogatives of leisure, authority, and sex diminished; they by no means disappeared. But men gained, too; their wives' employment lessened the pressure of being the sole family financial support. In return for their efforts, they were promised closer, more satisfying relationships with their wives and children. But in the case of both parenting and leisure, until feminism, men could remain helpers whose additional labor was discretional and voluntary, not essential or required.

With increased pressures and expectations, marriage was more fragile, and for many in an uncertain world, more essential. For working spouses marriage was where they looked for recognition and solace. In the postwar years, including the 1950s, marriage was an institution in transition, and yet the division of labor and the work of family life remained the most difficult pieces of the transformation.

In addition to their contemporary relevance, the difficulties couples had in integrating intimacy and companionship into their marriages cast doubt on our understanding of the history of companionate marriage. Even in the second half of the twentieth century, companionship may have long triumphed as the cultural ideal, but in reality couples negotiated and compromised over expectations and often settled for relationships that did not meet their own or their partners' desires. The continued shaping of democratic marriage patterns calls for a longer timeline. Postwar spouses may have been companions but not necessarily intimate, passionate, or equal ones, and this varied over the family cycle.[2]

The roots of postwar gender and social change lie in the baby boom family style of the 1950s. In the 1960s the parents of the baby boom did not reject the domesticity of their youth so much as they redrew its perimeters. Because of the very choices they made in the 1940s and 1950s, couples had new opportunities in the 1960s and 1970s. Older children, working mothers, and the possibility of divorce were all part of the next stage of the family cycle. Marriage still defined the structure of their lives and nearly all sought meaning there. But these marriages nonetheless provided scope for new roles. Conflict within marriage could and did lead to constructive changes. And when their children, the baby boomers, rejected youthful marriages, got divorced, or set out to redefine male and female roles, they did so partly in response to messages and examples they got at home from mom and dad.

But while critics of contemporary family life mistakenly harken back to the fifties family, the proponents of gender change rely on those same notions to chart how far we have come. They cloud the conflict and continuity in American homes today behind a hazy wishful glow of modern equality, symbolized by briefcase-bearing wives and pram-pushing husbands multi-tasking work and children thanks to car phones and take-out meals. The baby boomers may have set out to redefine roles, but they still do battle with a tradition-bound division of labor and gendered pay scales in their efforts to create egalitarian marriages, especially once children arrive. As sociological studies show, family life has changed, but gender roles remain the most difficult aspects to alter. Who performs the daily upkeep of household and family has proven most intractable.[3]

Today's couples share continuities with the parents of the baby boom when it comes to nurturing marriage and children at the same time. They are doing so at later ages in the life course that may make "togetherness" and "companionship" even more of a challenge. With regard to sexuality, contemporary Americans seem to be having second thoughts on permissiveness. In a recent poll, 66 percent said that greater "acceptance of sexual freedom" was an unwelcome change. The current publicity for Viagra points to a continued focus on performance, and the jokes that followed the announcement of this pharmaceutical aid reveal deep rifts in men's and women's views of sexuality. The issues couples did or did not talk about in the postwar marriages studied here still resonate.[4]

Individual needs and resources shift across the family cycle and as historical opportunities change. When we reduce postwar gender and family history to decade-long increments, these snapshot views diminish our understanding of that history. This longitudinal look inside families across the family cycle illustrates that despite gender inequities within the nuclear family and in the larger society, relationships possess underacknowledged room for maneuverability. Families are more elastic and less resistant to historical change than is traditionally assumed. Talk and conflict combined with changing access to resources, both economic and emotional, are the keys to this elasticity. In the kitchen, in the family room, and in the bedroom, couples battled the weight of tradition and did their best to elicit their demands and find satisfaction. In their successes as in their failures, the legacy of hope and disappointment the parents of the baby boom bequeathed to the next generation continues to shape family change. In fact, family members, as they go about the struggle to shape satisfactory lives, shape history.

Notes

INTRODUCTION

1. These and all other names of Institute of Human Development (IHD) study members are pseudonyms. Any similarity they bear to names of actual study participants is purely coincidental and unintended.

The case files at the Institute of Human Development contain transcripts from three interviews, Adult I, II, and III. The Guidance interviews at Adult I consisted of a high-low questionnaire and family history questionnaires called "Subject and Spouse" and "Subject and Parent." These are referred to in the footnotes by abbreviations H-L, S-S, and S-P. Oakland interviews at Adult I consisted of a numbered series of interviews cited as I-1, I-2, and so on, in the notes. There was only one interview at Adult II for all IHD subjects. In 1982–83, there were two interviews, a structured and a clinical interview. In my notes, S-I indicates the structured interview.

2. IHD Archives, Lois Dyer, S-S, 1960, 6.

3. IHD Archives, Dyer, 1960, 1982, 21. The institute is located at the University of California, Berkeley.

4. The IHD studies represent a multidisciplinary effort that involved medical doctors, psychologists, physiologists, sociologists, and economists. For other reexaminations of fifties family life, see Stephanie Coontz, *The Way We Never Were: American Families and the Nostalgia Trap* (New York: Basic Books, 1992), and Arlene Skolnick, *Embattled Paradise* (New York: Basic Books, 1991). A study of IHD subjects in "young" old age is now underway under the direction of Paul Wink at Wellesley College.

5. John Clausen, *American Lives: Looking Back at the Children of the Great Depression* (New York: Free Press, 1993), 38–39. My sample is derived from those who participated in all three adult interviews. Sixty-four Oakland study members met that criteria and 65 Guidance members did. I chose 50 from each. The IHD lost track of two-fifths of its subjects over the years. Those who withdrew or were lost to the IHD tended to be working class or experience family disruption, especially

those who left as youths. Others simply moved and lost contact with the IHD, some as late as when they retired. Many valued participation highly. On study participation, one member reflected, "It has given me a family that I belong to. . . . the children that I knew in grammar school, a lot of them are still a part of my life because the study has kept us together" (IHD Archives, Anne Matthews, S-I, 1982, 30).

6. Clausen, *American Lives*, chap. 2. Dorothy Eichorn, "Samples and Procedures," in *Present and Past in Middle Life* (New York: Academic Press, 1981), 33–41; Glen Elder, *Children of the Great Depression: Social Change in Life Experience* (Chicago: University of Chicago Press, 1974), 5. The records I examined from the 1950s are a mixture of verbatim transcription and paraphrasing on the part of the interviewers. All interviews for the 1968 and 1982 follow-ups were tape-recorded and transcribed.

7. Glen Elder, "Social History and Life Experience," in Eichorn et al., *Present and Past*, 27; Steven Mintz and Susan Kellogg, *Domestic Revolutions: A Social History of American Family Life* (New York: Free Press, 1988), 179; Steven McLaughlin et al., *The Changing Lives of American Women* (Chapel Hill: University of North Carolina Press, 1988), 60; Susan Householder Van Horn, *Women, Work and Fertility* (New York: New York University Press, 1988), 85; Andrew Cherlin, *Marriage, Divorce, Remarriage* (Cambridge: Harvard University Press, 1993), 34–43. In an overview of American family history, Daniel Scott Smith notes, "If the 1950s are taken as a baseline for the fundamental nature of the modern American family, the departure since the mid-60s becomes more striking and more troubling for those who were concerned about the forces behind the more recent developments or their implications. On the other hand, if the postwar era is regarded as an aberration, a momentary departure from past patterns, the changes since the 1960s do not appear to be so unusual in magnitude or worrisome in implication" ("Recent Change and Periodization of American Family History," *Journal of Family History* 20 [fall 1995]: 336). The demographic profile of the IHD study closely matches the national norms for most features. Of the study members queried in 1979, the mean age of marriage for women was 21 and for men 24. Most women had their first child two years after marriage and their last child at the median age of 31. They bore an average of 3.4 children in this short time. Arlene Skolnick, "Married Lives: Longitudinal Perspectives on Marriage," in Eichorn, *Present and Past*, 272; Janice B. Stroud, "Women's Careers: Work, Family, and Personality," in *Present and Past*, 388.

8. Elder, *Children of the Great Depression*, 64, 82, 114, 192, 195.

9. They represent a small birth cohort since American couples postponed or limited childbearing during the Depression; Richard Easterlin, *Birth and Fortune: The Impact of Numbers on Personal Welfare* (Chicago: University of Chicago Press, 1987), 16, 38.

10. Elaine Tyler May, *Homeward Bound: American Families in the Cold War Era* (New York: Basic Books, 1988), 90, 208. For a discussion of affluence and its threat to masculinity in the 1950s, see Jesse Berrett, "Feeding the Organization Man: Diet and Masculinity in Postwar America," *Journal of Social History* 30 (summer 1997): 805–25.

11. Stephanie Coontz, *The Way We Never Were: American Families and the Nostalgia Trap* (New York: Basic Books, 1992), 24–27, 29, 35, 76–78; May, *Homeward Bound*, 9; Stephanie Coontz, *The Way We Really Are: Coming to Terms with America's Changing Families* (New York: Basic Books, 1997), 43–46.

12. Wini Breines, *Young, White, and Miserable: Growing Up Female in the Fifties* (Boston: Beacon Press, 1992), 11–24, 45–46, 59, 83.

13. Betty Friedan, *The Feminine Mystique* (New York: Dell, 1974).

14. Joanne Meyerowitz, *Not June Cleaver: Women and Gender in Postwar America* (Philadelphia: Temple University Press, 1994).

15. The IHD Studies consist of the Berkeley Guidance Study, the Berkeley Growth Study, and the Oakland Growth Study (of adolescents). My sample is drawn from the guidance and Oakland studies only. The Berkeley Guidance Study drew subjects from the families of every third child born in a Berkeley hospital beginning in 1928–29. The Oakland study began with fifth-grade children who met the following criteria: willingness to participate and long-term Oakland residence; Elder, *Children of the Great Depression*, 321. The Berkeley study included a few (3 percent) minority families, two of whom are part of my sample, while the Oakland group was selected from Caucasian, English-speaking families by the institute at a time when Oakland's population was 92 percent white; Clausen, *American Lives*, 28–33. Interviews were carried out by clinical and research psychologists. Exposure to the University of California and the opportunities opened up to men who served in the armed forces (by the mid-1950s 70 percent of IHD men) led to educational advantages; Clausen, *American Lives*, 253. Dorothy Eichorn, "Overview" in *Present and Past*, 412. On Oakland Growth Study women's class mobility, see Elder, *Children of the Great Depression*, 316; for men, 160. While they may be comparatively more socioeconomically advantaged than most of their cohort, they measure out as similar in terms of IQ, personality characteristics, and physical health. For IHD study members as a whole, their divorce rate was lower than the national average, but if distinguished by age and sex, Oakland women and Berkeley men conformed to national rates of marital dissolution; Eichorn, *Present and Past*, 212–13. As to how representative IHD study members are of the midcentury American middle class, those who have written up IHD data before me have certainly made clear their assumptions of the universality of IHD subjects' experiences. I refer here to Glen Elder's *Children of the Great Depression* and John Clausen's *American Lives*. While there are other longitudinal studies of considerable size, scope, and duration, to my knowledge, no other study can claim to have followed 282 Americans for over 60 years in such breadth and rich detail.

16. Elder, "Social History and Life Experience," 4.

17. Ibid., 13–20.

18. Marilynn S. Johnson, *The Second Gold Rush: Oakland and the East Bay in World War II* (Berkeley: University of California Press, 1993), 35.

19. Eichorn, *Present and Past*, 34–35. On California, see David Farber, *The Age of Great Dreams: America in the 1960s* (New York: Hill & Wang, 1994), 53.

20. It is also important to note that my sample is drawn from a particularly

committed group of subjects who participated in all three adult interviews. At the least, their continued participation indicates a willingness to probe personal history and to understand motivations and influential life experiences. On the other hand, since the IHD was simply a part of life from childhood, a yearly interview was as normal as a yearly physical for this group. Adult participation was limited to a minimum four-hour interview, sometimes stretching over two days for loquacious subjects, every ten years. See Skolnick on "Psychological Gentrification," in *Embattled Paradise*, 16–18, and Elaine Tyler May, *Homeward Bound*, 187, 191. With regard to the content of IHD interviews, a primary concern for the institute at the 1957 interview of guidance study participants was for the interview subject to name life-long emotional high and low points. Often individual events like army induction and discharge as well as family dynamics figured in the responses and shed light on experiences of married life in the fifties. Of the limitations of IHD material Clausen writes, "If our data are somewhat deficient in showing the relationship of the individual to the larger society, however, they are much more adequate in depicting relationships among individuals, especially in the family" (*American Lives*, 12). Pondering the impact of life-long participation, one Oakland participant commented, "I would say definitely the study influenced the 200 of us. I've often wondered about that . . . because we're different people than if . . . we hadn't been kept so close socially" (IHD Archives, Grace Owens, 1982, 11).

21. IHD Archives, Lois Dyer, S-I, 1982, 16.

CHAPTER ONE

1. See Barbara Ehrenreich, *Hearts of Men: American Dreams and the Flight from Commitment* (Garden City: Anchor Books, 1983), 47, for a discussion of the *Playboy* view of marriage in the 1950s.

2. Betty Friedan, *The Feminine Mystique* (New York: Dell, 1974), 21, 59, 271. For another instance where trap is the metaphor of choice for discussing family life, see Richard Gordon and Katherine Gordon, *The Split-Level Trap* (New York: Max Gunther, Bernard Gels Association, 1960). In 1959, one writer warned prospective parents about the "trap" of parenthood so that "the trap won't be too much of a shock once they're in it" (B. M. Atkinson Jr., "What Dr. Spock Didn't Tell Us," *Ladies' Home Journal*, January 1959, 54–55, 57, 123–24).

3. Beth Bailey, *From Front Porch to Back Seat: Courtship in Twentieth-Century America* (Baltimore: Johns Hopkins University Press, 1989), 42; Steven Mintz and Susan Kellogg, *Domestic Revolutions: A Social History of American Family Life* (New York: Free Press, 1988), 179; IHD Archives. Oakland participants' wives married on average at 23, participants' husbands at 25. The wives of Berkeley men married at 22, on average. The men Berkeley women married had an average age of marriage of 26. These figures exclude two women and six men for whom date of birth was not available.

4. Mintz and Kellogg, *Domestic Revolutions*, 179; IHD Archives. These figures exclude couples who had no children (4) as well as those who adopted (4).

5. Wini Breines, *Young, White, and Miserable: Growing Up Female in the Fifties* (Boston: Beacon Press, 1992).

6. Edmund Bergler, M. D., *Conflict in Marriage* (New York: Harper & Bros., 1949), 174. See also Bergler, *Divorce Won't Help* (New York: Harper & Bros., 1948), 209. Frances Strain, *Marriage Is for Two* (New York: Longmans, Green & Co., 1955), 245. This viewpoint was encapsulated in the title of one of the key family sociology texts of the 1950s, Ernest W. Burgess and Harvey J. Locke, *The Family: From Institution to Companionship* (New York: American Book Co., 1953), cited in William G. Dyer and Dick Urban, "The Institutionalization of Equalitarian Family Norms," *Marriage and Family Living* 20 (February 1958): 53.

7. Strain, *Marriage Is for Two*, 119.

8. Constance Foster, "Six Threats to Happy Marriage," *Parents Magazine*, January 1956, 32–33, 62–63, 62. Sociologist Mirra Komarovsky also predicted problems in marriage because of postwar flux. She wrote, "With new and old patterns both in the air, it is all too human for each partner to reach for a double dose of privileges, those of old and those of the new role, leaving to the mate the double dose of obligation" (*Women in the Modern World: Their Education and Their Dilemmas* [Boston: Little, Brown & Co., 1953], 88). Sociologists William Dyer and Dick Urban compared single men and women to married men and women finding more divergence in the views between the sexes among the single than the married and suggested that "changes are made in behavior after persons are married as they begin to adjust the marital role expectations they held while single. Generally it appears the adjustment is towards equality although there are notable exceptions" (*Marriage and Family Living* 20: 58).

9. Robert Coughlan, "Changing Roles in Modern Marriage," *Life*, 23 December 1956, 118.

10. Komarovsky, *Women in the Modern World*, 250–51.

11. For a discussion of college marriage courses, see Bailey, *From Front Porch to Back Seat*, 126–40.

12. Paul H. Landis, *Making the Most of Marriage* (New York: Appleton-Century-Crofts, 1955), vi, 84, 77, 360.

13. Robert O. Blood Jr. and Donald M. Wolfe, *Husbands and Wives: The Dynamics of Married Living* (Glencoe, Ill.: Free Press, 1960), 17, 30.

14. As historian John Modell shows the transition to adulthood accelerated during and after World War II. Adulthood in the United States is signalled by such milestones, or in Modell's words "life course transitions," as leaving school, assuming employment, leaving the home of origin, marriage, and parenthood. In the 1940s and 1950s, these milestones were both reordered and compressed. See Modell, *Into One's Own: From Youth to Adulthood in the United States, 1920–1975* (Berkeley: University of California Press, 1989), 25, 36–38, 44, 52. See also Victor A. Christopherson, "College Marriage in Public and Private Institutions of Higher Education, 1943–1958," *Family Life Coordinator* 8 (March 1960): 49.

15. IHD Archives, Nan Meeker, I-1, 1959, 1; Blanche Warner, I-4, 1959, 13. Modell has parsed the impact of war by timing and age group: "Prewar economic recovery most potently improved marriage chances at the more modal marriage ages, for both men and women. The beginnings of the draft, in contrast, produced a marriage rush that was quite focused in age among younger men (many of whom no doubt hoped to avoid military service through family deferment) but not quite so focused among women. War itself produced a dramatic surge of relatively young marriage—again more so for men than for women—followed by a dearth most apparent in the ages of military service" (Modell, *Into One's Own,* 176). IHD interviews were open-ended. Much of the information here was volunteered in the process of lengthy conversations. Without formally coding them, for the most part I have grouped responses thematically to provide readers with a sense of how many study members expressed similar sentiments. However, the 1982 structured interview was coded by IHD staff, and when applicable I have included the relevant responses. The IHD data files contained the responses of 94 of my subjects and 72 of the spouses. In 1982, 30 percent of the Oakland men recalled that the war encouraged them to marry; half of the husbands of Oakland women said so as well.

16. IHD Archives, Malcom McKee, I-3, 1959, 12.

17. IHD Archives, Malcom McKee, I-3, 1959, 12.

18. IHD Archives, Stuart White, 1959, 5.

19. For a discussion of the war's impact on marriage, see Modell, *Into One's Own,* 162–212, and Ellen K. Rothman, *Hands and Hearts: A History of Courtship in America* (Cambridge: Harvard University Press, 1987), 301.

20. Walter Stokes, *Modern Pattern for Marriage: The Newer Understanding of Married Love* (New York: Rinehart & Co., 1948), 12.

21. "Subsidized Marriage," *Ladies' Home Journal,* December 1949, 58, 193. At the end of the decade the college marriage trend was still going strong. See Christopherson, *Family Life Coordinator* 8: 49–52.

22. Sidonie M. Gruenberg, "Why They Are Marrying Younger," *New York Times Magazine,* 30 January 1953, 17.

23. IHD Archives, Dorothy Simon, H-L, 1959, 6; Rita Frank, S-S, 1957, 6; Barbara Spalding, 1970, 22. Nearly a third of the Berkeley women recalled factoring parental pressure into their decision to marry; S-I, 1982.

24. IHD Archives, Denise Ames, 1982, 8. The younger Berkeley cohort reported feeling social pressure to marry. Half of the Berkeley women metnioned this as a factor in marital timing when asked; S-I, 1982.

25. IHD Archives, Diane Key, H-L, 1957, 3. Nine women from the IHD mentioned fear of becoming an old maid as a factor in their decision to marry. On the limited occupational horizon for postwar women, see Elaine Tyler May, *Homeward Bound: American Families in the Cold War Era* (New York: Basic Books, 1988), 83–87.

26. IHD Archives, Leonard Stone, S-I, 1983, 20; Ruth Wright, S-I, 1982, 18. Six couples mentioned eagerness to have sex as a motivation to marry. Other histo-

rians have uncovered similar motivations. May, *Homeward Bound*, 101. Many of the women Bret Harvey interviewed recalled that they married in order to become sexually active; *The Fifties: A Women's Oral History* (New York: HarperCollins, 1993), 75–78.

27. IHD Archives, Patricia James, S-I, 1982, 16; Elaine Hermann, 1971, 37; May Perkins, S-I, 1982, 11; Rose Little, S-I, 1982, 19; Jane Miller, 1970, 18. Arlene Skolnick writes, "The 1950s pattern of family formation required marriage as the price for living away from home and having sexual relations—at least for women" (*Embattled Paradise* [New York: Basic Books, 1991], 168). IHD Archives, Linda Anderson, 1971, 28. Seven women mentioned marrying young in order to leave their home of origin. See also May, *Homeward Bound*, 186 on similar motivations to marry.

28. IHD Archives, David Morris, 1969, 5. According to John Clausen, one-third of IHD men were married before age 23; *American Lives: Looking Back at the Children of the Great Depression* (New York: Free Press, 1993), 284.

29. Bailey, *From Front Porch*, 88–96; Richard Easterlin, *Birth and Fortune: The Impact of Numbers on Personal Welfare* (Chicago: University of Chicago Press, 1987); May, *Homeward Bound*. In my sample, 88 percent of the Oakland women were married by the age of 25, and 83 percent of the Oakland men were married by age 27. Three quarters of the Berkeley women in my sample were married by the age of 25 and 80 percent of the men were married by age 27.

30. IHD Archives, Gail Henderson, S-S, 1958, 21; Claire Manning, H-L, 1958, 6.

31. IHD Archives, Claudine Parker, 1982, 31; Patricia James, 1957, 2; Lloyd Andrews, H-L, 1958, 8–9.

32. IHD Archives, David Morris, 1969, 6; Rick Snyder, 1959, 4. Historian Barbara Ehrenreich writes, in the fifties "marriage was not only a proof of maturity, it was a chance to exercise one's maturity through countless tasks" (*The Hearts of Men*, 19).

33. IHD Archives, Lois Dyer, S-S, 1960, 19. Cynthia Thornton, H-L, 1958, 4; Patricia James, 1970, 47. Nine couples spoke of maturing or growing up during the first decade of marriage and seven others referred to themselves as immature or too young when they married. Four more recalled growing up after marriage when interviewed in 1970, and another in 1982.

34. IHD Archives, Marlene Hill, I-1, 1958, 20; Suzanne Miller, S-P, 1957, 2.

35. IHD Archives, Cynthia Thornton, H-L, 1958, 4.

36. IHD Archives, Clay Kent, S-S, 1959, 2; Judy Kent, S-S, 1959, 4. The seven women who quit school do not include women who opted for marriage directly out of high school or left school with AA or business degrees before marriage. IHD Archives, Claire Manning, 1957, 1; Caroline Good, 1982, 26. May, *Homeward Bound*, 79; Blanche Linden-Ward and Carol Hurd Green, *American Women in the 1960s: Changing the Future* (New York: Twayne Publishers, 1993), 68.

37. *The Oakland Tribune*, 8 June 1958, S-11.

38. Sociologist Valerie Kincade Oppenheimer suggests that "life cycle squeezes" drive women into the labor force. She writes, "The first occurs when young people are attempting to set themselves up as independent adults." This squeeze "occurs at a point in the life cycle when men's earnings are low" (*Work and the Family: A Study in Social Demography* [New York: Academic Press, 1982], 124).

39. IHD Archives, Evelyn Mitchell, 1958, 6.

40. IHD Archives, Evelyn Mitchell, 1972, 58; Patricia James, 1957, 2. Eleven women, or 20 percent, in my Guidance sample said they put their husbands through school; IHD Archives, 1958, 1970.

41. IHD Archives, Cynthia Thorton, H-L, 1958, 4; Ellen Collins, 1959, 1; Carl Gordon, H-L, 1959, 2, 5; Max Ames, H-L, 1958, 4.

42. IHD Archives, Mark Little, H-L, 1957, 3.

43. This will be discussed in the next chapter.

44. Erma Bombeck, *A Marriage Made in Heaven, or Too Tired for an Affair* (New York: HarperCollins, 1993), 1, 12.

45. IHD Archives, Doris Jenkins, I-1, 1960, 40.

46. IHD Archives, Cynthia Thornton, H-L, 1958, 4.

47. IHD Archives, Leonard Stone, S-I, 1983, 23; Claire Manning, 1958, 10.

48. IHD Archives, Brenda Jones, H-L, 1958, 6; Nan Meeker, I-5, 1959, 7.

49. IHD Archives, Janice Rogers, 1958, 4; John Anderson, H-L, 1958, 3.

50. IHD Archives, Ruth Wright, 1959, 13; Dorothy Simon, 1960, 21.

51. IHD Archives, Janice Rogers, H-L, 1958, 4, 5. Eight women reported anxiety over motherhood and homemaking responsibilities. Most voiced concern about inadequacy or failure.

52. IHD Archives, Lloyd Andrews, H-L, 1958, 9; Max Ames, H-L, 1959, 5.

53. IHD Archives, Leonard Stone, 1959, 5; Mark Little, 1958, 3.

54. IHD Archives, Sue White, 1959, 6.

55. IHD Archives, Mary Smith, S-I, 1982, 11.

56. IHD Archives, Mark Little, S-S, 1957, 6; Larry Sloan, 1958, 6.

57. IHD Archives, May Perkins, S-S, 1957, 2; Gail Henderson, 1958, 26; Connie Small, S-S, 1957, 4, 10.

58. IHD Archives, Connie Small, 1957, 4, 15; Gail Henderson, S-S, 1958, 8.

59. IHD Archives, Murray Borden, I-4, 1959, 15. The popular media affirmed sentiments favoring large families with births clustered together; Edith and Robert Simonds, "Babies? We Want Five," *Better Homes and Gardens*, April 1953, 216; Sidonie M. Gruenberg, "Why They Are Marrying Younger," *New York Times Magazine*, 30 January 1953, 17.

60. IHD Archives, Lois Dyer, S-S, 1960, 16.

61. IHD Archives, Martha Bentley, 1957, 2.

62. IHD Archives, Ellen Collins, 1959, 3.

63. IHD Archives, Mark Little, H-L, 1958, 4, 5.

64. IHD Archives, Max Ames, H-L, 1959, 4 and 1982, 42.

65. IHD Archives, Robert Mitchell, 1958, 7; Kurt Wolf, H-L, 1959, 5.

66. IHD Archives, Clay Kent, S-S, 1958, 8; Suzanne Miller, 1970, 5. Nine

couples reported men's anxiety with regard to their ability to fulfill family financial responsibilities.

67. IHD Archives, Stuart White, H-L, 1959, 7.

68. IHD Archives, Carl Gordon, H-L, 1959, 2.

69. IHD Archives, Cynthia Thornton, H-L, 1958, 5; Patricia James, 1957, 3.

70. IHD Archives, Marcia Sloan, 1969, 10, 16; Irene Lawrence, 1970, 13.

71. IHD Archives, May Perkins, S-S, 1957, 3; Evelyn Mitchell, 1958, 6.

72. IHD Archives, Rose Little, 1960, 3; Janice Rogers, 1963, 2; Sandra Thomas, 1982, 18; Ruth Wright, 1959, 8.

73. Ruth J. Tasch, "Interpersonal Perceptions of Fathers and Mothers," *Journal of Genetic Psychology* 87 (September 1955): 63.

74. Dyer and Urban, "The Institutionalization of Equalitarian Family Norms," *Marriage and Family Living* 20 (February 1958): 55–57; Marvin E. Olsen, "Distribution of Family Responsibilities and Social Stratification," *Marriage and Family Living* 22 (February 1960): 62, 65.

75. Arlene Skolnick observes, in the fifties, "The ideology of the strong male was at odds with the ideology of togetherness" (*Embattled Paradise*, 71).

76.. IHD Archives, Martha Bentley, 1957, 9; Gail Henderson, S-S, 1958, 27; Dennis Perkins, S-S, 1957, 9.

77. IHD Archives, Mary Smith, 1960, 14.

78. IHD Archives, Doris Jenkins, I-4, 1960, 44; Malcom McKee, I-3, 1959, 13.

79. IHD Archives, Leonard Stone, S-S, 1958, 18.

80. IHD Archives, Tom Cole, 1958, 12; Adam Walker, I-3; 1959, 60.

81. IHD Archives, Leonard Stone, 1958, 17.

82. IHD Archives, Thomas Williams, S-S, 1957; Theodore B. Johannis Jr., "Participation by Fathers, Mothers, and Teenage Sons and Daughters in Selected Family Economic Activity," *The Coordinator* 1 (September 1957): 15, 16.

83. IHD Archives, Dean Lawrence, 1958, 18; Howard Sims, I-4, 1958, 10.

84. IHD Archives, James Richards, 1958, 15; Claire Manning, 1960, 16.

85. IHD Archives, Alice Bremmer, 1958, I-4, 13; I-3, 15. The men in Glen Elder's Oakland sample were divided 60/40 between male authority and shared decision making when it came to large economic decisions. Interestingly, it was men whose families experienced tough economic times during the Great Depression who reported shared authority most frequently, perhaps because their parents responded to the Depression as a team; Elder, *Children of the Great Depression: Social Change in Life Experience* (Chicago: University of Chicago Press, 1974), 198–99.

86. John A. Clausen, *American Lives*, 198–99; Dyer and Urban, *Marriage and Family Living* 20: 55; Theodore B. Johannis Jr. and James M. Rollins, "Teenager Perception of Family Decision Making," *The Coordinator* 6 (June 1959): 71, 73, 74.

87. Dyer and Urban, *Marriage and Family Living* 20: 58, 57. May found that women in the Kelly Longitudinal Study also chafed against culturally approved male authority; May, *Homeward Bound*, 88, 200.

88. On young couples as cultural innovators, see Modell, *Into One's Own*, 213.

89. Robert O. Blood Jr., "The Division of Labor in City and Farm Families," paper read at the December, 1955, meeting of the Michigan Sociological Society, cited in Marvin E. Olsen, "Distribution of Family Responsibilities and Social Stratification," *Marriage and Family Living* 22 (February 1960): 60.

90. Mary Thom, ed., *Letters to Ms. 1972–1982* (New York: Henry Holt & Co., 1987), 211. IHD Archives, Gail Henderson, S-I, 1982, 13.

CHAPTER TWO

1. Betty Friedan, *The Feminine Mystique* (New York: Dell Publishing, 1974); F. Ivan Nye and Lois Wladis Hoffman, *The Employed Mother in America* (Chicago: Rand McNally, 1963); *Report to the President's Commission on the Status of Women* (Washington, D.C.: U.S. Government Printing Office, 1963). For a discussion of the response to Friedan, see Elaine Tyler May, *Homeward Bound: American Families in the Cold War Era* (New York: Basic Books, 1988), epilogue. For a discussion of the commission and its impact, see Rosalind Rosenberg, *Divided Lives: American Women in the Twentieth Century* (New York: Hill & Wang, 1992), 184–86; on the 1950s and early 1960s as staging grounds for feminist revival, see William Chafe, *The American Woman: Her Changing Social, Economic, and Political Role, 1920–1970* (New York: Oxford University Press, 1974), 225, 234; Valerie Kincade Oppenheimer, *Work and the Family: A Study in Social Demography* (New York: Academic Press, 1982), 30. For a discussion of the President's Commission on the Status of Women as a "new frontier" for women, see Cynthia E. Harrison, "A 'New Frontier' for Women: The Public Policy of the Kennedy Administration," *Journal of American History* 67 (December 1980): 630–45.

2. For married women with children aged six to seventeen the rate of participation was even higher—43 percent; *Historical Statistics of the United States: Colonial Times to 1970* (Washington, D.C.: United States Department of Commerce, Bureau of the Census, 1975), Series D 29–41, 131, Series D 63–74, 134.

3. Steven D. McLaughlin et al., *The Changing Lives of American Women* (Chapel Hill: University of North Carolina Press, 1988), 206, 223; see p. 214, Appendix D to compare this longitudinal study with another National Longitudinal Survey of women born 1928–32.

4. Employment peaked in 1969 when these women were still in their prime but no longer had very young children at home. Retirement accounts for lower rates of participation—31 percent—for the older cohort of women in 1982. Still, of the younger cohort, almost two-thirds were hard at work at age 56. John A. Clausen and Martin Gilens, "Personality and Labor Force Participation across the Life Course: A Longitudinal Study of Women's Careers," *Sociological Forum* 5 (December 1990): 602–3; IHD Archives.

5. Carl N. Degler, *At Odds: Women and the Family from the Revolution to the Present* (New York: Oxford University Press, 1980), 418; William H. Chafe, *The American Woman*, 135–48.

6. Historian Sonya Michel argues that the government and social welfare discourse surrounding child care for women workers during World War II actually enhanced beliefs in the essential role and responsibility of women in the home; "American Women and the Discourse of the Democratic Family in World War II," in Margaret Randolph Higonnet et al., *Behind the Lines: Gender and the Two World Wars* (New Haven: Yale University Press, 1987), 154–67; Chafe, *The American Woman*, 151–71, esp. 169–71.

7. As of 1994, 61 percent of married women worked; see Cynthia Costello and Barbara Kivimae, eds., *The American Woman, 1996–97: Where We Stand, Women and Work* (New York: W. W. Norton & Co., 1996), 51. While in 1940 only 15.2 percent of married women worked, in 1945 the figure was 24 percent; Ralph E. Smith, "The Movement of Women into the Labor Force," in Ralph E. Smith, ed., *The Subtle Revolution: Women at Work* (Washington, D.C.: Urban Institute, 1979), 3–7. See Elaine Tyler May, *Homeward Bound*, chaps. 2 and 3, for a discussion of the cultural response to disruption in gender roles in the 1930s and 1940s. For a discussion of World War II propaganda and the campaign to mobilize women workers, see Maureen Honey, *Creating Rosie the Riveter: Class, Gender, and Propaganda during World War II* (Amherst: University of Massachusetts Press, 1984).

8. Historian Claudia Goldin writes, "The 1950s mark a sharp break in the way the labor market accommodated married women, older women, and women with household responsibilities. . . . after 1950 the marriage bar vanished . . . and part-time work became widespread. The factors that account for these changes amount to nothing short of a revolution in the demographics of labor supply" (Claudia Goldin, *Understanding the Gender Gap: An Economic History of American Women* [New York: Oxford University Press, 1990], 174). After 1960 the growth in part-time work continued, as did women's participation in it. The number of part-time workers increased at a pace three times that of full-time workers between 1965 and 1977. As of 1977 women represented 70 percent of that workforce; Nancy S. Barrett, "Women in the Job Market: Unemployment and Work Schedules," in Smith, *Subtle Revolution*, 81.

9. The majority of women taking jobs in the first two decades after the war were over 35 and no longer had young children at home. See Ethel Klein, *Gender Politics: From Mass Consciousness to Mass Politics* (Cambridge: Harvard University Press, 1984), 33, and Goldin, *Understanding the Gender Gap*, 205. Historian Susan Hartmann also notes transitional undercurrents promoting the expansion of women's roles during the 1950s. Susan Hartmann, "Women's Employment and the Domestic Ideal," in Joanne Meyerowitz, ed., *Not June Cleaver: Women and Gender in Postwar America, 1945–1960* (Philadelphia: Temple University Press, 1994), 84–100.

10. Winifred D. Wandersee, *On the Move: American Women in the 1970s* (Boston: Twayne Publishers, 1988), xviii, 127, 129; Blanche Linden-Ward and Carol Hurd Green, *American Women in the 1960s: Changing the Future* (New York: Twayne Publishers, 1993), 92.

11. For an example of the daughters-as-historical-agents view: "However their

mothers' lives had turned out, many daughters of the fifties early recognized that they needed an independent identity, one that challenged the Feminine Mystique's emphasis on marriage and motherhood. Fear of becoming an 'ordinary housewife'—in the words of one sixties feminist writer—is what fueled the female generation gap" (Ruth Rosen, "The Female Generation Gap: Daughters of the Fifties and the Origins of Contemporary American Feminism," in Linda K. Kerber, Alice Kessler-Harris, and Kathryn Kish Sklar, eds., *U.S. History as Women's History: New Feminist Essays* [Chapel Hill: University of North Carolina, 1995] 316). Or "The gap between the mothers' ideology and their experience is, in fact, a motif in the younger women's stories; the older women's lives could not be unambivalently embraced by the younger" (Wini Breines, *Young, White, and Miserable: Growing Up Female in the Fifties* [Boston: Beacon Press, 1992], 48). And, "The catalyst for a profounder criticism and a mass mobilization of American women proved to be the young female participants in the social movements of the 1960s. These daughters of the middle class had received mixed, paradoxical messages about what it meant to grow up to be women in America" (Sara Evans, *Personal Politics: The Roots of Liberation in the Civil Rights Movement and the New Left* [New York: Vintage, 1980], 22).

12. Joanne Meyerowitz, "Women and Gender in Postwar America," 1945–1960," and "Beyond the Feminine Mystique: A Reassessment of Postwar Mass Culture 1946–1958," in *Not June Cleaver*, 2–3 and 229–62. On the contradictions in Friedan's version of her own history and how that helped her to reach her audience better, see Daniel Horowitz, "Rethinking Betty Friedan and *The Feminine Mystique*: Labor Union Radicalism and Feminism in Cold War America," *American Quarterly* 48 (March 1996): 1–42. For a discussion of women's discontent in the Cold War era, see Eva Moskowitz, "'It's Good to Blow Your Top': Women's Magazines and a Discourse of Discontent, 1945–1965," *Journal of Women's History* 8 (fall 1996): 66–97.

13. Meyerowitz, *Not June Cleaver*, 238; Moskowitz, *Journal of Women's History* 8: 67, 77, 78, 87, 89, 91; Friedan, *The Feminine Mystique*, 14. Even at the time, acceptance of women workers received notice. A study of popular magazines in 1958 examined 35 articles concerning working mothers and found that "the dominant message was that both sets of responsibilities could be met by a woman with determination and energy" (M. G. Hatch and D. L. Hatch, "Problems of Married Working Women as Presented by Three Popular Working Women's Magazines," *Social Forces* 37 [1958]: 148–53, cited in Alberta Engvall Siegel and Miriam Bushkoff Hass, "The Working Mother: A Review of Research," *Child Development* 34 [September 1963]: 522).

14. Chafe makes this point clearly in *The American Woman*, chap. 9.

15. Gerry Murray Engel, "I Chose Work," *Good Housekeeping*, 7 January 1953, 49. In the late 1950s, sociological studies showed increasing acceptance for working mothers as children matured. In one study, 42 percent of the women polled condoned the employment of mothers with preschool children and 49 percent approved employed mothers of school-age children. For mothers of high school students, the approval was 66 percent; H. M. Glenn, "Attitudes of Women Regarding

Gainful Employment of Married Women," *Journal of Home Economics* 51 (1959): 247–53, cited in Siegel and Hass, *Child Development* 34: 520. Joanne Meyerowitz found that women's public achievement was celebrated in 1950s magazines; *Not June Cleaver*, 234–35.

16. "Working Wives," *Life*, 5 January 1953, 75; *Womanpower: A Statement by the National Manpower Council* (New York: Columbia University Press, 1957), 16. This view, which still maintained the primacy of motherhood, was echoed in the President's Commission on the Status of Women report; see Harrison, *Journal of American History* 67: 644.

17. Bernice Fitz-Gibbon, "The Woman in the Gay Flannel Suit," *The New York Times Magazine*, 29 January 1956, 15; David Yellin, "I'm Married to a Working Mother," *Harper's*, July 1956, 35.

18. Dorothy Barclay, "Case for Mothers Who Go to Work," *The New York Times Magazine*, 4 October 1953, 51; Frances Strain, *Marriage Is for Two* (New York: Longmans, Green & Co., 1948), 102. Writer Hannah Lees expressed a similar opinion; "Are You Too Much Mother?" *Parents Magazine*, April 1957, 54.

19. David Yellin, *Harper's*, July 1956, 36.

20. Robert Coughlan, "Changing Roles in Modern Marriage," *Life*, 23 December 1956, 116.

21. Sloan Wilson, "The Woman in the Gray Flannel Suit," *The New York Times Magazine*, 15 January 1956, 15.

22. Ibid., 36, 38; Clifford R. Adams, "Making Marriage Work," *Ladies' Home Journal*, September 1954, 26.

23. Benjamin Spock, *The Common Sense Book of Baby and Child Care* (New York: Duell, Sloan & Pearce, 1957), 570.

24. Yellin, *Harper's*, July 1956, 35; Dorothy Thompson, "The Employed Woman and Her Household," *Ladies' Home Journal*, September 1952, 11, 14.

25. Gertrude Samuels, "Why Twenty Million Women Work," *The New York Times Magazine*, 9 September 1951, 35; *Womanpower*, 33.

26. Edmund Bergler, M. D., *Divorce Won't Help* (New York: Harper & Bros., 1948), 209; Strain, *Marriage Is for Two*, 116.

27. IHD Archives, Ava Michaels, I-8, 1958, 2. In the 1950s financial need was "the most acceptable reason for a woman to work." In one study of 50 middle- and upper-middle-class working mothers, just over half worked "as a means of achieving cultural, status, educational and health goals for the family and children not otherwise available" (M. R. Yarrow, "Maternal Employment and Childrearing," *Children* 8 [1961]: 226, cited in Siegel and Haas, *Child Development* 34: 524). In order to protect the anonymity of participants in the IHD study, in the pages that follow I avoid specific reference to the jobs that women held. Most working women were clustered in the female sector of the labor market whether they pursued pink-collar jobs or careers in the familiar female professions. A few women found work in predominantly male fields—drafting, electronics, and other skilled work.

28. "The concentration of child-rearing in the early years of marriage is diffi-

cult to explain if women were planning their whole lives around the marital and maternal role" (Susan Householder Van Horn, *Women, Work, and Fertility* [New York: New York University Press, 1988], 122). IHD Archives, Janice Rogers, 1963, 5; Alice Bremmer, I-5, 1958, 12, 14; James Richards, 1958, 7. Of the Oakland IHD women in Glen Elder's study a quarter followed what he termed a "conventional pattern of employment," that is, work prior to marriage and not returning. Yet in 1964 one-third of this conventional group told the IHD that they had "plans to seek employment in the near future" (*Children of the Great Depression* [Chicago: University of Chicago Press, 1974], 212–13).

29. IHD Archives, Katie Ryder, I-3, 1960, 17.

30. "Are We Wasting Women?" *Life*, 28 July 1961, 36B.

31. Friedan, *The Feminine Mystique*, 11.

32. Betty Friedan, "The Crisis in Women's Identity," speech, delivered at the University of California, San Francisco, 1964, and "Woman: The Fourth Dimension," in *It Changed My Life: Writings on the Women's Movement* (New York: W. W. Norton & Co., 1985), 66, 34.

33. Friedan, *The Feminine Mystique*, 332–33.

34. Elizabeth Douvan, "Employment and the Adolescent," in F. Ivan Nye and Lois Wladis Hoffman, *The Employed Mother in America*, 146, 153. For a brief summary of the research in *The Employed Mother*, see Ronald J. Burke and Tamara Weir, "Relationship of Wives' Employment Status to Husband, Wife and Pair Satisfaction and Performance," *Journal of Marriage and the Family* 38 (May 1976): 280.

35. Hilda Sidney Krech, "The Identity of Modern Woman," *The Nation*, 20 September 1965, 127. This was a common observation in 1965. David Riesman, author of *The Lonely Crowd*, predicted that women who "put their professional interests to simmer on the back of the stove during the early family-building years" would reemerge from this "familism" to "refurbish their professional concerns" (David Riesman, "Two Generations," in Robert Jay Lifton, ed., *The Woman in America* [Boston: Houghton Mifflin Co., 1965], 96).

36. Lois Benjamin, "How to Be a Working Mother without Really Crying," *Ladies' Home Journal*, May 1966, 101; Nannette E. Scofield, "When Mother Goes Back to Work," *The New York Times Magazine*, 15 December 1968, 95.

37. "The Reentry Problem," *Time*, 20 March 1972, 86–87; Hazel Erskine, "The Polls: Women's Role," *Public Opinion Quarterly* 35 (summer 1971): 282–87; "Opinion Roundup," *Public Opinion* 3 (December/January 1980): 33, cited in Ethel Klein, *Gender Politics*, 42.

38. IHD Archives, Mary Smith, 1982, 31; Betty Morris, 1970, 35. Amy Chase, an exception to the overall postwar pattern, remained a homemaker through most of her married life. One reason she stayed away from the work world was her conviction that she would not be hired: "Lord knows who would hire me since I've been a housewife all these years. I don't know how to do anything" (IHD Archives, Amy Chase, 1969, 35).

39. IHD Archives, Blanche Warner, 1969, 10; Evelyn Mitchell, 1972, 62.

40. IHD Archives, Meg Fisher, 1969, I-2, 70. IHD Archives, Sylvia Gould, 1970, 23; 1982, 24. Nancy S. Barrett, "Women in the Job Market: Occupations, Earnings, and Career Opportunities," in Smith, *Subtle Revolution*, 46. Economic historian Claudia Goldin has linked midlife labor-force participation to youthful participation for cohorts of women born 1900 to 1910. It is likely that work experience in young adulthood had a similar impact on cohorts born during 1920–30; Goldin, *Understanding the Gender Gap*, 147, 148.

41. IHD Archives, Ruth Wright, 1971, 26.

42. IHD Archives, Martha Bentley, 1970, 56; Betty Morris, 1982, 1.

43. IHD Archives, Maureen Gordon, 1970, 5, 13, 16.

44. In the 1970s, "Women's magazines gave women permission to work. However, women's work still had to be rationalized within the good of the family" (Kathryn Keller, *Mothers and Work in Popular American Magazines* [Westport: Greenwood Press, 1994], 99). It is important to note that while time spent with children diminished after they went to school, homemakers did not have any less household labor to perform. As historian Ruth Schwartz Cowan concludes, "Most American housewives did not enter the job market because they had enormous amounts of free time on their hands. Rather, American housewives . . . discovered that, with the help of a dishwasher, a washing machine, and an occasional frozen dinner, they could undertake that employment without endangering their family's living standards" (Ruth Schwartz Cowan, *More Work for Mother: The Ironies of Household Technology from the Open Hearth to the Microwave* [New York: Basic Books, 1983], 208).

45. IHD Archives, Meg Fisher, 1969, 12. In 1970, Didi Jones said, "I was just worn out. After ten years of raising a family and working both, I was just always exhausted. So, when the opportunity came to work part-time," she jumped on it. IHD Archives, Didi Jones, 1970, 21.

46. IHD Archives, Judy Kent, 1971, 8, 9; Erma Bombeck, *A Marriage Made in Heaven, Or Too Tired for an Affair* (New York: HarperCollins, 1993), 90, 97.

47. This integration, without compensatory shifts in the household division of labor, resulted in "overload for wives." So concluded two sociologists who reviewed the sociological literature on women and housework in 1979; see Sandra L. Hofferth and Kristin A. Moore, "Women's Employment in Marriage," in Smith, *Subtle Revolution*, 115.

48. Susan R. Orden and Norman M. Bradburn, "Working Wives and Marriage Happiness," *American Journal of Sociology* 74 (January 1969): 397, 398.

49. IHD Archives, Ruth Wright, 1971, 26; Karen Lewis, 1958, 5.

50. IHD Archives, Judy Kent, 1971, 15; Lois Dyer, 1982, 9; Maureen Gordon, 1982, 36.

51. IHD Archives, Harriet Pollard, 1970, 18; Marlene Hill, 1970, 31.

52. For a sobering analysis of how women's salaries were spent in the 1970s, see Clair Vickery, "Women's Economic Contribution to the Family," in Smith, *Subtle Revolution*, 160–62, 177–78. Vickery argues that taxes, clothing, and transportation

costs rise with women's employment, significantly cutting into a family's financial gains when they went to work. IHD Archives, Sharon Richards, 1982, 21; Gene Lewis, S-I, 1982, 13; Ruth Wright, 1971, 29.

53. IHD Archives, Lorraine Sherwood, 1969, 12; Caroline Wood, 1970, 15; Floyd Michaels, 1970, 30.

54. IHD Archives, Anne Matthews, 1970, 31.

55. IHD Archives, Ruth Wright, S-I, 1982, 13; May Perkins, 1970, 65. Thirteen women mentioned they enjoyed the sociability they found at work.

56. IHD Archives, Irene Lawrence, 1982, 18; Nina Harris, S-I, 1982, 16; May Perkins, 1982, 12.

57. IHD Archives, May Perkins, 1982, 13, 14. Feminist economists in the 1970s studied the value of homemakers' labor to their families by pricing their services at minimum wage. In 1973 dollars, that value in a two-child family was estimated at $7,000 per year; Kathryn E. Walker, "Household Work Time: Its Implication for Family Decisions," *Journal of Home Economics* 65 (October 1973): 7–11, cited in Sandra L. Hofferth and Kristin A. Moore, "Women's Employment and Marriage," in Smith, *Subtle Revolution*, 112, n. 43.

58. IHD Archives, Marlene Hill, 1982, 37; Alice Bremmer, I-3, 1958, 14 and 1982, 3, 39. Nearly a quarter of those who worked cited independence as an important benefit.

59. IHD Archives, Gail Henderson, 1958, 12, and S-I, 1982, 8; Anne Matthews, S-I, 1982, 10.

60. IHD Archives, Ava Michaels, I-8, 1958, 6; Thelma Morton, 1970, 31.

61. A brief look at the numbers of part-time female workers of the same cohort as the IHD women shows clearly that this cohort (born 1920–41) continued to increase its labor-force participation over time. In 1965 there were 1,681,000 women aged 22–44 voluntarily working part time. In 1977, there were 1,877,000 part-time female workers aged 45–64; Nancy Barrett, "Women and the Job Market: Unemployment and Work Schedules," in Smith, *Subtle Revolution*, 84.

62. Studies in the 1970s showed, "Working wives had higher self-esteem and self-confidence, and a greater sense of personal competence and personal autonomy" (Burke and Weir, " *Journal of Marriage and the Family* 38: 280). The association of self-confidence and employment is also supported by social science research on working mothers in F. Ivan Nye, "Effects on Mother" in Lois Wladis Hoffman and F. Ivan Nye, *Working Mothers* (San Francisco: Jossey-Bass, 1974), 224.

63. IHD Archives, Ava Michaels, S-I, 1982, 7; Barbara Spalding, S-I, 1982, 10; Anne Matthews, 1982, 22; Evelyn Mitchell, 1983, 1. Thirty-two percent of the women working in 1982 mentioned that gaining a sense of personal efficacy made their jobs satisfying; S-I, 1982.

64. IHD Archives, Martha Bentley, 1970, 55; Maureen Gordon, S-I, 1982, 9. Thirty-six percent of the women working in 1982 mentioned fulfillment or making a contribution made their jobs satisfying. Half said simply that the work was interesting or fun; S-I, 1982.

65. IHD Archives, Judy Kent, 1982, 13; Blanche Warner, 1981, 11; Mary Smith, S-I, 1982, 10. More than half of the women working in the 1980s reported personal satisfaction as a benefit they derived from their jobs. Research psychologists have studied a cohort of women roughly 15 years younger than the women discussed here. They found that women's individualism and nonconformance to norms increased over the life course; Brent W. Roberts and Ravenna Helson, "Changes in Culture, Changes in Personality: The Influence of Individualism in a Longitudinal Study of Women," *Journal of Personality and Social Psychology* 72 (March 1997): 641–51. They have also found increased independence and confidence among women in their early 50s; Ravenna Helson and Paul Wink, "Personality Change in Women from the Early 40s to the Early 50s," *Psychology in Aging* 7 (March 1992): 46–55.

66. Bombeck, *A Marriage Made in Heaven*, 85, 86, 88. Social science studies in the 1970s showed that while housework remained the primary responsibility of working wives, the household labor of other family members did increase when wives took jobs. Adolescent children's availability might limit husbands' involvement. Nonetheless, women's employment tended to mean that decisions about the allocation of labor would be made based on availability and preference rather than traditional role prescription; Stephen J. Bahr, "Effects on Power and Division of Labor in the Family," in Hoffman and Nye, *Working Mothers*, 184.

67. IHD Archives, John Anderson, 1970, 39. Ironically, his second wife worked their entire marriage in part to help him meet his child support payments; Glenn Dyer, S-I, 1982, 10.

68. IHD Archives, David Morris, 1982, 38; Rick Snyder, 1960, 8; Joan Sinclair, I-7, 1959, 15; S-I, 1982, 8. The distinction Andrew Sinclair drew, however, was about wage-earning work only, for within a few years Joan was working for his small business and once the children were raised, Joan worked right alongside him.

69. IHD Archives, Steven Downs, 1982, 20.

70. IHD Archives, May Perkins, 1982, 14; Dale George, 1970, 33. One study of 189 Canadian couples in the 1970s found that men whose wives worked registered greater marital dissatisfactions than did men with homemaking wives. Since some of those dissatisfactions were job-related, their dissatisfaction may have been related to the family's overall economic situation and the factors propelling a woman into employment, rather than solely the fact of her employment. Still, the findings indicated that marriage to homemaking wives was important to men's definitions of marital satisfaction; Burke and Weir, *Journal of Marriage and the Family* 38: 283.

71. IHD Archives, Alice Bremmer, 1969, 32, and 1982, 30.

72. IHD Archives, Gordon James, 1958, 12; David Nichols, S-I, 1983, 11; S-I, 1982.

73. IHD Archives, Ken Harris, S-I, 1982, 13.

74. IHD Archives, Edward Martin, S-I, 1982, 12; Frank Ryder, 1981, 25; Diane Key, 1970, 49.

75. IHD Archives, Glen Dyer, 1982, 14, 36; Lois Dyer, 1982, 44. Wives' paychecks increased discretionary income for couples; this tended to be used "to improve husband-wife sociability" (Orden and Bradburn, *American Journal of Sociology* 74: 401).

76. IHD Archives, Dean Lawrence, 1970, 19, and 1982, 19. By 1982, only one working woman reported her husband disapproved of her employment outright. More than half said their husbands approved; S-I, 1982.

77. IHD Archives, Philip Pollard, 1970, 25; Dan Bentley, S-I, 1982, 15.

78. IHD Archives, Alice Bremmer, 1982, 30. Stephen J. Bahr, "Effects on Power and Division of Labor," in Hoffman and Nye, *Working Mothers*, 167–81.

79. IHD Archives, Herbert Henderson, 1982, 25.

80. On masculine domesticity in the 1950s, see Robert Rutherdale, "Dads, You're Gonna Love This," unpublished paper given at the Third Carleton Conference on the History of the Family, 1997. Political scientist Ethel Klein writes, "When market activities became more salient to women's lives and to their self-definition, issues such as female unemployment, low pay, low advancement opportunities, and the sex segregation of occupations became matters of great concern. . . . the development of a new self-image of women as workers allowed for the recognition and rejection of unfair treatment" (Klein, *Gender Politics*, 46).

81. Surveying women in 1964, David Riesman assumed that they would quietly continue in their "effort to lead a full, multidimensional life without storming the barricades at home or abroad." He underestimated the conflict between multidimensional goals and sexist obstacles that could not accommodate them; Riesman, "Two Generations," in Lifton, *The Woman in America*, 97. Ethel Klein compares poll results to labor force participation rates in the 1960s and concludes, "Labor force participation increased rapidly for over a decade before attitudes toward working women became favorable, which suggests that feminism is more likely to result from nontraditional behaviors rather than the other way around" (Klein, *Gender Politics*, 109). Valerie Kincade Oppenheimer found that shifts in attitudes lagged behind behavioral changes, indicating that changes in behavior have gradually brought about changes in sex norms; see *Work and the Family: A Study in Social Demography*, 28 –31.

CHAPTER THREE

1. After Robert Young's death in the summer of 1998, journalists evaluated his influence on postwar parents' psyches and the ironic contrast between his small-screen and off-screen lives. Off screen Young struggled with alcoholism and depression. Of 1950s sitcoms, columnist Ellen Goodman wrote, "Their middle-class subdivisions are our Eden, their nuclear families the cultural baseline against which we judge all other families, especially our own. And all other parents, especially ourselves"; "The Father Who Knew Best," *The San Francisco Chronicle*, 28 July 1998, A19.

2. Margaret Marsh, *Suburban Lives* (New Brunswick: Rutgers University Press, 1990); Robert Griswold, *Fatherhood in America: A History* (New York: Basic Books, 1993), 119–60; Ralph La Rossa, *The Modernization of Fatherhood: A Social and Political History* (Chicago: University of Chicago Press, 1997), 2.

3. On middle-class residential patterns and their impact on family life, see Margaret Marsh, *Suburban Lives*, 76–83. See also John Gillis, *A World of Their Own Making: Myth, Ritual, and the Quest for Family Values* (New York: Basic Books, 1996), chap. 9. On increased leisure time, see Elaine Tyler May, *Great Expectations: Marriage and Divorce in Post-Victorian America* (Chicago: University of Chicago Press, 1980), 137–55. For the role of psychologists in shaping the ideals of fatherhood in the 1920s, see Robert Griswold, *Fatherhood in America*, 121–37. On men's desire to parent actively, see La Rossa, *The Modernization of Fatherhood*, 2.

4. On the impact of World War II on father-child relationships, see William M. Tuttle Jr., *Daddy's Gone to War: The Second World War in the Lives of America's Children* (New York: Oxford University Press, 1993).

5. As Griswold shows, fixing fatherhood in the 1950s and 1960s was linked to correcting youth and social problems; *Fatherhood in America*, 8, 186.

6. For more on the suburban family style, see Kenneth Jackson, *The Crabgrass Frontier* (New York: Oxford University Press, 1985). Benjamin Spock, M. D., *The Common Sense Book of Baby and Child Care* (New York: Pocket Books, 1946). I have quoted from the 1957 edition, published by Duell, Sloan & Pearce. For an admiring and insightful overview of Spock's contributions to postwar family life, see Ann Hulbert, "Dr. Spock's Baby: Fifty Years in the Life of a Book and the American Family," in *The New Yorker*, 20 May 1996, 82–92. IHD participants joined with other Americans in embracing Spock's advice and later in criticizing its results. Crystal Robertson said she "went through about five copies until they were dog-eared," until finally she "didn't have to go out and buy any new copies because I knew the book." Judy Kent commented, "I really feel that one of the greatest crimes was Dr. Spock" (IHD Archives, Crystal Robertson, 1970, 22; Judy Kent, 1971, 32). On the appeal of Spock's advice for anxious parents in an anxious age, see Michael Zuckerman, "Dr. Spock: The Confidence Man," in Charles E. Rosenberg, ed., *The Family in History* (Philadelphia: University of Pennsylvania Press, 1975), 179–207. William Graebner offers a different take on Spock, noting Spock's own anxieties about both social and individual instability; "The Unstable World of Benjamin Spock: Social Engineering in a Democratic Culture, 1917–1950," *Journal of American History* 67 (December 1980): 612–29. As of 1976, Spock's book had sold over 28 million copies; Nancy Pottisham Weiss, "Mother, the Invention of Necessity: Dr. Benjamin Spock's Baby and Child Care," *American Quarterly* 19 (winter 1977): 520.

7. O. Spurgeon English and Constance Foster, "How Good a Family Man Is Your Husband?" *Parents Magazine*, September 1952, 37. In 1949, Rachel Ann Elder noted the evolution of a new family type, the "developmental" family. This family she argued was "based on inter-personal relations of mutual affection, companionship and understanding, with a recognition of individual capabilities, desires and

need for the development of each member of the family, be he father, mother or child" ("Traditional and Developmental Conceptions of Fatherhood," *Marriage and Family Living* 11 [summer 1949]: 98). Other researchers saw changes in the "modern" family as well; see Ruth Jacobson Tasch, "The Role of the Father in the Family," *Journal of Experimental Education* 20 (June 1952): 319–61.

8. Margaret Mead, "What Is Happening to the American Family?" *Journal of Social Casework* 28 (1947): 329, cited in Robert H. Bremner, "Families, Children, and the State," in Bremner and Gary W. Reichard, eds., *Reshaping America: Society and Institutions, 1945–1960* (Columbus: Ohio State University Press, 1982), 7.

9. Robert Coughlan, "Changing Roles in Modern Marriage," *Life,* 23 December 1956, 118; Edward Streeter, "Have Fathers Changed?" *The New York Times Magazine,* 9 May 1954, 14.

10. M. Robert Gomberg, "Father as Family Man," *The New York Times Magazine,* 6 September 1953, 34; Ruth Newburn Sedam, "Who Wants to Go Back to the Good Old Days?" *Parents Magazine,* October 1956, 38.

11. Harold Justin, "It's a Man's Job, Too!" *Parents Magazine,* September 1951, 165; English and Foster, "Father's Changing Role," *Parents Magazine,* October 1951, 44; English and Foster, *Parents Magazine,* September 1952, 81; Loyd W. Rowland, "Father's Role," *The New York Times Magazine,* 31 July 1949, 27.

12. Spock, *The Common Sense Book of Baby and Child Care,* 18.

13. Ibid.; English and Foster, "How to Be a Good Father," *Parents Magazine,* June 1950, 86.

14. English and Foster, *Parents Magazine,* October 1951, 45; Marina Farnham, "Helping Boys to Be Boys and Girls to Be Girls," *Parents Magazine,* January 1953, 35, 62; English and Foster, *Parents Magazine,* October 1951, 45. On Spock as a key disseminator of psychoanalytic concepts of family life, see A. Michael Sulman, "The Humanization of the American Child: Benjamin Spock as a Popularizer of Psychoanalytic Thought," *Journal of the History of the Behavioral Sciences* 9 (July 1973): 258–65. In addition to psychoanalytic concerns, psychologists pondered the political ramifications of fathering styles. One study identified permissive fathering with healthy personality development and men favoring restrictive styles with inadequacies and a list of characteristics associated with the "authoritarian personality"; Jack Block, "Personality Characteristics Associated with Fathers' Attitudes toward Child-Rearing," *Child Development* 26 (March 1955): 41–48. On sex roles and adult men, see Barbara Ehrenreich, *The Hearts of Men: American Dreams and the Flight from Commitment* (New York: Anchor Books, 1983), 14–15. In a study of 85 urban fathers, Ruth Tasch found that while men did not see themselves as imparting sex-typed behavior to their children, they did treat their daughters and sons differently; *Journal of Experimental Education* 20: 327–31.

15. Newburn Sedam, *Parents Magazine,* October 1956, 38. For an in-depth discussion of the meaning of recreation in Canadian baby boom families, see Robert Rutherdale, "'Dads, You're Gonna Love This': Advertising, Oral History and Masculine Domesticity in Canada, 1945–1965," unpublished paper, presented at the Third Carleton Conference on the History of the Family, Ottawa, 1997.

16. Spock, *The Common Sense Book of Baby and Child Care,* 17–18; English and Foster, "What's Happening to Father?" *Better Homes and Gardens,* 30 April 1952, 205. Other voices supported this view: "Tenderness, gentleness, a capacity to empathize with others, a capacity to respond emotionally and to rationalize at leisure, to value a love object more than the self, and to find a living experience in the experiences of others is not the prerogative of women alone; it is a human characteristic"; Irene M. Josselyn, M. D., "Cultural Forces, Motherliness, and Fatherliness," *American Journal of Orthopsychiatry* 26 (April 1956): 268.

17. English and Foster, *Parents Magazine,* June 1950, 84, 86; English and Foster, *Parents Magazine,* October 1951, 153, 156.

18. English and Foster, *Parents Magazine,* June 1950, 87; Dorothy Barclay, "What Every Father Should Know," *The New York Times Magazine,* 11 June 1950, 47.

19. Loyd W. Rowland, *The New York Times Magazine,* 31 July 1949, 27; Streeter, *The New York Times Magazine,* 9 May 1954, 14. Arlene Skolnick sees postwar men constructing their own versions of domestic masculinity: "The suburban fathers of the 1950s were domestic in different ways than earlier generations of men: not only were they spending more time at home but they also found ways to carve out niches of masculinity around the house" (*Embattled Paradise: The American Family in an Age of Uncertainty* [New York: Basic Books, 1991], 112).

20. Justin, *Parents Magazine,* September 1951, 164; Willard D. Lewis, "When Daddy Comes Home," *Parents Magazine,* May 1950, 46; Andrew Takas, "What Children Need from Dad," *Parents Magazine,* May 1953, 77. Images of playful fathers reached fathers in other ways. In his study of twentieth-century advertising, Bruce Brown found that magazine advertisements commonly depicted fathers playing with their children; *Images of Family Life in Magazine Advertising: 1920–1978* (New York: Praeger, 1981), 48. Regarding the postwar concern with fatherhood, May writes, "The outpouring of attention to fatherhood in the popular media belies an undercurrent of uncertainty: were fathers really involved in childrearing?" (*Homeward Bound: American Families in the Cold War Era* [New York: Basic Books, 1988], 147).

21. Gomberg, *The New York Times Magazine,* 6 September 1953, 34; Bruno Bettelheim, "Fathers Shouldn't Try to Be Mothers," *Parents Magazine,* October 1956, 129, 126, 40. Another critic disparaged the emphasis on play because it diminished the actual role men could have in childrearing. "Being considered an animated plaything, too fragile to tolerate the realities of the home or too limited in knowledge to be a wise parent, is not especially conducive to an effective expression of the mature self that is an essential component of fatherliness" (Josselyn, *American Journal of Orthopsychiatry* 26: 269.

22. Spock, *The Common Sense Book of Baby and Child Care* 18; Selma Lentz Morrison, "Father Needs Your Help," *Parents Magazine,* October 1950, 32; English and Foster, *Parents Magazine,* October 1951, 44; English and Foster, *Parents Magazine,* September 1952, 77.

23. For a discussion of the home as haven for men in the 1950s, see May, *Homeward Bound,* 205.

24. Erma Bombeck, *A Marriage Made in Heaven, Or Too Tired for an Affair* (New York: HarperCollins, 1993), 43, 51.

25. Among men in the Oakland Study queried in 1964, Glen Elder found work "was valued more highly than family activity," but that "leisure and community roles" ranked significantly lower than family activity in men's "activity preferences" (*Children of the Great Depression* [Chicago: University of Chicago Press, 1974], 186–87).

26. IHD Archives, Ernest Johnson, I-2, 1958, 4; Howard Sims, I-4, 1958, 11; Adam Walker, I-2, 1959, 71; Tasch, *Journal of Experimental Education* 20: 352. John Clausen characterized IHD men's "involvement in the paternal role" as "seldom intense," explaining that young fathers were "struggling with both occupational and marital adaptation during the same period" (*American Lives: Looking Back at the Children of the Great Depression* [New York: Free Press, 1993], 255).

27. IHD Archives, Scott Parker, S-S, 1957, 3.

28. IHD Archives, John Thompkins, I-5, 1958, 3; Malcom McKee, I-3, 1959, 16; Dale George, I-3, 1959, 5. On the Sears study, see Griswold, *Fatherhood in America*, 204; G. Gurin, J. Veroff, and S. Feld, *Americans View Their Mental Health: Joint Commission on Mental Illness and Health* (New York: Basic Books, 1960), cited in Joseph Veroff and Sheila Feld, *Marriage and Work in America: A Study of Motives and Roles* (New York: Van Nostrand Reinhold Co., 1970), 126.

29. IHD Archives, Dean Lawrence, H-L, 1958, 5–7; Dennis Perkins, S-P, 1957, 2. Two more men said in 1970 that they improved on their fathers' examples. Robert Griswold noted a similar desire to be more affectionate than their own fathers among participants in the Sears's study at Stanford; *Fatherhood in America*, 204. In Rachel Elder's study of 32 Iowa fathers, she discovered that one-third wanted to be "better" than their own fathers and another third wanted to be "different." Most significant, and perhaps most indicative of a change in male attitudes toward involvement in childrearing, the parent postwar fathers "many said they tried to be like" was mother; *Marriage and Family Living* 11 (summer 1949): 100, 106. In Tasch's study, very few men rated their own fathers as participants in child care, whereas for themselves they ranked that role only after "companion," "economic provider," and "guide and teacher" (*Journal of Experimental Education* 20: 353).

30. IHD Archives, Leonard Stone, S-S, 1958, 11; Gordon James, S-S, 1958, 12, 21. Exactly how "lots of husbands" fathered in the 1950s is difficult to determine. One study of 1027 Florida families, while it did find that most men were most active in behaviors traditionally associated with male family roles, also noted that "more than one-third of the fathers" cared for their children when they were sick, a task the author saw as traditionally female. And while fathers lagged considerably behind mothers, they did "help children with school work" and "see children do homework." Two-thirds also saw to it that "children have fun" (Theodore B. Johannis Jr., "Participation by Fathers, Mothers and Teenage Sons and Daughters in Selected Child Care and Control Activity," *The Coordinator* 6 [December 1957]: 31–32).

31. IHD Archives, Robert Mitchell, 1958, 3, 5.

32. Tasch, *Journal of Experimental Education* 20: 347; Elder, *Marriage and Family Living* 11 (summer 1949): 100.

33. IHD Archives, Gordon James, S-S, 1958, 8. Tasch's 85 fathers criticized themselves for not having enough time for their children. Tasch wrote, "Daytime absence from the home and absorption in occupational success may appear to present a dilemma since even though fathers enjoy spending time with their children, the amount of time they can spend is prescribed to some extent by job pressures." But then she went on to let busy fathers off the hook. "Doing things with children in the time they have available, appears to be more important than the consideration of how much time they spend with their children." Here she echoed the experts; Tasch, *Journal of Experimental Education* 20: 358.

34. IHD Archives, Dean Lawrence, 1958, 2.

35. IHD Archives, Leonard Stone, 1958, 9.

36. IHD Archives, Sam Arthur, I-3, 1959, 16; Joseph Maxwell, I-3, 1958, 31; Milly Benson, I-3, 1959, 8. By their own or their wives' report, seven men voiced strictly traditional attitudes toward childrearing.

37. IHD Archives, Grant Thornton, S-S, 1959, 17; Tom Cole, 1958, 7; Scott Parker, S-S, 1958, 15.

38. IHD Archives, James Evans, I-3, 1959, 16. William G. Dyer and Dick Urban, "The Institutionalization of Equalitarian Family Norms," *Marriage and Family Living* 20 (February 1958): 55; Tasch, *Journal of Experimental Education* 20: 353. See also Ruth J. Tasch, "Interpersonal Perceptions of Fathers and Mothers," *Journal of Genetic Psychology* 87 (September 1955), 61. A 1960 study of 391 women found that while a third of the husbands put children to bed and taught children manners, just over 10 percent bathed and fed preschool children; Marvin E. Olsen, "Distribution of Family Responsibilities and Social Stratification," *Marriage and Family Living* 22 (February 1960): 64. Griswold surveyed studies of the sharing of household tasks and concludes, "Fathers in the 1950s continued to profit from the gender-based division of labor so central to the structure of twentieth-century family relationships." Fatherhood for men was defined as fun, not as work; Griswold, *Fatherhood in America*, 194.

39. A much later study of male participation in household work supports the contention that the presence of small children in the home is a strong predictor of male involvement in domestic labor. But hours spent at work was another strong variable. For baby boom fathers these demands fell coterminously; Shelley Coverman, "Explaining Husbands' Participation in Domestic Labor," *Sociological Quarterly,* 26 (April 1985): 92.

40. IHD Archives, Meg Fisher, I-3, 1958, 1; Judy Kent, S-S, 1959, 24. Eight wives specifically praised their husbands' parenting in the 1950s interviews. By 1964, social scientist David Riesman could observe, "The young husband has become as much by his own volition as by pressure on him, part of the maternal task force, helping his wife with the children on all occasions and not only on such

ceremonial ones as a trip to the circus or being a spectator (as in the movie *Executive Suite*) at a Little League baseball game" ("Two Generations," in Robert Jay Lifton, ed., *The Woman in America* [Boston: Houghton Mifflin Co., 1965], 79).

41. IHD Archives, Claudine Parker, S-S, 1958, 6, 11; May Perkins, S-S, 1958, 3.

42. IHD Archives, Claudine Parker, S-S, 1958, 9.

43. IHD Archives, Janice Rogers, S-S, 1958, 17; Milly Benson, I-3, 1959, 8; Georgeanne Gaynor, I-9, 1959, 17.

44. IHD Archives, May Perkins, S-S, 1957, 5. Six wives described emotional or physical tasks they performed in order either to provide relaxing evenings for their husbands (feeding the children before he came home) or to involve them with parenting (planning an event).

45. IHD Archives, Dorothy Simon, H-L, 1959, 8.

46. IHD Archives, Janice Rogers, S-S, 1958, 17.

47. IHD Archives, Dean Lawrence, S-S, 1958, 7; Tom Cole, 1958, 6; Cynthia Thornton, S-S, 1959, 17; Claudine Parker, S-S, 1958, 11.

48. IHD Archives, Gordon James, S-S, 1958, 8; Lloyd Andrews, 1958; Gary Simon, 1959, 5.

49. IHD Archives, Dale George, I-2, 1959, 2; Ron Chase, I-9, 1958, 3. These parenting differences are confirmed by one study. Based on data gathered in 1957, Joseph Veroff and Sheila Feld concluded, "Marriage and parenthood are prescribed ways for him to anchor his life, to establish his adult validity, but it is in day-to-day contact with the business world and the social world outside of the home that men seem to seek their broad interpersonal gratifications. A man without a wife or without children has no anchor, but a man without friends is deprived of his daily social satisfactions" (*Marriage and Work*, 339).

50. Benjamin Spock, M.D., "Fathers as Disciplinarians," *Redbook*, April 1969, 26, 31.

51. T. Berry Brazelton, M. D., "What Makes a Good Father," *Redbook*, January 1970, 74, 122. Popular literature in the 1960s and 1970s was bolstered by continuing psychological research that built a strong case for fatherly involvement. As an example, see the series of articles by psychologist Paul Mussen and his co-authors. In 1960 Mussen and Luther Distler saw stronger masculine role identification in boys whose fathers were affectionate, companionable, and permissive with them than among more distant authoritarian fathers—based on observation of 32 children and interviews with their mothers; Paul Mussen and Luther Distler, "Child-Rearing Antecedents of Masculine Identification in Kindergarten Boys," *Child Development* 31 (March 1960): 89–100. A 1963 study supported the thesis that nurturant fathers raised masculine-identified sons; Paul Mussen and Eldred Rutherford, "Parent-Child Relations and Parental Personality in Relation to Young Children's Sex-Role Preferences," *Child Development* 34 (September 1963): 589–607.

52. "On Being an American Parent," *Time*, 15 December 1967, 30–31. Psychologist Uri Bronfenbrenner reported, "We have found that children who reported their parents away from home for long periods of time rated significantly lower on

such characteristics as responsibility and leadership. Perhaps because it was more pronounced, absence of the father was more critical than that of the mother, particularly in its effect on boys" ("The Split-Level American Family," *Saturday Review*, 7 October 1967, 61).

53. Clausen, *American Lives*, 467.

54. IHD Archives, Adult II survey, 1969. Thanks to Barbara Burek for gathering this information for me.

55. IHD Archives, Norman Smith, 1960, 4; Edward Martin, 1970, 9. Historians Robert Griswold and Elaine Tyler May suggest that as consumption took a central place in defining middle-class status and the democratic American way, breadwinning became all the more important in the decades after World War II; Griswold, *Fatherhood in America*, 197, 198, and May, *Homeward Bound*, 17, 18.

56. IHD Archives, Dean Lawrence, 1970, 27; Scott Clinton, 1970, 4.

57. IHD Archives, Russell Weber, 1969, 11; Malcom McKee, 1970, 35; Bill Mills, 1969, 25, 5. Nearly one quarter of the men volunteered that they did not spend enough time with their children in the 1969–71 interviews.

58. IHD Archives, Leonard Stone, 1971, 16, 50; Richard Gaynor, 1969, 16.

59. IHD Archives, Ken Harris, 1970, 13.

60. IHD Archives, Clay Kent, 1970, 27; Dean Lawrence, 1970, 27; Gary Simon, 1971, 34.

61. IHD Archives, Glen Dyer, 1969, 4, 17; George Rogers, 1969, 21; Carl Gordon, 1970, 6. Of baby boom fatherhood in Canada, historian Robert Rutherdale writes, "Fatherhood in the domestic setting was portrayed as an active and creative role, shaped by gendered preferences for certain practices, pursuits, and patterns of family relations. Fathers were expected to spend time with their families, but chose to do so in a consumer-based economy that allowed them to express their manliness in many forms, from the backyard grass cutter to the family vacation traveler" ("'Dads, You're Gonna Love This,'" Third Carleton Conference on the History of the Family, Ottawa, 1997, 52–53).

62. IHD Archives, Hal Powell, 1970, 17; Peter Wood, 1970, 5.

63. IHD Archives, Thomas Williams, 1969, 25, 4; Philip Pollard, 1970, 15; Burt Hill, 1970, 9; Charles Bremmer, 1969, 11. This finding is in keeping with other studies of men in the 1970s. A 1976 study reported that "Men say they are not as good fathers as they would like to be because they are not as close to their children and do not spend time with them or interact with them enough" (Joseph Veroff, Elizabeth Douvan, Richard A. Kulka, *The Inner American: A Self-Portrait from 1957 to 1976* [New York: Basic Books, 1981], 219).

64. IHD Archives, Herbert Henderson, 1971, 13. One study of parent socialization and political values of children by sex concluded, "Although the sample was small, in general, the mothers had about equal influence over sons and daughters, while fathers exerted little influence over either child with regard to the eight issue areas we investigated." And "Our findings suggest that mothers still dominate in the sphere of child-rearing; fathers have not attained parity in parental influence."

The study looked at 73 families; Alfred P. Fengler and Vivian Wood, "Continuity between Generations: Differential Influence of Mothers and Fathers," *Youth and Society* 4 (March 1973): 368, 370.

65. IHD Archives, Miriam Stone, 1971, 32; Lois Dyer, 1971, 47; May Perkins, 1958, 16; Mary Smith, 1971, 21. For IHD couples as a whole, this stage of the family cycle—with adolescent children present in the home—was a difficult one. Clausen noted that "fully half of the Guidance Study mothers" noted "dealing with the children" as a source of "major disagreement with their husbands" (*American Lives*, 430). Marjorie F. Lowenthal and David A. Chiriboga, "Transition to the Empty Nest: Crisis, Challenge or Relief?" *Archives of General Psychiatry* 26 (1972), cited in Jessica Field Cohen, "Male Roles in Mid-Life," *Family Coordinator* 28 (October 1979): 468.

66. IHD Archives, Patricia James, 1970, 5; Marie Weber, 1969, 28, 33.

67. IHD Archives, Fred Adams, 1970, 34.

68. Harry and Sandy Chapin, "Cats in the Cradle," *Verities and Balderdash*, Elektra Records, 1974. Thanks to the Harry Chapin Fan Page: http://www.littlejason.com/chapin/info/html. One reviewer of research on males in midlife noted, "Males who adhere to the masculine role description may find themselves, in mid-life, questioning their achievements and accomplishments and bemoaning the inadequacy of their familial and other interpersonal relationships" (Cohen, *Family Coordinator* 28 [October 1979]: 466).

69. "Where Have all the Fathers Gone?" *McCall's*, November 1972, 46; Robert B. McCall, "The Importance of Fathers," *Parents*, August 1980, 82; "Do Fathers Make Good Mothers," *McCall's*, February 1977, 65; "Working Fathers," *Ms.*, May 1974, 54–55, 111; Jack McGarvey, "It's a Bird, It's a Plane, It's Super-Two," *Parents Magazine*, January 1976, 35–37, 70. For a contemporaneous overview of research and perspectives on fathering in the 1970s, see Robert A. Fein, "Research on Fathering: Social Policy and an Emergent Perspective," *Journal of Social Issues* 34 (winter 1978): 122–35. Griswold discusses the feminist and therapeutic discourse surrounding fatherhood in the 1980s and 1990s; *Fatherhood in America*, 247–52.

70. Clausen, *American Lives*, 466, 464.

71. IHD Archives, Jane Mills, 1982, 25; Claire Manning, 1982, 30; Nina Harris, S-I, 1982, 25; Dina Powell, S-I, 1982, 14. Of the respondents to the third IHD interview, Clausen writes, "Clinical interviews in the wives' 50s and 60s elicited deep-seated resentment from many women" toward their husbands' family roles; Clausen, *American Lives*, 466.

72. IHD Archives, Nina Harris, S-I, 1982, 25.

73. IHD Archives, Janice Rogers, S-I, 1982, 9; Irene Lawrence, 1982, 6; Marlene Hill, 1982, 31.

74. IHD Archives, Louis Miller, 1982, 27; Greg Fox, 1982, 22; Hal Powell, 1982, 40; Clausen, *American Lives*, 464.

75. IHD Archives, Bill Mills, S-I, 1982, 15; Ken Harris, 1982, 19; Sam Arthur, 1982, 10; John Thompkins, 1970, 27.

76. IHD Archives, Grant Thornton, 1982, 10.

77. IHD Archives, Ken Harris, S-I, 1982, 12. Anthony Astrachan mentions a similar desire among the "older fathers" he interviewed for his study of men adapting to gender role change; *How Men Feel: Their Response to Women's Demands for Equality and Power* (Garden City: Anchor Books, 1986), 256.

78. IHD Archives, Andrew Sinclair, 1982, 34.

79. Author's notes. In contrast, thirteen men characterized themselves as good, involved fathers. A few of these still thought they could have done more.

80. Samuel Osherson wrote, "The interviews I have had with men in their thirties and forties convince me that the psychological or physical absence of fathers from their families is one of the great underestimated tragedies of our times" (*Finding Our Fathers: The Unfinished Business of Manhood* [New York: Free Press, 1986], 4).

81. John Gillis, "Making Time for Family: The Invention of Family Time(s) and the Reinvention of Family History," *Journal of Family History* 21 (January 1996): 12.

82. Gillis's perceptive observation that "Family time presents itself to us as a neutral cultural practice, when in fact, it is an ideologically constituted form of prescription" sheds light on the experience of men and women shaping families in the postwar era; ibid., 17.

83. Sociological studies showed that young families in the 1970s still had a long way to go when it came to shared parenting. A 1976 survey of parents of children under 12 years old or younger found that mothers did more child-care than fathers even among dual-career couples. The same survey also showed that men claimed to help more than their wives felt they did. Overall, the surveyors reported, "traditional definitions of father as material provider and moral authority, and mother as socioemotional provider and daily caretaker still hold sway and infuse people's conceptions, performance, and experience of parenthood" (Veroff, Douvan, and Kulka, *The Inner American*, 178–80, 217). Another study found paternal involvement to be 34 percent that of mothers; Michael E. Lamb, "The Emergent American Father," *The Father's Role: Cross-Cultural Perspectives* (Hillsdale, N.J.: Lawrence Erlbaum Associates, 1987), 10. Robert Bly, one of the "fathers" of the men's movement, wrote, "Not seeing your father when you are small, never being with him, having a remote father, an absent father, a workaholic father, is an injury" (*Iron John: A Book about Men* [New York: Vintage Books, 1992], 31). Astrachan noted, "In men's meetings I have been struck by the pathos and the passion with which men talk about compensating for a father's sins in their relations with their own children, sometimes for the wounds inflicted but more often for the emotional absence during their childhoods" (*How Men Feel*, 232, 241).

84. When the next generation of IHD children (the children of the subjects of this book) were queried, researchers found that "There are fewer children, wives tend to be employed, and husbands and wives share in the same tasks rather than having a sharp division of labor" (Clausen, *American Lives*, 206).

CHAPTER FOUR

1. Otis Stiese, "Live the Life of McCall's," *McCall's*, May 1954, 27.

2. Carroll Smith-Rosenberg, "The Female World of Love and Ritual: Relations between Women in Nineteenth-Century America," in *Disorderly Conduct: Visions of Gender in Victorian America* (New York: Oxford University Press, 1985), 53–76.

3. On women's sphere, see Nancy Cott, *The Bonds of Womanhood* (New Haven: Yale University Press, 1977); for opposing views on the mutuality of nineteenth-century middle-class marriage, see Carl Degler, *At Odds: Women and the Family from the Revolution to the Present* (New York: Oxford University Press, 1980); and Carroll Smith-Rosenberg, "The Female World of Love and Ritual," *Disorderly Conduct: Visions of Gender in Victorian America*. Recently historians of gender have called into question earlier historians' emphasis on nineteenth-century prescriptions for separate spheres, arguing that in fact gender conventions were far more flexible in practice than historians allow; see Laura McCall and Donald Yacovone, eds., *A Shared Experience: Men, Women, and the History of Gender* (New York: New York University Press, 1998).

4. Elaine Tyler May argues that by the 1920s the pressures of performing each gender role in marriage also were enhanced; see *Great Expectations* (Chicago: University of Chicago Press, 1980), 156. On marriage in the 1920s, see also Paula Fass, *The Damned and the Beautiful: American Youth in the 1920s* (New York: Oxford University Press, 1979), 64–83.

5. May, *Great Expectations*, 90; John D'Emilio and Estelle B. Freedman, *Intimate Matters: A History of Sexuality in America* (New York: Harper & Row, 1988), 265–74.

6. Steven Mintz and Susan Kellogg, *Domestic Revolutions: A Social History of American Family Life* (New York: Free Press, 1988), 180.

7. One observer characterized postwar families as "based on inter-personal relations of mutual affection, companionship, and understanding, with a recognition of individual capabilities, desires and needs for the development of each member of the family, be he father, mother or child" (Rachel Ann Elder, "Traditional and Developmental Conceptions of Fatherhood," *Marriage and Family Living* 11 [summer 1949]: 98). Sanford Brown, "May I Ask You a Few Questions about Love?" *The Saturday Evening Post*, 3 December 1966, 239.

8. Historian Marty Jezer posits that in the 1950s the concept of the nuclear family functioned to deny atomization within the family and that "Americans fastened onto the idea of togetherness" to deny loneliness. In fact togetherness was designed in a sense to counter, not deny loneliness; Marty Jezer, *The Dark Ages*, (Boston: South End Press, 1982), 222.

9. Stiese, *McCall's*, May 1954, 27.

10. Helen P. Glenn, "Up to Now: The Story of a Marriage," *Parents Magazine*, August 1954, 98.

11. Marjorie Holmes, "What Became of the Man I Married?" *Better Homes and Gardens*, May 1952, 257.

12. Dorothy Barclay, "Family Palship—with an Escape Clause," *The New York Times Magazine*, 18 November 1956, 48; Jean R. Komaiko, "So I'm Not a Perfect Parent," *Parents Magazine*, October 1956, 113–14.

13. Joseph Veroff and Sheila Feld, *Marriage and Work in America: A Study of Motives and Roles* (New York: Van Nostrand Reinhold Co., 1970), 74.

14. IHD Archives, Maureen Gordon, 1970, 8. In order to protect IHD participants' confidentiality I have avoided explicit reference to actual family size.

15. Describing the backyard barbecue, signpost of togetherness, Benita Eisler writes, "And just as surely, this type of meal—the menu, setting, early hour, and conveniently unbreakable tableware—tell us that children—even very young children—were included" (*Private Lives: Men and Women of the Fifties* [New York: Franklin Watts, 1986], 186); IHD Archives, Judy Kent, S- S, 1959, 12.

16. IHD Archives, Philip Pollard, H-L, 1957, 9, 11; Veroff and Feld, *Marriage and Work in America*, 121.

17. *McCall's*, May 1954, 27.

18. "Up to Date or Out of Date?" *McCall's*, June 1954, 32.

19. As historian Glenna Matthews observes, the fifties housewife was the "chief votary" of the "cult" of togetherness; *Just a Housewife* (New York: Oxford University Press, 1987), 196. IHD Archives, George Rogers, S-S, 1959, 8. Glen Elder looked at IHD Oakland women in 1964 and found that "Compared to men in the sample, their sentiments and gratifications were more committed to a single sphere of life; family activity ranked well above even the combined importance of work and leisure as a source of accomplishment, enjoyment and interest" (*Children of the Great Depression* [Chicago: University of Chicago Press, 1974], 223).

20. IHD Archives, Gail Henderson, S-S, 1958, 4. Five couples specifically mentioned togetherness as the feature distinguishing their own family from that of their parents. Like fatherhood, this trend helped postwar Americans define themselves as modern and middle class.

21. IHD Archives, Judy Kent, S-S, 1959, 20. Clay Kent, S-S, 1959, 9. A little more than a decade later Clay did "need" to get away from the family and announced his decision to file for divorce.

22. IHD Archives, David Morris, S-S, 1957; Leonard Stone, S-S, 1958, 5.

23. IHD Archives, Gail Henderson, 1958, 7; Sally Williams, S-S, 1958, 6; Karen Lewis, 1958, 5; Lloyd Andrews, S-S, 1958, 5; Betty Morris, S-S, 1959, 6; Ruth Wright, 1959, 4; Hank Jones, S-I, 1958, 10. Theodore B. Johannis Jr., "Participation by Fathers, Mothers and Teenage Sons and Daughters in Selected Social Activity," *The Coordinator* 7 (December 1958): 25. This article also hinted at the temporal confinement of togetherness, noting that "teenagers look outside of the family circle for much of their social activity."

24. IHD Archives, Connie Small, 1957, 6.

25. IHD Archives, Judy Kent, S-S, 1959, 23; Claire Manning, 1960, 6.

26. IHD Archives, Dean Lawrence, S-S, 1958, 12.

27. Historian Rochelle Gatlin also notes the discrepancy between a prescriptive

emphasis on both romantic attachment and women's domestic work in marriage in *American Women Since 1945* (Jackson: University of Mississippi Press, 1982), 55; Robert O. Blood Jr. and Donald M. Wolfe, *Husbands and Wives: The Dynamics of Married Living* (Glencoe: Free Press, 1960), 174.

28. IHD Archives, Janice Rogers, 1963, 3. For another discussion of women's isolation in postwar suburban homes, see Mary Ryan, *Womanhood in America* (New York: Franklin Watts, 1983), 270–76. She writes, "In point of fact, then, few couples fulfilled the emotional and social stipulations of the heterosexual imperative. The suburbs remained sex-segregated social space for most of the daylight hours" (276). See also Gatlin, *American Women,* 53.

29. IHD Archives, Dennis Perkins, S-S, 1957, 8; James Evans, 1959, 8.

30. Sociologists Robert O. Blood Jr. and Donald M. Wolfe, in their 1960 study of marriage noted, "When Americans think of marriage, they think of companionship more than anything else" (Blood and Wolfe, *Husbands and Wives,* 150). Rochelle Gatlin writes, "Marriage became a more important relationship because husbands and wives were likely to share a longer period together" (*American Women,* 50). The importance of the relationship between husbands and wives was heightened partly because it took up a greater portion of the life course.

31. Betty Friedan, *It Changed My Life: Writings on the Women's Movement* (New York: W. W. Norton & Co., 1985), 14.

32. IHD Archives, Meg Fisher, 1969, 21.

33. IHD Archives, Sam Arthur, 1970, 34, 1982, 10.

34. IHD Archives, Ernest Johnson, 1981, 14.

35. When women directed criticism at their husbands' jobs, generally, it was with reference to how their participation as fathers rather than as husbands was affected. For a full discussion see chap. 3.

36. IHD Archives, Amy Chase, 1969, 37; Helen Evans, S-I, 1982, 18. Gatlin points to other forces emphasizing the mother-child relationship over that of husband-wife: "Female domesticity was encapsulated within the myth of motherhood. As housework became less interesting, women invested more emotional commitment and time in mothering" (Gatlin, *American Women,* 69).

37. IHD Archives, Meg Fisher, 1969, 34; Tom Fisher, S-I, 1982, 18.

38. IHD Archives, Max Ames, 1970, 53; Patricia James, 1970, 13.

39. IHD Archives, Ken Harris, 1970, 17.

40. IHD Archives, Howard Sims, 1982, 17.

41. IHD Archives, Grant Thornton, 1970, 31; Cynthia Thornton, 1982, 40; May Perkins, 1970, 22, 84.

42. IHD Archives, Maureen Gordon, S-I, 1982, 12; Roberta Johnson, S-I, 1981, 13.

43. IHD Archives, James Evans, S-I, 1982, 12.

44. IHD Archives, Connie Douglas, 1969, 36; Aileen Ross, I-6, 1958, 7; Karen Lewis, 1982, 40; Ken Harris, S-I, 1982, 16.

45. IHD Archives, Don Baldwin, 1971, 38.

46. IHD Archives, Rodney Scott, 1970, 5, 16, 1982, 28.

47. IHD Archives, Hank Jones, 1982, 18. Over a quarter of couples in 1982 said that marital companionship had recently increased.

48. Jessica Field Cohen, "Male Roles in Mid-Life," *Family Coordinator* 28 (October 1979): 468. IHD Archives, Eugene Good, 1982, 19.

49. IHD Archives, Edward Martin, 1970, 3; James Evans, S-I, 1982, 5; Blanche Warner, 1969, 5.

50. IHD Archives, Sally Williams, 1969, 34; Dale George, 1970, 17.

51. IHD Archives, May Perkins, 1970, 75 and 1982, 37; Mary Smith, 1970, 75 and 1982, 52; Irene Lawrence, 1982, 25; Olivia Adams, 1970, 18.

52. IHD Archives, Malcom McKee, S-I, 1982, 7; Scott Clinton, 1970, 21.

53. Cohen, *Family Coordinator* 28 (October 1979): 468. IHD Archives, Nina Harris, 1969, 15; Frank Ryder, S-I, 1982, 18; Katie Ryder, 1970, 21.

54. IHD Archives, Didi Jones, 1970, 20; Hank Jones, 1982, 13; John Thompkins, S-I, 1982, 13.

55. IHD Archives, Hal Powell, 1982, 72; May Perkins, 1982, 21. A. P. Fengler, "Attitudinal Orientations of Wives toward Their Husbands' Retirement," *International Journal of Aging and Human Development* 6 (1975): 139–152, cited in Patricia M. Keith and Timothy H. Brubaker, "Male Household Roles in Later Life: A Look at Masculinity and Marital Relationships," *The Family Coordinator* 28 (October 1979): 500. Couple togetherness remained an important determinant of marital satisfaction for men of this generation; Carolyn L. Funk, *Perceptions of Marital Togetherness and Companionship* (Santa Monica, Calif.: Rand Corporation 1988), 2.

56. IHD Archives, Roberta Johnson, 1981, 26; Georgeanne Gaynor, 1969, 40. O. Brim, "Theories of the Male Mid-life Crisis," *Counseling Psychologist* 6 (1976): 6, quoted in Cohen, *Family Coordinator* 28 (October 1979): 467. One study found that over time, husbands tend to increase appreciation for joint leisure activities. Wives on the other hand demonstrate greater preference for independent activities. Jay A. Mancini and Dennis K. Orthner, "Recreational Sexuality Preferences among Middle-Class Husbands and Wives," *The Journal of Sex Research* 14 (May 1978): 102.

57. IHD Archives, Kay Patterson, 1983, 23.

58. IHD Archives, Joe Maxwell, 1982, 32; Eleanor Maxwell, S-I, 1982, 18; Gordon James, 1982, 37.

59. IHD Archives, Milly Benson, 1982, 32.

60. IHD Archives, Meg Fisher, 1982, 1; Malcom McKee, 1982, 13, 21. Patricia M. Keith and Timothy H. Brubaker, *The Family Coordinator* 28 (October 1979): 499, 500.

61. IHD Archives, 1969, 54, 47; 1983, 68.

62. IHD Archives, 1959, S-S, 4.

63. IHD Archives, 1959, S-S, 5, 6, 1960, S-P, 4, 1969, 41.

64. IHD Archives, 1982, 14–15, 1969, 38. This is the most extreme case of domestic violence I found in the 100 IHD families in my sample. Other couples reported domestic violence between themselves or toward their children. In a few cases divorce provided the ultimate resolution. In two cases violence erupted

around the issue of male children's rebellion and drug abuse in the 1960s and 1970s and the father's alcohol abuse, with wives victimized as well.

65. Historian Laura E. Nym Mayhall connects the Disney film *Mary Poppins* closely to the postwar concept of togetherness. Mary Poppins departs only when both parents are fully engaged in a fun-filled outing with their children at the park; "Domesticating Emmeline: The Figure of the Suffragette in Anglo-American Political Discourse and Popular Culture, 1930–1993," *National Women's Studies Association Journal* 11 (summer 1999).

66. IHD Archives, Rita Frank, S-I, 1982, 20.

CHAPTER FIVE

1. *The New Yorker Album of Cartoons, 1925–1975* (New York: Viking Press, 1978). On the origins of the term sexual revolution, popular by 1963, see Beth Bailey, "Sexual Revolution(s)," in David Farber, ed., *The Sixties: From Memory to History* (Chapel Hill: University of North Carolina Press, 1994), 235–62.

2. *The New Yorker Album of Cartoons, 1925–1975*. Thanks to Elizabeth Haiken for suggesting these images to me.

3. As George Chauncey documents in *Gay New York: Gender, Urban Culture, and the Making of the Gay Male World, 1890–1940* (New York: Basic Books, 1994) and Joanne Meyerowitz in *Women Adrift: Independent Wage Earners in Chicago, 1880–1930* (Chicago: University of Chicago Press, 1988), the economic and residential configurations of urban life also made possible new forms of homosexual culture. See also Kathy Peiss, *Cheap Amusements: Working Women in New York City, 1880–1920* (Philadelphia: Temple University Press, 1985).

4. Bailey writes, "Dating moved courtship into the public world, relocating it from family parlors and community events to restaurants, theaters, and dance halls" (Beth L. Bailey, *From Front Porch to Back Seat: Courtship in Twentieth-Century America* [Baltimore: Johns Hopkins University Press, 1989], 13). See also Paula Fass, *The Damned and the Beautiful* (New York: Oxford University Press, 1977), 75, 269.

5. Fass, *The Damned and the Beautiful*, 79; Elaine Tyler May, *Great Expectations: Marriage and Divorce in Post-Victorian America* (Chicago: University of Chicago Press, 1980), 158.

6. Christina Simmons, "Companionate Marriage and the Lesbian Threat," in Kathryn Kish Sklar and Thomas Dublin, eds., *Women and Power in American History: A Reader* (Englewood Cliffs, N.J.: Prentice-Hall, 1991), 2:183–94. Of the 1920s marriage manuals, Margaret Jackson writes, "This suggests that the 'problem' with which marriage manuals were really grappling was not so much sexual maladjustment as feminism, and the threat, or in some cases perhaps the reality, of men's loss of power in heterosexual relationships" (*The Real Facts of Life: Feminism and the Politics of Sexuality, c. 1850–1940* [London: Taylor & Francis, 1994], 162).

Margaret Sanger, *Happiness in Marriage* (1926; Old Saybrook: Applewood Books, 1993), 6.

7. Fass, *The Damned and the Beautiful*, 74, 288–90. As to new marital ideals in the 1920s, Christina Simmons writes, "How well this new ideology of marriage described the typical patterns of people's sexual lives requires investigation, but no one could have remained totally isolated from its power" (Simmons, in Sklar and Dublin, *Women and Power in American History*, 2:191). Steven Seidman, *Romantic Longings: Love in America, 1830–1980* (New York: Routledge, 1991), 77, 91. According to historian Jonathan Ned Katz, Americans constructed heterosexuality itself in these years, that is a male-female relationship based on the sex-love impulse as distinguished from procreative view of sexuality and a "true love," spiritual view of love during the nineteenth century; *The Invention of Heterosexuality* (New York: Dutton, 1992), 83–93. John D'Emilio and Estelle Freedman, *Intimate Matters: A History of Sexuality in America* (New York: Harper & Row, 1988), 242; Blanche Linden-Ward and Carol Hurd Green, *American Women in the 1960s: Changing the Future* (New York: Twayne Publishers, 1993).

8. D'Emilio and Freedman, *Intimate Matters*, 246, 268, 286. For a survey of twentieth-century patterns of premarital sex, see Leonard Beeghley, *What Does Your Wife Do? Gender and the Transformation of Family Life* (Boulder, Colo.: Westview Press, 1996), 18–25.

9. Jane Lewis and Kathleen Kiernan discuss changes in British sexual behavior and government policies in these decades arguing that "the new sexual morality of the 1960s advocated a new basis for sexual relationships that resulted in the abandoning of the priority accorded marital stability in favor of securing better personal relationships. But most advocates of the new morality felt that this would strengthen marriage rather than undermine it" ("The Boundaries between Marriage, Nonmarriage, and Parenthood: Changes in Behavior and Policy in Postwar Britain," *Journal of Family History* 21 [July 1996]: 385).

10. Beth Bailey notes, "The sexual revolution was not one movement. It was instead a set of movements, movements that were closely linked, even intertwined, but which often made uneasy bedfellows" (Bailey, in David Farber, ed., *The Sixties*, 238). IHD Archives, Maureen Gordon, 1959, S-S, 3.

11. Seidman, *Romantic Longings*, 93, 126.

12. Alfred C. Kinsey et al., *Sexual Behavior in the Human Female* (Philadelphia: W. B. Saunders Co., 1953), 7, 328, 568, 12. Kinsey's personal life embodied the very public-private split he argued against in his studies, biographer James Jones has found. Kinsey privately immersed himself in what Jones terms a "sexual utopia" of extramarital sex, homosexuality, masochism, and exhibitionism; "Dr. Yes," *The New Yorker*, 25 August and 1 September 1997, 99–113. For another discussion of sexuality during the 1950s, see Elaine Tyler May, *Homeward Bound: American Families in the Cold War Era* (New York: Basic Books, 1988), 114–34. At the time Kinsey's report was seen as a step toward a more public discussion of sexuality and away from reticence; see Rochelle Gurstein, *The Repeal of Reticence: A History of America's*

Cultural and Legal Struggles over Free Speech, Obscenity, Sexual Liberation, and Modern Art (New York: Hill & Wang, 1996), 252–59. But at the same time that Kinsey sparked public talk of sex, he also, according to historian David Allyn, made a case for the "privatization of morality," wherein the state stepped back as regulator of morals and thus sexual behavior, abetting the transition to "the laissez faire enthusiasm" about sex after 1960. Allyn demonstrates that Kinsey focused on private, not public forms of sexuality; "Private Acts/Public Policy: Alfred Kinsey, the American Law Institute and the Privatization of American Sexual Morality," *Journal of American Studies* 30 (December 1996): 406, 414–17, 428.

13. Paul Landis, *Making the Most of Marriage* (New York: Appleton-Century-Crofts, 1955), 395.

14. Barbara Benson, "What Women Want to Know about the Kinsey Book," *Ladies' Home Journal*, September 1953, 52; Landis, *Making the Most of Marriage*, 331.

15. Clifford R. Adams, "Making Marriage Work: What Factors Favor Good Sexual Adjustment and a Happy Marriage?" *Ladies' Home Journal*, August 1958, 28; Abraham Stone, "What Husbands Don't Know about Sex," *Ladies' Home Journal*, November 1956, 187.

16. Clifford R. Adams, "Making Marriage Work: Differences in Understanding and Knowledge of Sex Can Cause Serious Conflict," *Ladies' Home Journal*, July 1955, 28.

17. Adams, *Ladies' Home Journal*, August 1958, 28.

18. Abraham Stone, M. D., as told to Joan Younger, "What Wives Don't Know about Sex," *Ladies' Home Journal*, May 1956, 72; Abraham Stone, "What Every Wife Should Know," *Ladies' Home Journal*, May 1956, 127.

19. Abraham Stone, M. D., "What Husbands Don't Know about Sex," *Ladies' Home Journal*, November 1956, 66, 67, 187; Clifford R. Adams, "Making Marriage Work: We Agree on Almost Everything Except Sex," *Ladies' Home Journal*, June 1957, 50.

20. Stone, *Ladies' Home Journal*, May 1956, 72; Henry B. Safford, M. D., "Tell Me, Doctor," *Ladies' Home Journal*, September 1956, 50; Dorothy Thompson, "Do We Misunderstand Romantic Love?" *Ladies' Home Journal*, December 1955, 11.

21. In 1966 sociologist Jessie Bernard observed, "The current sexual renaissance reflects an era which encourages—compels or coerces, some might say—women to equal if not out-do men in the enjoyment of the male sex act" ("The Fourth Revolution," *Journal of Social Issues* 22 [April 1966]: 80).

22. Erma Bombeck, *A Marriage Made in Heaven Or Too Tired for an Affair* (New York: HarperCollins, 1993), 7. Thirteen couples reported to the IHD that at least one partner had engaged in premarital sex. The Nicholses married because Rosalyn was pregnant. Margaret Reed's mother insisted she use a diaphragm after she "got in trouble" before she married, and in 1958, Reed already planned to do the same with her own daughter instead of "making them get married." In twenty-two couples, at least one partner was a virgin when he or she married, and several stated that their spouses were too. Others may simply have been unwilling to say. In the

Kelly Longitudinal Study of couples who dated in the 1930s and 1940s, the majority had not had premarital sex, although 40 percent had; May, *Homeward Bound*, 120. In a study of college students' attitudes toward premarital sex, half of the men and a fifth of the women had sex prior to marriage; Alfred J. Prince and Gordon Shipman, "Attitudes of College Students toward Premarital Sex Experience," *The Coordinator* 6 (June 1958): 57. Behavior and attitudes were not necessarily congruent, social scientists found. One 1960 study of premarital intimacy found that 41 percent of both men and women who had engaged in intercourse during engagement felt that they had gone "too far"; Robert R. Bell and Leonard Blumberg, "Courtship Stages and Intimacy Attitudes," *The Family Life Coordinator* 8 (March 1960): 62. A survey of 100,000 married women in the 1970s found that among women over forty (who came of age in the 1950s and before) 68 percent reported having premarital sex; Carol Tavris and Susan Sadd, *The Redbook Report on Female Sexuality* (New York: Delacorte Press, 1975), 33.

23. IHD Archives, Doris Jenkins, 1960, I-4, 15; Joan Sinclair, 1959, I-4, 24; Judy Kent, 1959, S-S, 13. This testimony is similar to that reported by Elaine Tyler May in her study of marriage in the 1950s; *Homeward Bound*, 126. Forty percent of a sample of Wisconsin college students felt that "their sex education had been inadequate" (Prince and Shipman, *The Coordinator* 6 [June 1958]: 57). To protect confidentiality of IHD participants, I have avoided mention of specific family size and actual number of years married.

24. IHD Archives, Gary Simon, 1959, 4; Jack Stevens, I-4, 1959, 9.

25. IHD Archives, Janice Rogers, S-S, 1958, 13; Dean Lawrence, S-S, 1958, 6; Kay Patterson, I-3, 1959, 8.

26. IHD Archives, Dennis Perkins, S-S, 1957, 3; Gary Simon, 1959, 4.

27. IHD Archives, Kay Patterson, I-3, 1959, 8; Didi Jones, 1958, 18; Marie Weber, 1958, 85.

28. IHD Archives, Clay Kent, S-S, 1959, 10.

29. IHD Archives, Nan Meeker, I-3, 1959, 19.

30. IHD Archives, Cynthia Thornton, H-L, 1958, 4; Dorothy Simon, 1962, 4.

31. IHD Archives, Judy Kent, 1970, 16.

32. IHD Archives, Betsy Downs, 1982, 16; May, *Homeward Bound*.

33. D'Emilio and Freedman remark, "The baby boom made the need for contraception more pressing, precisely at a moment when its use seemed less threatening. Wives who had two, three, or four children while still in their twenties could hardly be accused of seeking contraceptive devices in order to avoid their biological destiny, or to escape the confines of home" (*Intimate Matters*, 249). May notes that during the 1950s doctors, Protestant and Jewish clergymen, and politicians endorsed birth control as a method of spacing or postponing births within marriage; *Homeward Bound*, 150–52. IHD Archives, Claire Manning, S-S, 1958, 6; Dean Lawrence, S-S, 1958, 6; 1970, 35–36; Irene Lawrence, 1970, 68. Among Catholic women, aged 18–39, in 1955, a third did not conform to church doctrine concerning contraception. By 1965, 53 percent of Catholic women who participated in a national survey did not conform; Raymond H. Potvin, Charles F. Westoff, and

Norman B. Ryder, "Factors Affecting Catholic Wives' Conformity to Their Church Magisterium's Position on Birth Control," *Journal of Marriage and the Family* 30 (May 1968): 263; D'Emilio and Freedman, *Intimate Matters*, 252.

34. IHD Archives, Eleanor Maxwell, 1982, 22–23; Crystal Robertson, 1982, 17; Sandra Thomas, 1982, 14; Sally Williams, 1969, 54. Social scientist David Riesman observed, "Having watched so many young couples where the husband is a graduate student and the wife still in college begin having children when it is most inconvenient, I have come to suspect among non-Catholics a certain casualness about birth control, perhaps reflecting the cult of spontaneity or a kind of Russian roulette where the stakes are not very great!" (David Riesman, "Two Generations," in Robert Jay Lifton, *The Woman in America* [Boston: Houghton Mifflin Co., 1965], 88).

35. A fertility survey of the United States showed that, for the period 1960–65, "55 percent of all births . . . were unintended—19 percent unwanted and 36 percent mistimed" (L. A. Bumpass and C. F. Westoff, "Unwanted Births and U.S. Population Growth," *Family Planning Perspectives* 2 [July-August 1970]: 9, in Jacqueline Darroch Forrest and Susheela Sing, "The Sexual and Reproductive Behavior of American Women, 1982–1988," *Family Planning Perspectives* 22 [September-October 1990]: 214). Elise F. Jones, "Comparisons: The United States and Britain," *Family Planning Perspectives* 11 (March-April 1979): 136.

36. D'Emilio and Freedman, *Intimate Matters*, 250; Linden-Ward and Green, *American Women in the 1960s*, 338–41. For a brief account of the origins of the birth control pill, including early trials in Puerto Rico, see Linda Grant, *Sexing the Millennium: Women and the Sexual Revolution* (New York: Grove Press, 1994), 44–59. IHD Archives, Owen Wright, 1982, 32, 25.

37. IHD Archives, Walter Small, 1971, 19; Claudine Parker, 1971, 42; Dennis Perkins, 1970, 26; Linden-Ward and Green, *American Women in the 1960s*, 341. Surgical sterilization was also becoming common in middle America: "In 1976, 30 percent of married couples with a wife of childbearing age were sterile, about two-thirds of them because of surgical sterilization" (Theodore Caplow et al., *Middletown Families: Fifty Years of Change and Continuity* [New York: Bantam Books, 1983], 187).

38. One study of sterilization in the 1970s found that "the female partners of couples who have never used any contraceptive method are the *most* likely to obtain a sterilization" (Charles F. Westoff and James McCarthy, "Sterilization in the United States," *Family Planning Perspectives* 11 [May-June 1979] 147, 149).

39. "Sex in the Magazines," *Newsweek*, 24 August 1959.

40. On Hefner, see Barbara Ehrenreich, *Hearts of Men: American Dreams and the Flight from Commitment* (Garden City: Anchor Books, 1983), chap. 4. On Brown, see Barbara Ehrenreich, Elizabeth Hess, and Gloria Jacobs, *Re-Making Love: The Feminization of Sex* (Garden City: Anchor Books, 1986) and John Modell, *Into One's Own: From Youth to Adulthood in the United States, 1920–1975* (Berkeley: University of California Press, 1989), 3–5. Lawrence Lipton, *The Erotic Revolution: An Affirmative View of the New Morality* (Los Angeles: Sherbourne Press, 1965), 9,

36. Sanford Brown, "May I Ask You a Few Questions about Love?" *Saturday Evening Post*, 3 December 1966, 27.

41. William H. Masters and Virginia E. Johnson, *Human Sexual Response* (Boston: Little, Brown & Co., 1966), 6, 27.

42. Vern L. Bullough, *Science in the Bedroom: A History of Sex Research* (New York: Basic Books, 1994), 201–4. In 1962, Albert Ellis decried the emphasis on the vaginal orgasm in contemporary marriage manuals, calling it a myth; *American Sexual Tragedy* (New York: Lyle Stuart, 1962), 96–97.

43. "Sex: How to Read All about It," *Newsweek*, 24 August 1970, 38.

44. "The Intimate Hours," *Ladies' Home Journal*, June 1978, 50.

45. "Sex and Marriage," *Redbook*, September 1970, 85; Theodore I. Rubin, M. D., "What Women Ask about Sex," *Ladies' Home Journal*, March 1975, 22, 24; "Sex and Marriage, a *Redbook* discussion with Dr. William H. Masters and Mrs. Virginia E. Johnson," *Redbook*, September 1970, 84. A 1973 self-help book was entirely devoted to the subject of dialogue in marriage, including a section on "Leveling and Sex—Honesty in the Bedroom," that counseled, "Total honesty should be the creed of the bedroom"; Cathrina Bauby, *Between Consenting Adults: Dialogue for Intimate Living* (New York: Macmillan, 1973), 143.

46. Harriet La Barre, "How to Say No to Your Husband," *Ladies' Home Journal*, June 1975, 44, 111.

47. "Battle of the Sexes," *Newsweek*, 7 August 1967, 52.

48. Adelaide Bry, "How to Keep Love in Long Marriages," *Ladies' Home Journal*, April 1975, 64.

49. Alan E. Nourse, M. D., "Sexual Compatibility," *Ladies' Home Journal*, February 1975, 74 (excerpt from *Ladies' Home Journal Family Medical Guide* [New York: Harper & Row, 1973]).

50. Vance Packard, *The Sexual Wilderness: The Contemporary Upheaval in Male-Female Relationships*, (New York: David McKay Co., 1968) 55, 73, 273–78; "Sex in the Magazines," *Newsweek*, 24 August 1959, 56.

51. *Redbook*, September 1970, 87.

52. Tavris and Sadd, *The Redbook Report on Female Sexuality*, 61; Anthony Pietropinto, M. D., and Jacqueline Simenauer, *Husbands and Wives: A Nationwide Survey of Marriage* (New York: Times Books, 1979), 88.

53. IHD Archives, Rick Snyder, S-S, 1960, 4. Clay Kent, 1970, 40.

54. IHD Archives, Martha Bentley, 1970, 54; Michelle Anderson, 1970, 19. It wasn't just married couples in their forties who had trouble communicating freely about their sexuality. In response to a 1972 article on women's sexuality in *Ms.* a male reader wondered, "Where, may I ask, are men supposed to acquire all this knowledge (it may surprise some sexually frustrated women that we are not born with a Casanova's know-how)? From women who don't openly discuss sexual problems, don't tell their men where things feel best on their bodies, don't use their mouths and hands freely, and don't generally initiate new techniques—yet still expect full sexual satisfaction?" (Mary Thom, ed., *Letters to Ms. 1972–1987* [New York: Henry Holt & Co., 1987], 3).

55. IHD Archives, Kevin Jenkins, 18, 1970; Alex Comfort, M. D., *The Joy of Sex—A Cordon Bleu Guide to Lovemaking* (New York: Crown Publishing, 1972), 235. Postwar women, too, saw "premarital" restraint as contributing to difficulty later on; May, *Homeward Bound*, 129.

56. IHD Archives, Doris Jenkins, 13, 1970. A 1972 study of women (average age 34.5) found that 8 percent of respondents "never had orgasm during coitus" (Robert R. Bell and Phyllis L. Bell, "Sexual Satisfaction among Married Women," *Medical Aspects of Human Sexuality* 6 [December 1972]: 142). Seven percent of the women responding to the *Redbook* questionnaire in 1974 considered themselves "non orgasmic"; Tavris and Sadd, *The Redbook Report on Female Sexuality*, 72. Interestingly, in a 1980s study results showed that women of this generation may have benefited both from the sexual revolution and their years of experience. "When asked whether they had ever experienced orgasm during lovemaking, 13% of women ages 18 to 26, 3% of women ages 51 to 64 and 9% of women over age 65 said No" (Samuel S. Janus and Cynthia L. Janus, *The Janus Report on Sexual Behavior* [New York: John Wiley & Sons, 1993], 19).

57. IHD Archives, Adam Walker, 1970, 54; Virginia Walker, 1970, 24. The stereotypes were supported by sociological data in the 1970s. Theodore Caplow found that "Whenever some degree of sexual frustration was seen as characterizing a marriage, it was the husband who defined himself (or was defined by his wife) as being more amorous" (Caplow et al., *Middletown Families*, 177). Another study found that 45 percent of the husbands and 26 percent of the wives indicated that sex and affection was one of their five favorite activities, in a study of patterns of marital leisure. The authors of the study also acknowledged that gendered definitions of sex as "play" or leisure activity not just gender preferences for sex itself might be at work; J. A. Mancini and Dennis K. Orthner, "Recreational Sexuality Preferences among Middle-Class Husbands and Wives," *Journal of Sex Research* 14 (May 1978): 100, 104.

58. IHD Archives, Malcom McKee, 1970, 10.

59. IHD Archives, Celia McKee, 1971, 17. In fact in 1982, four individuals declined to answer questions about their sexual relationships.

60. IHD Archives, Paul Meeker, 1970, 25 and 1982, 15; Nan Meeker, 1970, 53, 55 and 1982, 17. In the national survey the remaining 80 percent rated their sex lives "very good" or "satisfactory to good" in roughly equal proportions. The study also found that "the sexual revolution has not annihilated the conservative population. Four out of five married people do not employ objects or techniques that might be termed far-out, kinky, or unconventional" (Pietropinto and Simenauer, *Husbands and Wives*, 78, 85). An earlier study, in 1965, had this to report about upper middle-class marriage: "the overriding fact seems to be that for the majority, by the middle years, sex has become almost nonexistent, something to be stifled, or a matter about which they are downright afraid and negative" (John F. Cuber with Peggy B. Harroff, *The Significant Americans: A Study of Sexual Behavior among the Affluent* [New York: Appleton-Century, 1965], 172).

61. IHD Archives, Liz Arthur, 1970, 45–46.

62. IHD Archives, Liz Arthur, 1970, 30.

63. IHD Archives, Mary Smith, 1971, 31, S-I, 1982. Anthony Astrachan found men over fifty, who as they came to terms with aging's effects on sexuality, were unable to let go of old beliefs about male performance, despite new information about the pleasures of nonpenetrative eroticism. Astrachan wrote, "But they hadn't been able to bring that information to life in their own lives and they were not happy in their sexual relationships" (Anthony Astrachan, *How Men Feel: Their Response to Women's Demands for Equality and Power* [Garden City: Anchor Books, 1986], 283).

64. IHD Archives, 1971, 19, 25–26.

65. IHD Archives, Crystal Robertson, S-I, 1982, 20. Women's magazines picked up this message; see Harriet La Barre, *Ladies' Home Journal*, April 1975, 44.

66. IHD Archives, Lloyd Andrews, S-I, 1982, 16.

67. IHD Archives, Nan Meeker, 1982, 17; Paul Meeker, 1982, 15. Middletown couples also made it clear to researchers that discussing sex was difficult. Caplow et al., *Middletown Families*, 178–79. In their national study of marriage, Pietropinto and Simenauer found that the most common ways of dealing with sexual problems were "'learning to cope,' 'ignoring it,' or other ways of expressing passive acceptance" (*Husbands and Wives*, 106).

68. IHD Archives, Barbara Clinton, 1970, 22. Tavris and Sadd, *The Redbook Report on Female Sexuality*, 103, 106.

69. IHD Archives, Kevin Jenkins, 1982, 60. A survey of 4,066 men in the 1970s showed that "just over half of all the men discuss their preferences in sex with their partners sooner or later. Just under half never do." Willingness to discuss sexual matters was less apparent among older men. Those most willing to talk were under thirty (60 percent), and of midlife men 40–54, 49 percent discussed their preferences. Significantly, 51 percent of the married men in the study said "they did *not* talk to their wives" (Anthony Pietropinto, M. D., and Jacqueline Simenauer, *Beyond the Male Myth: What Women Want to Know about Men's Sexuality* [New York: Times Books, 1977], 144–45). These figures all hover at about half, indicating both the spread of ideas about communication, and resistance to them. Of the letters that came in response to the *Redbook* survey of female sexuality, the authors of the resulting book commented, "Oddly, in spite of, or maybe because of, all the talk about sex in the last decade, it is as difficult as ever for people to express their real desires to the person closest to them. Many find it easier to talk to an impersonal questionnaire than to the familiar stranger in their bedroom" (Tavris and Sadd, *The Redbook Report on Female Sexuality*, 23).

70. IHD Archives, Marie Weber, 1982, 41, 53. Theodore Rubin wrote, "I suggest that you discuss it with him openly and honestly" (*Ladies' Home Journal*, March 1975, 22).

71. IHD Archives, Thelma Morton, S-I, 1982, 13, Alice Bremmer, S-I, 1982, 12; Grace Owens, S-I, 1982, 11. Nineteen couples reported having ceased sexual relations in 1982. One quarter reported a decrease in sexual satisfaction. A reader

of *Ms.* complained about the glorification of sex in later life, writing, "I am fifty. . . . I am aware that sex can be enjoyed as long as there is life and that, for women especially, sexual pleasure tends to increase with age. But this is only a case of increasing expectations leading to greater frustration and bitterness" (Thom, ed., *Letters to Ms. 1972–1987*, 11).

72. IHD Archives, Kevin Jenkins, 1982, 58. Mancini and Orthner, *The Journal of Sex Research* 14: 101.

73. IHD Archives, Leonard Stone, S-I, 1983, 23. A quarter of the 1982 respondents said they ignored or accommodated sexual problems in their relationships; another quarter said they worked on them together; five couples reported seeking professional help; S-I 1982. Sociologists found "most respondents are not seriously upset about their sex lives": 27 percent of those queried in 1976 reported that they were "often" or "sometimes" "upset" about their sexual relationship with a spouse; Joseph Veroff, Evelyn Douvan, and Richard A. Kulka, *The Inner American: A Self Portrait from 1957 to 1976* (New York: Basic Books, 1981), 168.

74. Phillip Shaver and Jonathan Freeman, "Your Pursuit of Happiness," *Psychology Today*, August 1976, 28, 31.

75. "Mrs. Ford and the Affair of the Daughter," *Ladies' Home Journal*, November 1975, 118.

76. IHD Archives, Mary Smith, 1982, 42; George Rogers, 1982, 16; Rita Frank, 1982, 26; Betty Morris, 1982, 13; Dean Lawrence, 1982, 30. Norval D. Glenn and Charles N. Weaver, "Attitudes toward Premarital, Extramarital, and Homosexual Relations in the U.S. in the 1970s," *Journal of Sex Research* 15 (May 1979): 112, 115.

77. IHD Archives, Connie Small, 1970, 14; Gail Henderson, 1971, 34.

78. IHD Archives, Keith Warner, 1969, 32; Anne Matthews, S-I, 1982, 20; Ava Michaels, 1982, 30.

79. *The New Yorker Cartoon Album*, 1978 (Frank Modell, 1972).

80. Bombeck, *A Marriage Made in Heaven*, 139. Indeed, a 1989 report on a 1970 survey of sex and morality questioned the very utility of the term sexual revolution; Albert D. Klassen et al., *Sex and Morality in the U.S.: An Empirical Enquiry under the Auspices of the Kinsey Institute* (Middletown, Conn.: Wesleyan University Press), 4–6.

81. And it continues to be so for younger generations. Lillian Rubin concludes, "The bedroom is one of the primary places where women and men meet as adversaries, where unspoken negotiations go on as they seek to get something they want" (*Erotic Wars: What Happened to the Sexual Revolution?* [New York: Farrar, Straus & Giroux, 1990], 23).

82. Conservatism should not just be seen as a trait of older generations. The author of a 1964 survey of college students remarked, "underlying feelings of caution, control, and inhibition are often overlooked," concluding that "when one examines carefully the supposed sexual revolution, the changes that have occurred do not seem to be quite that impressive" (Mervin B. Freedman, "The Sexual Behavior of American College Women: An Empirical Study and an Historical Survey,"

Merrill-Palmer Quarterly of Behavior and Development 11 [January 1965]: 44, 45). The 1970 Kinsey survey also found that "background influences" or "generational effects might outweigh sexual experiences in determination of sexual morality," indicating that as of 1970 a sexual revolution was far from universal, when it came to norms and morality; Klassen et al., *Sex and Morality in the U.S.*, 83.

83. Peter Laipson, "'Kiss without Shame, for She Desires It': Sexual Foreplay in American Marital Advice Literature, 1900–1925," *Journal of Social History* 30 (spring 1996): 507–25. With regard to the "discourse of foreplay" in advice literature, Laipson writes, "Middle-class women gained the possibility of pleasure but at the cost of sexual autonomy; middle-class men maintained the promise of authority but at the expense of a sometimes paralyzing expectation of sexual performance." The new set of rules governing foreplay "did not work exclusively or entirely to the advantage or disadvantage of either sex" (509).

84. Stephanie Coontz, *The Way We Never Were* (New York: Basic Books, 1992), 185, 199. In 1990, sociologist Lillian Rubin questioned the utility of "sex talk" and sexual information. Why, she asked do "our sexual difficulties continue to support a thriving sex therapy business? Could it be that all the noise about sex has served mainly to foster uneasiness and confusion, while also helping to create a set of impossible expectations" (Rubin, *Erotic Wars*, 188–89).

85. Beth Bailey writes, "The sexual revolution was not only about sex. It was about the struggle for power and for freedom, equality, and autonomy—a struggle in which sex played a key role" (*From Front Porch to Back Seat*, 142).

86. Fifty-one percent of couples in a 1976 study responded to the question "How often have you wished that your spouse understood you better?" with the reply "often" or "sometimes," leading the authors to conclude, "Despite active exchange in marriage, most people hold an ideal for marital interaction which is grander than they are able to realize in their own marriage." They state, "Most people are satisfied with their sexual fulfillment in marriage, but the advertising has left them with a vague sense that their marriages could be larger and richer in social exchange" (Veroff, Douvan, and Kulka, *The Inner American*, 168). These patterns continue in the 1990s. According to a recent survey of American sexuality, "The general picture of sex with a partner in America shows that Americans do not have a secret life of abundant sex. If nothing else, the startlingly modest amounts of partnered sex reveal how much we as a society can deceive ourselves about other people's sex lives." They also found a "persistent inability to talk about sex" (Robert T. Michael, John H. Gagnon, Edward O. Laumann, and Gina Kolata, *Sex in America: A Definitive Survey*, [Boston: Little, Brown & Co., 1994], 122, 152).

CHAPTER SIX

1. One woman in this study remarked, "All of our friends are getting divorced in the last six months"; IHD Archives, Ruth Wright, 1971, 16.

2. Gerard Jones, *Honey, I'm Home! Sitcoms, Selling the American Dream* (New York: Grove Wadenfeld, 1992), 194.

3. "The Divorce of the Year," *Newsweek*, 12 March 1973, 49.

4. This rate is slightly higher than IHD divorce rates as of 1979 for 232 subjects when 19 percent had been divorced. At least one of the divorces in my sample occurred after 1979. For the IHD as a whole, 65 percent of those divorced remarried. Arlene Skolnick, "Married Lives: Longitudinal Perspectives on Marriage," in *Past and Present in Middle Life* (New York: Academic Press, 1981), 272. This figure is close to the 27 percent of IHD men who were divorced by 1982; John Clausen, *American Lives: Looking Back at the Children of the Great Depression* (New York: Free Press, 1993), 290. For American women, average duration of first marriage peaked with the cohort of women born between 1928 and 1932, at 31.1 years, largely because of early marriage and increases in longevity, which countered changes in divorce behavior. See Steven D. McLaughlin et al., *The Changing Lives of American Women* (Chapel Hill: University of North Carolina Press, 1988), 62. These figures do not include spouses' marital experiences prior to or after marriage to subjects, although several participants' spouses had been previously married. In a few cases, the IHD did locate and interview spouses at least once after a divorce. IHD data show early marriage to be a significant factor in divorce. Richard C. Rockwell, Glen H. Elder Jr., and David J. Ross, "Psychological Patterns in Marital Timing and Divorce," *Social Psychology Quarterly* 42 (December 1979): 403. Tsipora Peskin analyzed IHD data to compare Oakland and Guidance Study members with regard to divorce. She concluded that the younger Guidance Study men, relatively unscarred by the Depression were less dependent on marriage and more likely to opt for individual fulfillment through divorce. Jack Horn, "Personality and Divorce," *Psychology Today*, October 1976, 143.

5. United States Department of Commerce, Bureau of the Census, *Historical Statistics of the United States: Colonial Times to 1970* (Washington, D.C., 1975), 64.

6. Lenore Weitzman, in *The Divorce Revolution* (New York: Free Press, 1985), uses this term in reference to the changes in divorce law and practice in the United States after the adoption of no-fault statutes, but scholars also use the term more broadly to address the increase in marital dissolution since the 1960s; McLaughlin et al., *The Changing Lives of American Women*, 60–61. United States Department of Commerce, Bureau of Census, *Historical Statistics*, 64.

7. Andrew J. Cherlin, *Marriage, Divorce, Remarriage* (Cambridge: Harvard University Press, 1992), 22–23, 25, 67. Couples in this study bridge two marital cohorts—late Depression and wartime marriages (the Oakland subjects) and postwar and 1950s marriages (the Berkeley subjects). Cherlin's table (p. 22) of projected proportion of marriages begun in each year that will end in divorce ranges between .25 and .3 for marriages begun roughly between 1945 and 1955—projections consistent with the 24/100 couples who dissolved their marriages in my sample.

8. Glenda Riley, *Divorce: An American Tradition* (New York: Oxford University Press, 1991), 156, 62, 55.

9. Elaine Tyler May, *Great Expectations* (Chicago: University of Chicago Press, 1980), 47, 156.

10. Elaine Tyler May, *Homeward Bound: American Families in the Cold War Era* (New York: Basic Books, 1988), 185–86, 203–4. For a thorough discussion of the historiography of American divorce reform and an analysis of divorce codes and beliefs since 1920, see J. Herbie DiFonzo, *Beneath the Fault Line: The Popular and Legal Culture of Divorce in Twentieth-Century America* (Charlottesville: University Press of Virginia, 1997).

11. Kingsley Davis, "Divorce Downswing," *The New York Times Magazine*, 8 May 1955, 67.

12. The argument about the discrepancy between behavior and statute and divorce echoed a similar push for reform of codes governing sexual behavior. Historian David Allyn writes, "Kinsey revealed the wide gap between moral idealism and sociological reality. His implicit suggestion—to revise moral codes rather than struggle hopelessly to change behavior—guided psychiatrists and legal experts as they sought to make American society more rational" ("Private Acts/Public Policy: Alfred Kinsey, the American Law Institute and the Privatization of American Sexual Morality," *Journal of American Studies* 30 [December 1996]: 428).

13. Of laws that demanded marital fault, Glenda Riley concludes, "In flaunting the adversarial system, collusive couples practiced a form of what was later called no fault divorce. . . . Collusion remained in force thus establishing in practice what later no-fault legislation would recognize by statute" (*Divorce*, 144). For a more detailed discussion of the New York way of divorce at midcentury, see DiFonzo, *Beneath the Fault Line*, 88–91.

14. David R. Mace, "We Urgently Need a Brand-New Approach to Divorce," *McCall's*, April 1962, 48; Monrad B. Paulsen, "For a Reform of the Divorce Laws," *The New York Times Magazine*, 13 May 1962, 22, 32, 36, 40.

15. Edmund Bergler, M. D., *Conflict in Marriage* (New York: Harper & Bros., 1949), 119, 215; Howard Whitman, "Divorce Granted," *Reader's Digest*, October 1954, 15; John Bartlow Martin, "A Little Nest of Hate," *Saturday Evening Post*, 22 November 1958, 36.

16. Frances Bruce Strain, *Marriage Is for Two* (New York: Longmans, Green & Co., 1955), 183. In Britain, similar notions of marriage and divorce were percolating. Historians Jane Lewis and Kathleen Kiernan write, "In line with the belief that truly moral behavior could come only from within, rather than from regulations imposed by an external authority, it became impossible to defend keeping 'an empty shell' marriage in being" ("The Boundaries between Marriage, Nonmarriage, and Parenthood: Changes in Behavior and Policy in Postwar Britain," *Journal of Family History* 21 [July 1996]: 378).

17. Herbert Gold, "Divorce as a Moral Act," *Atlantic*, November 1957, 117; see also, Art Buchwald, "What Is Your Divorce Potential?" *McCall's*, October 1963, 86; Midge Decter, "The Young Divorcee," *Harper's*, October 1962, 167.

18. Margaret Mead, "Double Talk about Divorce," *Redbook*, May 1968, 47. Di-

Fonzo argues that the "two generations of readily divorced Americans" that accumulated between 1920 and 1940 had reduced the fears of a punitive divorce court: "When the required penance of social ostracism disappeared between the two World Wars, the divorce court lost its menacing aspect and took on the bland coloration of a registry" (*Beneath the Fault Line*, 92). The general public seems not to have shared the reformers' fervor over the divorce codes. Only about 13 percent of those polled by Gallup in 1966 felt that contemporary statutes were too stringent; Cherlin, *Marriage, Divorce, Remarriage*, 46.

19. Paul W. Alexander, "Divorce without Guilt or Sin, " *The New York Times Magazine*, 1 July 1951, 14–16, 14; Alexander was, according to DiFonzo, a prime proponent behind the therapeutic divorce movement; *Beneath the Fault Line*, 114. John Bartlow Martin, "Effort to Save a Troubled Marriage," *Saturday Evening Post*, 8 November 1958, 36, 39, 141–42, 36; Martin, "The Depths of Scandal" *Saturday Evening Post*, 15 November 1958, 45, 76, 80. Weitzman, *Divorce Revolution*, 16–20. For a legal assessment of divorce reform since no-fault, see Stephen Sugarman and Herma Hill Kay, eds., *Divorce Reform at the Crossroads* (New Haven: Yale University Press, 1991). DiFonzo argues that in fact the main logic behind reforming the fault system was to institute a more therapeutic divorce process that might catch salvageable marriages and thus preserve marital stability rather than augment divorce; DiFonzo, *Beneath the Fault Line*, 112.

20. IHD Archives, Rodney Scott, 1969, 36. The film *The Best Years of Our Lives* (1946) depicts the crumbling of a war marriage.

21. IHD Archives, Marlene Hill, 1982, 25; Marie Weber, 1969, 48.

22. John Clausen, *American Lives: Looking Back at the Children of the Great Depression* (New York: Free Press, 1993), 423. Six subjects were divorced more than once. IHD Archives.

23. I am grateful to Lisa Rubens for suggesting the term "divorce card." IHD Archives, Steven Downs, I-4, 1958, 8.

24. IHD Archives, Karen Lewis, 1959, 17. In May's examination of the Kelly Longitudinal Study data from the 1950s in *Homeward Bound*, she found that almost half of the women and a third of the men had considered divorce at some point in marriage, further evidence that divorce permeated marriage after the war and did so in a gendered manner; *Homeward Bound*, chap. 8.

25. IHD Archives, David Nichols, 1970, 77; Rick Snyder, 1971, 18.

26. IHD Archives, Connie Small, 1970, 26; Rita Frank, S-I, 1982, 19.

27. IHD Archives, Aileen Ross, 1970, 7; Malcom McKee, 1982, 33.

28. IHD Archives, Hazel Drew, 1982, 15; Sam Arthur, 1970, 38; S-I, 1982, 13; Laura Gilbert, S-I, 1982, 10. According to John Clausen, in 1970, 10 percent of IHD men had considered divorce "several" times, while "nearly half" of the women "had at one time considered divorce" (*American Lives*, 209, 428). By 1982, 22 percent of the Oakland couples said they had thought seriously of divorce. Far fewer of the Berkeley couples said they had thought of divorce, perhaps because those that thought of it had already followed through and divorced; S-I, 1982.

29. Of the California reforms, DiFonzo writes, "the division of no-fault conceived by the reformers, that scrupulous trial courts—not impulsive couples—would determine the right to a divorce, never materialized." Instead the result was "divorce on demand" (DiFonzo, *Beneath the Fault Line*, 168, 170). "Do-It-Yourself Divorce," *Newsweek*, 8 November 1971, 71; Barbara Falconer, "California: Is Divorce without Guilt Working?" *McCall's*, April 1974, 41. Accompanying no-fault statutes were new laws requiring judges to treat men and women "equally" in divorce settlements, the rejection of a "lifetime" right to alimony, regulations regarding the division of marital property, and new views about custody, traditionally allocated to women. See Deborah L. Rhode and Martha Minow, "Reforming the Questions, Questioning the Reforms: Feminist Perspectives on Divorce Law," in Sugarman and Kay, *Divorce Reform at the Crossroads*, 191–210. Lester Velie, "What's Killing Our Marriages?" *Reader's Digest*, June 1973, 152–56, 154. Mel Kantzler, *Creative Divorce: A New Opportunity for Personal Growth* (New York: M. Evans, 1973).

30. "The Broken Family: Divorce U.S. Style," *Newsweek*, 12 March 1973, 47–48, 50, 55, 57, 47.

31. R. DeWolfe, "Myths of American Marriage," *The Nation*, 23 April 1973, 527–29, 527. Margaret Mead, "Too Many Divorces, Too Soon," *Redbook*, February 1974, 72, 74.

32. Mackey Brown, "Keeping Marriage Alive through Middle Age," *McCall's*, January 1973, 73, 138–40, 73.

33. *Newsweek*, 12 March 1973, 50; "Surge in Divorces: New Crisis in Middle Age," *U.S. News and World Report*, 20 December 1976, 56. Betty Friedan, "To Marry Now Is an Act of Hope and Courage," *It Changed My Life: Writings on the Women's Movement* (New York: W. W. Norton & Co., 1985), 238, 14.

34. Mackey Brown, *McCall's*, January 1973, 138; "End of a Marriage," *Good Housekeeping*, February 1974, 75, 134, 137–40; 134.

35. *Good Housekeeping*, February 1974, 140.

36. "Drop-Out Wife," *Life*, 17 March 1972, B-41; "The Broken Family," *Newsweek*, 50; *Good Housekeeping*, February 1974, 75.

37. Richard Boeth, "Connubial Blitz," *Newsweek*, 12 March 1973, 56.

38. IHD Archives, Ken Harris, 1970, 15; Nick Manning, 1982, 28.

39. IHD Archives, Claire Manning, 1970, 20.

40. IHD Archives, Leonard Stone, 1983, 20.

41. IHD Archives, Clay Kent, 1970, 44; Murray Borden, 1982, 11.

42. IHD Archives, Dale George, 1982, 19; Leonard Stone, 1983, 19.

43. IHD Archives, Jack Stevens, 1970, 31; Evelyn Mitchell, 1970, 57, 65, and 1972, 56.

44. IHD Archives, Barbara Spalding, 1982, 24.

45. IHD Archives, Evelyn Mitchell, 1972, 8; Nancy Cole, 1970, 33; Tom Cole, 1969, 9.

46. IHD Archives, Barbara Spalding, 1970, 8; Judy Kent, 1982, 18.

47. IHD Archives, Judy Kent, 1982, 36; Philip Pollard, 1982, 44.

48. IHD Archives, Sue White, 1970, 27; Jack Stevens, 1970, 10, 30.

49. IHD Archives, Milt Fitzgerald, S-I, 1982, 21.

50. IHD Archives, Philip Pollard, 1970, 11. Pollard rejected marriage, choosing to live with his next partner without marriage. After divorce, Pollard and White both embraced the ethos of the counterculture, rejecting conventional nine-to-five-jobs and living arrangements. IHD Archives, White, 1970; Mitchell, 1971.

51. Benita Eisler, *Private Lives: Men and Women of the Fifties* (New York: Franklin Watts, 1986), 300. Based on the 1970 census, two sociologists concluded that highly educated women had a higher rate of marital disruption. Not surprisingly, women with five or more years of education tended to be employed. Resulting economic independence was one factor. Sharon K. Houseknecht and Graham B. Spanier, "Marital Disruption and Higher Education among Women in the United States," *Sociological Quarterly* 21 (summer 1980): 388.

52. IHD Archives, Hazel Drew, 1970, 24, 17.

53. IHD Archives, Nancy Cole, 1970, 20.

54. IHD Archives, Barbara Spalding, 1970, 1982, 25.

55. IHD Archives, Marlene Hill, 1982, 36–37, 39; Sue White, 1969, 30.

56. IHD Archives, Mabel Baldwin, 1970, 11. In Lillian B. Rubin's 1979 study of midlife women, the divorced women whom she queried did mention problems after divorce, but she concluded that "theirs are not lives of one long lament. Indeed, very few pine for the marriage that's gone regardless of whether they left or were left." Rubin's subjects ranged in age from 35 to 54 and IHD women were within that range in the late 1970s. Divorcees made up 22 percent of her subjects. These women had been married on average 19.5 years; Rubin, *Women of a Certain Age: The Midlife Search for Self* (New York: Harper & Row, 1979), 139, 214.

57. IHD Archives, Connie Small, 1970, 8, 1982, 17. Based on their research in the late 1970s and early 1980s, Philip Blumstein and Pepper Schwartz commented, "It may seem unconscionably cynical to say that wives stay in marriages because they cannot support themselves outside them, but our data show there is some validity to this" (*American Couples: Money, Work, Sex* [New York: William Morrow & Co., 1983], 309).

58. For more on the economic costs of divorce for women, see Weitzman, *Divorce Revolution*, and Terry Arendell, *Mothers and Divorce: Legal, Economic, and Social Dilemmas* (Berkeley: University of California Press, 1986). IHD Archives, Judy Kent, 1982, 38–40.

59. IHD Archives, Judy Kent, 1971, 39; Betsy Downs, 1969, 16; Crystal Robertson, 1982, 21.

60. IHD Archives, Victor Gilbert, 1982, 27; Claire Manning, 1982, 24.

61. IHD Archives, Russell Weber, 1982, 15, 41.

62. IHD Archives, Leonard Stone, 1983, 23.

63. IHD Archives, Rose Little, S-I, 1982, 21; Herbert Henderson, 1982, 12; Dan Bentley, S-I, 1982, 13.

64. IHD Archives, Lois Dyer, 1982, 17; Amy Chase, 1969, 33; Jane Mills, S-I, 1982, 15; Catherine Hudson, 1982, 18.

65. IHD Archives, Patricia James, 1970, 20.

66. IHD Archives, Betsy and Steven Downs, 1969, 49.

67. IHD Archives, Joseph Maxwell, S-I, 1982, 16; Ben Robertson, S-I, 1982, 16.

68. IHD Archives, Patricia James, 1982, 29.

69. IHD Archives, Dan Bentley, 1970, 34; Sam Arthur, S-I, 1982, 13; Kevin Jenkins, 1982, 13.

70. IHD Archives, Frank Ryder, S-I, 1981, 19; Gail Henderson, S-I, 1982, 13.

71. IHD Archives, Ernest Johnson, 1981, 15; Barbara Clinton, 1982, 21.

72. IHD Archives, Andrew Sinclair, 1970, 7.

73. Heidi Hartmann, "Changes in Women's Economic and Family Roles in Post–World War II United States," in Lourdes Beneria and Catharine R. Stimpson, *Women, Households, and the Economy* (New Brunswick: Rutgers University Press, 1987), 33–64.

74. IHD Archives, 1982, 2, 17, 21.

CHAPTER SEVEN

1. John Mack Carter, "The New Feminism," *Ladies' Home Journal*, August 1970, 63; "Liberating the Journal," *Newsweek*, 3 August 1970, 44. For a discussion of radical feminists' relationship with the media, see Theresa Kaminski, "'Contesting Feminism': Radical Feminist Publications and Mainstream Magazines," *Journal of American Studies Association of Texas* 28 (October 1997): 14–37.

2. My analysis of the oppositional portrayal is based on a survey of early 1970s media coverage of radical feminism and informed by the work of Susan J. Douglas in *Where the Girls Are: Growing Up Female in the Mass Media* (New York: Times Books, 1994), 221–44. For a discussion of the anti-ERA campaign, see Barbara Ehrenreich, *The Hearts of Men: American Dreams and the Flight from Commitment* (Garden City: Anchor Books, 1983), 144–68.

3. IHD Archives, Crystal Robertson, S-I, 1982, 8.

4. IHD Archives, Blanche Warner, 1969, 5.

5. Sociologist Lillian Rubin's study of midlife women revealed similar trends. She wrote, "With children in the teenage years, they have more freedom than ever before, but it's not enough to satisfy. Instead a taste of freedom opens up a hunger for more—not just for more time for themselves, but for the opportunity, finally, to claim themselves." Half of these women were employed; Lillian B. Rubin, *Women of a Certain Age: The Midlife Search for Self* (New York: Harper & Row, 1979) 11, 18.

6. Ninety percent of college-educated women in a 1964 survey endorsed the idea that "Parents should encourage just as much independence in their daughters as in their sons" (Karen Oppenheim Mason, John L. Czajka, and Sara Arber, "Change in U.S. Women's Sex-Role Attitudes, 1964–1974," *American Sociological*

Review 41 [August 1976]: 587). Political scientist Ethel Klein concluded that based on 1972 electoral polls, "Having a working mother left both men and women more open to feminism." The impact was apparently stronger on men. The mothers of the baby boom shaped the values of both men and women of the next generation; Ethel Klein, *Gender Politics* (Cambridge: Harvard University Press, 1984), 114.

7. IHD Archives, Sally Williams, 1982, 6; Blanch Warner, I-3, 1959, 14. Sociologist Alice Rossi examined a 1962 Gallop poll touting the satisfaction of American married women and questioned the "gloss" of the "rosy perspective" the summation portrayed. She asked, "If these women were so satisfied with their lives, why does only 10% of the sample want their daughters to live the same life they have? Instead these women say they want their daughters to get more education and to marry later than they did" ("Equality between the Sexes: An Immodest Proposal," in Robert J. Lifton, ed., *The Woman in America* [Boston: Houghton Mifflin, 1965], 127).

8. IHD Archives, Thelma Morton, I-3, 1958, 12; May Perkins, S-S, 1957, 6. In Glen Elder's discussion of IHD Oakland women, one-third, as compared to two-thirds of Oakland men, reported that their parents' hopes for them included higher education; *Children of the Great Depression* (Chicago: University of Chicago Press, 1974), 204.

9. IHD Archives, Marlene Hill, I-3, 1958, 10; Crystal Robertson, 1970, 36.

10. IHD Archives, Olivia Adams, 1970, 38; Doris Jenkins, 1970, 13; Sylvia Gould, 1970, 38.

11. IHD Archives, Laura Gilbert, 1970, 19.

12. IHD Archives, Nina Harris, 1969, 24. Fourteen mothers said they wanted their daughters to have something to fall back on.

13. IHD Archives, Barbara Spalding, 1970, 26.

14. IHD Archives, Connie Small, 1970, 21. A 1972 study of mothers' influence on their daughters' attitude found that college-aged daughters of nonworking mothers devalued "female competence" more than did the daughters of working mothers. It is significant that the chief variable found to affect assumptions about a dual role for women (employment and family) is the mother's attitude toward the dual role and her success at carrying it out. Thus, by posing one model of the work-family combination, baby boom mothers shaped their daughters or did so through their attitudes and opinions, even if they did not model such behavior themselves; Grace K. Baruch, "Maternal Influences upon College Women's Attitudes toward Women and Work," *Developmental Psychology* 6 (January 1972): 34.

15. IHD Archives, Crystal Robertson, S-I, 1982, 24; May Perkins, 1982, 31.

16. The years 1964–70, before the feminist movement attracted a mass following, were nonetheless a period of significant change in women's sex role attitudes, shedding light on the roots of the explosion of liberal feminism's popularity in the early 1970s. Between 1964 and 1970 older cohorts of women changed their sex role attitudes: "Even before widespread media attention to the women's movement was common, college-educated women in the United States were changing their

attitudes toward the traditional roles of the sexes" (Mason, Czajka, and Arber, *American Sociological Review* 41: 587–88).

17. For example, readers of *Newsweek* learned that "a 60-woman *posse* 'seized' the Statue of Liberty" (emphasis mine); "Ladies' Day," *Newsweek*, 24 August 1970, 16; IHD Archives, Grace Owens, 1971, 42; Klein, *Gender Politics*, 125, 126.

18. IHD Archives, Doris Jenkins, 1970, 49–51.

19. IHD Archives, Connie Small, 1970, 17. For an astute analysis of the housewife's view of ERA and feminism, see Barbara Ehrenreich, *Hearts of Men*, 144–61.

20. Louis Harris and Associates, *The 1972 Virginia Slims American Women's Opinion Poll* (New York: Louis Harris and Associates, 1972), 2, 23, cited in Jessie Bernard, "Age, Sex and Feminism," *Annals of the American Academy of Political and Social Science* 415 (September 1974): 121, 132.

21. Karen Oppenheim Mason and Larry L. Bumpass, "U.S. Women's Sex Role Ideology," *American Journal of Sociology* 80 (March 1975): 1218.

22. IHD Archives, Connie Small, 1970, 8; 1982, 17. This finding led the authors of a 1974 study to conclude that "employment, not marital disruption was the determining factor in the liberation of women's attitudes" (Mason, Czajka, and Arber, *American Sociological Review* 41:583). Political scientist Ethel Klein described single, separated, or divorced women as "significantly more feminist than widowed or married women in 1972." But, she did not distinguish between views toward the home and workplace; Ethel Klein, *Gender Politics*, 107.

23. IHD Archives, Mary Smith, 1982, 18.

24. IHD Archives, Barbara Clinton, 1982, 40.

25. IHD Archives, Virginia Walker, S-I, 1982, 12; Roberta Johnson, S-I, 1982, 16; Alice Bremmer, S-I, 1982, 15; Martha Bentley, S-I, 1982, 12. One of the women in Rubin's study commented, "It was the women's movement that made it possible for me to consider making a serious commitment to a life aside from the family" (*Women of a Certain Age*, 209). While most women stated that the movement had not influenced their marriages, 18 percent of the Oakland women in my sample interviewed in 1982 said the movement had "some" impact on their marriages, and a third of the Berkeley women said it had "some" impact as well; S-I, 1982.

26. IHD Archives, Crystal Robertson, S-I, 1982, 22; Rita Frank, 1982, 20; Helen Evans, 1982, 42.

27. IHD Archives, Patricia James, 1982, 10; Janice Rogers, 1982, 12; May Perkins, 1982, 10.

28. IHD Archives, Laura Gilbert, 1982, S-I, 11.

29. IHD Archives, Crystal Robertson, S-I, 1982, 16; Blanche Warner, S-I, 1982, 18. Ten women reported that the movement had influenced them to speak up and shape more equitable relationships with their husbands.

30. IHD Archives, Leonard Stone, 1983, S-I, 24, 27; Betty Stone, 1983, 19–20.

31. IHD Archives, Tom Fisher, S-I, 1982, 17; Norman Smith, S-I, 1982, 15. Klein's analysis of 1972 polls shows that "Men with employed wives were more

sensitive to women's rights and the need to end discrimination than were men whose wives were homemakers" (*Gender Politics,* 109).

32. IHD Archives, Albert Morton, S-I, 1982, 18; Hank Jones, S-I, 1982, 15.

33. IHD Archives, Gary Simon, S-I, 26; Scott Clinton, 1970, 20 and S-I, 1982, 20. Eighteen men said they supported the principle of equality for women.

34. IHD Archives, Scott Clinton, S-I, 1982, 20; Dennis Perkins, S-I, 1982, 19; Rodney Scott, S-I, 1982, 1, 7.

35. IHD Archives, Victor Gilbert, S-I, 1982, 19; Murray Borden, S-I, 1982, 16; Fred Adams, S-I, 1982, 13. Harris and Associates, *The 1972 Virginia Slims American Women's Opinion Poll,* 2, 4, cited in Bernard, *Annals of the American Academy of Political and Social Science* 415: 124.

36. IHD Archives, Diane Key, 1970, 61; Irene Lawrence, 1982, 21; Connie Douglas, 1982, 12; Harris and Associates, *The 1972 Virginia Slims American Women's Opinion Poll,* 2, 4, cited in Bernard, *Annals of the American Academy of Political and Social Science* 415:124. Klein points out that "group action goes against the prevailing sentiment in a democracy that 'anyone who tried hard can succeed.'" Individual success can also predispose people to disdain protest activities; Klein, *Gender Politics,* 123, 127. Twenty-four women in my sample explicitly affirmed the principle of equal pay for equal work.

37. IHD Archives, 1970, 17, S-I, 1982, 14.

38. IHD Archives, 1982, 13–14.

39. IHD Archives, Marlene Hill, 1982, 50. Klein found that employed women in 1972 were "more likely to be feminist than women who worked at home." Of employed women, those in higher status occupations were more feminist. Regardless of age, "Positive work experience stimulated feminist support among all working women" (Klein, *Gender Politics,* 108–9). In 1972, 26 percent of women who "supported feminist arguments did not sympathize with the women's liberation movement because of the image that the activists were attributing to feminism" (131).

40. IHD Archives, Gail Henderson, S-I, 1982, 14; Alice Bremmer, 1982, 42.

41. IHD Archives, Lois Dyer, 1982, 33, 22, 42. Klein, *Gender Politics,* 110.

42. Sociologist Jessie Bernard commented, "It is not, however, the specific details of the ERA which are most significant; they may well be left to experts on law and legislation. . . . It is more significant as a symbol of the changes in roles now in process in our society than as a statement of the actual changes themselves" (*Annals of the American Academy of Political and Social Science* 415: 137).

43. On women's anti-ERA activism, see Barbara Ehrenreich, *The Hearts of Men,* 144–65; IHD Archives, Steven Downs, 1982, 32; Rick Snyder, S-I, 1982, 19.

44. IHD Archives, Alice Bremmer, S-I, 1982, 14; Charlotte Thompkins, 1982, 13; Milly Benson, S-I, 1982, 14; Lisa Sims, S-I, 1982, 14; Crystal Robertson, 1982, 32.

45. IHD Archives, Michelle Anderson, 1982, 49.

46. Wini Breines, *Young, White, and Miserable: Growing Up Female in the Fifties* (Boston: Beacon Press, 1992), 47–83.

47. For a discussion of how American women in the 1990s perceive feminism, see Sherrye Henry, *The Deep Divide: Why American Women Resist Equality* (New York: Macmillan Publishing Co., 1994).

EPILOGUE

1. Gerard Jones, *Honey, I'm Home! Sitcoms, Selling the American Dream* (New York: Grove Wadenfeld, 1992).

2. Historian Christina Simmons says of the prescriptions for marriage in the 1920s, "Companionate marriage represented the attempt of mainstream marriage ideology to adapt to women's perceived new social and sexual power" ("Companionate Marriage and the Lesbian Threat," in Kathryn Kish Sklar and Thomas Dublin, eds., *Women and Power in American History* [New York: Prentice Hall, 1991], 2:186).

3. Arlie Hochschild with Anne Machung, *The Second Shift* (New York: Avon Books, 1989).

4. Tom W. Smith, "Attitudes toward Sexual Permissiveness: Trends, Correlates, and Behavioral Connections," in Alice S. Rossi, ed., *Sexuality across the Life Course* (Chicago: University of Chicago Press, 1994), 92.

Selected Bibliography

Arendell, Terry. *Mothers and Divorce: Legal, Economic and Social Dilemmas.* Berkeley: University of California Press, 1986.

Bailey, Beth. *From Front Porch to Back Seat: Courtship in Twentieth-Century America.* Baltimore: Johns Hopkins University Press, 1989.

Bergler, Edmund, M. D. *Conflict in Marriage.* New York: Harper & Bros., 1949.

———. *Divorce Won't Help.* New York: Harper & Bros., 1948.

Bernard, Jessie. *The Future of Marriage.* New York: Bantam Books, 1978.

Blood, Robert O., Jr., and Wolfe, Donald M. *Husbands and Wives: The Dynamics of Married Living.* Glencoe, Ill.: Free Press of Glencoe, 1960.

Bombeck, Erma. *A Marriage Made in Heaven, or Too Tired For an Affair.* New York: HarperCollins, 1993.

Breines, Wini. *Young, White, and Miserable: Growing Up Female in the Fifties.* Boston: Beacon Press, 1992.

Bremner, Robert H., and Gary W. Reichard. *Reshaping America: Society and Institutions, 1945–1960.* Columbus: Ohio State University Press, 1982.

Bullough, Vern. *Science in the Bedroom: A History of Sex Research.* New York: Basic Books, 1994.

Caplow, Theodore, et al. *Middletown Families: Fifty Years of Change and Continuity.* New York: Bantam Books, 1983.

Carter, Paul. *Another Part of the Fifties.* New York: Columbia University Press, 1983.

Cavan, Ruth Shonle. *American Marriage — A Way of Life.* New York: Thomas Y. Crowell Co., 1959.

Chafe, William H. *The American Woman: Her Changing Social, Economic and Political Role.* New York: Oxford University Press, 1974.

Cherlin, Andrew. *Marriage, Divorce, Remarriage.* Cambridge: Harvard University Press, 1981.

Clausen, John A. *American Lives: Looking Back at the Children of the Great Depression.* New York: Free Press, 1993.

Coontz, Stephanie. *The Way We Never Were: American Families and the Nostalgia Trap*. New York: Basic Books, 1992.

Corneau, Guy. *Absent Fathers, Lost Sons: The Search for Masculine Identity*. Boston: Shambhala, 1991.

Cott, Nancy. *The Bonds of Womanhood*. New Haven: Yale University Press, 1977.

Cowan, Ruth Schwartz. *More Work for Mother: The Ironies of Household Technology from the Open Hearth to the Microwave*. New York: Basic Books, 1983.

D'Emilio, John, and Estelle Freedman. *Intimate Matters: A History of Sexuality in America*. New York: Harper & Row, 1988.

Degler, Carl. *At Odds: Women and the Family in America from the Revolution to the Present*. New York: Oxford University Press, 1980.

DiFonzo, J. Herbie. *Beneath the Fault Line: The Popular and Legal Culture of Divorce in Twentieth-Century America*. Charlottesville: University of Virginia Press, 1997.

Diggins, John Patrick. *The Proud Decades: America in War and in Peace*. New York: W. W. Norton & Co., 1988.

Dinnerstein, Myra. *Women between Two Worlds: Midlife Reflections on Work and Family*. Philadelphia: Temple University Press, 1992.

Easterlin, Richard. *Birth and Fortune: The Impact of Numbers on Personal Welfare*. 2d ed. Chicago: University of Chicago Press, 1987.

Ehrenreich, Barbara, Elizabeth Hess, and Gloria Jacobs. *Remaking Love*. Garden City: Anchor Books, 1986.

Ehrenreich, Barbara. *The Hearts of Men: American Dreams and the Flight from Commitment*. Garden City: Anchor Books, 1983.

Eichorn, Dorothy H., et al. *Present and Past in Middle Life*. New York: Academic Press, 1986.

Eisler, Benita. *Private Lives: Men and Women of the Fifties*. New York: Franklin Watts, 1986.

Elder, Glen. *Children of the Great Depression: Social Change in Life Experience*. Chicago: University of Chicago Press, 1974.

English, O. Spurgeon, and Constance J. Foster. *Fathers Are Parents, Too*. New York: G. P. Putnam's Sons, 1951.

Ernst, Morris L., and Loth, David. *For Better or Worse: A New Approach to Marriage and Divorce*. New York: Harper & Bros., 1952.

Fass, Paula S. *The Damned and the Beautiful*. New York: Oxford University Press, 1979.

Filene, Peter. *Him/Her/Self: Sex Roles in Modern America*. New York: Harcourt Brace Jovanovich, 1974.

Fout, John C., and Maura Shaw Tantillo, eds. *American Sexual Politics: Sex, Gender, and Race since the Civil War*. Chicago: University of Chicago Press, 1993.

Friedan, Betty. *The Feminine Mystique*. New York: Dell Publishing, 1983.

———. *It Changed My Life: Writings on the Woman's Movement*. New York: W. W. Norton & Co., 1985.

Gatlin, Rochelle. *American Women since 1945.* Jackson: University Press of Mississippi, 1987.

Gerson, Kathleen. *No Man's Land: Men's Changing Commitments to Family and Work.* New York: Basic Books, 1993.

Gillis, John. "Making Time for Family: The Invention of Family Time and the Reinvention of Family," *Journal of Family History* 21, no. 1 (1996): 4–21.

Glick, Paul. *American Families.* New York: John Wiley & Sons, 1957.

Goldin, Claudia. *Understanding the Gender Gap: An Economic History of American Women.* New York: Oxford University Press, 1990.

Gordon, Richard E., and Gordon, Katherine. *The Split Level Trap.* New York: Max Gunther, Bernard Gels Association, 1960.

Griswold, Robert L. *Fatherhood in America: A History.* New York: Basic Books, 1993.

Hartmann, Heidi I. "Changes in Women's Economic and Family Roles in Post–World War II United States," in Lourdes Beneria and Catharine R. Stimpson, eds., *Women, Households, and the Economy.* New Brunswick: Rutgers University Press, 1987.

Harvey, Brett. *The Fifties: A Woman's Oral History.* New York: HarperCollins Publishers, 1993.

Havemann, Ernest, and Patricia Salter West. *They Went to College: The College Graduate in America Today.* New York: Harcourt, Brace & Co., 1952.

Henry, Sherrye. *The Deep Divide: Why American Women Resist Equality.* New York: Macmillan Publishing Co., 1994.

Honey, Maureen. *Creating Rosie the Riveter: Class, Gender, and Propaganda during World War II.* Amherst: University of Massachusetts Press, 1984.

Hoschild, Arlie, with Anne Machung. *The Second Shift: Working Parents and the Revolution at Home.* New York: Viking Press, 1989.

Jackson, Kenneth T. *The Crabgrass Frontier.* New York: Oxford University Press, 1985.

Jackson, Margaret. *The Real Facts of Life: Feminism and the Politics of Sexuality, c. 1850–1940.* London: Taylor & Francis, 1994.

Jezer, Marty. *The Dark Ages.* Boston: South End Press, 1982.

Johnson, Marilynn S. *The Second Gold Rush: Oakland and the East Bay in World War II.* Berkeley: University of California Press, 1993.

Johnston, Carolyn. *Sexual Power: Feminism and the Family in America.* Tuscaloosa: University of Alabama Press, 1992.

Jones, Gerard. *Honey, I'm Home! Sitcoms, Selling the American Dream.* New York: Grove Wadenfeld, 1992.

Jones, Landon Y. *Great Expectations: America and the Baby Boom Generation.* New York: Coward, McCann & Geghegan, 1980.

Kaledin, Eugenia. *Mothers and More: American Women in the 1950s.* Boston: Twayne Publishers, 1984.

Katz, Donald. *Home Fires: An Intimate Portrait of One Middle-Class Family in Postwar America.* New York: HarperCollins, 1992.

Katz, Jonathan Ned. *The Invention of Heterosexuality*. New York: Dutton, 1992.

Keller, Kathryn. *Mothers and Work in Popular American Magazines*. Westport: Greenwood Press, 1994.

Kennedy, Susan Estabrook. *If All We Did Was Weep at Home: A History of White Working-Class Women in America*. Bloomington: Indiana University Press, 1979.

———. *Out to Work: A History of Wage-Earning Women in the United States*. New York: Oxford University Press, 1982.

Kerber, Linda K., Alice Kessler-Harris, and Kathryn Kish Sklar, eds. *U.S. History as Women's History: New Feminist Essays*. Chapel Hill: University of North Carolina, 1995.

Kessler-Harris, Alice. *A Woman's Wage: Historical Meanings and Consequences*. Lexington: University of Kentucky Press, 1990.

Kinsey, Alfred C. *Sexual Behavior in the Human Female*. Philadelphia: W. B. Saunders Co., 1953.

Klein, Ethel. *Gender Politics: From Mass Consciousness to Mass Politics*. Cambridge: Harvard University Press, 1984.

Komarovsky, Mirra. *Women in the Modern World: Their Education and Their Dilemmas*. Boston: Little, Brown & Co., 1953.

La Rossa, Ralph. *The Modernization of Fatherhood: A Social and Political History*. Chicago: University of Chicago Press, 1997.

Laipson, Peter. " 'Kiss without Shame, for she Desires it': Sexual Foreplay in American Marital Advice Literature, 1900–1925." *Journal of Social History* 30 (spring 1996): 507–25.

Landis, Paul. *Making the Most of Marriage*. New York: Appleton-Century-Crofts, 1955.

Leuchtenburg, William. *A Troubled Feast: American Society since 1945*. Boston: Little, Brown, & Co., 1983.

Light, Paul Charles. *Baby Boomers*. New York: W. W. Norton & Co., 1988.

Linden-Ward, Blanche, and Carol Hurd Green. *American Women in the 1960s: Changing the Future*. New York: Twayne Publishers, 1993.

Marsh, Margaret. *Suburban Lives*. New Brunswick: Rutgers University Press, 1990.

Matthews, Glenna. *Just a Housewife*. New York: Oxford University Press, 1987.

May, Elaine Tyler. *Homeward Bound: American Families in the Cold War Era*. New York: Basic Books, 1988.

———. *Great Expectations: Marriage and Divorce in Post-Victorian America*. Chicago: University of Chicago Press, 1980.

May, Lary. *Recasting America*. Chicago: University of Chicago Press, 1984.

McLaughlin, Steven D., et al. *The Changing Lives of American Women*. Chapel Hill: University of North Carolina Press, 1987.

Meyerowitz, Joanne, ed. *Not June Cleaver: Women and Gender in Postwar America*. Philadelphia: Temple University Press, 1994.

Meyerowitz, Joanne. "Beyond the Feminine Mystique: A Reassessment of Post-war Mass Culture." *Journal of American History* 79 (1993): 1455–1483.

Michel, Sonya. "American Women and the Discourse of the Democratic Family in World War II." In Margaret Randolph Higgonet, ed. *Behind the Lines: Gender and the Two World Wars*. New Haven: Yale University Press, 1987.

Miller, Douglas T., and Marion Nowak. *The Fifties: The Way We Really Were*. Garden City: Doubleday, 1977.

Mintz, Steven, and Susan Kellogg. *Domestic Revolutions: A Social History of American Family Life*. New York: Free Press, 1988.

Modell, John. *Into One's Own: From Youth to Adulthood in the United States, 1920–1975*. Berkeley: University of California Press, 1989.

Nye, F. Ivan, and Hoffman, Lois Wladis. *The Employed Mother in America*. Chicago: Rand McNally & Co., 1963.

Oakley, J. Ronald. *God's Country: America in the Fifties*. New York: Dembner Books, 1986.

Oppenheimer, Valerie Kincade. *Work and the Family: A Study in Social Demography*. New York: Academic Press, 1982.

Packard, Vance. *The Sexual Wilderness: The Contemporary Upheaval in Male-Female Relationships*. New York: David McKay Co., 1968.

Riley, Glenda. *Divorce: An American Tradition*. New York: Oxford University Press, 1991.

Rothman, Ellen K. *Hands and Hearts: A History of Courtship in America*. Cambridge: Harvard University Press, 1987.

Rubin, Lillian B. *Women of a Certain Age: The Midlife Search for Self*. New York: Harper & Row, 1979.

———. *Erotic Wars: What Happened to the Sexual Revolution?* New York: Farrar, Straus & Giroux, 1990.

Rupp, Leila J., and Verta Taylor. *Survival in the Doldrums: The American Women's Rights Movement, 1945 to the 1960s*. New York: Oxford University Press, 1987.

Ryan, Mary P. *Womanhood in America*. New York: Franklyn Watts, 1983.

Seidman, Steven. *Romantic Longings: Love in America, 1830–1980*. New York: Routledge, 1991.

Skolnick, Arlene. *Embattled Paradise: The American Family in an Age of Uncertainty*. New York: Basic Books, 1991.

Smith-Rosenberg, Carroll. *Disorderly Conduct: Visions of Gender in Victorian America*. New York: Oxford University Press, 1985.

Smith, Ralph E. *The Subtle Revolution: Women at Work*. Washington, D.C.: Urban Institute, 1979.

Snarey, John. *How Fathers Care for the Next Generation: A Four-Decade Study*. Cambridge: Harvard University Press, 1993.

Spock, Benjamin, M. D. *The Common Sense Book of Baby and Child Care*. New York: Duell, Sloan, & Pearce, 1957.

Stacey, Judith. *Brave New Families: Stories of Domestic Upheaval in Late Twentieth Century America*. New York: Basic Books, 1990.

Stearns, Peter N. *Be a Man: Males in Modern Society*. New York: Holmes & Meier Publishers, 1979.

Stokes, Walter. *Modern Pattern for Marriage: The Newer Understanding of Married Love*. New York: Rinehart & Co., 1948.

Strain, Frances Bruce. *Marriage Is for Two*. New York: Longmans, Green & Co., 1955.

Tuttle, William M. *Daddy's Gone to War: The Second World War in the Lives of America's Children*. New York: Oxford University Press, 1993.

Van Horn, Susan Householder. *Women, Work and Fertility*. New York: New York University Press, 1988.

Verhoff, Joseph, Elizabeth Douvan, and Richard Kulka. *The Inner American: A Self-Portrait from 1957 to 1976*. New York: Basic Books, 1981.

Wandersee, Winifred D. *On the Move: American Women in the 1970s*. Boston: Twayne Publishers, 1988.

White, Kevin. *The First Sexual Revolution*. New York: New York University Press, 1993.

Wittner, Lawrence. *Cold War America*. New York: Praeger Press, 1974.

Womanpower: A Statement by the National Manpower Council. New York: Columbia University Press, 1957.

Index